Biology Living Systems

Probing Levels of Life
Laboratory Manual

Paul J. Hummer, Jr.
Hood College
Frederick, MD

Albert Kaskel
Evanston Township High School
Evanston, IL

James E. Kennedy
Ohio Dominican College
Columbus, OH

Raymond F. Oram
The Peddie School
Hightstown, NJ

GLENCOE
McGraw-Hill
New York, New York   Columbus, Ohio   Woodland Hills, California   Peoria, Illinois

A GLENCOE PROGRAM

Biology

Living Systems

Student Edition
Teacher Wraparound Edition
Study Guide, SE and TE
Investigating Living Systems, SE and TAE
Probing Levels of Life, SE and TAE
Assessment
Videodisc Correlations
Science and Technology Videodisc Series Teacher Guide
Transparency Package
Concept Mapping
Exploring Environmental Issues
Critical Thinking/Problem Solving
Spanish Resources
Lesson Plans
Computer Test Bank

Cover Photograph: Green Darner: Frank Cocco

Send all inquiries to:

GLENCOE DIVISION
Macmillan/McGraw-Hill
936 Eastwind Drive
Westerville, OH 43081

ISBN 0-02-826299-9

Printed in the United States of America

4 5 6 7 8 9 10 066 05 04 03 02 01 00 99

Preface

Probing Levels of Life investigates the various levels of life from the molecular activities of cells to organisms interacting with the physical factors in the environment. During the investigations, students manipulate scientific equipment, make observations, collect and record data, and explain results based on their collected data. All the main topics of biology are presented in this laboratory program.

The major features of *Probing Levels of Life* include

- use of scientific equipment and supplies;
- use of models or simulations to simplify or illustrate abstract concepts;
- performance objectives for the students that provide a guide for quickly determining what is expected of them during investigations;
- keeping of all laboratory records—observations, data, graphs, diagrams, answers, and conclusions—in a separate, student-supplied notebook;
- collection of both individual and class data to arrive at valid conclusions;
- step-by-step instructions given in paragraph form;
- extensive use of living organisms; and
- development of science skills and scientific literacy.

Using this laboratory program, students become "involved" with science—learning firsthand about biology. Students learn the value of making accurate observations and of recording accurate data in arriving at valid conclusions. The directions for each investigation are clear and concise. With some teacher assistance and supervision, students can become actively involved in discovering biological principles and concepts.

Probing Levels of Life includes three types of investigations.

1. Investigations in which students work with substances or specimens and actually perform experiments. In these investigations, each student collects his or her own data. Because differences in data arise from physiological and structural variations in living organisms, class data and averages are used in arriving at valid conclusions.
2. Investigations in which students observe and make conclusions about living and preserved specimens without actual experimentation.
3. Model building and problem-solving investigations. Through use of models and simulations, difficult or abstract concepts are explained.

The time necessary to complete almost every investigation is one laboratory period. Some investigations, however, involve daily or weekly observations. Moreover, special investigations have been designed to take you and your classes outside the school to observe organisms in their own environment.

The 84 investigations in this manual are representative of the topics covered in most introductory biology courses. *Probing Levels of Life* follows the sequence of *BIOLOGY: Living Systems* and reinforces concepts presented in that text.

To The Student

The door to the real world of biology can be opened for you as you work in the biology laboratory. *Probing Levels of Life* is a tool that you can use to make your laboratory work both worthwhile and enjoyable.

The laboratory investigations are designed to achieve the following:

- to develop an interest in the study of biology;
- to reinforce important concepts and ideas covered in your text;
- to allow you to verify some of the scientific information learned through lectures or text readings;
- to acquaint you with some modern tools and techniques being used by today's biological scientists; and
- to allow you to apply the principles of biology learned in the classroom to everyday life.

The laboratory investigations are designed to give you firsthand experiences as a student scientist. Acting as a scientist, you will conduct investigations using the steps employed by experienced scientists as they solve problems. The observations and data collected by both you and other class members during an investigation will be evaluated to help you draw logical conclusions.

Each investigation in *Probing Levels of Life* has the five parts listed below. An understanding of the purpose of each of these parts will make your laboratory experience easier.

1. **Introduction**—The introduction is in a box directly below the title of each investigation. These paragraphs give you needed background information or interesting historical information.
2. **Objectives**—The last paragraph of the introduction contains the purpose of each investigation. This section begins with "In this investigation, you will. . ." and tells you what you are expected to learn. When you are finished with the investigations, you should reread this section to see if you have accomplished the stated objectives.
3. **Materials**—The organisms, solutions, and equipment needed to complete the investigation are listed in the materials section.
4. **Procedure**—The procedure, in paragraph form, gives you step-by-step instructions which lead you through the investigation. Making observations and recording data in a notebook are necessary parts of this section. Sample tables and graphs serve as models for you to use in recording your observations and data in your notebook. Labeled diagrams are also included in this section to aid you in completing the investigation. Many investigations have safety cautions listed in the procedure sections. Be sure to read and follow these statements.
5. **Formulating Generalizations**—In this section you draw conclusions about the investigation just completed. By answering a series of questions, you will be able to interpret your data and form accurate conclusions.

In addition to the cautions in the investigations, this manual contains a list of safety rules on the inside back cover. Below the rules is a table listing common laboratory injuries and what you should do if such an injury were to occur. Safety in the laboratory is your responsibility. Read these sections over now. Familiarity with the correct laboratory procedures will help ensure your safety as well as the safety of others.

A year of investigating how the various levels of life function can be a rewarding experience. This book has been designed to make biology both understandable and exciting. Have a good year!

Table of Contents

Safety Symbols

The *Biology: Living Systems* Program uses several safety symbols to alert you to possible laboratory dangers. These safety symbols are explained below. Be sure that you understand each symbol before you begin an investigation.

 DISPOSAL ALERT This symbol appears when care must be taken to dispose of materials properly.	 ANIMAL SAFETY This symbol appears whenever live animals are studied and the safety of the animals and the student must be ensured.
 BIOLOGICAL SAFETY This symbol appears when there is danger involving bacteria, fungi, or protists.	 RADIOACTIVE SAFETY This symbol appears when radioactive materials are used.
 OPEN FLAME ALERT This symbol appears when use of an open flame could cause a fire or an explosion.	 CLOTHING PROTECTION SAFETY This symbol appears when substances used could stain or burn clothing.
 THERMAL SAFETY This symbol appears as a reminder to use caution when handling hot objects.	 FIRE SAFETY This symbol appears when care should be taken around open flames.
 SHARP OBJECT SAFETY This symbol appears when a danger of cuts or puncture caused by the use of sharp objects exists.	 EXPLOSION SAFETY This symbol appears when the misuse of chemicals could cause an explosion.
 FUME SAFETY This symbol appears when chemicals or chemical reactions could cause dangerous fumes.	 EYE SAFETY This symbol appears when a danger to the eyes exists. Safety goggles should be worn when this symbol appears.
 ELECTRICAL SAFETY This symbol appears when care should be taken when using electrical equipment.	 POISON SAFETY This symbol appears when poisonous substances are used.
 PLANT SAFETY This symbol appears when poisonous plants or plants with thorns are handled.	 CHEMICAL SAFETY This symbol appears when chemicals used can cause burns or are poisonous if absorbed through the skin.

Life: Common Characteristics

1

Earth is teeming with many different kinds of living things. During your course in biology you will investigate the structure, function, development, heredity, and evolution of organisms. You will also investigate the function of organisms in the biological community.

The purpose of this investigation is to observe and record specific data about various living things. From these observations and data you will attempt to formulate generalizations about organisms.

Materials (*per class*)

labeled specimens of living things
microscopes
hand lenses
rulers as needed

Procedure

Before your class period, construct a table similar to Table 1. Your teacher will tell you how many specimens to prepare for. The numbers in the table refer to questions to be answered.

TABLE 1. OBSERVATIONS OF ORGANISMS
SPECIMEN 1
Name:
1.
2. a.
b.
c.
3.
4.
5.
6.
7.
8.
SPECIMEN 2
Name:
1.
2. a.
b.
c.
3.
4.
5.
6.
7.
8.

During the class period, observe each specimen carefully. Answer the following questions for each specimen. Answer the questions only on the basis of your observations. If you cannot answer a question from your observations, write "c.a." (cannot answer) in the table.

1. What are the physical characteristics of the specimen?
2. What evidence did you see of
   a. growth and development?
   b. maintenance and repair?
   c. reproduction?
3. Is the organism unicellular (composed of one cell) or multicellular (composed of many cells)?
4. Is the specimen a producer (an organism capable of making its own food) or a consumer (an organism unable to produce its own food)?
5. List any organs that you can observe.
6. An adaptation is a special feature that enables the organism to survive in its environment. List any adaptations you observe.
7. What community or communities might the specimen be able to live in—forest, grassland, desert, pond, or others you can think of?
8. What special features make this specimen different from other specimens observed?

Formulating Generalizations

You have just completed a series of observations of living things. Some of the specimens were probably familiar to you; others were not. Your collected data now become important because you can formulate generalizations about the specimens.

Answer the following questions about your observations of the specimens.

1. Which one of the nine questions was most difficult to answer on the basis of your observations? Why?
2. Which questions were the least difficult to answer? Why?
3. How many of the observed specimens can probably live in more than one community?
4. Give an example of an adaptation that you observed and explain how it helps the organism to survive.
5. What features helped you identify the specimen as a producer or consumer?
6. What features helped you identify some consumers as decomposers?
7. Why are organisms broadly classified as producers and consumers instead of plants and animals?
8. How does each organism fit into the food chain of the community in which it lives?
9. Define life based on your observations.
10. Which of the five processes—growth, development, reproduction, maintenance, and repair—would be the hardest to observe? Why?
11. How are you able to distinguish between a unicellular and a multicellular organism?

Life In A Square Meter Community

2

Living things are in a state of constant interaction with each other and their environment. Soil is "home" for many forms of life—some are microscopic (not visible to the unaided eye) and others are macroscopic (visible to the unaided eye). Organisms inhabiting the soil have special adaptations that enable them to survive. They are more diverse and more numerous per given area than organisms on top of the soil, in water, or in the air. Living things can alter the physical and chemical factors of the soil. At the same time, the structure and chemistry of the soil affect the number of organisms found there.

The purpose of this investigation is to observe and collect specimens from a square meter plot of a community near your school and to observe the interactions between organisms and the soil.

Materials (*per team of four students*)

- cord or string—1 ball
- graph paper—4 sheets
- hand lens
- probe or pencil
- meter stick—2
- newspaper
- large plastic bags—6
- small shovel or trowel
- specimen jars—8
- large nails or stakes—4

Procedure

Using a meter stick, cord or string, and four stakes, mark off a square-meter plot (Figure 1) in a community near your school. Make a sketch (top view) of your square-meter plot on graph paper. Show major features such as areas covered by leaves, rocks, and small plants. Record the date, time, and weather conditions (rainfall, temperature changes, etc.) that may have recently affected this area. Make the following observations of your square-meter community.

FIGURE 1

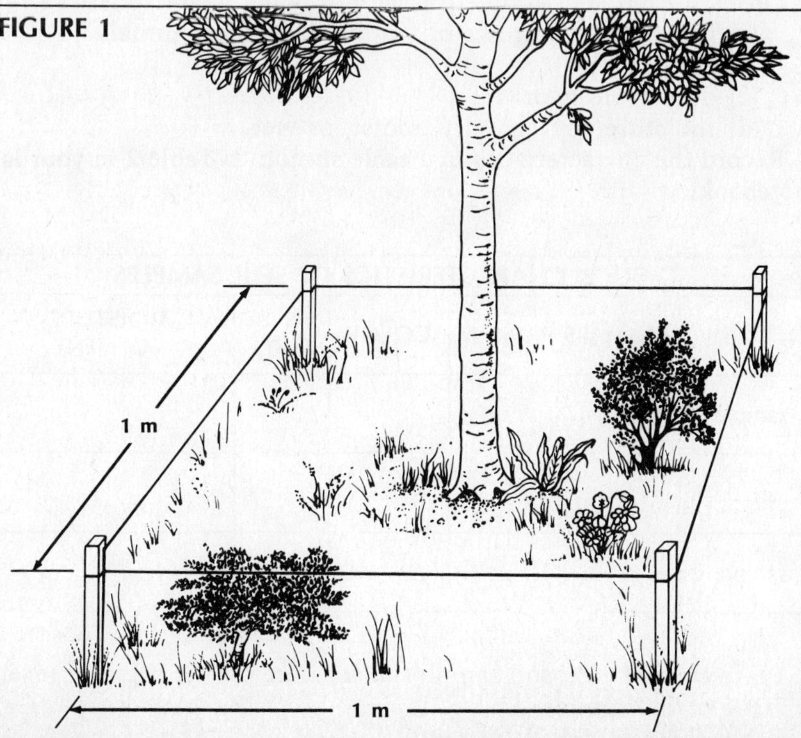

Observation of Plant and Plantlike Communities

Record the presence and number of the following plant types in a table similar to Table 1.

(a) Trees—woody plants with one stem, 0.5 to 30 m in height
(b) Shrubs—low woody plants with two or more stems protruding from the ground, 0.5 to 3.0 m in height
(c) Herbaceous plants—nonwoody, green plants such as ferns and grasses that wither and die in winter, 0.1 to 1 m in height
(d) Floor covering—fallen leaves and stems; herbaceous plants such as mosses; lichens and fungi

If you desire to collect any part of a plant or a complete plant, your teacher will explain preservation techniques. Be sure to check with your teacher before touching or removing plants.

TABLE 1. PLANTS IN THE SQUARE METER COMMUNITY

	TREES	SHRUBS	HERBACEOUS PLANTS	FLOOR COVERING
number				

Observation of Animal Communities

If present, collect a sample of fallen leaves and place it in a large plastic bag.

Remove a soil sample from your community by inserting the shovel vertically into the soil in four places to form a square with each side the width of the shovel. Then, carefully pry the block of soil loose from the bottom. Try to remove the soil sample in one piece. Place the sample on a piece of newspaper. Remove two or three other soil samples from your plot. Place each soil sample on a different piece of newspaper.

Observe each soil sample for the following characteristics:

(a) presence of burrows of worms and other animals
(b) color
(c) detectable odor
(d) moisture content: dry, moist, or wet.

Record the characteristics in a table similar to Table 2 in your lab notebook.

TABLE 2. CHARACTERISTICS OF SOIL SAMPLES

	ANIMALS PRESENT	COLOR	ODOR	MOISTURE CONTENT
sample A				
sample B				
sample C				

Place each of your soil samples in separate plastic bags to prevent mixing of the samples.

Label the samples A, B, and C.

In the classroom or at home, observe each soil sample and fallen leaf sample (if you have one) for animals. Place each sample on a piece of newspaper and carefully sort through it with a probe (pencil). Make a table similar to Table 3 in your lab notebook and record the presence and number of the following animal types:

(a) without legs
(b) with two pairs of legs
(c) with three pairs of legs
(d) with four pairs of legs
(e) with more than four pairs of legs
(f) others.

You will need a hand lens to observe some of the animals. Make a separate list of animals for each soil and fallen leaf sample.

After you make the observations, the animals may be preserved in small jars. Use preservatives recommended by your teacher. **CAUTION:** *Some preservatives are harmful. Avoid breathing fumes.* If you wish to keep live specimens, set up a terrarium and place the animals inside.

Formulating Generalizations

1. Which plant types are more abundant in your community? Why?
2. Were any of the plants or plantlike organisms consumers (parasites or saprophytes)?
3. Which plant or plantlike organisms appear to contribute most to food production by photosynthesis? Why?
4. Describe any special adaptations that your soil animals have.
5. Using Table 3, list which type of animal is most abundant in each soil sample.
6. List the common names for the organisms you found in your soil samples.
7. List a possible food chain for the area surrounding your plot.
8. How do you think color, odor, and moisture of soil would affect the plants and animals in a community?

TABLE 3. NUMBER OF ANIMALS

	NO LEGS	TWO PAIRS OF LEGS	THREE PAIRS OF LEGS	FOUR PAIRS OF LEGS	MORE THAN FOUR PAIRS	OTHERS
leaf sample						
soil sample A						
soil sample B						
soil sample C						

3 The Compound Microscope—A Biological Tool

Some living things are too small to be seen with the unaided eye. Therefore, you cannot observe them directly. In future laboratory exercises you will observe not only tiny specimens but also internal structures of living things. Such observations are possible by using an instrument called a microscope. A microscope contains a series of lenses which enlarge the image of a specimen many times its normal size. There are many types of microscopes, each with a specific magnification range.

In this investigation you will identify the parts of a compound microscope, develop skill in using the compound microscope, and describe the optical properties of a microscope. You will also construct and observe wet mount slides.

Materials (*per student*)

absorbent cotton
cloth or paper towel
microscope
coverslip
dropper
lens paper
magazine with print and photos
glass slide
pencil with eraser
probe
scissors
water
dish soap

Procedure

Part A. Preliminary Observations and Light Adjustment

Remove a microscope from the storage area by placing one hand beneath the base and firmly grasping the arm of the microscope with the other hand. Carry the microscope close to your body to help

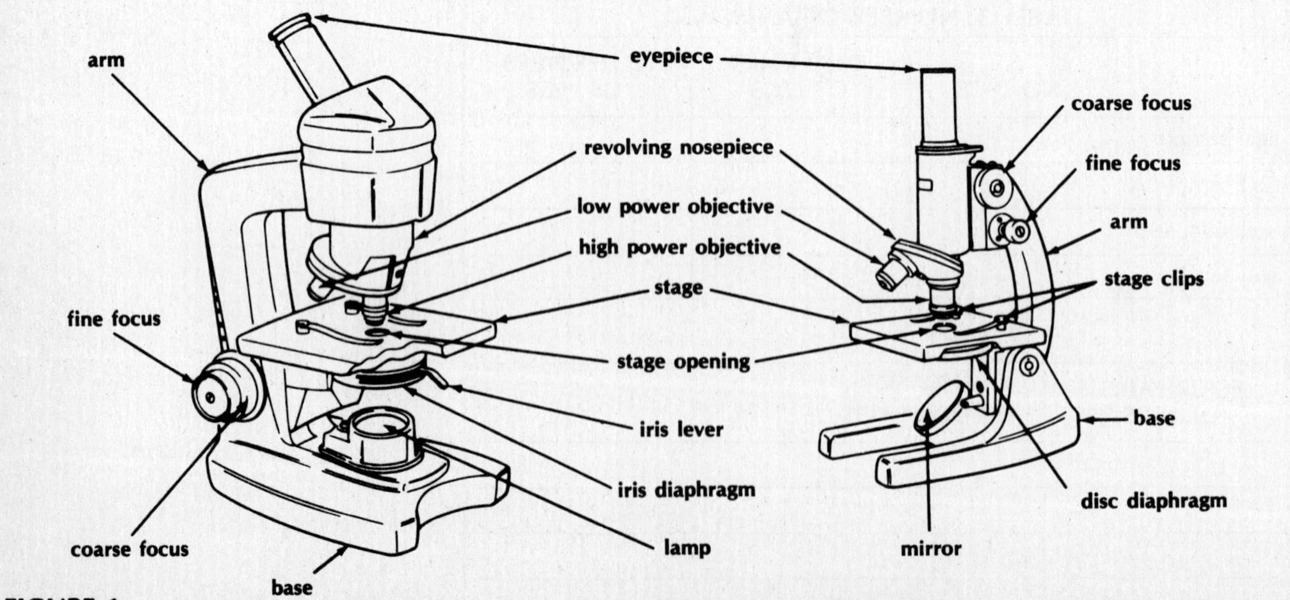

FIGURE 1

TABLE 1. FUNCTIONS OF THE PARTS OF A MICROSCOPE	
PART	FUNCTION
eyepiece	contains lenses for magnification
arm	supports body tube
body tube	maintains a set distance between eyepiece and objective lens
coarse focus	moves body tube up and down
fine focus	sharpens the image, used to focus
nosepiece	contains high and low power objective lenses
stage	supports the slide being viewed
stage clips	hold the slide in place on the stage
diaphragm	regulates light from mirror or light source
mirror	reflects light through diaphragm
base	supports microscope

prevent excess bumping and jarring of the instrument. Place the microscope on the table with the arm toward you and the stage away from you. Identify the parts of the microscope (Figure 1). As you identify the parts, note and learn the function of each part (Table 1).

Part B. Preparing a Wet Mount

Materials observed with a microscope are placed on a glass slide. For most preparations, a thin piece of glass or plastic called a coverslip is placed over the materials on the slide. Water is usually placed between the slide and coverslip. A slide prepared in this manner is called a wet mount.

Rinse a slide and coverslip in slightly soapy water. Wipe both sides of each gently with a clean cloth or paper towel. After cleaning, always handle slides by the edge rather than the flat surface so you will not have any smudges that interfere with observations.

Select a paper square from the printed material provided. Look on both sides of the paper for the smallest letter "e" that you can find. Place the paper square (smallest print side up) in the center of the slide and add a drop of water with a dropper. Place the cover slip at a 45° angle over the drop of water and the paper. Using a probe, gently lower the coverslip onto the slide. If air bubbles are present, gently tap the coverslip directly over the bubbles with the eraser of a pencil (Figure 2).

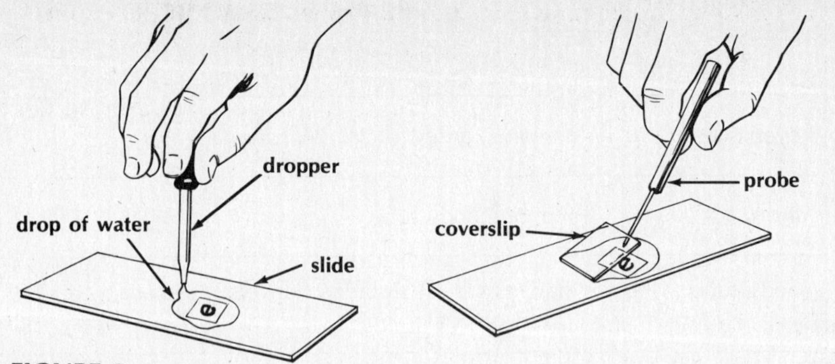

FIGURE 2

Part C. Focusing the Microscope and Determining Magnification

Raise the body tube of the microscope using the coarse focus until the objective lens is about 2 to 3 cm above the opening in the stage. Revolve the nosepiece so the low power objective (10X) is directly in line with the body tube. The objective lens is properly in line when you hear a "click." When the objective is in proper position, slight pressure on the side of the objective will not move it. If the lens is not locked in place, you will not be able to focus properly, nor will you see the entire field of view. The low power lens should now be directly above the opening in the stage. Adjust the diaphragm and mirror so the greatest amount of light is coming through the opening in the stage.

Place the wet mount slide on the stage. Position the slide so that you can read the letter normally from behind the microscope and so the letter is in the exact center of the stage opening. Fasten the stage clips on the slide so it will stay in position. Use the coarse focus to lower the body tube until it stops. Do not force the body tube to go any farther.

Some microscopes do not have automatic stops. If yours does not have an automatic stop, lower the body tube using the coarse focus while looking from the side of the microscope. Lower the body tube until the distance between the bottom of the objective and the coverslip is about 5 mm.

From the side, note the distance between the low power lens and the top of the coverslip. This length is known as the *working distance.* Observe the specimen through the eyepiece to become familiar with the field of view. Because the field of view is probably out of focus, raise the body tube by using the coarse focus while looking through the eyepiece. When the letter comes into view, use the fine focus knob to bring the slide into proper focus. By adjusting the diaphragm, the proper amount of light for viewing is attained. In your lab notebook, make a sketch of the letter as observed.

Observe what happens to the position of the letter as you move the slide. Move the slide toward your left hand. Recenter the letter and move the slide away from the arm of the microscope.

Questions:

1. How did the letter's position appear when viewed through the microscope as compared to its actual position on the slide?
2. What happened to the letter when you moved the slide to the left? Away from the microscope's arm?

3. From your observations through the microscope, if you see a living thing moving from the bottom to the top of the field of view, what do you know about the organism's real direction of travel?
4. In general, how is the orientation of an object changed when viewed through a compound microscope?

To observe the letter on high power, place the letter in the center of the low power field of view, sharpen the focus, and rotate the nosepiece until the high power lens "clicks" in line with the body tube. If the high power objective touches the coverslip, raise the body tube with the coarse focus. If the image is out of focus, turn the fine focus knob. *Never focus on high power with the coarse focus knob.* Make a sketch of your observations in your lab notebook.

Questions:

5. Upon switching to high power, did the letter change position? Explain your answer.
6. Explain the change in the size of the image.
7. When you switched to high power, what happened to the brightness of the field of view? Give a reasonable explanation.

Make a chart similar to Table 2. Locate a number followed by an "X" on each of the two objective lenses and eyepiece. The number tells how many times each lens magnifies an object. Record the magnification of each lens on the chart. To compute the total magnification of an image, multiply the magnification of the eyepiece by the magnification of the objective lens. For example, to determine the magnification with low power, multiply the eyepiece (4X) by the low power objective (10X). The total magnification is 40X the original size. Use the data from your chart to compute total magnification of the image on low and high power.

TABLE 2. LENS POWER

LENS	MAGNIFICATION
Eyepiece	10X
Low Power	10X
High Power	43X

Question:

8. What is the total magnification of the image with your microscope on low power? On high power? (Check your answers with your teacher before proceeding further.)

Part D. Resolving Power and Depth of Focus

The capability of a microscope to provide fine detail is known as resolving power. Depth of focus is the vertical amount of the specimen that is in focus at one time.

Revolve the nosepiece so the low power objective is over the opening on the stage. While looking at the low power objective, turn the coarse focus knob away from you. Record in your lab notebook whether the low power objective moves up or down. Now turn the coarse focus toward you and record whether the low power objective moves up or down.

Prepare a wet mount using two different colored threads. Place a piece of colored thread on the slide. Add a second thread of a different color on top of the first thread. Place the second thread at an angle so it forms the letter "X." (See Figure 3.) Record in your lab notebook which thread is superimposed on the other.

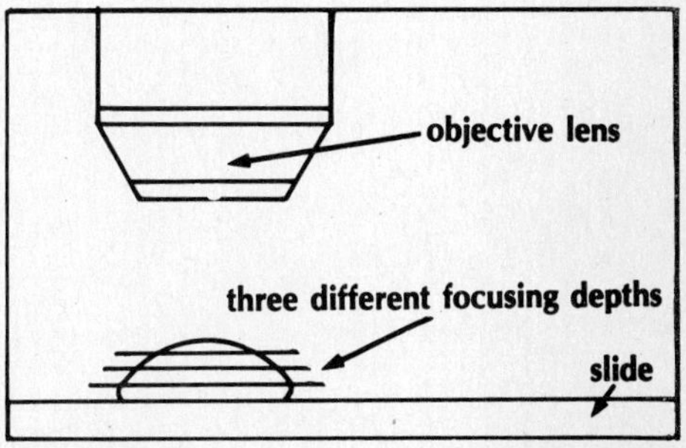

FIGURE 3

Using low power, locate the area where the one thread is superimposed on the other thread and forms an "X." Move the coarse focus until one of the threads comes into sharp focus. The other thread should be slightly out of focus. Turn the fine focus until the second thread comes into fine focus. The first thread should now be out of focus. This procedure shows the depth of focus of a microscope.

Make a wet mount of a small piece of paper from a photograph in a magazine and place the wet mount on the stage of the microscope. Observe the material on low and then high power. Make a sketch in your lab notebook of what you have observed on low or high power. This procedure shows the resolving power of the microscope.

Questions:

9. Which thread came into focus first, the one on the top or the one on the bottom?
10. How can you determine which piece of thread overlays the other?
11. Explain what happens when a thread that was in focus when the fine adjustment knob is turned back and forth. Use the term "depth of focus" in your answer.
12. Describe the magnified image of the photograph that you observed. Use the term "resolving power" in your answer.
13. Does the objective lens move closer to or farther away from the object being magnified when the focus knob is turned away from you?
14. Does the objective lens move closer to or farther away from the object being magnified when the focus knob is turned toward you?

Formulating Generalizations

1. A student places a wet mount on the stage of the microscope. Which direction should the student move the slide in order to see objects on the left side of the slide? On the right side?
2. A microscope's eyepiece has a magnification of 4X. The low power objective has a magnification of 12X, and the high power objective has a magnification of 50X. What is the total magnification of this scope under low power? Under high power?
3. A student makes a wet mount using pond water. When the student looks through the scope, he sees no organisms. Explain several things that may be wrong and how the student can correct the problem.
4. As you observe a moving unicellular organism, the organism seems to disappear and then reappear. Explain what may have happened.
5. How is it possible that part of a cell can be clearly in focus while another part of the same cell is not in focus?
6. A student locates the nucleus of a cell under low power. How can the student be certain that the nucleus will be visible when the objective is switched to high power?

Microscopic Measurement

4

Some living things can be observed with the unaided eye and measured with a millimeter ruler. Some living things are so large that they are measured in meters. Before the discovery of water microbes that were "one thousand times smaller than the eye of a louse," humans had no need for a smaller unit of measurement than the millimeter.

In your study of biology, it will be important for you to estimate the length, width, and diameter of microscopic living things or body parts of macroscopic living things.

In this investigation, you are to compute the diameter of the field of view (in micrometers) of your microscope on both low and high powers and compute the diameter of pollen grains and the length and width of a rotifer in micrometers. Also, you are to compare the optical properties of a stereomicroscope with the optical properties of a compound microscope, and determine the diameter of the field of view (in mm) of a stereomicroscope.

Materials *(per team of two students)*

microscope
coverslip
preserved insect
dropper
fresh flower
glass slide
pollen grains of one type of flower
probe
rotifer culture
scalpel
stereomicroscope
transparent plastic ruler (mm scale)
water
watch glass

Procedure

Part A. Determining the Diameter of the Field of View of a Microscope

To measure the field of view of a microscope you must use a unit called a micrometer (μm). A micrometer equals 0.001 mm.

Questions:

1. How many micrometers are there in one mm?
2. Could you visually divide a millimeter into the number of micrometers calculated in question 1? Why or why not?

Place the millimeter section of a plastic ruler over the center of the stage opening of a compound microscope. Using low power of the microscope, locate the measured lines of the ruler in the center of the field of view by using first the coarse focus knob and then the fine focus knob. Move the ruler so that one of the lines representing a millimeter is visible at one edge of the field of view (Figure 1). Remember, the distance between two lines is one millimeter. Estimate the diameter (in mm) of the field of view on low power.

Calculate the diameter in micrometers. Record the diameter in your lab notebook.

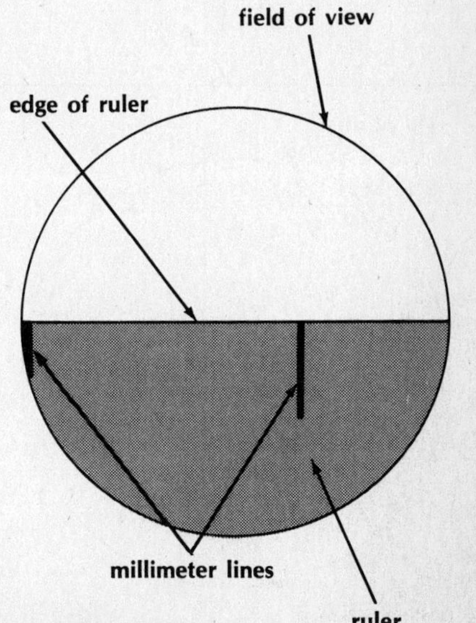

FIGURE 1

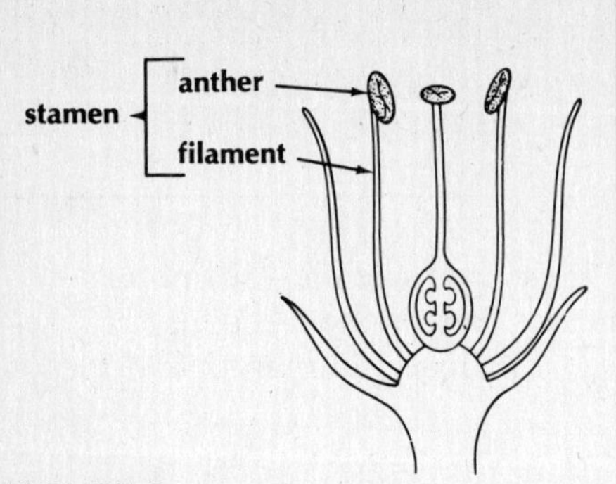

FIGURE 2

Because the high power field of view is less than one millimeter, it will be difficult to estimate the diameter by this technique. To calculate the diameter of the high power field, (*a*) divide the magnification of your high power field (usually 43X) by the magnification of the low power field (10X). Then (*b*) divide the diameter of the low power field in micrometers by the answer to *a*. The answer to *b* is the diameter of the high power field in micrometers.

Sample problem:

Low power field (magnification) = 10X
High power field (magnification) = 40X
Low power field (diameter in micrometers) = 2000 μm

a. $\frac{40X}{10X} = 4$

b. $\frac{2000 \text{ micrometers}}{4} = 500 \text{ micrometers}$

The diameter of the high power field of view is 500 micrometers.

Calculate the diameter of the high power field of view of your microscope by following these steps. Record the diameter in your lab notebook.

Part B. Measuring Living Material Viewed With a Microscope

Pollen grains

Remove the stamen (Figure 2) from a flower and open the anther with a probe and scalpel. **CAUTION:** *Scalpel is sharp. Cut away from fingers to avoid cuts.* Place some dustlike pollen grains on a clean slide. Make a wet mount of the pollen and observe the slide on both low and high powers. Calculate the diameter of a pollen grain by estimating how many grains could be placed end to end across the field of view (Figure 3). Then divide the diameter of the field of view by the number of grains.

Sample problem:

Diameter of low power field of view = 1500 μm
Pollen grains across field of view = 10 grains

$$\frac{1500 \text{ micrometers}}{10 \text{ pollen grains}} = 150 \ \mu m \text{ per pollen grain}$$

The diameter of a pollen grain is approximately 150 μm.

Make a wet mount of other types of pollen grains and calculate their diameters. Record the diameters in your lab notebook.

Rotifers

Some living things can change shape; consequently, they can change size. Make a wet mount of a rotifer (Figure 4). Observe the specimen with low power. Calculate the length and width of a rotifer. While observing the specimen, tap the slide with your pencil until the rotifer shrivels.

Questions:

3. Which was harder to calculate, the length of the rotifier or a pollen grain?
4. Why is it important to observe living specimens for a longer period of time than you did the letter in Investigation 3?

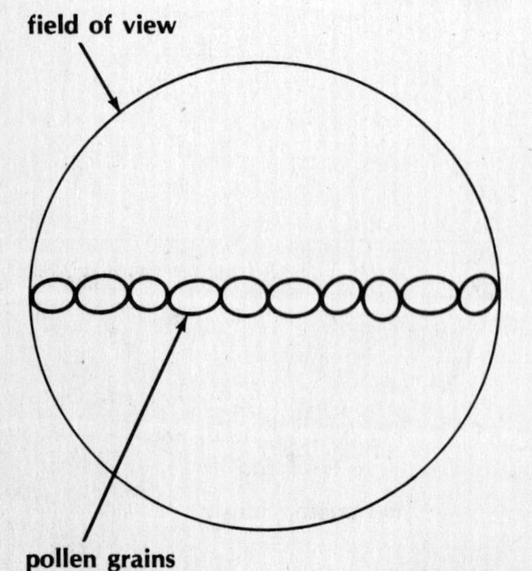

FIGURE 3

Question:

5. Considering the resolving power and depth of focus of your microscope, how are your observations of the rotifer different from the threads observed during Investigation 3?

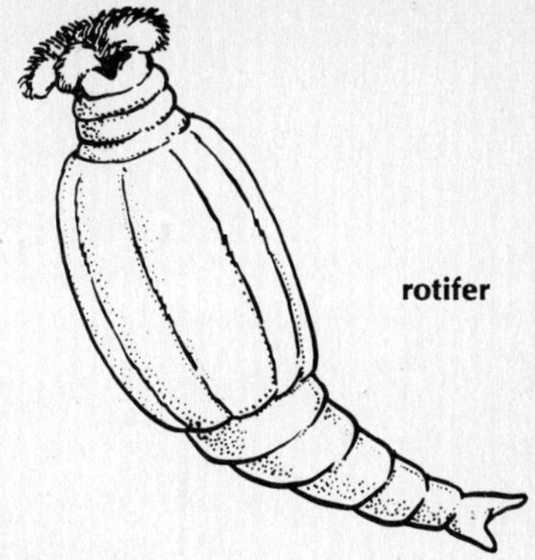

FIGURE 4

Part C. The Stereomicroscope

Some living things are too large to be viewed with a compound microscope and too small to be viewed with the unaided eye. For such living things, a stereomicroscope can be used (Figure 5). With a stereomicroscope, a biologist can see not only length and width but also depth because there are two lens systems. Specimens observed with this type of microscope are opaque. Therefore, reflected light is used rather than transmitted light. A compound microscope uses transmitted light, light that goes through the specimen. With a plastic ruler, measure the field of view of a stereomicroscope.

Questions:

6. Is the field of view of your stereomicroscope larger or smaller than that of a compound microscope?
7. Is the working distance and depth of focus of this microscope more or less than the compound microscope? Why?

Use a stereomicroscope to observe a preserved insect. Place a preserved insect in a watch glass and place the watch glass on the stage of the stereomicroscope. Move the specimen to the right. Compare the direction of movement of the insect with what you observed when you moved a specimen to the right under the compound microscope.

Question:

8. In what direction does the specimen appear to move when viewed under the stereomicroscope?

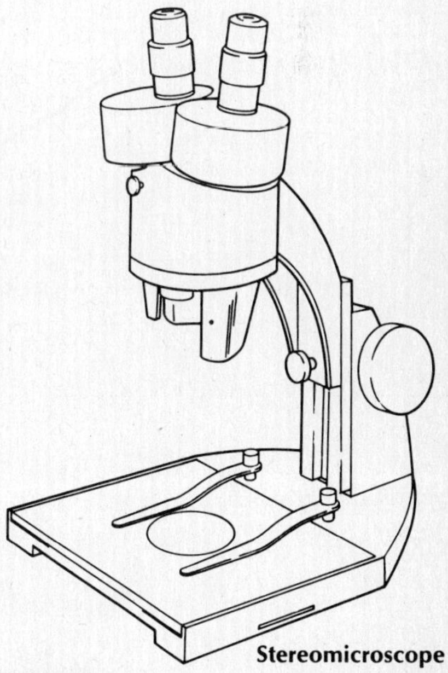

FIGURE 5

Formulating Generalizations

1. A student measures a specimen under low power to be 600 μm wide. How many millimeters wide is this specimen?
2. A specimen observed under low power is estimated to be 200 micrometers long. The student changes to the high power lens. What will happen to the size in micrometers of this specimen?
3. The sizes of several living organisms are listed below. Tell which microscope, compound or stereo, you would use to observe the organisms properly.
   a. 10 mm in length
   b. 10 000 μm in length
   c. 80 μm in width
   d. 660 μm in length
4. How do compound and stereomicroscopes differ in their use of light?
5. What types of objects are best viewed using a stereomicroscope?

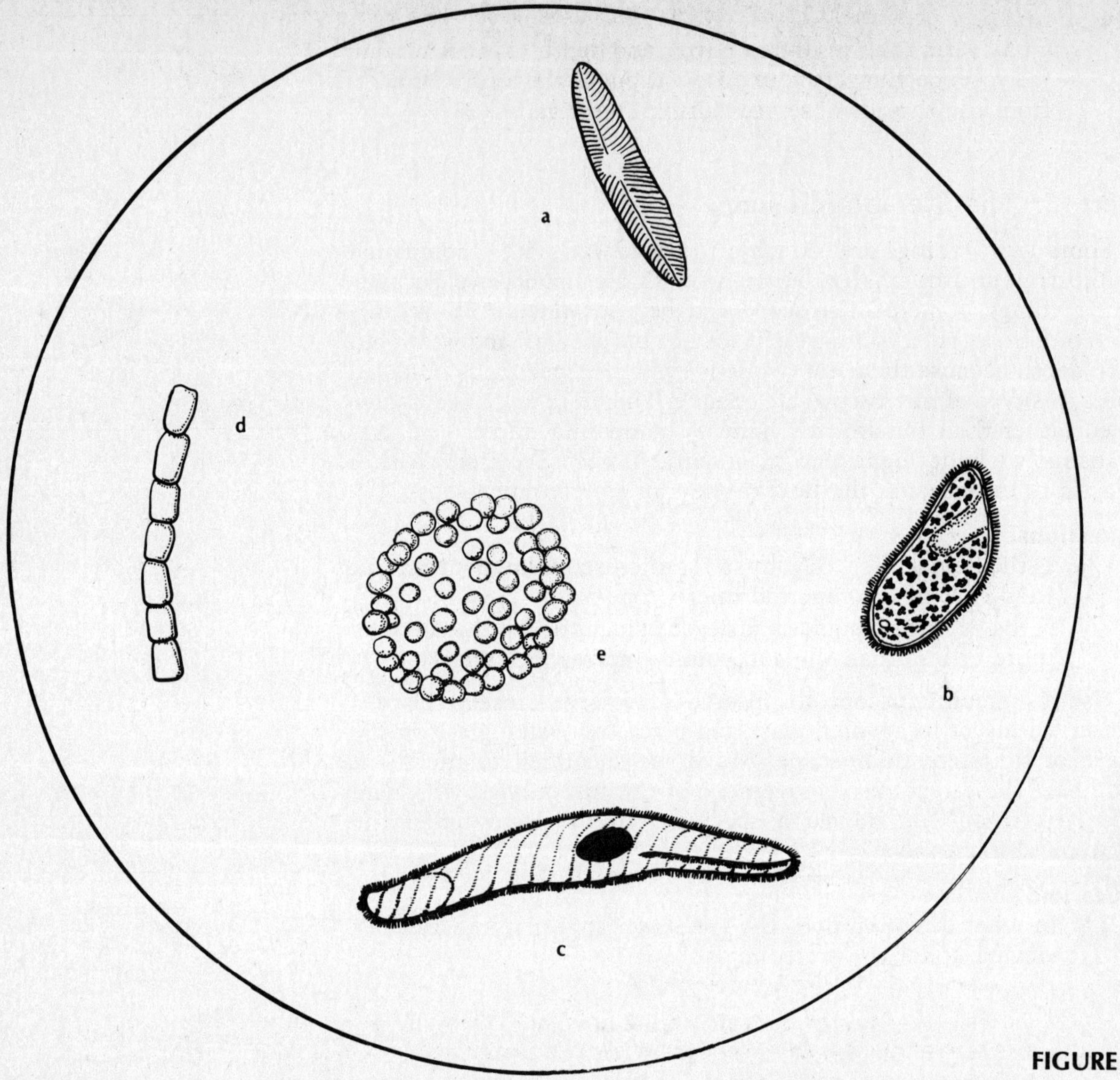

FIGURE 6

Figure 6 shows organisms as seen through the high power field of view in a microscope. Use the formulae in this laboratory investigation, Figure 6, and the microscope data below to answer questions 6 through 11.

Microscope Data

Eyepiece = 15X
Low power objective = 10X
High power objective = 50X
Diameter of low power field of view = 1.5 mm

6. How many micrometers in width is organism A?
7. How many micrometers in length is a cell in D?
8. How many micrometers in length is organism B?
9. How many micrometers in length is organism C?
10. How many micrometers in diameter is a cell of organism E?
11. How many micrometers in diameter is the high power field of view?

Detecting Compounds Made By Living Things

5

Specific compounds are necessary for life processes such as growth, development, reproduction, maintenance, and repair. Scientists have developed a series of chemical tests to determine the presence or absence in food samples of the building blocks of living things. In testing the substances and foodstuffs available, you should realize that the materials had a biological origin—they were made by producers or consumers. There are many compounds present in living organisms. However, you will perform tests for only four of these compounds: sugar, starch, protein, and fat.

In this investigation you are to use specific chemical tests to verify the presence of starch, sugar, protein, and fat in known solutions. Then you are to use these specific chemical tests to determine the presence of protein, fat, sugar, or starch in food samples. These tests are generally qualitative tests for the four substances. A qualitative test is one in which you observe the presence (or absence) of a substance. A few of the tests also indicate the relative amount of a substance present by the intensity of the color of the test solution. This is called a quantitative test.

Materials *(per team of two students)*

Benedict's solution—2 mL
burner
graduated cylinder—10 mL size
Gram's iodine solution—2 mL
known solutions:
  cooking oil (fat)—2 mL
  egg white (protein)—2 mL
  glucose solution (sugar)—2 mL
  starch suspension—2 mL
softened food samples
biuret reagent—3 mL (10 drops/test)
paper bag (cut in five pieces 10 cm × 10 cm)
Sudan III—2 mL
test tube holder
test tube rack
test tubes—4

Procedure

Part A. Background Information

Several solutions of food substances and food samples that have been soaked and softened in water have been prepared. If you bring any material from home make sure it is thoroughly softened before testing. Test each substance for starch, sugar, protein, and fat by using the following tests. Use a clean test tube for each test. When heating a sample, turn the open end of the test tube away from yourself and other students. The solutions may boil rapidly and spurt from the test tube. Pass the test tube gently through the flame (Figure 1). **CAUTION:** *use extreme care when working with an open flame. Secure long hair and loose clothing. Do not point tube towards yourself or another student while heating.*

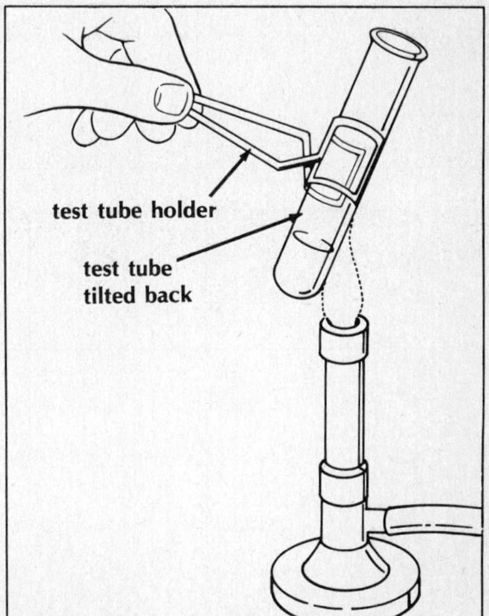

FIGURE 1

Record the results of each test in a table similar to Table 1. Use the symbols in Table 2 to record your results from each test.

Part B. Starch Test

Presence of starch can be detected by adding Gram's iodine to a food sample. **CAUTION:** *If iodine spillage occurs, rinse with water.* Place 3 to 5 drops of Gram's iodine in a test tube containing 2 mL of starch suspension. A change in color of the solution from red-brown to blue-black indicates the presence of starch. Concentration of starch is indicated by the intensity of the blue-black color. A dark color indicates the presence of much starch.

Part C. Sugar Test

Presence of a simple sugar (monosaccharide) can be detected by adding Benedict's solution to the sample and heating it. Place 6 to 8 drops of Benedict's solution into a test tube containing 2 mL of sugar solution. Heat the material gently by passing the test tube through the flame (Figure 1). Upon heating, the material will change to a green (+), yellow (+ +), orange (+ + +), or brick red (+ + + +) color as an indicator of the quantity of certain sugars present.

Part D. Protein Test

Presence of protein can be detected by adding biuret reagent to a food sample and heating it. **CAUTION:** *Biuret reagent is corrosive; it will burn skin. Be careful when pouring biuret reagent into a test tube.* Place 10 drops of biuret reagent in a test tube containing 2 mL of uncooked egg white. Heat the material gently until it boils. Allow the tube to cool. The presence of protein is indicated by a change from a blue to a purple colored solution.

Part E. Brown Paper Test

One way to test for the presence of fat is to rub the food sample on brown paper. Place a small drop of cooking oil on a 10 cm × 10 cm piece of brown paper. Rub the oil over an area 5 cm in diameter. Allow the paper to dry in a warm place. The presence of fat is indicated by a translucent spot on the paper. Hold the paper toward a light source to see the spot.

TABLE 1. TEST RESULTS

MATERIAL TO BE TESTED	STARCH TEST (A)	SUGAR TEST (B)	PROTEIN TEST (C)	FAT TEST	
				PAPER TEST	SUDAN III TEST (D)

TABLE 2. KEY TO TEST RESULTS	
SUGAR TEST RESULTS:	
− blue (no sugar) + green + + yellow	+ + + orange + + + + brick red (most sugar)
STARCH, FAT, AND PROTEIN TEST RESULTS:	
− specific molecule absent + specific molecule present	

Sudan III Test

Another test for the presence of fat is to add Sudan III to the sample. Place 2 mL of cooking oil and 2 mL of water into a test tube. Place 4 mL of water into a second test tube. Add three drops of Sudan III to both test tubes. Shake both test tubes gently. The presence of fat is indicated by a pink color diffused throughout the cooking oil. If no fat is present, the material in the test tube will be the same pink color throughout.

Part F. Testing Unknown Foods

Test each softened food sample for the presence of starch, protein, fat, and sugar. Place 1 mL of each food sample into each of four test tubes. Label the tubes A, B, C, and D. Use the tests described in Parts A-E of this investigation to determine the type of each food sample. Record your results in your data table using the symbols listed in Table 2.

Formulating Generalizations

1. If a substance has sugar present but it tests negative for sugar, what does this tell you about the structure of the molecule?
2. Suppose a student added Benedict's solution to a test tube containing glucose and allowed it to stand for fifteen minutes. The student noticed no color change in the test tube. Explain why this happened.
3. Why was Sudan III added to a test tube containing only water?
4. In the test for protein, why do some tubes show a light purple color while others show a dark purple color?
5. In the test for sugar, why do some tubes show a green color while others show a brick red color?
6. Name any of the softened foods that had more than one compound present.
7. What factors hindered the four different tests? How could these factors be corrected?
8. Why do cartons and cans containing foods have labels that give the amounts of sugars, fats, proteins, and starches present?

6 Molecules Of Biological Importance

Carbon, oxygen, nitrogen, and hydrogen are four elements that combine in many ways to form many of the molecules in organisms. In some organisms, these elements make up over 90% of the weight of the organisms. Other elements are present in organisms but in smaller amounts.

Hydrocarbons constitute a large group of organic compounds. They contain the elements hydrogen and carbon. Often another atom, other than carbon or hydrogen, or a group of atoms is substituted on the hydrocarbon molecule. This substitute group of atoms is called a functional group.

The chemical properties of an organic molecule are determined by the functional group. CH_4 is a gas called methane. By removing one hydrogen atom and adding a hydroxyl group (—OH), the substance becomes CH_3OH, methyl alcohol. Methyl alcohol is a liquid.

For convenience, biochemists use the letter "R" to represent the part of a molecule other than the functional group. The R can also be used to show the location of the functional group in a molecule. For example, CH_3OH could be written R—OH where R stands for CH_3. In this way, the complete structural formula does not have to be written.

Although you may be unfamiliar with the synthesis of organic molecules by organisms, this knowledge will become more important as you continue your study of biology.

Given the molecular formulas of nine molecules of biological importance, you are to determine the two-dimensional structural formulas of the molecules and write the two-dimensional formula for each compound in your lab notebook. You will also build three-dimensional models of these compounds.

Materials *(per student)*

polystyrene balls (black, red, blue, green)
toothpicks

Procedure

With the help of Tables 1, 2, and 3, use the molecular formulas of the following compounds to write two-dimensional structural formulas of each compound.

1. C_2H_5OH — ethyl alcohol
2. H_2O — water
3. $C_3H_5(OH)_3$ — glycerol
4. CH_3COOH — acetic acid
5. NH_2CH_2COOH — glycine (amino acid)
6. $CO(NH_2)_2$ — urea
7. $CH_3COCOOH$ — pyruvic acid
8. CH_3CHO — acetaldehyde
9. $CH_3CH_2CH_2COOH$ — butyric acid

Example: CH_3OH, methyl alcohol

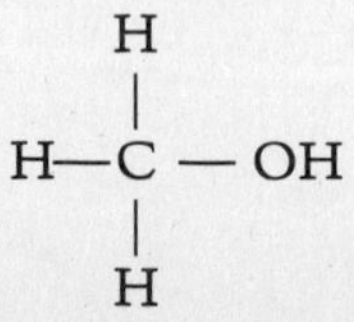

TABLE 1. NUMBER OF BONDS PER ELEMENT
carbon (C) = 4
hydrogen (H) = 1
oxygen (O) = 2
nitrogen (N) = 3 or 4 (usually 3)

Build three-dimensional models of each compound. Use different colored balls to represent specific atoms and toothpicks to represent chemical bonds.

Color code for balls:

C = black   H = blue
O = red   N = green

Formulating Generalizations

1. Which element forms the "backbone" of most two-dimensional organic compounds?
2. Which of the nine molecules that you built are not organic models? Explain.
3. How are the pyruvic acid, butyric acid, and acetic acid molecules different from each other?
4. Look at the formulas of the hydrocarbons in Table 2. What do the prefixes pent-, hex-, hept-, oct-, and dec- mean?
5. Using the structural formula and names of functional groups, tell why glycine is called an amino acid.
6. What does the prefix of the hydrocarbon molecule, for example hex- of hexane, tell you about that molecule?

TABLE 2. ALKANE HYDROCARBONS

NAME	MOLECULAR FORMULA
methane	CH_4
ethane	C_2H_6
propane	C_3H_8
butane	C_4H_{10}
pentane	C_5H_{12}
hexane	C_6H_{14}
heptane	C_7H_{16}
octane	C_8H_{18}
nonane	C_9H_{20}
decane	$C_{10}H_{22}$

TABLE 3. FUNCTIONAL GROUPS

GROUP NAME	FORMULA	STRUCTURAL FORMULA	EXAMPLE
alcohol	R—OH	R—OH	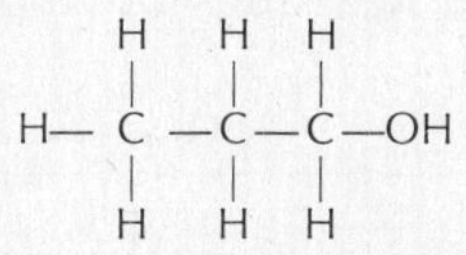
carboxylic acid (organic acid)	R—COOH	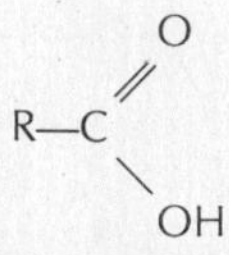	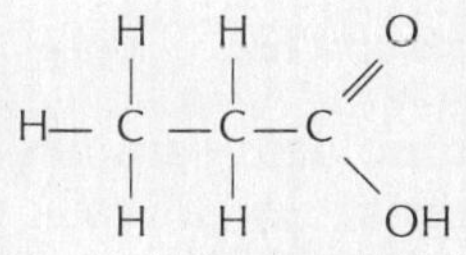
amine	R—NH_2	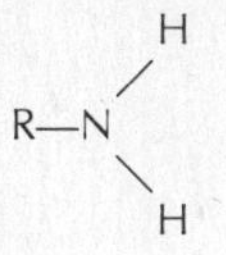	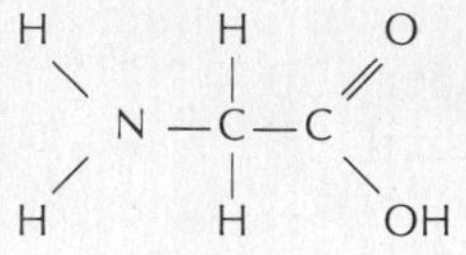
aldehyde	R—CHO	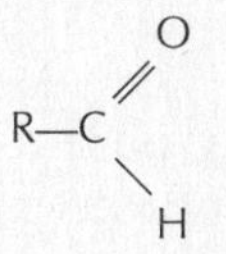	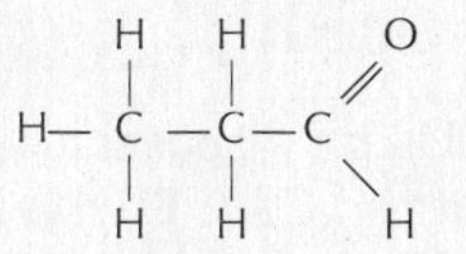

7 Amino Acid Chromatography

Solutes can be separated from solvents and identified by various chemical and physical means or a combination of both. A Russian scientist, Tswett, developed a technique to separate compounds from a solution. This technique is called chromatography. Tswett worked with plant pigments.

Chromatography is a physical process in which compounds are separated from a solution. A common feature in any chromatographic method is the use of two phases. One phase is stationary, the other is mobile. The stationary phase can be solid or liquid. The mobile phase can be a liquid or gas. The mixture to be separated is distributed between the two phases. In this investigation you will use paper chromatography.

In paper chromatography, the solution is "spotted" near the edge of a piece of filter paper and allowed to dry. The filter paper is then placed in a container of a specific solvent. The spots of dried solution are placed slightly above the solvent level. The filter paper absorbs the solvent and the component parts of the dried solution will "move" upward at a specific rate in relationship to the moving solvent.

Unknown solutes from a solution or its component parts may be identified by computing the R_f value of the known components in the solvent systems. The R_f value is the ratio of the distance traveled by the solute to the distance traveled by the solvent. By comparing R_f values of unknown components with the R_f values of known components, an unknown substance can be identified.

In a prior investigation, you learned to identify proteins. In this investigation, you will identify some amino acids, which are building blocks of proteins. By comparing the R_f value of an unknown amino acid with the R_f values of known amino acids, you will identify the unknown amino acid.

Materials *(per student or team)*

- amino acid samples—2
- disposable gloves
- filter paper strips (5 × 15 cm)—2
- jars with lids—2
- ninhydrin solution
- paper clips—2
- pencil
- plastic straws—2
- pump spray bottle
- ruler, metric
- solvent
- toothpicks, flat—2
- hood

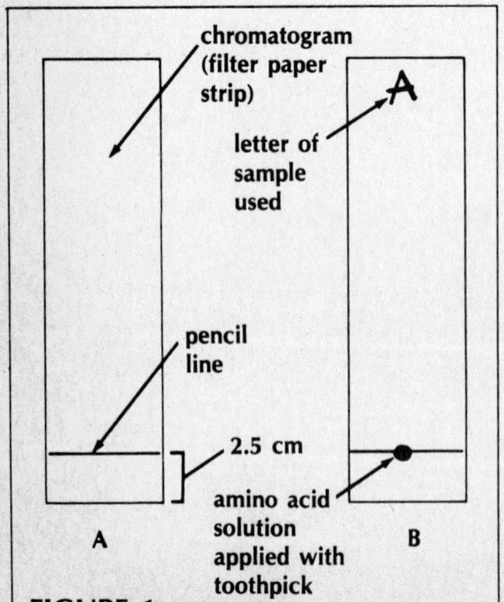

FIGURE 1

Procedure

Using disposable gloves, obtain two filter paper strips (chromatograms). **CAUTION:** *Do not touch filter paper with your bare hands. Chemicals in sweat can interfere with results.* With a pencil, draw a line 2.5 cm from the bottom of each chromatogram (Figure 1A). Dip the wide end of a flat toothpick into one unknown amino acid solution. Touch the wet end of the toothpick to the middle of the pencil line drawn on the chromatogram (Figure 1B). The amino acid solution will be transferred from the toothpick to the chromatogram and will appear as a wet spot about 0.5 to 1 cm in diameter. Discard the used toothpick. With a pencil, write the letter of the sample you

TABLE 1. DATA CHART FOR UNKNOWN AMINO ACIDS					
LETTER OF SAMPLE OF AMINO ACID	A. DISTANCE TRAVELED BY AMINO ACID	B. DISTANCE TRAVELED BY SOLVENT	R_f VALUE $\frac{A}{B}$	COLOR OF AMINO ACID	NAME OF UNKNOWN AMINO ACID

used at the top of the chromatogram (Figure 1B). Also record this letter in your lab notebook in a data chart similar to Table 1. Repeat the above procedure using the second chromatogram and a second unknown amino acid solution.

Using Figures 2 and 3 as guides, roll the lettered end of one chromatogram around a straw. Place the chromatogram into an *empty* jar. Adjust the paper on the straw so that the chromatogram just touches the bottom of the jar when the straw supporting the paper strip is placed across the mouth of the jar. Paper clip the chromatogram around the straw in this position. Repeat this procedure for the second chromatogram.

Remove the chromatograms from the empty jars. Pour solvent into each jar to a depth of 1 cm. **CAUTION:** *DO NOT breathe fumes from solvent. If spillage occurs, rinse with water and call your teacher.* Place the chromatograms back into the jars and rest the straws on the jar mouths. Gently place a lid on top of each jar (the straws should be sticking out from underneath the lids). The jar lids will help keep the air inside the jars saturated with solvent. Your finished assembly should look like Figure 3. Allow the jars to sit for at least 15 minutes.

At the end of 15 minutes, remove the chromatograms from the jars. Using a pencil, draw a line to indicate how far the solvent has moved up each chromatogram. This line is called the leading edge of the solvent (Figure 4).

Air dry the chromatograms under a hood by moving them back and forth. Using a pump spray bottle, spray the area between the leading

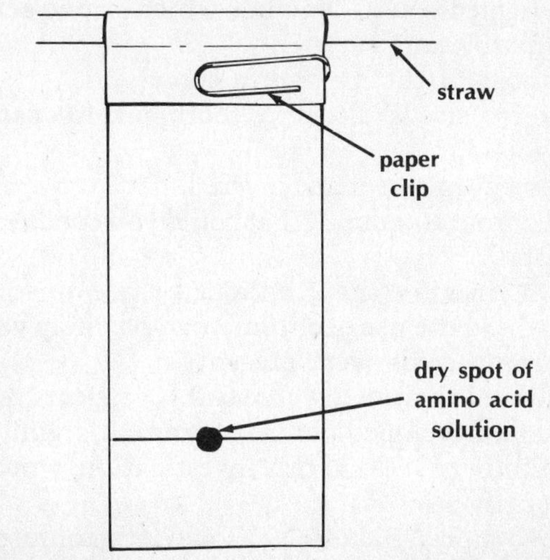

FIGURE 2

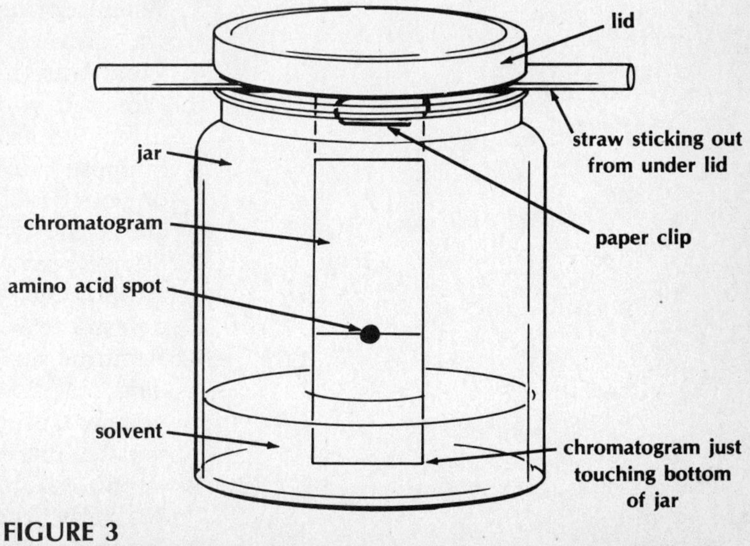

FIGURE 3

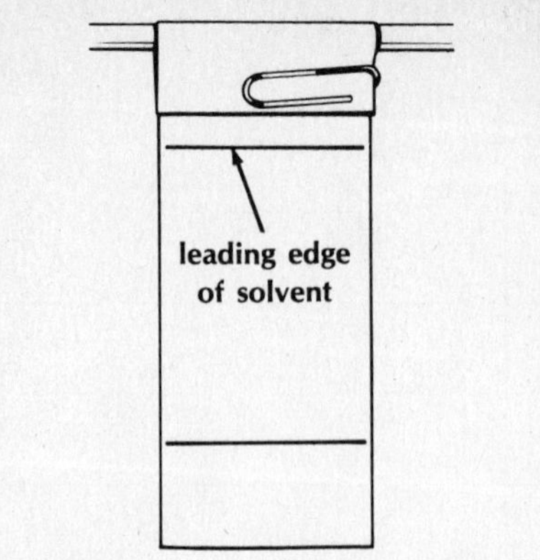

FIGURE 4

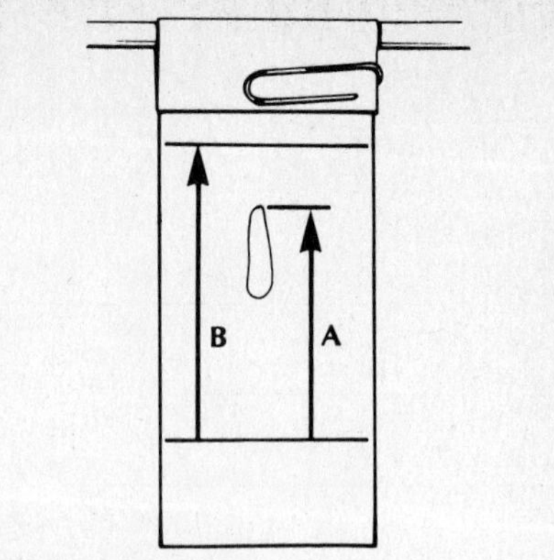

FIGURE 5

edge and the bottom pencil line of each chromatogram with ninhydrin solution. **CAUTION:** *Ninhydrin is toxic. Do not inhale fumes. Spray solution under a hood only.* Air dry the chromatograms again.

After air drying, place the chromatograms near a lighted incandescent bulb for three to five minutes. A colored spot will appear on each chromatogram. The spots represent a specific amino acid. Outline the spots with a pencil.

On both chromatograms, measure the distance from the top of the colored spot to the bottom pencil line (A on Figure 5). Also measure the distance from the leading edge of the solvent to the bottom pencil line (B on Figure 5). Record these distances in your data chart. Using the formula

$$\frac{\text{Distance traveled by amino acid solution (A)}}{\text{Distance traveled by the solvent (B)}} = R_f,$$

compute the R_f values for your two unknown amino acids. Identify the unknowns by comparing your R_f values and the colors of your amino acids to those listed in Table 2.

TABLE 2. R_F VALUES OF AMINO ACIDS

AMINO ACID	COLOR	R_f
Serine	Reddish purple	0.50
Proline	Yellow to orange	0.59
Lysine	Dark purple	0.69
Alanine	Reddish purple	0.75
Leucine	Light reddish purple	1.00

Formulating Generalizations

1. How many spots were present for each of the developed amino acids on the chromatograms?
2. What were the two amino acids that were found on your chromatograms?
3. What information helped you to conclude which amino acid was on each chromatogram?
4. What was the purpose of the ninhydrin spray?
5. Why did you have to use a different toothpick for each unknown amino acid?
6. Suppose you saw one purple spot and one red spot 2 cm apart on your developed chromatogram. What could you conclude about the two spots?
7. Suppose you had a mixture that contained three to four amino acids, how would the use of chromatography help you determine what amino acids were present?
8. Arginine, an amino acid with an R_f value of 0.70, appears as a dark purple spot on a developed chromatogram. If arginine were one of the unknowns used in this investigation, would you be able to identify it?
9. Suppose arginine has an R_f value of 0.59. Could it be confused with any other unknown amino acids in this investigation?
10. What is the practical value of chromatography to a scientist?

Extracellular Enzymes

8

Enzymes are catalysts that aid chemical reactions. A catalyst's function is to change the rate of reaction. Enzymes are composed of biological materials called proteins. Enzymes take part in necessary biochemical processes that occur in the cells of all organisms. Enzymes are specific. Each enzyme has a function to perform in a cell. In most cases, enzymes will aid only one reaction.

Some enzymes can move through the cell membrane into the surrounding medium, or environment. Such an enzyme is called an extracellular enzyme. An extracellular enzyme breaks down (or digests) complex molecules into smaller molecules. The smaller molecules can then be absorbed through the cell membrane. These molecules can be metabolized within the cell for energy.

In this investigation, you are to distinguish the degree of extracellular digestion that occurs as a result of bacterial growth on agar plates containing starch or milk.

Materials *(per student or team)*

broth cultures:
- *Bacillus cereus*
- *Bacillus subtilis*
- *Escherichia coli*
- yeast suspension

glass marking pencil
incubator
iodine solution—15 mL
5% skim milk agar—15 mL
0.2% starch agar—15 mL
0.4% starch agar—15 mL
0.8% starch agar—15 mL
sterile cotton swabs—8
sterile petri dishes—4

Procedure

Part A. Hydrolysis (Digestion) of Starch

CAUTION: *Bacteria may cause infection. Keep hands away from face throughout this investigation. Do not chew gum or eat while carrying out the procedure. Wash hands immediately after finishing procedure.*

Obtain a petri dish of each starch solution concentration. Divide each dish into four sectors by marking on the bottom of the dish with a glass marking pencil. Label each petri dish with your name and the starch concentration. Inoculate each dish by dipping a sterile cotton swab into a broth culture, slightly opening the lid, and gently swabbing a sector of the starch agar in the dish (Figure 1). Using a new sterile swab for each culture, inoculate each sector of all four dishes. Place *B. subtilis* on sector 1, *E. coli* on sector 2, *B. cereus* on sector 3, and yeast on sector 4. In your lab notebook, record the concentration of starch and the culture swabbed on each sector in a data table similar to Table 1. Incubate the dishes inverted at 37°C for 48 hours.

Test each petri dish for starch hydrolysis by flooding the dish with iodine solution. **CAUTION:** *If iodine spillage occurs, rinse with water.* After one minute, drain off the iodine into a sink. An unstained area around a culture indicates digestion of starch by the organism. Record which organisms did and did not digest starch. Record in your lab notebook whether starch digestion is affected by the concentration of starch in the plates. Record the degree of differences noted in each concentration in your data chart.

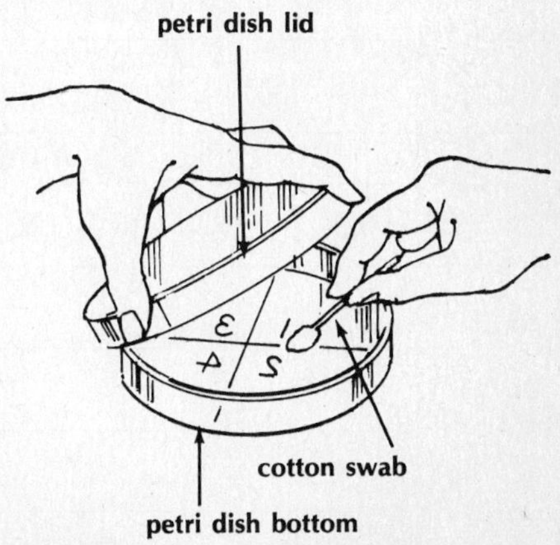

FIGURE 1

Part B. Hydrolysis (Digestion) of Milk Proteins

Obtain a skim milk agar dish. Divide the dish into four sectors by marking on the bottom of the dish with a glass marking pencil. Inoculate each sector with the different cultures as you did in Part A. Label the petri dish with your name and "milk agar" to differentiate it from starch agar. In your lab notebook, record the culture swabbed on each sector in a data chart similar to Table 2.

Incubate the dish inverted for four days at 37°C to ensure maximum growth. A clear area immediately surrounding an area of growth is evidence of protein hydrolysis. Record which organisms did and did not digest protein in your data chart.

Formulating Generalizations

1. Why were the petri dishes inverted during incubation? (HINT: Consider the water droplets that condensed on the lids of the petri dishes.)
2. Did any type of microorganism digest starch better than another? If so, which one?
3. Is starch digestion gradual? Explain the evidence you have to support your answer.
4. Which microorganisms did not appear to digest starch at all?
5. What does your answer to question 4 tell you about the enzyme used in starch digestion?
6. On which dish did starch digestion appear most complete? Explain your answer.
7. Which microorganisms appeared to digest milk proteins? Explain your answer.
8. Which microorganisms digested both starches and proteins? Why?

TABLE 1. HYDROLYSIS OF STARCH

% STARCH	CULTURE TYPE	OBSERVATIONS

TABLE 2. HYDROLYSIS OF MILK PROTEINS

% SKIM MILK	CULTURE TYPE	OBSERVATIONS

Qualitative And Quantitative Plasmolysis

9

Water passes through cell membranes from areas of high water concentration to areas of lower water concentration. This movement of water is called osmosis. If a cell is placed in an environment in which the concentration of water is less than that inside the cell, water will flow from the cytoplasm through the membrane into the environment. The cytoplasm of the cell shrinks. In an animal cell, the entire cell shrivels. In a plant cell, the cytoplasm shrinks away from the cell wall. This water removal is called plasmolysis.

A scientist can observe the effects of water loss by observing the shrinking of a cell's cytoplasm with a microscope. This observation is a qualitative measurement. In measuring the amount of water loss in grams, a scientist makes a quantitative measurement.

The purpose of this investigation is to observe the qualitative effects of plasmolysis in *Elodea* cells and to quantitatively measure the rate of plasmolysis in potato slices.

Materials *(per student)*

Part A

- *Elodea* sprigs
- microscope
- glass slide
- coverslip
- water
- dropper
- 5% sodium chloride solution—5 mL
- 10% sodium chloride solution—5 mL
- distilled water
- paper towel

Part B

- white potatoes—2
- beakers, 250-mL—4
- balance
- paper towel
- glass marking pencils or labels
- distilled water—75 mL
- 5% sodium chloride solution—75 mL
- 10% sodium chloride solution—75 mL
- 15% sodium chloride solution—75 mL
- single-edge razor blade

Procedure

Part A. Qualitative Plasmolysis

Make a wet mount of an *Elodea* leaf (see Investigation 10). Locate epidermal cells on low power and then on high power of your microscope. Place two drops of 5% sodium chloride solution along one edge of the coverslip. Draw the salt solution across the slide by placing a small section of a paper towel on the opposite side of the coverslip (Figure 1). Observe the effects of the solution on the cells. Replace the sodium chloride solution with distilled water in the same manner that the sodium chloride was added. Observe the results in high power.

Make another *Elodea* wet mount and repeat this procedure using a 10% sodium chloride solution.

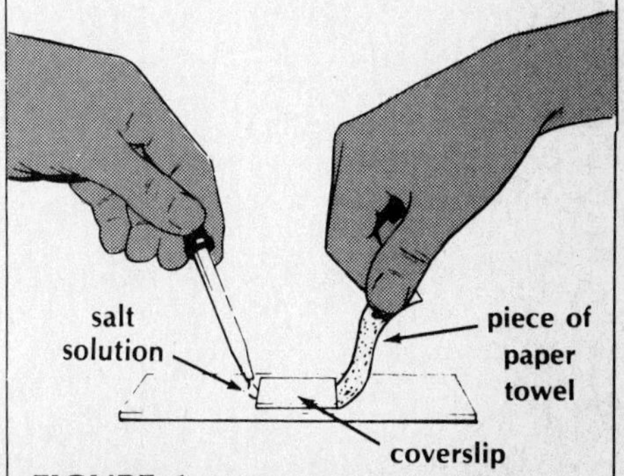

FIGURE 1

Part B. Quantitative Plasmolysis

Cut a white potato into 8 to 12 slices. Each piece should be about 1 cm thick. Determine the mass of the potato slices in stacks of three. Record the mass of each stack of three potato slices in a table similar to Table 1 in your lab notebook. Put a stack of potatoes into each of four beakers. Label the beakers A, B, C, and D. To beaker A, add 75 mL of distilled water; to beaker B, add 75 mL of 5% sodium chloride solution; to beaker C, add 75 mL of 10% sodium chloride solution; and to beaker D, add 75 mL of 15% sodium chloride solution. After 20 minutes, remove the potato slices from the beakers. Quickly blot the slices with a paper towel and determine the mass of each stack. In the table, record the mass of each stack after soaking. In rows 3 and 4 of the table, indicate the amount of increase or decrease in mass of each stack. Calculate the percent change by using the formula:

$$\frac{\text{Amount of increase or decrease}}{\text{Mass before}} \times 100 = \%\ \text{change}$$

Observe the appearance of each slice of potato. Record a brief description of the potato slices in your lab notebook.

TABLE 1. CHANGE IN MASS OF POTATO STACKS

	BEAKER A	BEAKER B	BEAKER C	BEAKER D
mass before				
mass after				
amount of increase				
amount of decrease				
percent change				

Formulating Generalizations

1. What happened to the cytoplasm of the leaf cells when salt solution was added to the *Elodea* wet mount? Why?
2. When the salt solution was replaced by distilled water in the *Elodea* wet mount, did the cells recover? Why or why not?
3. Was there any difference in the effect on the *Elodea* cells between the 5% and 10% salt solutions? Explain.
4. Which potato stack gained the most mass after 20 minutes of immersion? Which potato stack lost the most mass?
5. Give reasons for what happened to each stack of potato slices in the various solutions.
6. What might have been the result with the potato slices if the immersion time were lengthened?
7. What would happen to your cells if you were to drink salt water? Explain.

Basic Cell Structure

10

Some cells are visible to the unaided eye, but most are microscopic. They range from 0.1 micrometers to several centimeters in diameter. Most cells average between 10 to 15 micrometers in diameter. Fifty cells 10 micrometers in diameter would be able to fit side by side across the period at the end of this sentence.

All cells have an outer boundary called a cell membrane. The cell membrane holds the parts of a cell, or organelles, inside in the same way a plastic bag holds material. The cell membrane controls what enters and leaves the cell. Plant cells have a thick, rigid cell wall covering the outside of the membrane. The stiff cell wall adds support to a plant.

Inside the cell is a jellylike material called cytoplasm. Many metabolic reactions take place in the cytoplasm and several organelles are found in the cytoplasm. Most cells have a spherical object inside the cytoplasm called the nucleus. The nucleus contains genetic material and controls the cell's activities. Some cells also contain small round parts called plastids. Plastids that contain chlorophyll are called chloroplasts. The number of plastids in cells varies. Using a light microscope, you can see the cell wall, cell membrane, nucleus, cytoplasm, and plastids in those cells that have these parts.

In this investigation, you are to observe and locate parts within several types of cells. You are to measure the length and width (diameter) of each type of cell in micrometers. You are to record what parts are present or absent in each type of cell.

Materials *(per student or team)*

microscope
probe
Protococcus culture on bark
glass slide
coverslip
water
toothpick
stain (methylene blue or iodine)
paper towels
dropper
Amoeba culture
prepared *Allium* root slide, longitudinal section
slime mold culture
onion bulb
forceps
Elodea sprig

Procedure

Observe each cell type as directed below. For each type of cell perform the following and record your results in a table similar to Table 1. Measure the length, width, and/or diameter of each cell. Record the presence or absence of the listed organelles and structures that you observe. Compare each cell that you observe with the drawings (Figures 2 through 7) provided for you and list any differences in organelles present and/or their shapes that you observe.

Cell Types

A. *Protococcus.* With a probe, gently scrape some green scum from a piece of bark containing *Protococcus.* The green scum is *Protococcus.* Place the *Protococcus* on a clean, dry slide and prepare a wet mount. Observe the cells with low power and then with high power. The nucleus should appear as a large dark body in the center of the cell. The chloroplasts are elongated green bodies within the cytoplasm.

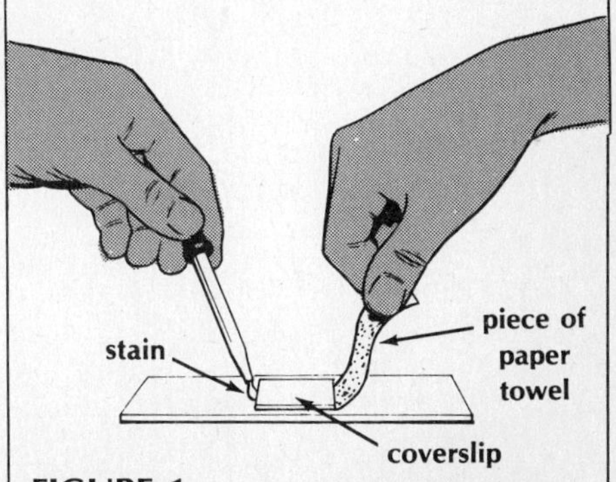

FIGURE 1

FIGURE 2

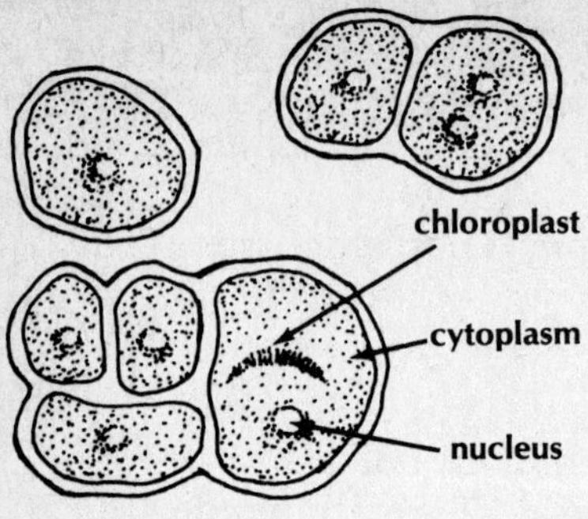

Protococcus

FIGURE 3

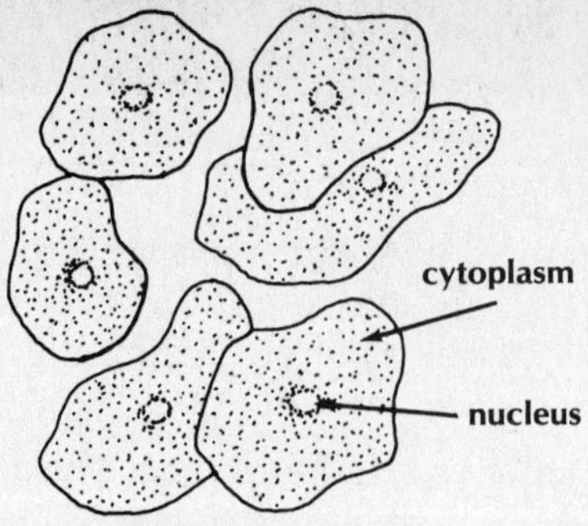

Cheek Cells

FIGURE 4

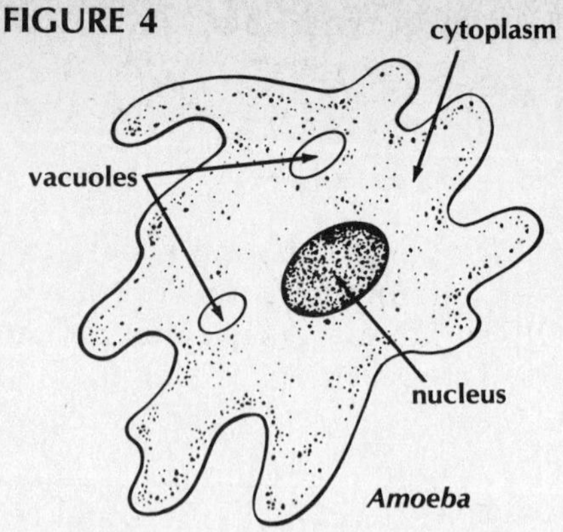

Amoeba

B. Cheek cells. With a clean, flat toothpick, gently scrape the inside of your cheek. Rub the toothpick on a clean, dry slide. Add a drop of water and a coverslip. Examine the wet mount with low power and then with high power.

A stain will be needed with this type of cell to make cell structures visible. You will not have to destroy your wet mount to stain the cells. Raise the body tube of the microscope about 2 cm and put the low power objective back in position. Add a drop of stain along one edge of the coverslip. Place a small section of a paper towel on the opposite side of the coverslip (Figure 1). The stain will be drawn across the slide by capillary action. After the cells have been stained, observe them again with low power and high power. In future labs, this technique can be used to do "on the spot" staining. **CAUTION:** *If stain spillage occurs, rinse with water.*

C. Amoebae. Use a dropper to transfer a drop from an *Amoeba* culture to a clean, dry slide. Add a coverslip to make a wet mount. Observe the amoebae with low power and then high power.

TABLE 1. CHARACTERISTICS OF DIFFERENT CELL TYPES

CELL TYPE	STRUCTURES (PRESENT OR ABSENT)						MOTILITY (PRESENT OR ABSENT)	DIMENSIONS (MICROMETERS)
	Cell Wall	Membrane	Nucleus	Cytoplasm	Plastids	Others		
Protococcus								

D. Meristematic and protective cells. Place a prepared slide of a longitudinal section of an *Allium* root on the stage of your microscope. Using low power, locate the meristematic and protective tissue (Figure 5). Meristem cells are easily distinguished from other cells because their nuclei occupy nearly one-half of the cell and are nearly square in shape. Some of these cells will have chromatin. In others, the chromatin has condensed into rod-shaped bodies called chromosomes. Protective cells have shapes and contents different from meristematic cells. Fill in the table for both types of cells.

E. Slime mold. Remove the top half of a petri dish from a slime mold culture. Place the bottom half, containing agar and a slime mold culture, on the stage of your microscope. Center a part of the plasmodium (the slimy mass of material) over the hole in the stage. Using low power, examine the plasmodium of the slime mold. **CAUTION:** *DO NOT run the objective into the agar. Use low power only.*

F. Onion epidermis. Remove a scale from an onion that has already been cut in quarters. Peel the thin, *inner* layer of the scale away using forceps or your fingernail. Place the tissue on a clean, dry slide. Add a drop of water and a coverslip to make a wet mount. Observe the onion epidermis with low power and then with high power.

Repeat the staining procedure used for cheek cells. Again, observe the cells with low and high powers. Use the stained cells to fill in the table.

G. *Elodea*. Remove a young leaf near the growing tip of an *Elodea* sprig. Put the leaf on a slide and add a drop of water. Add a coverslip to make a wet mount. Observe the leaf with low and then high power. Observe the cells along the margin and those directly in the middle of the leaf. Record any differences. Look for movement of chloroplasts within the cells.

FIGURE 5

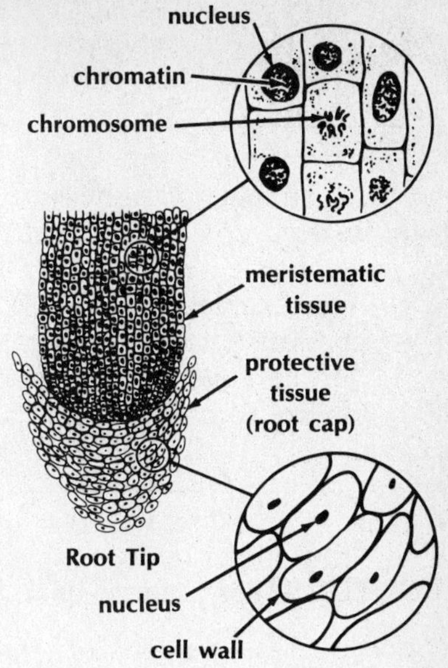

FIGURE 6

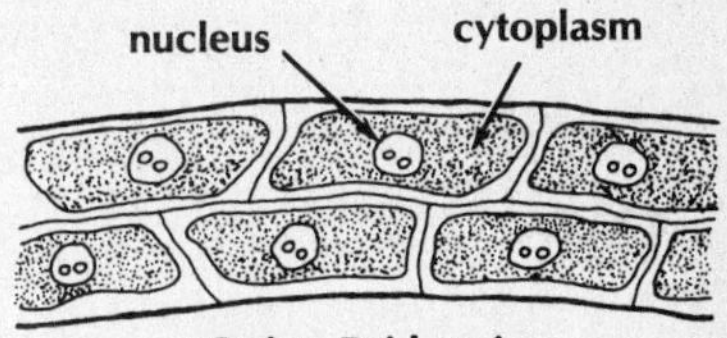

Onion Epidermis

FIGURE 7

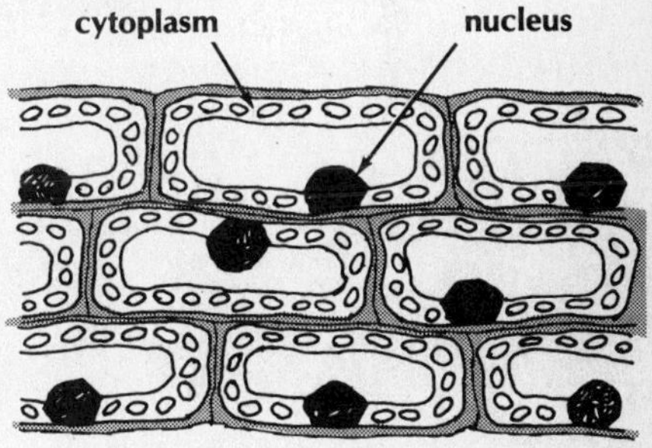

Elodea Leaf

Formulating Generalizations

1. How are the samples of the *Amoeba* and cheek cells similar?
2. What three organelles do cheek cells, slime mold cells, and *Amoeba* cells have in common?
3. What two organelles are visible in *Protococcus, Allium* root, *Elodea*, and onion epidermis?
4. Which cells have green plastids? What is the function of green plastids?
5. Why was the nucleus not visible in *Elodea* cells?
6. In which cells did you see movement of cytoplasm?
7. What is the function of movement of cytoplasm?
8. What features of the root tip cells of *Allium* enabled you to tell the difference between the meristematic and protective cells?
9. Which specimens appeared to be unicellular?
10. Which specimens appeared to be multicellular?
11. What cell parts became more visible after stain was added?
12. The cell theory states that (1) all organisms are composed of cells or cell fragments which are the basic units of structure and function, and (2) all cells are produced from other cells. Which cell types observed verify the second statement of the cell theory? Explain.

11 Measurement of Chemical Energy in Food

A biologist can measure the amount of chemical energy in foodstuffs by burning the food. Breaking down molecules transfers the energy stored in the molecules to heat energy. The heat energy released from burning food can be used to heat water. The change in temperature of the water enables biologists to compute the energy change. Because of some inefficiency in the apparatus that is used, some heat will be lost to the environment.

In this investigation, you are to measure the amount of heat released when a nut is burned. You are to calculate the amount of heat released in calories per gram in each sample.

Materials *(per student or team)*

balance
cork, large
graduated cylinder, 10 mL
matches
ring stand
straight pin
test tube, medium size
test tube clamp
water
thermometer
various nuts (8 mm × 8 mm), unshelled—2 of each type

Procedure

Find the mass of a nut and record it in your lab notebook in a table similar to Table 1. Place the nut on the end of a pin inserted in a cork (Figure 1). Attach the test tube to the clamp. Place exactly 10 mL of water into the test tube. Record the temperature of the water in your data table. Ignite the nut with a match. **CAUTION:** *Use extreme caution with lighted matches.* Be sure the nut is not below the test tube when you light the nut. After the nut is ignited, place the test tube about 1 cm above the burning nut (Figure 1).

Make sure the test tube is directly over the burning sample. **CAUTION:** *The test tube will absorb heat. Do not touch the test tube with your fingers.* Unscrew the clamp from the ring stand to move the test tube.

If complete burning does not occur, relight the nut. When burning is complete, measure the temperature of the water in the test tube. Record this temperature in your table.

Repeat the investigation using another sample of the same kind of nut. If time permits, use other types of nuts. Using the information in the calculations section on page 31, calculate the number of calories in each sample of nut. Calculate the average number of calories in each type of nut (average your two samples). Record the calories in your data table and write your results on the chalkboard. Compare your results with those of your classmates. Compute class averages for each type of nut and record these in your notebook.

FIGURE 1

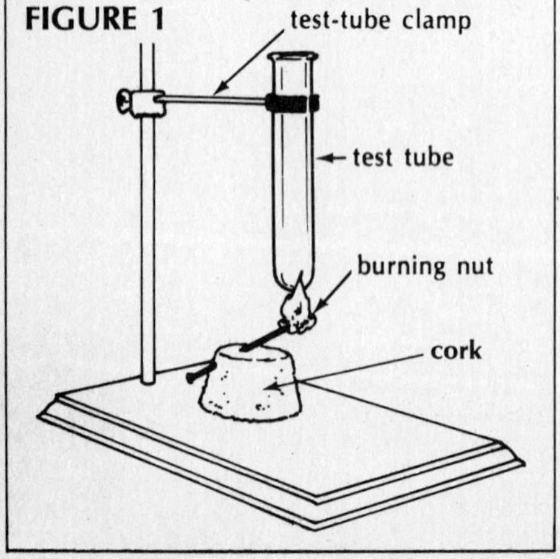

Calculations

Energy of molecules can be measured in units called calories. A calorie is the amount of energy needed to raise the temperature of 1 mL of water one Celsius degree. A kilocalorie is the amount of energy needed to raise the temperature of 1000 mL of water (1 liter) one Celsius degree. The calorie is always written in lowercase (calorie). A kilocalorie is sometimes called a large calorie. A large calorie is

TABLE 1. CALCULATION OF KILOCALORIES				
	NUT 1 TRIAL 1	NUT 1 TRIAL 2	NUT 2 TRIAL 1	NUT 2 TRIAL 2
mass of sample				
mass of water				
initial water temperature				
final water temperature				
calories				
calories/gram				
kilocalories				
class average				

written with a capital letter (Calorie). The latter is the unit usually used to describe the food we eat. The calories in a food sample can be calculated from the amount of temperature increase of the water. The number of calories equals the mass of the water (in grams) multiplied by the difference in the temperature of the water multiplied by the known amount of heat needed to raise the temperature of water one degree. One milliliter of water equals one gram. Therefore, the volume of water is easily changed to mass.

Sample problem:

The following data were collected from a calorimeter experiment:

amount of water = 10 g
initial temperature of water = 18°C
final temperature of water = 30°C

How many calories were in the food sample?

calories = (mass of water) × (temperature change) × (calories needed to heat 1 g of water)

calories = (10 g) × (30° − 18°) × (1 cal/g−C°) = 120 calories

Formulating Generalizations

1. What is the relationship of a calorie to the chemical energy stored in foods?
2. Given the number of calories per gram of the sample, compare your data with the given data (Table 2). What difference do you notice? Give several possible reasons for your error.
3. How do your data compare with the class data? Explain any differences.
4. Most people can live on 1600 kilocalories per day. How many grams of peanuts would you have to eat to obtain this many kilocalories? How many grams of sugar?
5. Would a diet of peanuts or sugar be a proper way of getting your required calories? Explain.
6. Why are snack foods sometimes called junk foods?
7. Grizzly bears are known to eat the fatty parts of many animals. What property of the fatty tissues makes them a good food source for the bears?

TABLE 2. KNOWN VALUES	
SAMPLE	KILOCALORIES/GRAM
sugar	4.1
almond	6.9
pecan	6.6
peanut	5.8
walnut	6.2

12 Yeast Fermentation

In 1837, Theodore Schwann noticed that yeasts grew on fruits. He was the first person to associate fermentation with microorganisms. In 1857, Louis Pasteur observed the action of bacteria in milk. The bacteria changed "sweet milk" into "sour milk" by fermentation. Fermentation is a process in which microorganisms convert sugar to alcohol or organic acids in the absence of oxygen.

Louis Pasteur saved the wine industry of France by his research. He noted that microorganisms, such as yeasts and molds, were essential in producing good wines. If these organisms were not present on the fruit, wine would not be produced or it would be sour. The souring resulted from the introduction of unwanted types of microorganisms into the wine vats.

In this investigation, you are to measure the amount of waste product, carbon dioxide, that occurs as a result of fermentation. You are to calculate the parts per million of carbon dioxide by using an indicator.

Materials *(per team of two students)*

flasks, 250-mL—2
0.4% sodium hydroxide solution —50 mL
2-hole stoppers—2
2% sterile sucrose solution—200 mL
rubber tubing—30 cm
glass tubing—40 cm
phenolphthalein solution —1.0 mL
graduated pipette, 5-mL
tap water
pinch clamp
narrow stem funnel
clock or watch
dropper
incubator
distilled water—200 mL
dry yeast—1 pkg
beaker, 150-mL
glass marking pencil

Procedure

Part A. Yeast Fermentation

Obtain a flask of sterile sucrose solution and label it Flask A. Remove the aluminum foil cover from the longer glass tube and add a short piece of rubber tubing (Figure 1). Place a pinch clamp on the rubber tubing. Make sure that the pinch clamp is closed so that no air enters the flask. Place 1 g of dry yeast into Flask A with the sucrose solution and replace the rubber stopper. Put 100 mL of distilled water in a second flask labeled B. Then connect the two flasks in the following way. Remove the foil from the shorter piece of glass tubing

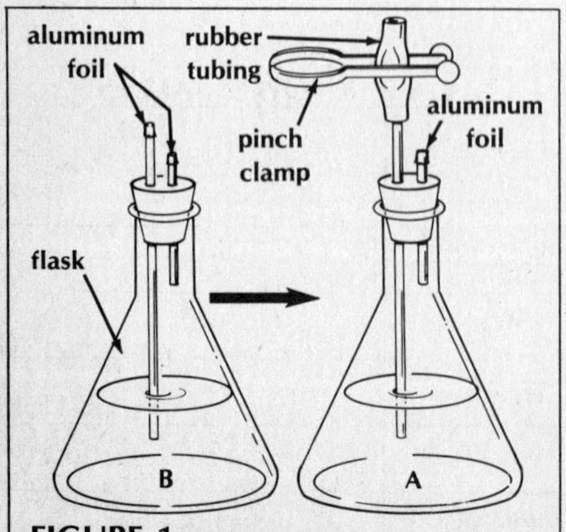

FIGURE 1

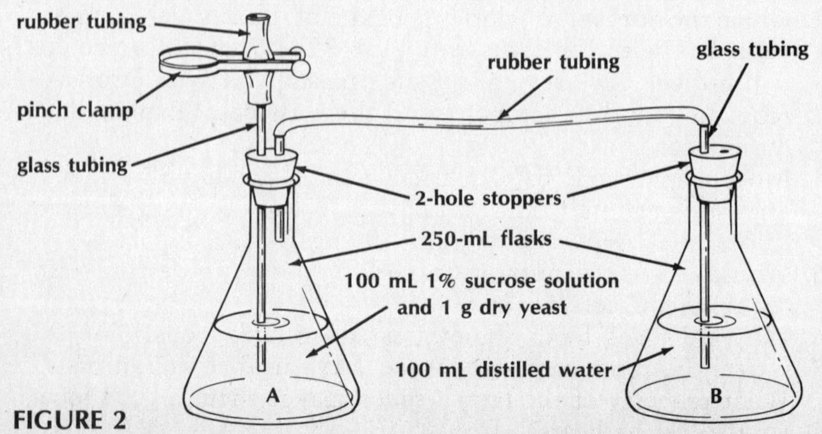

FIGURE 2

on Flask A. Connect one end of the rubber tubing to the shorter glass tube of Flask A, and the other end to the tubing in Flask B (Figure 2).

Incubate the flasks at 30°C for 24 hours. After 24 hours of incubation, note the bubbling of gas in Flask B. This gas is carbon dioxide. It is an end product of yeast fermentation. In the remaining part of the investigation you will measure the quantity of carbon dioxide given off and compare your measurement with those of other members of your class.

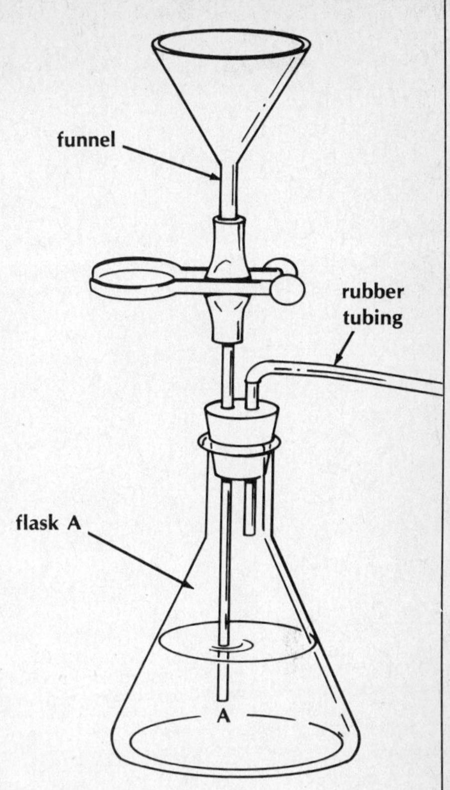

FIGURE 3

Part B. Calculation of Quantity of Carbon Dioxide

Attach a narrow stem funnel to the rubber tubing connection of Flask A (Figure 3). Using a beaker, fill the funnel with tap water. Slowly release the pinch clamp to allow the water to enter Flask A. This will force carbon dioxide gas from Flask A to Flask B. When Flask A is filled to within 1 cm of the short glass tube, close the clamp. Remove the stoppers from both flasks.

Test Flask B for carbon dioxide gas in this way. Add 5 drops of phenolphthalein to Flask B. Using a graduated pipette, add sodium hydroxide solution to the flask drop by drop (Figure 4). Count the drops as you add them. **CAUTION:** *Sodium hydroxide can cause burns. If spillage occurs, rinse with water and call your teacher immediately.* Gently swirl the flask after each drop is added. Continue to add and count sodium hydroxide drops until a faint pink color occurs and lasts for three minutes. The pink color indicates the presence of carbon dioxide. Convert the number of drops to milliliters. Ten drops equals approximately one milliliter. Record the number of milliliters of sodium hydroxide solution added to the flask to obtain the pink color.

Carbon dioxide is usually measured in parts per million (ppm). A solution containing one part per million of carbon dioxide contains one particle of carbon dioxide in a total of one million particles of water. Each mL of sodium hydroxide solution chemically combines with 100 parts per million of carbon dioxide. To compute the parts per million of carbon dioxide in the flask, multiply the number of mL of sodium hydroxide solution used by 100. This calculation will give the number of carbon dioxide molecules present in parts per million of water (Example: 3.5 mL NaOH $\times$ 100 $=$ 350 ppm of CO_2).

Compare your data with data from the rest of the class. Record your data on a class data chart, then find the class average.

Test 100 mL of fresh, sterile 2% sucrose solution for the presence of carbon dioxide as a control.

Compute the ppm of carbon dioxide in Flask B. Compute the ppm of carbon dioxide in the fresh, sterile 2% sucrose solution. Compute the ppm of carbon dioxide given off by each gram of yeast.

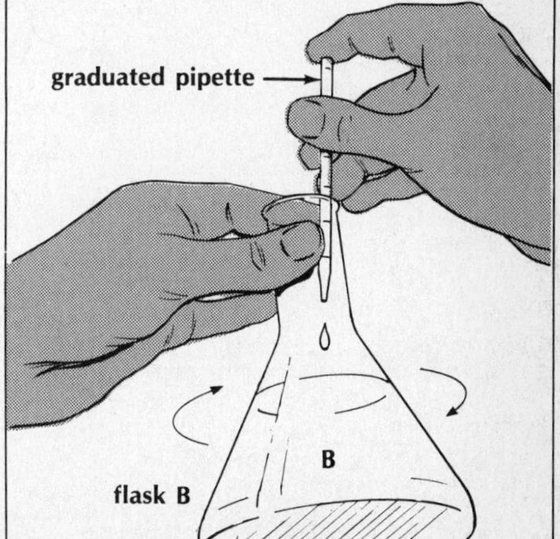

FIGURE 4

Formulating Generalizations

1. Why was no air allowed to enter Flask A?
2. What process formed the carbon dioxide in Flask B?
3. There are two types of respiration, aerobic and anaerobic. List the two reactants present in each type of respiration.
4. List the two end products of both types of respiration.
5. What end product is alike in each reaction? What reactant is alike?
6. Which type of respiration occurred in Flask A? Explain.
7. Biologists sometimes call this reaction alcohol fermentation. Why?
8. Was carbon dioxide present in the fresh sucrose solution prior to adding yeast? Explain.

Analysis Of Plant Pigments

13

Plant leaves are various colors because they contain several pigments. Different pigments in a leaf absorb different wavelengths of light. Pigments can affect the function of a leaf. Chlorophyll is the pigment associated with photosynthesis. Other pigments—carotene (orange), xanthophyll (yellow), and anthocyanin (red)—are usually present in a leaf. However, their appearance is often masked by chlorophyll. Their functions are uncertain but some may be involved in absorbing light and transferring the energy to chlorophyll. All of the pigments are found in plastids except anthocyanin which is dissolved in the cytoplasm.

In this investigation, you are to separate the various pigments of the leaf by means of paper chromatography. You are to compute the R_f values of the pigments and identify each pigment. You are to arrange the pigments in order of their speed of separation from slowest to fastest. Recall the techniques of chromatography in Investigation 7.

Materials *(per student or team)*

Coleus plant
Zebrina plant
mortar and pestle
filter paper (about 5 × 15 cm)
ruler
pencil
solvents—three types
paper clip
straw
capillary tubes — 2
developing tank (large jar)
aluminum foil
scalpel or sharp knife
small beaker
stapler
forceps
dropper
acetone — 4 to 6 mL

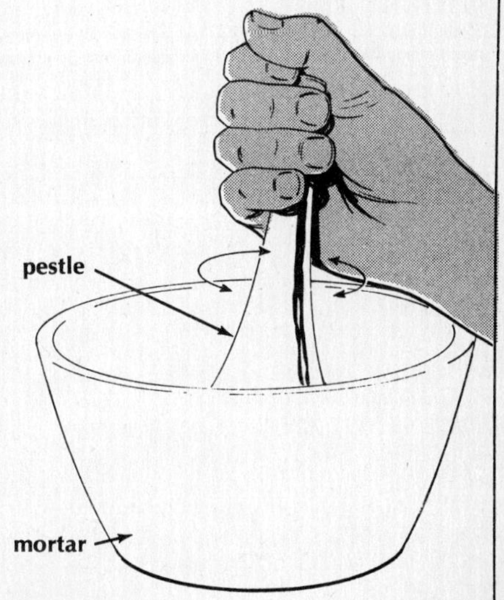

FIGURE 1

Procedure

Part A. Preparation of Leaf Extract

Cut two leaves from a *Coleus* or *Zebrina* plant into 1 cm × 1 cm squares. **CAUTION:** *Be careful with the knife or scalpel. Slice away from your fingers to avoid cuts.* Put the pieces of leaf in a mortar. Add 4 to 6 mL of acetone to the leaves and crush them until the material is finely ground (Figure 1). **CAUTION:** *Do not inhale fumes from acetone. If spillage occurs, rinse with water.* Place the material in a small beaker and cover it with aluminum foil.

Part B. Setting up a Chromatogram

Follow the procedure of Investigation 8 applying the following modifications:

1. Mark two X's on the bottom line of the filter paper. Each X should be 1.5 cm from the nearest edge. Using a dropper, place one drop of pigment extract between the two X's (Figures 2, 3, and 4).

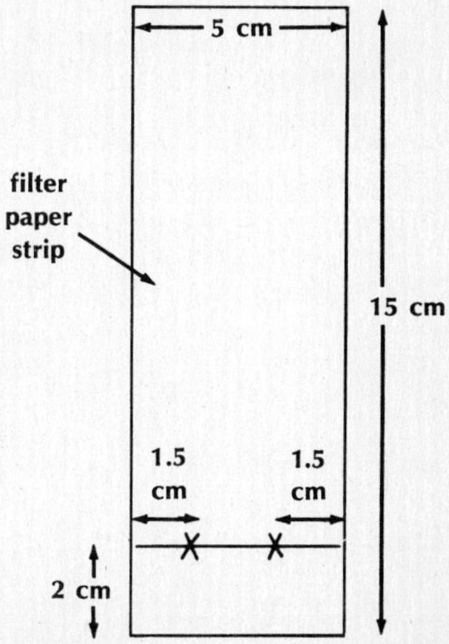

FIGURE 2

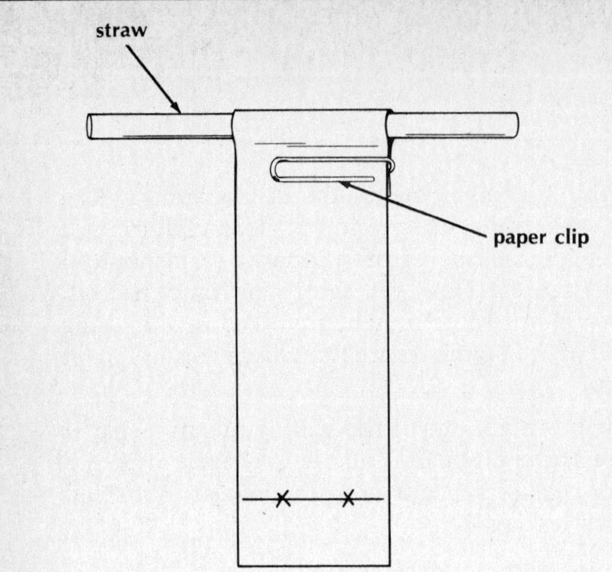

FIGURE 3

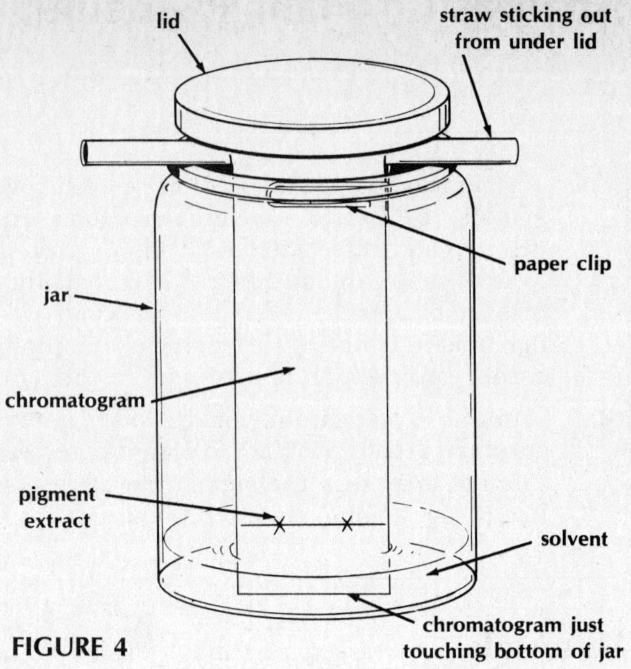

FIGURE 4

2. CAUTION: *The solvents being used are highly flammable and hazardous if inhaled. Do not allow the solvent to come near a flame. Do not inhale any of the solvents.*

3. Your teacher will assign a particular solvent for you to use for your chromatogram.

4. Allow the chromatogram to develop until the solvent reaches the top pencil line or until the end of the lab period.

5. No spraying of the chromatogram is necessary.

6. Outline the various pigment spots with pencil because they will fade with time.

7. Compute the R_f value for each pigment. (See Investigation 7.)

Formulating Generalizations

1. What does the appearance of more than one band for each pigment indicate?
2. Did any pigments not visible in the leaf appear on the developed chromatogram?
3. Were all pigments soluble in all solvents used? List any pigments and solvents that did not show solubility.
4. If any did not move, give a reasonable explanation.
5. How do you account for the various R_f values of the pigments?
6. Compare the R_f values you obtained with another student's values for the same solvent. Describe the differences in R_f values obtained by students using the same solvents. Why did these differences occur?
7. Compare your R_f values with students' values using the other solvents. Write a rule explaining the differences in the R_f values of the solvents.
8. List the pigments according to their rate of separation from slowest to fastest in your solvent.
9. List the pigments according to their rate of separation from slowest to fastest in each of the other solvents.

Some Aspects Of Photosynthesis

14

In 1648, Jean Van Helmont described a reason for gain in weight of a plant growing in soil. Van Helmont dried 200 pounds of soil in an oven. He placed this soil in an earthenware pot. To the pot he added rainwater and a five pound willow shoot. During the next five years he watered the plant with rainwater and distilled water. He covered the rim of the pot with a metal plate. This prevented dust from entering the soil. After five years, Van Helmont weighed the dry soil and the plant. The plant gained 164 pounds. Because the soil lost only about 2 ounces, he assumed the increase in weight came from water alone.

Our knowledge today tells us that he was right in assuming that the soil did not turn into plant material. He was wrong in assuming that all the plant material added came from water. Scientists since Jean Van Helmont have determined the proper reactants and products of photosynthesis.

Over 100 years later, another scientist found that oxygen from a plant would allow a mouse to live in a bell jar with no outside air. A few years later it was determined that light was necessary for oxygen production, and the process of carbon dioxide absorption by plants was described. From these humble beginnings, ideas about the process of photosynthesis began to be tested at great length.

In this investigation, you will determine whether or not light is necessary for photosynthesis. Also, you will calculate the rate of photosynthesis by counting the number of bubbles coming from *Elodea* per minute and determine if the gas is oxygen.

Materials *(per team of two students)*

aluminum foil
scissors
potted *Coleus* plants—3
potted kidney bean plants—3
beakers, 250-mL—2
95% alcohol—90 mL
600-mL beaker
iodine solution—50 mL
petri dishes—2
water
electric hot plate (or burner)
beaker, 1000-mL (or large jar)
test tube (or ignition tube)
0.5% sodium bicarbonate solution—1000 mL
Elodea sprig
short stem funnel
rubber stoppers—3
100 or 200 watt electric lamp
cm ruler
wooden splint
graph paper—1 sheet
match
glass tubing—12 cm

Procedure

Part A. Light—Necessary or Unnecessary for Photosynthesis?

Cut four pieces of aluminum foil 15 cm × 15 cm. **CAUTION:** *Always be careful when using scissors.* Using two of the pieces, cover

FIGURE 1

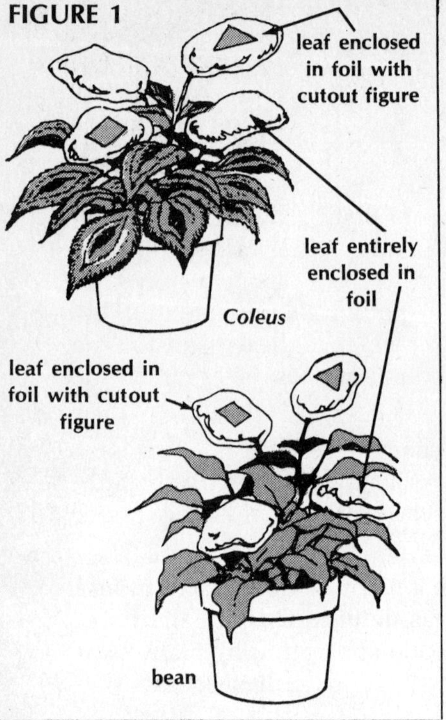

one healthy leaf of a *Coleus* plant and one leaf of a kidney bean plant with aluminum foil. Cover both the top and bottom of each leaf so no light reaches the leaf. In the middle of the other two pieces of foil, cut out a geometric shape not exceeding 2 cm across. Cover another leaf of each plant with this foil by placing the cut out opening on the upper surfaces of the leaf (Figure 1). Make sketches of the leaves covered with foil with the cut out openings. Place these plants in direct sunlight for two or three days.

Place the other potted bean and *Coleus* plants in a dark area for two or three days. Do not cover any of the leaves with aluminum foil.

After two or three days, gently remove the foil from each leaf and remove those leaves from the plants. Remove another uncovered leaf from each plant that was kept in the light. Keep these six leaves separated so you know which were covered and which were uncovered.

Place the leaves in boiling water for three to four minutes to kill the tissue. **CAUTION:** *Be careful around open flames or hot plates. Make sure all loose clothing and hair are secured.*

Place 90 mL of 95% alcohol in a 250-mL beaker. Place a piece of U-shaped glass tubing in the bottom of the 600-mL beaker. Fill the 600-mL beaker one third full of water. Place the 250-mL beaker in the 600-mL beaker (Figure 2). Transfer the leaves to the alcohol and place the entire assembly on the hot plate. **CAUTION:** *Do not place the alcohol directly on a hot plate as it can ignite or boil away rapidly.* Gently boil the water until the chlorophyll is removed from the leaves (about five minutes). Spread each leaf flat in a petri dish and cover it with iodine solution. After five minutes, pour off the iodine.

Locate areas of starch formation in each of the leaves. Make sketches in your lab notebook.

Also after two to three days, remove three leaves from each plant that was placed in the dark. Boil the leaves and test for starch in the same manner as you did for the leaves wrapped in aluminum foil. Make sketches in your lab notebook.

Part B. Rate of Photosynthesis

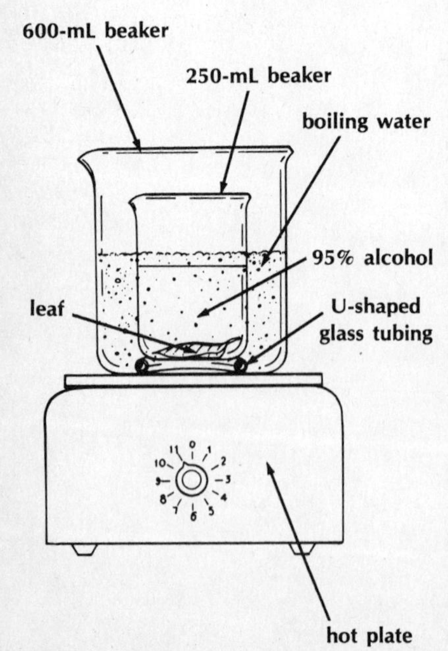

FIGURE 2

Fill a 1000 mL beaker (or battery jar) three-fourths full with 0.5% sodium bicarbonate solution. Gently crush the cut end of the stem of an *Elodea* sprig. Place the sprig of *Elodea* in the funnel. Support the funnel on three rubber stoppers in the beaker (or battery jar) as in Figure 3. Make sure the small end of the funnel is under the solution. Fill a test tube (or ignition tube) with water and invert it over the funnel. Do not allow any water to run out of the tube.

Place a lamp 10 cm from the side of the beaker and turn it on. When bubbles begin to escape at a steady rate, count the number of bubbles that escape each minute for five minutes. Record your results in a table similar to Table 1 in your lab notebook. After the five-minute period, turn off the lamp.

After a few minutes, move the lamp so it is 20 cm from the beaker and turn it on. Count and record the number of bubbles that escape every minute for five minutes. Then, turn off the lamp.

Repeat this procedure with the lamp 30 cm from the beaker. Raise the test tube enough so you can place your thumb over the mouth of the test tube. However, do not raise the test tube above the water before covering the mouth. Lift the tube vertically out of the water. Allow the remaining water to flow slowly from the tube. Holding the test tube mouth down, place a glowing splint into it. If oxygen is present, the splint will ignite.

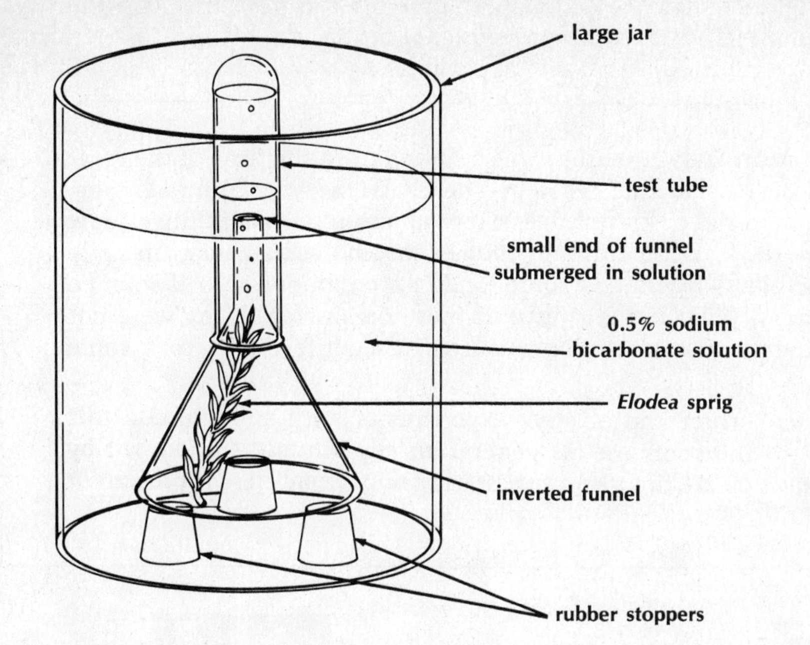

FIGURE 3

TABLE 1. NUMBER OF BUBBLES

TIME (minutes)	DISTANCE (cm)		
	10	20	30
1			
2			
3			
4			
5			
Totals			
Average			

Construct a graph showing the number of gas bubbles that escaped per minute at each given distance (Figure 4).

FIGURE 4

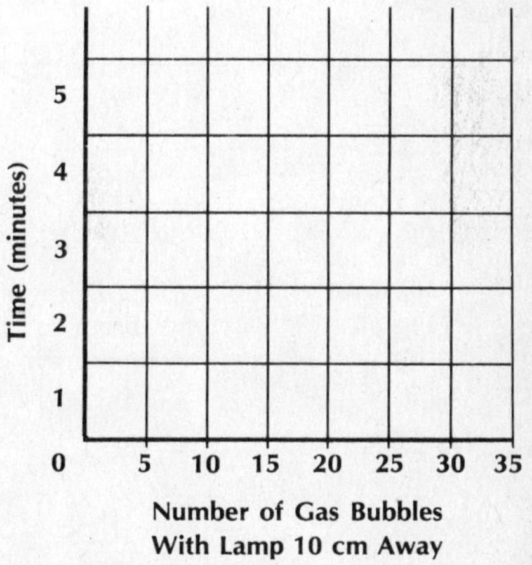

Formulating Generalizations

1. In what area of each uncovered kidney bean leaf exposed to light was starch formed?
2. In what area of the uncovered *Coleus* leaf exposed to light was starch formed?
3. What effect did being covered with foil have on the leaves?
4. What is the role of light in photosynthesis?
5. Explain your results with the plant placed in the dark.
6. Of what importance is chlorophyll in photosynthesis?
7. Do you have any evidence that chlorophyll is essential to photosynthesis?
8. What was the purpose of crushing the *Elodea* sprig?
9. Was oxygen given off by the *Elodea*? How do you know?
10. Does the rate of gas escape increase or decrease as distance from the light source becomes greater? Explain your answer.

15 Spontaneous Generation

Historically, spontaneous generation of living things was believed from the time of the great philosophers of early Greece until the time of Louis Pasteur—nearly twenty-two hundred years. Assume that you have no written material or knowledge of reproduction of living things. How would you respond when you see a frog crawling from the mud or see a horse hair snake in a pile of horse manure containing horse hairs? If you add some food to a container, it will soon be teeming with microscopic life forms. What is the source of these organisms? They were not present in the fresh food. If spontaneous generation occurred, then life came from some nonliving thing.

In this investigation, you will construct and observe experiments with suitable controls similar but not exactly identical to the spontaneous generation experiments conducted by Needham, Spallanzani, and Pasteur. You are to write a rule stating why cloudiness is present or absent in five flasks.

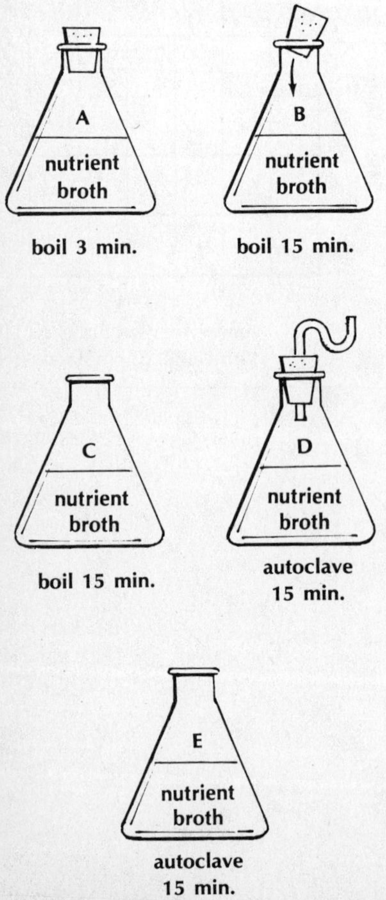

FIGURE 1

Materials *(per student or team)*

autoclave
beakers, 600-mL—1
burner and ring stand (or electric hot plate)
glass tubing—10 cm
distilled water
Erlenmeyer flasks, 250-mL—5
glass marking pencil
nutrient broth powder
rubber stopper (one-hole)
rubber stoppers (solid)—2
stirring rod

Procedure

Add 4.5 g of nutrient broth powder to a 600-mL beaker containing 550 mL of distilled water. Gently heat the beaker until the powder goes into solution. Stir the contents of the flask with a stirring rod. Pour 100 mL of nutrient broth into each of five flasks. Label the flasks A, B, C, D, and E.

Do the following for each of the flasks:

Flask A: Needham's Experiment: Boil the contents of the flask for three minutes and then seal the flask with a solid rubber stopper. **CAUTION:** *Flask and contents are hot. Do not touch flask with unprotected hand. Secure all loose clothing and hair if you are using an open flame.*

B: Spallanzani's Experiment: Boil the contents of the flask for 15 minutes with a stopper angled loosely in the neck of the flask so some air enters. After boiling, allow the flask to cool slightly and then place the stopper tightly in the neck.

C: Spallanzani's Control: Boil the contents of the flask for 15 minutes and leave open.

D: Pasteur's Continuous Air Experiment: Autoclave the contents of the flask at 15 pounds of pressure for 15 minutes.

E: Pasteur's Control: Autoclave the contents of the flask at 15 pounds of pressure for 15 minutes. Do not cover.

Check each flask for clarity after completing the above procedures. Place the five flasks in an inconspicuous area of the classroom as designated by your teacher. Observe your cultures 24 hours and 48 hours after preparation. Then observe them one week later. Record all observations of any changes in your lab notebook in a table similar to Table 1.

After one week, open the flasks and smell the contents of each. Record your observations.

Formulating Generalizations

At the end of one week:

1. Why were all the flasks of nutrient broth heated at the beginning of the experiment?
2. Which of the flasks were cloudy at the end of one week? Explain why they were cloudy.
3. What condition is similar in some of the cloudy flasks?
4. What condition in one of the cloudy flasks was unlike the others?
5. Which of the flasks were clear at the end of one week? Explain why they were clear.
6. Which of the flasks that admitted air did not turn cloudy? Explain why they were not cloudy.
7. How do you explain the difference in cloudiness of flasks A and B?
8. Although flasks B and C were boiled for the same amount of time, why would you expect a difference in cloudiness in these two flasks?
9. What would a person who believes in spontaneous generation say is the cause for no cloudiness in flask B?

TABLE 1. OBSERVATIONS OF THE FLASKS

FLASK	24 HOURS	48 HOURS	1 WEEK	ODOR AFTER 1 WEEK
A				
B				
C				
D				
E				

16 Significance Of Time And Mitosis

Mitosis is a process that distributes replicated chromosomes to new nuclei. Usually, mitosis is accompanied by cell division, or division of the cytoplasm. Mitosis followed by cell division results in the formation of two daughter cells. Each daughter cell receives a set of chromosomes identical to that of the parent cell. The formation of new cells allows growth and repair in multicellular organisms. In unicellular organisms, mitosis followed by cell division is essentially reproduction.

The time it takes for a cell to complete mitosis, from prophase to telophase, varies with each type of tissue and with the surrounding environmental or metabolic temperature. Usually mitosis time for most cells ranges from 20 minutes to just over an hour depending on the cell type. Dividing cells respond to a biological clock mechanism. That is, cells in some phases of mitosis are more numerous at specific times during a 24 hour cycle than are cells in other phases.

During this investigation, you are to be guided by two assumptions concerning the amount of time for each phase of cell division. Assume that (1) the total time it takes for mitosis to occur in onion root tips is the maximum for all phases (Table 1), and (2) all cells counted came from root tips grown under the same conditions and were cut and preserved at the same time. From these assumptions, you are to test the following hypothesis: the amount of cells in a given phase of mitosis is equal to the length of time required for completion of the phase. For example at 10°C, if 75 minutes are required to complete prophase, then 75 out of 110 cells observed should be in prophase (Table 1).

Materials *(per student or team)*

microscope
prepared slide of *Allium* root tip, longitudinal section

Procedure

Study the physical features of each stage of mitosis as shown in Figures 1 and 2.

Place a prepared slide of a longitudinal section of an *Allium* root tip on the stage of a microscope. Locate the meristematic area of the root on low power. Revolve the nosepiece to high power and observe the cells. Record the number of cells in each stage of mitosis out of the first 110 cells. *Do not count cells in interphase.* Record your observations in a table in your lab notebook similar to Table 1.

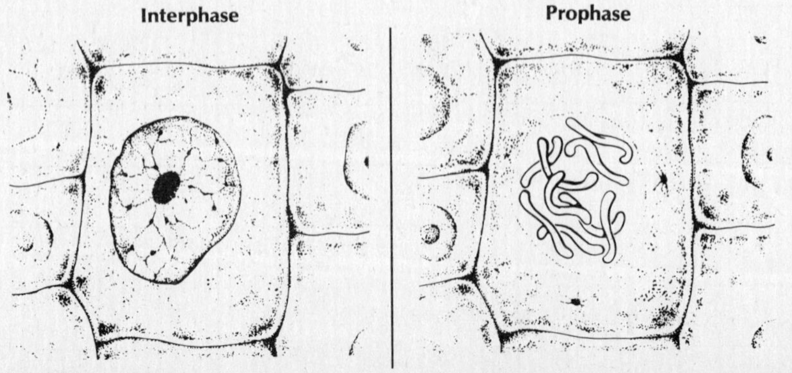

FIGURE 1

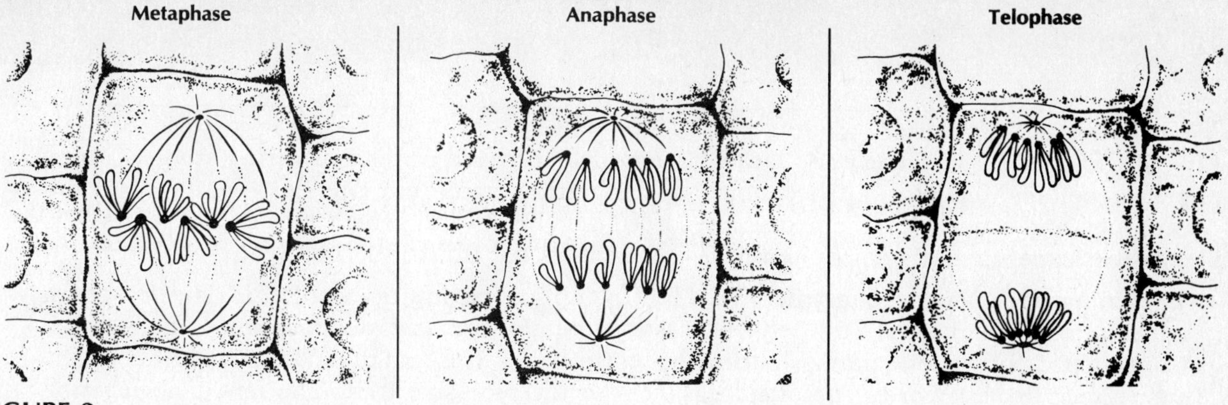

FIGURE 2

Record your data on the chalkboard along with the rest of the class. Record the average of the class data for each phase of mitosis in your notebook.

Formulating Generalizations

1. List three changes that take place in the cell during prophase.
2. What happens to the chromosomes in a cell during metaphase?
3. What happens to each chromosome and centromere during anaphase?
4. List three changes that take place in a cell during telophase.
5. Of the 110 cells you observed, which stage of mitosis had the most cells present? Explain why these cells were present in the greatest amount.
6. Of the 110 cells that you observed, which stage of mitosis had the least cells present? Explain why these cells were observed the least?
7. Which stage of mitosis takes the greatest amount of time?
8. From your data, do you support the hypothesis posed in the introduction? Explain.
9. Do class data support this hypothesis? Explain.

TABLE 1. TIME FOR MITOSIS AND NUMBER OF CELLS IN EACH PHASE IN ONION ROOT TIPS

PHASE OF MITOSIS	NUMBER OF MINUTES NEEDED TO COMPLETE EACH PHASE AT 10°C	NUMBER OF CELLS EXPECTED IN SLIDES (AT 10°C)	NUMBER OF CELLS OBSERVED	
			YOUR DATA	CLASS DATA
Prophase	75	75		
Metaphase	15	15		
Anaphase	8	8		
Telophase	12	12		
Total	110	110		

17 Probability And Mendelian Genetics

Gregor Mendel is called the "father of genetics" because of his pioneering studies. Many people before Mendel published notes on hereditary traits, but Mendel's work was more thorough and exact. He observed and recorded data on several generations of pea plants. His classical experiments with garden peas were conducted from 1856 to 1864.

From his data, Mendel constructed the law of dominance, law of segregation, law of random fertilization, and law of independent assortment. In the law of dominance, he showed mathematically that one trait is dominant over the other. The trait that does not show up in the appearance or behavior of the offspring is called the recessive trait. The law of segregation indicates that during gamete (sex cell) formation, the genes controlling a particular trait are separated. Each gamete will contain one gene of each pair.

The law of random fertilization shows that any male gamete can fertilize any female gamete for a particular species. The law of independent assortment involves two pairs of genes on different chromosomes. During gamete formation, one gene enters a gamete independently of the others. From these laws and on the basis of probability, expected ratios of genotypes and phenotypes can be calculated.

Since Mendel's work was discovered, many new concepts of genetics have been formed. However, his laws are still valid. By using the laws of probability, you can determine how often an event should occur, or the expected results. Sometimes outside factors alter the expected results. Therefore, the number of times that the events actually occur are called the observed, or actual, results.

In this investigation, you are to construct Punnett squares of two genetic crosses to determine the expected offspring. You are to determine (by tossing coins) whether the observed results are the same as the expected results.

Materials *(per student)*

nickels—2
pennies—2

Procedure

Part A. Monohybrid Cross

A monohybrid cross is a cross in which only one trait is being considered. Assume that a cross was made between two pea plants. Both plants had the genotype *Rr* (*R* = round seed, *r* = wrinkled seed). Thus, they were heterozygous (with one dominant gene and one recessive gene for each trait) for seed coat shape.

To determine the expected results from this cross, construct and fill in a Punnett square in your lab notebook. Fill in each box of the Punnett square by putting the proper gene combinations together from each parent. A completed Punnett square shows the distribution of the expected results. In this case, the Punnett square is for the cross *Rr* × *Rr*. The capital letters represent dominant genes while the lower case letters represent recessive genes. In a monohybrid cross, a Punnett square shows how many times a certain genotype is expected to appear in four offspring. A Punnett square can be used for offspring of multiples of four by multiplying the results by the appropriate number of offspring.

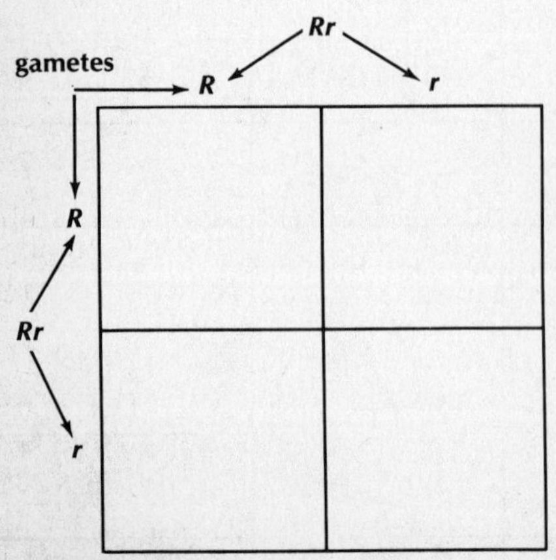

FIGURE 1

Questions:

1. If you were to get four different offspring from this cross, list the different genotypes and the number of each genotype you would expect.
2. Using four offspring, list the different phenotypes and the number of each phenotype you would expect.
3. Suppose you were to get 32 offspring from this cross, how many of each genotype and phenotype would you expect?

A set of observed, or actual, results that represents results of a monohybrid cross can be obtained by tossing coins. Toss a penny 32 times and record in your notebook in a table similar to Table 1 whether each toss is heads or tails as penny A. Record your results after each toss. Toss a second penny 32 times and again record the results in the table as penny B.

Assume that the two coins represent male and female gametes of two pea plants. Because both plants are *Rr*, there are two possible gametes for each plant, *R* and *r*. Whether or not a gamete will be *R* or *r* is determined by chance. The same is true for tossing a coin: it can land either heads or tails. Therefore, heads can represent the dominant gene, *R*, and tails can represent the recessive gene, *r*. In the table in your notebook, write the symbol *R* beside each head, and write *r* beside each tail. Thus, the table represents the 32 possible male gametes (penny A) of one pea plant and 32 possible female gametes (penny B) of the second pea plant.

Now, assume that the corresponding number of each toss of both pennies represents a union of a male gamete and a female gamete. Again the possible combinations are by chance. In the table, record the resulting genotype and phenotype for each possible zygote. The results represent 32 offspring of the pea plants. Thus, the genotypes and phenotypes from the coin toss represent observed results of the cross.

In a table similar to Table 2 in your lab notebook, record summaries of the expected results (question 3) and the observed results. Copy your results (total heads and tails and genotype combinations) of the monohybrid cross on the chalkboard. Collect the class data and record it in a table similar to Table 3 in your notebook. Calculate the average of the class data and record the average in the table. Calculate the expected results for the total class and record these results in the table.

TABLE 1. INDIVIDUAL DATA FOR MONOHYBRID CROSS

TRIAL OR GAMETE NUMBER	PENNY A (MALE GAMETE)	PENNY B (FEMALE GAMETE)	GENOTYPE OF ZYGOTE	PHENOTYPE OF ZYGOTE
1	heads (*R*)	tails (*r*)	*Rr*	round
2				
32				

TABLE 2. SUMMARY OF EXPECTED AND OBSERVED RESULTS					
	NUMBER OF OFFSPRING				
	genotype			phenotype	
	RR	*rR* or *Rr*	*rr*	round	wrinkled
expected					
observed					

TABLE 3. CLASS DATA FOR MONOHYBRID CROSS						
	EXPECTED GENOTYPES			OBSERVED GENOTYPES		
	RR	*Rr*	*rr*	*RR*	*Rr*	*rr*
Student 1						
Student 2						
Student 32						
Total						
Average						

Part B. Dihybrid Cross

A dihybrid cross is a cross in which two factors or traits are being considered together at the same time. Assume that a cross was made between two guinea pigs which are heterozygous for color and coat texture, *BbRr* (*B* = black, b = albino; *R* = rough coat, *r* = smooth coat).

Determine the expected results by constructing and completing a Punnett square for the cross *BbRr* × *BbRr* in your lab notebook. In a dihybrid cross, the Punnett square shows 16 offspring.

Question:

4. If you get 32 offspring, how many would you expect to be black and rough, black and smooth, albino and rough, and albino and smooth?

Observed results of a dihybrid cross can be represented by tossing four coins. Because there are four possible genes in a dihybrid cross, two coins are needed to represent the genes and their possible combinations in the gametes. Let the pennies represent the possible

TABLE 4. INDIVIDUAL DATA FOR DIHYBRID CROSS						
TRIAL OR GAMETE	MALE GAMETE		FEMALE GAMETE		ZYGOTE	
	PENNY A	NICKEL A	PENNY B	NICKEL B	GENOTYPE	PHENOTYPE
1						
2						
32						

TABLE 5. SUMMARIES OF INDIVIDUAL DATA FOR EXPECTED AND OBSERVED RESULTS				
	POSSIBLE PHENOTYPE COMBINATIONS FROM COIN TOSSES			
	BLACK, ROUGH	BLACK, SMOOTH	ALBINO, ROUGH	ALBINO, SMOOTH
Expected offspring				
Observed offspring				

TABLE 6. CLASS DATA FOR DIHYBRID CROSS				
	PHENOTYPE AND GENOTYPE			
	HEAD-HEAD *BR*	HEAD-TAIL *Br*	TAIL-HEAD *bR*	TAIL-TAIL *bb*
Student 1				
Student 2				
Total observed				
Average				
Total expected				

genes for *B* and *b*. A toss of heads is *B* (black) and tails is *b* (albino). Let the nickels represent the possible genes for *R* and *r*. A toss of heads is *R* (rough) and tails is *r* (smooth). Beside the heads and tails in the table write the appropriate symbol, *B*, *b*, *R*, or *r*. Assume that penny A and nickel A represent the possible male gametes, and penny B and nickel B represent the possible female gametes.

As in Part A, assume that each toss of all four coins represents the union of a male gamete and a female gamete with both factors represented. Toss two pennies and two nickels. Record the results of each toss (heads or tails) in your notebook in a table similar to Table 4 as to (a) whether each coin is heads or tails, (b) the gene it represents, and (c) the resulting genotype and phenotype.

Toss the four coins 31 more times and record the results in your table. Record in your notebook in a table similar to Table 5 summaries of the expected results (question 4) and the observed results. Copy your results (total of each of 4 phenotypes observed) of the dihybrid cross on the chalkboard. Collect the class data and record it in a table similar to Table 6 in your notebook. Calculate the expected results for the total class and record these results in the table.

Formulating Generalizations

1. Out of 32 tosses of the "female" penny (monohybrid cross of Part A), how many heads and tails did you expect?
2. Out of 32 tosses of the "male" penny (monohybrid cross of Part A), how many heads and tails did you expect?
3. Were your answers to Questions 1 and 2 the same or different? Explain.
4. Did you obtain the expected monohybrid results? If you did not, how many more or less did you observe?
5. Which sample, your data or class data, was closer to the expected results for both monohybrid and dihybrid crosses? Explain.
6. Out of 32 tosses with the penny and the nickel (dihybrid cross), how many heads and tails did you expect?
7. Did you obtain the expected dihybrid results? If you did not, how many more, or less, did you observe?
8. What Mendelian laws are operating in Part A (monohybrid cross) if the expected genotypes and phenotypes are obtained in the observed results?
9. What Mendelian laws are operating in Part B (dihybrid cross) if the expected genotypes and phenotypes are obtained in the observed results?
10. What size would the sample have to be to ensure that the observed will always equal the expected?

Drosophila Genetics

18

To determine the genotypes of parents (P_1) it is sometimes essential to record the results of genetic crosses for several generations (F_1, F_2). Mendel had this problem in working with peas. Human geneticists have difficulties because it sometimes takes 25 years or more to get the results from one generation.

Fruit flies, *Drosophila,* are excellent experimental animals for studies in genetics. They have a short life cycle at room temperatures (10 days from eggs to adults), have large numbers of offspring, and can be grown on easily prepared media. Also the apparatus needed to raise them is simple and they have distinct phenotypic variations that are easily observed.

Fruit flies are common pests because they lay eggs in fruit. A female can lay 300 to 500 eggs in 10 days. *Drosophila* eggs are elliptical in shape and contain two small projections on one end. These projections enable the eggs to float in liquid media. Depending on temperature, eggs usually hatch into larvae within 24 to 48 hours. Larvae eat continually. As they eat, they form channels in solid media. After four days, a larva enters a stage called the pupa. During this pupal period, wings, legs, and a head develop. An adult emerges from the pupa on the tenth day as a light-colored, fragile insect. The wings expand and the fly darkens in a few days.

In this investigation, you are to differentiate between male and female *Drosophila* by examining living specimens. Also you are to cross a female of one phenotype with a male of another phenotype and obtain F_1 and F_2 generations.

Materials *(per team)*

- anesthetizer (pill container and funnel)
- commercial anesthetic
- 3 × 5 white index card
- camel's hair brush
- stereomicroscope
- morgue (baby food jar and motor oil)
- transparent tape or glass marking pencil (for labels)
- absorbent cotton
- *Drosophila* flies in a vial
- culture of wild-type flies growing in medium
- culture of mutant strain of flies growing in medium
- culture vials containing fresh medium—2
- sheet of white notebook paper

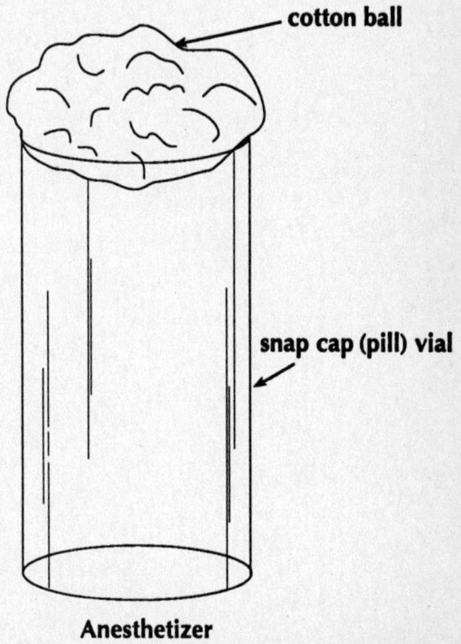

FIGURE 1

Procedure

Part A. Handling *Drosophila*

You will be given a vial containing *Drosophila* to examine. To examine the flies you can make them immobile by using a commercial anesthetic. Set up an anesthetizer as shown in Figure 1. **CAUTION:** *Do not inhale fumes.* Use the following steps to immobilize the *Drosophila* in your vial:

1. Place 2 drops of anesthetic on the cotton ball and replace the cotton ball on the vial.
2. Tap the bottom of the vial containing flies sharply on the palm of your hand to drive the flies to the bottom.

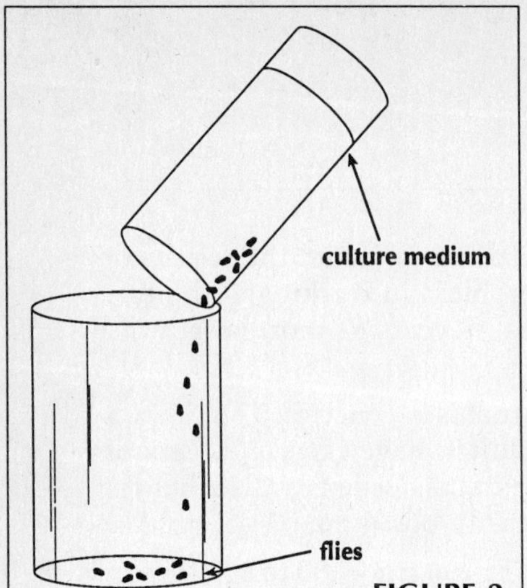

FIGURE 2

3. Remove the cotton plug from the culture vial and from the anesthetizer. Invert and tap the culture vial so the flies fall down into the bottom of the anesthetizer (Figure 2).
4. Remove the culture vial and replace the cotton plug into the anesthetizer so the fumes cannot escape.
5. After the flies stop moving, wait 25 seconds. Then remove the flies from the anesthetizer by dumping the flies on a sheet of notebook paper. Let the flies remain in the anesthetizer for 3 to 5 minutes. If necessary, while observing the flies, place them in the anesthetizer for 10 to 15 seconds. (If flies are killed, their wings will extend at right angles to their bodies.)

Place the anesthetized flies on a 3 × 5 white index card. Use a camel's hair brush with crushed bristles (Figure 3) to move the flies. Observe the flies with a stereomicroscope. Distinguish between males and females by referring to Figure 4. After your observations, either discard the flies in the morgue (jar containing motor oil) or put them back in the vial. Follow the directions of your teacher.

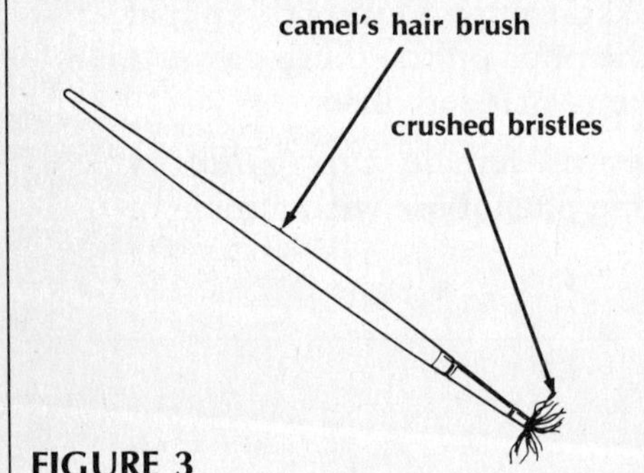

FIGURE 3

Part B. P_1 Mating

With a stereomicroscope, examine the different mutant cultures of *Drosophila* provided by your instructor. Observe the mutant characteristic of each type of *Drosophila* so you will recognize the phenotype.

Make a cross between the two strains of *Drosophila*. Put two or three virgin females of one strain in a vial containing fresh culture media. Your teacher will give you virgin females. Add two or three males from the other strain to this culture media. Label the culture vial with the type of female and type of male, your name, and the date.

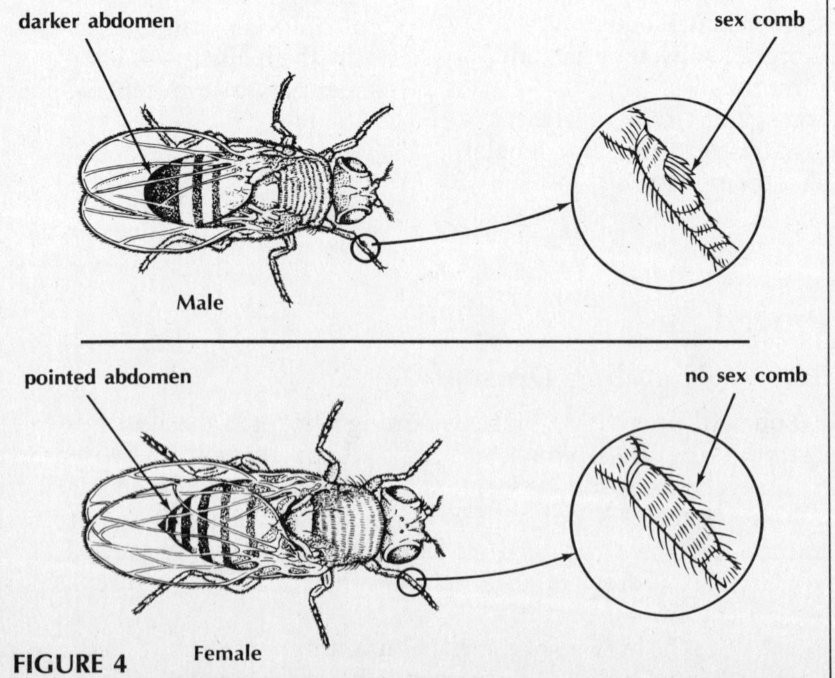

FIGURE 4

TABLE 1. INDIVIDUAL DATA				
Cross: ____________ ♂ × ____________ ♀ (genotype) ____________ ♂ × ____________ ♀ (phenotype) ____________ ♂ × ____________ ♀ (gametes) Date of mating ____________ Date of larva emergence ____________ Date of pupa formation ____________ Date of adult emergence ____________				
	OBSERVATIONS			
	♂		♀	
DATE	PHENOTYPE	NUMBER	PHENOTYPE	NUMBER

TABLE 2. CLASS DATA				
Cross: ______ ♂ × ______ ♀				
	OBSERVATIONS			
	♂		♀	
STUDENT	PHENOTYPE	NUMBER	PHENOTYPE	NUMBER
1				
2				
3				
Totals				

Decide which of the two crosses you will make and which your partner will make before proceeding. One of you should cross females of the wild type with males of the mutant strain. The other should cross males of the wild type with females of the mutant strain.

When you observe larvae in your culture, remove the parent flies. When F_1 adult flies begin to emerge, etherize and examine them daily. Record the number of each type of fly in your lab notebook in a table similar to Table 1. Place all flies not needed for Part C in the morgue. Record data for all the adults that emerge within ten days. Put your data on the chalkboard under the cross designating the male and female you used. Compare your data with data from the rest of the class. Record the class data for your cross in a table similar to Table 2.

Part C. F_1 Mating

After a few F_1 adults have emerged from the P_1 cross, place two or three pairs of F_1 flies in a vial of fresh medium. Label the vial with the type of cross, the date, and your name.

When larvae of this cross emerge, remove the adults. When F_2 adults emerge, etherize them and examine them daily. Record the data as you did for Part B in your lab notebook in another table similar to Table 1. Place all flies in the morgue. Record the data for all adults that emerge within ten days. Place your data on the chalkboard under the cross designating the male and female you used. Record the class data for your cross in another table similar to Table 2.

Formulating Generalizations

1. List the chief differences between male and female *Drosophila.*
2. What are the differences between the two *Drosophila* strains?
3. Construct Punnett squares for your P_1 and F_1 crosses.
4. How many phenotypes were observed in the F_1 generation?
5. How many phenotypes were observed in the F_2 generation?
6. Which law(s) of Mendel is (are) represented in this investigation?
7. From your data of the P_1 and F_1 crosses, did you get the expected ratios? Explain.
8. From the class data of the P_1 and F_1 crosses, did you get the expected ratios? Explain.
9. Were the class results or your individual data closer to the expected? Explain.
10. Why do you think you used virgin females for this investigation?
11. How would your results have been different if you had not used a virgin female?

DNA Models

19

Deoxyribonucleic acid (DNA) is the molecule responsible for hereditary traits. Francis Crick and James D. Watson worked in the early 1950's to unravel the molecular structure of the DNA molecule.

DNA can be compared to a "twisted" ladder. The uprights or sides of the ladder are composed of phosphate groups and sugar molecules. There is an almost endless repetition of these substances. Each rung of the ladder is composed of a pair of nitrogen compounds called bases. DNA molecules are composed of combinations of four bases. They are guanine, cytosine, adenine, and thymine. A deoxyribose molecule, phosphate group, and base form a nucleotide.

In the "rungs" of the DNA ladder, cytosine always pairs with guanine, and thymine always pairs with adenine. Base pairing of these four bases results in specific sequences of nucleotides on a chromosome which account for differences in genes. A gene may contain thousands of these base pairs.

In this investigation, you are to construct a two-dimensional model of a DNA molecule. You are to determine the sequence of bases, deoxyribose, and phosphate groups from the sketch given. Also, you are to construct a three-dimensional model of a DNA molecule.

Materials *(per student)*

- scissors
- construction paper—1 sheet of each of 8 different colors
- poster board
- glue
- colored toothpicks*
- polystyrene balls*
- jelly beans*
- corks*

*You will have to determine the number you need.

Procedure

Part A. Two-Dimensional Model

Using a different color for each structure in Figure 1, trace and cut out the appropriate number of each structure on construction paper. Make the number of each molecule that is indicated below each structure. **CAUTION:** *Always be careful with scissors.*

Using the portion of a DNA molecule shown in Figure 2 as a guide, construct a two-dimensional DNA model. Glue the construction paper molecule to a piece of poster paper. Start your model so it is like Figure 2. Then, complete the model of the DNA molecule by determining sequences of remaining bases, deoxyribose molecules, phosphate groups, and bonds needed to form a molecule with 12 nucleotide pairs.

FIGURE 1

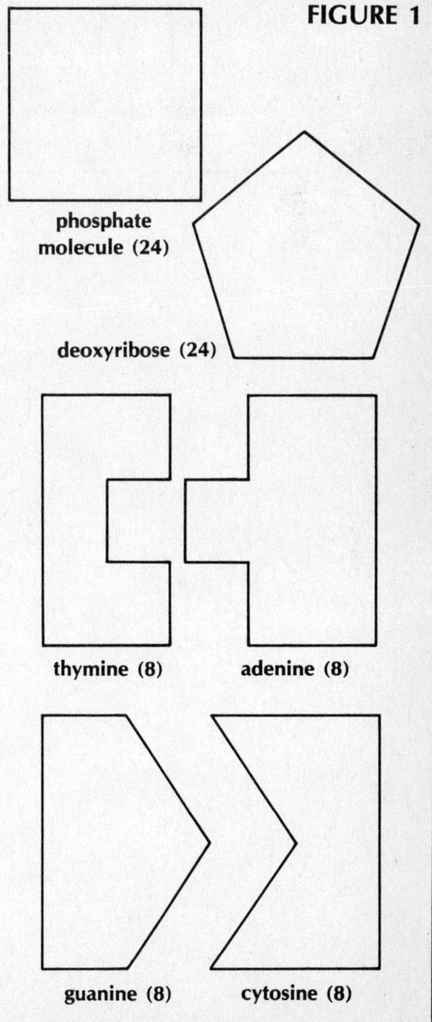

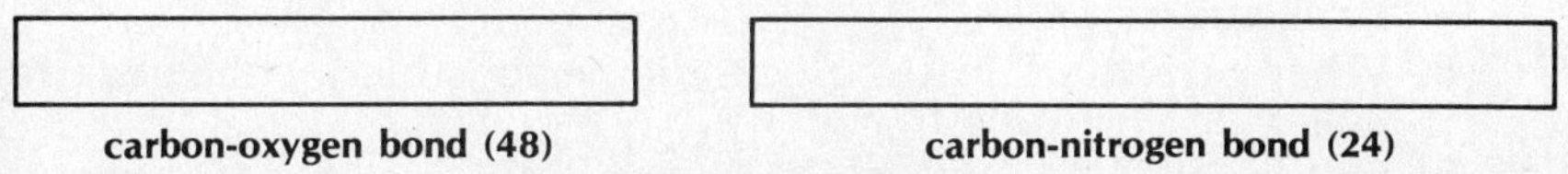

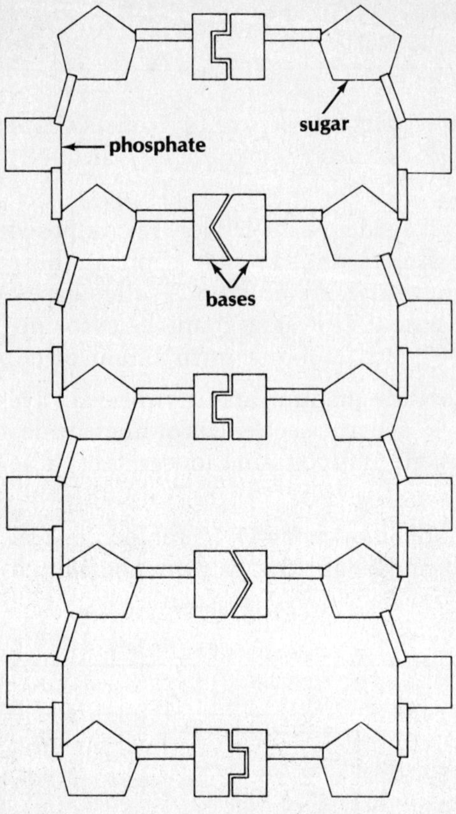

Portion of a DNA Molecule

FIGURE 2

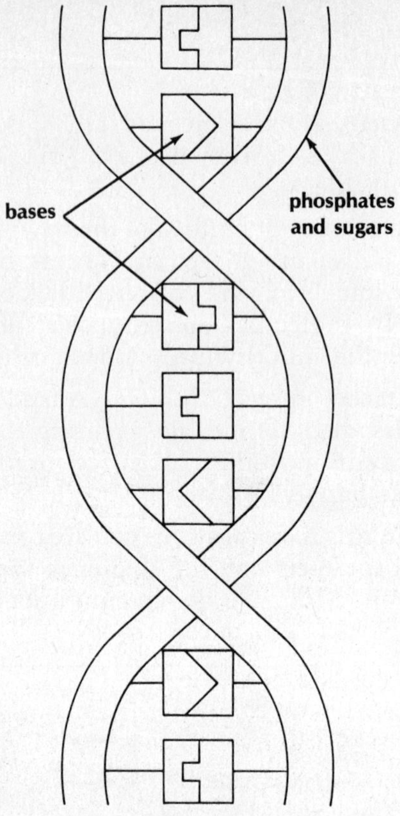

Twisted Ladder

FIGURE 3

Part B. Three-Dimensional Model

In reality, a DNA molecule is three dimensional. The ladder-like structure is twisted (Figure 3).

Using materials such as toothpicks, polystyrene balls, corks, jelly beans, and so on, construct a three-dimensional model of a DNA molecule. Construct the model so it is a three-dimensional model of the two-dimensional model you constructed in Part A.

Formulating Generalizations

1. What three parts make up a DNA molecule?
2. What makes up a nucleotide?
3. What bases are found in a DNA molecule?
4. What is the significance of base pairing?
5. What reasons are there that guanine can not bond to adenine and cytosine can not bond to thymine?
6. Of what importance is the phosphate group in the structure of DNA?
7. Of what importance is the deoxyribose molecule in the structure of DNA?
8. What part of a DNA molecule is responsible for the genetic code?
9. What role do the four bases play in the structure of a DNA molecule?

Modeling Protein Synthesis

20

DNA directs protein synthesis. Proteins are composed of different kinds of amino acids. These amino acids are arranged in long chains. Each chain may be several hundred amino acid units long. The chemical and physical properties of proteins are determined by the number, type, sequence, and arrangement of the amino acids.

The four bases in DNA determine the kinds of amino acids in a protein molecule. Each of the 20 kinds of amino acids is coded for by a specific sequence (or sequences) of three bases in the DNA molecule. For example, the sequence CAC (cytosine-adenine-cytosine) in a DNA molecule codes for the amino acid histidine. Several amino acids have more than one specific code (Table 1).

DNA does not directly synthesize protein. Ribonucleic acid (RNA) is also involved. RNA is a single stranded molecule similar to DNA. Main differences between DNA and RNA are that the DNA base, thymine, is replaced by the base uracil in RNA, and the sugar in RNA is ribose rather then deoxyribose. One type of RNA carries the three base message, or codon, from DNA to ribosomes. Because this type of RNA is a messenger, it is called messenger RNA (mRNA). Ribosomes, the sites of protein synthesis, are cellular organelles made of another type of RNA.

Protein synthesis occurs when mRNA leaves the nucleus and attaches to a ribosome in the cytoplasm. Another type of RNA, transfer RNA (tRNA), carries specific amino acids to the mRNA. The three-base code of tRNA is called an anticodon. An anticodon correlates directly with a specific mRNA codon. The anticodon is at one point on the tRNA and a specific amino acid attaches at another point. Messenger RNA codons and tRNA anticodons pair up bringing specific amino acids close together at the ribosome. Bonds form between the amino acids and form proteins.

In this investigation, you are to use Table 1 and index cards with codon units to construct a protein molecule that is twenty-five amino-acid units long. You are to simulate the building of the protein molecule by using mRNA and tRNA models.

Materials *(per team)*

small index cards—56
cord, 150 cm long—2 pieces
transparent tape—1 roll
large index card—1
paper clips—4
masking tape
scissors
rectangles cut from colored
  card stock, 2 × 5 cm:
  red—28
  yellow—28
  green—27

Procedure

Part A. Gathering Data

Print each mRNA codon from Table 1 on separate small index cards. Print only one codon unit per card. Do not repeat any codon. Remove the following cards from the stack: UAA, UAG, and UGU. You will use any one of these codons to stop protein synthesis.

Shuffle the remaining 57 index cards with the codon units face down. Draw the top card. Record the mRNA amino acid codon as the

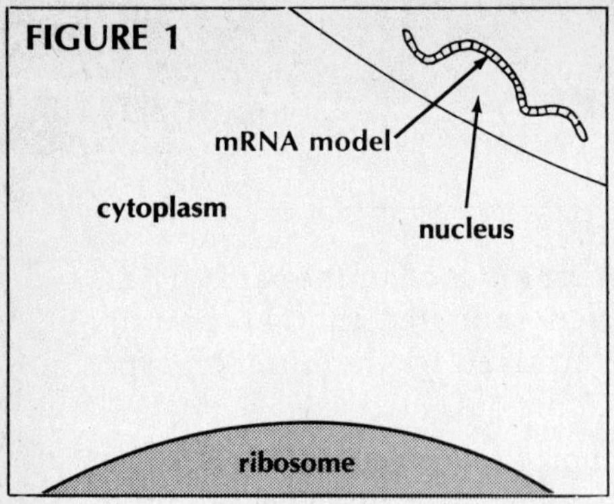

number 1 amino acid codon in your lab notebook in a table similar to Table 4 on page 58. Place the card back in the deck and reshuffle the cards. Draw the top card again. Record the mRNA amino acid codon in the table as the number 2 amino acid codon. Repeat this procedure for a total of 25 times.

Using Table 1, determine the 25 amino acids represented by the 25 codons drawn from the deck. Record the names of these amino acids in the table in your lab notebook. For example, if the first card you drew was AUC, the amino acid is isoleucine.

For each amino acid listed in the table, determine the anticodon unit for the corresponding tRNA molecule. Use Table 2 to determine which bases will pair with each other. For example, the isoleucine mentioned above would have the anticodon "UAG." Why is UAG the anticodon for AUC?

Part B. Assembling the Model

Number each set of yellow, red, and green rectangles 1 to 25. From the data in your table, print the mRNA codons on the corresponding yellow cards. Assuming the example above, on yellow card 1 should be printed "AUC." From the data in your table, print the amino acid on the corresponding red cards. For example, on red card 1 should be printed "isoleucine," the amino acid for "AUC" in the example above. Using the data from the table, print the anticodons on the

TABLE 1. AMINO ACID CODONS

AMINO ACID	mRNA CODON OR TRIPLET CODE
Alanine	GCA, GCG, GCC, GCU
Arginine	CGA, CGG, CGC, CGU, AGA, AGG
Asparagine	AAC, AAU
Aspartic Acid	GAC, GAU
Cysteine	UGC, UGU
Glutamic Acid	GAA, GAG
Glutamine	CAA, CAG
Glycine	GGC, GGU, GGA, GGG
Histidine	CAC, CAU
Isoleucine	AUC, AUU, AUA
Leucine	CUA, CUG, CUC, CUU, UUA, UUG
Lysine	AAA, AAG
Methionine	AUG
Phenylalanine	UUC, UUU
Proline	CCA, CCG, CCC, CCU
Serine	AGU, AGC, UCA, UCC, UCG, UCU
Threonine	ACA, ACG, ACU, ACC
Tryptophan	UGG
Tyrosine	UAC, UAU
Valine	GUA, GUG, GUC, GUU
Stop	UAA, UAG, UGA

TABLE 2. PAIRING BASES OF mRNA, tRNA, and DNA		
mRNA BASE	tRNA BASE	DNA BASE
uracil (U)	adenine (A)	adenine (A)
cytosine (C)	guanine (G)	guanine (G)
guanine (G)	cytosine (C)	cytosine (C)
adenine (A)	uracil (U)	thymine (T)

TABLE 3.	
CARD COLOR	MOLECULE REPRESENTED
yellow	mRNA nucleotides
red	amino acids
green	anticodons

corresponding green cards. Yellow cards represent mRNA nucleotides, red cards represent amino acids, and green cards represent tRNA nucleotides (Table 3).

Attach two blank yellow cards to the end of a piece of cord. Place the cord on the table with two blank yellow cards to your left. Print "mRNA" on the first card and "AUG" on the second card. AUG starts protein synthesis. When found elsewhere in a protein, AUG codes for methionine.

Let your laboratory table represent a cell. "Mark off" appropriate areas showing the nucleus, cytoplasm, and a ribosome using masking tape (Figure 1). Place the mRNA model inside the nucleus.

Transfer the mRNA from the nucleus to the surface of the ribosome. Place the green cards and red cards in the area marked "cytoplasm." Make sure they are in order from 1 to 25. Place the second piece of cord parallel to the mRNA molecule. To the left end of the cord, attach two blank red cards with transparent tape. Print "new protein" on the first card and "start" on the second card.

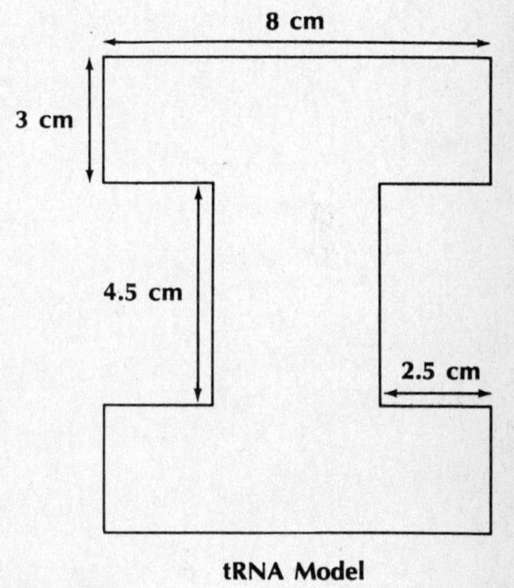

FIGURE 2

Part C. Protein Synthesis

Cut out a tRNA molecule model from a piece of construction paper using the dimensions indicated on Figure 2. Use the construction paper model of a tRNA molecule to transfer specific amino acids from the cytoplasm to the ribosome where the new protein is being synthesized. For each codon, there is a specific tRNA molecule. However, in this investigation, you will use one tRNA model. Different anticodon cards will be attached to it to represent the specific tRNA for each amino acid. Using paper clips, attach the first anticodon card and amino acid card to the tRNA molecule. Move the tRNA molecule from the cytoplasm to the first codon unit of mRNA.

FIGURE 3

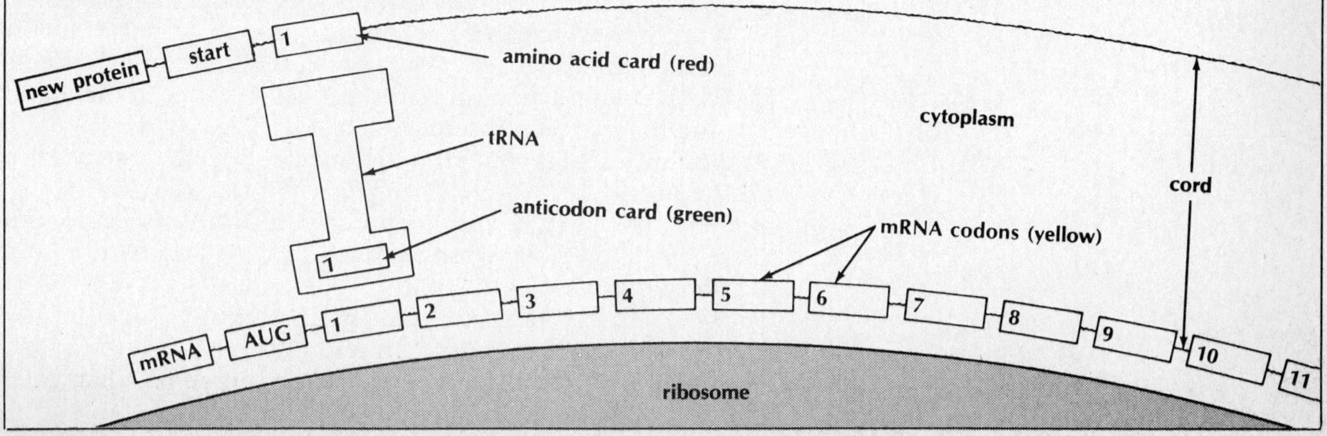

Remove the amino acid from tRNA and attach it to the cord labeled "new protein" beside the first mRNA codon unit (Figure 3).

Return the tRNA molecule to the cytoplasm. Remove the anticodon unit. Attach the second amino acid card and anticodon unit card. Move the tRNA molecule to the number 2 codon unit of mRNA and transfer the amino acid to the "new protein" cord beside the sécond mRNA codon unit.

Return the tRNA to the cytoplasm and repeat the procedure for the other 23 mRNA codon units. Now choose one of the "stop" codons (UAG, UGA, or UAA) and add as the last card on the mRNA. Determine the anticodon of the codon you chose. On a green card write the word "stop" and place it on the tRNA model. Carry this to the new protein and add this as the last card to the right. At the end of this procedure, you will have a protein that is 25 amino acid units long.

TABLE 4. CODONS, AMINO ACIDS, AND ANTICODONS

CARD NUMBER	mRNA CODON	AMINO ACID	ANTICODON
start			
1			
2			
25			
stop			

Formulating Generalizations

1. How do codons and anticodons differ?
2. How do mRNA and tRNA differ?
3. How do mRNA and tRNA work together during protein synthesis?
4. Were any of the amino acids repeated more than two times in your protein molecule? How is this replication possible?
5. What would happen if a cell made a protein in such a random manner that you used? Could such proteins be used by a cell?
6. What would happen if red blood cells produced "random" proteins instead of hemoglobin?
7. How different is your protein from those of other members of the class?
8. What would happen to a protein if a tRNA molecule were to "pick up" the wrong amino acid and carry it to the ribosome?
9. What effect might a "misinterpretation" have on the organism containing the protein? Why?
10. If an organism synthesized the "wrong" protein, what would the change in the genetic code be called?

Detecting Chromosome Problems By Karyotyping

21

Humans, like all other organisms, have a specific number of chromosomes. In 1956, it was discovered that humans had 46 chromosomes in each of their body cells. Prior to that time it was thought that humans had 48 chromosomes.

How is it possible to see chromosomes? Cells are removed from the amnion that surrounds a fetus. These cells are grown in a special solution and photographed just before they divide into two new cells. The photograph of the chromosomes is enlarged and each chromosome is cut out of the photograph and arranged in matched pairs. Each chromosome of a pair has the same size and appearance. This arrangement of chromosomes is called a karyotype.

Sometimes a child inherits an extra chromosome or has a missing chromosome. A chromosome may have an extra section attached on one arm or a section may be missing. All of these conditions seen in chromosomes are called chromosomal mutations. A karyotype can show differences in chromosome number and mutations that occur in chromosomes. If a human geneticist finds a chromosomal mutation in the karyotype of an unborn child, the parents can be informed about the mutation and what effect it will have on the child.

In this investigation you will cut out and arrange (in pairs) the chromosomes of two different karyotype sheets like those used by a human geneticist. One of the karyotypes shows a normal pattern, the other an abnormal pattern. Using your finished karyotypes, you are to determine the type of chromosomal mutation present in the abnormal pattern.

Materials *(per student)*

scissors
glue
2 pages of chromosomes
2 charts for mounting chromosomes

Procedure

Part A. Normal Karyotype

Obtain a page of chromosomes from your teacher labeled "Normal Human Karyotype." This page is a duplicate of an actual photograph of chromosomes in metaphase as seen through a microscope. Two of the chromosomes, the sex chromosomes, are unshaded. These were left unshaded because they can be confused easily with another chromosome of the same size.

Prepare a karyotype of these chromosomes by cutting out each chromosome with scissors. **CAUTION:** *Always be careful with scissors.* Cut out the chromosomes so they will look like the chromosomes in Figure 1. Set the unshaded chromosomes aside and arrange the shaded chromosomes in pairs from longest to shortest. Use the location of the centromere to determine which chromosomes make up a pair. The centromere holds the two chromatids together in a chromosome.

Before transferring the pairs of chromosomes to a blank karyotype chart, place two small drops of glue above each number. See Figure 2. Place the longest pair of chromosomes on the glue in the upper left hand corner at position 1. These chromosomes are called pair one. Place the next longest pair at position 2. The remainder of the chromosomes (pairs 3–22) should be placed on the karyotype chart (Figure 3). Finally, place the unshaded sex chromosomes in the place provided in the lower right corner.

Part B. Abnormal Human Karyotype

Obtain a second page of chromosomes from your teacher labeled "Abnormal Human Karyotype." Prepare a second karyotype as you did the first karyotype. Use a second blank karyotype chart on which to glue the matched pairs.

Formulating Generalizations

1. How many chromosomes are present in the karyotype in Part A?
2. How many matched pairs of chromosomes are present in the karyotype in Part A?
3. Do any of the pairs of chromosomes in Part A have chromosomes of two different sizes? Explain your answer.
4. What is the sex of the unborn child in Part A?
5. What was the advantage of having the sex chromosomes unshaded?
6. How many chromosomes are present in the karyotype in Part B?
7. What is the sex of the unborn child in Part B?
8. Which chromosomes appear to be abnormal?
9. What type of chromosomal problem will the unborn baby have? (Consult Chapter 11 of your text.)
10. Were the cells used in making both karyotypes from a somatic cell or a gamete? Explain your answer.
11. What can we find out about an unborn child by using the karyotype procedure?

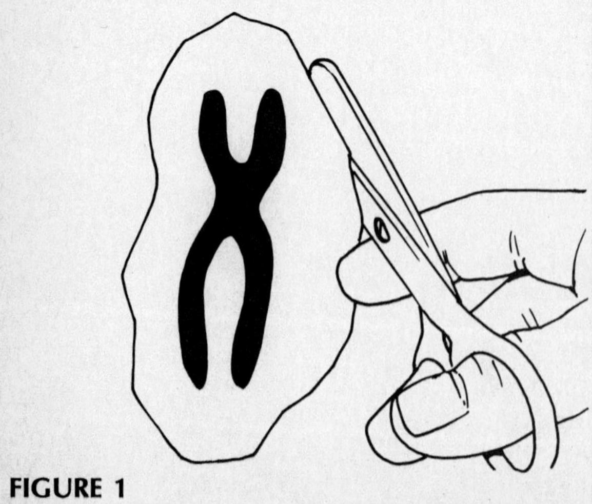

FIGURE 1

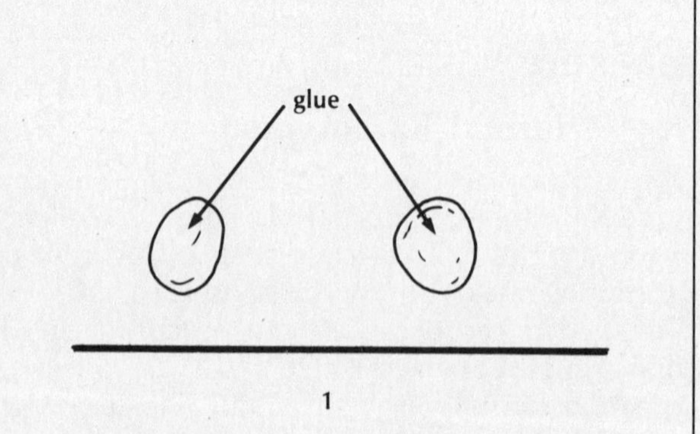

FIGURE 2

Human Pedigree Genetics

22

Progress in human genetics has proceeded slowly. A geneticist uses experimental results to verify the genotypes and phenotypes of living organisms. In humans, the generation time is about 15 to 40 years. Also, the time involved for a new generation to show a certain trait can be several decades. For example, diabetes mellitus in some people may not show up for 30 or 40 years. Other organisms have shorter generation times. For example, fruit flies are easy to study because new generations develop in only ten to twelve days. Traits in these organisms show up much sooner.

Genotypic and/or phenotypic data of human genetic patterns are usually presented as a diagrammed chart called a pedigree. Some pedigree symbols are shown in Table 1. A pedigree shows several generations of a family and the people who married into the family (Figure 1). Each person in a pedigree can be identified by the Roman numeral for the generation and by an individual number. One difficulty in making a pedigree chart is that sometimes the information is obtained from only a few members of the family. Therefore, it could be inaccurate or unreliable.

Today, geneticists are able to provide a service called "genetic counseling." Families affected with unfavorable traits such as sickle cell anemia or PKU can be given advice about the chances of their future children having these traits.

In this investigation you are to analyze three family pedigrees. From these pedigrees, you are to determine whether the gene for the trait listed is dominant or recessive and determine the genotype and phenotype of each individual in the family.

Procedure

Study each of the following pedigrees of families with certain hereditary traits. Determine whether each of the traits is dominant or recessive. Determine the genotype and phenotype of each individual in each pedigree. Record the genotypes and phenotypes in your lab notebook.

TABLE 1. PEDIGREE CHART SYMBOLS

SYMBOL	MEANING
□	male
○	female
■ or ●	affected individual
□ or ♀	stillbirth
○⁄\□	fraternal twins

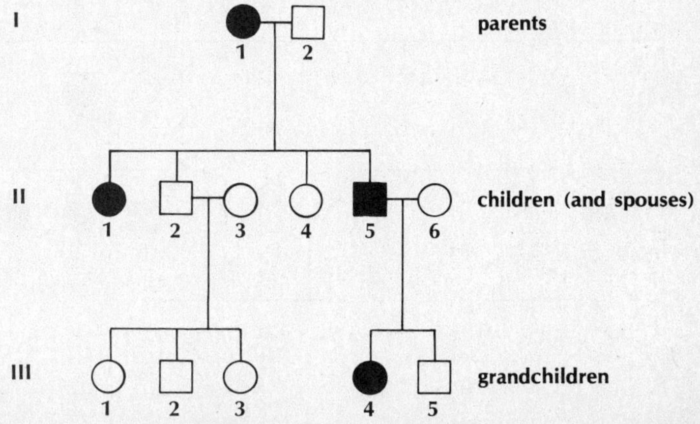

FIGURE 1

Pedigree A. Deaf Mutism

One form of deafness in humans is a type in which the individual inherits not only deafness but also the inability to talk. Use symbols *D* for dominant, *d* for recessive.

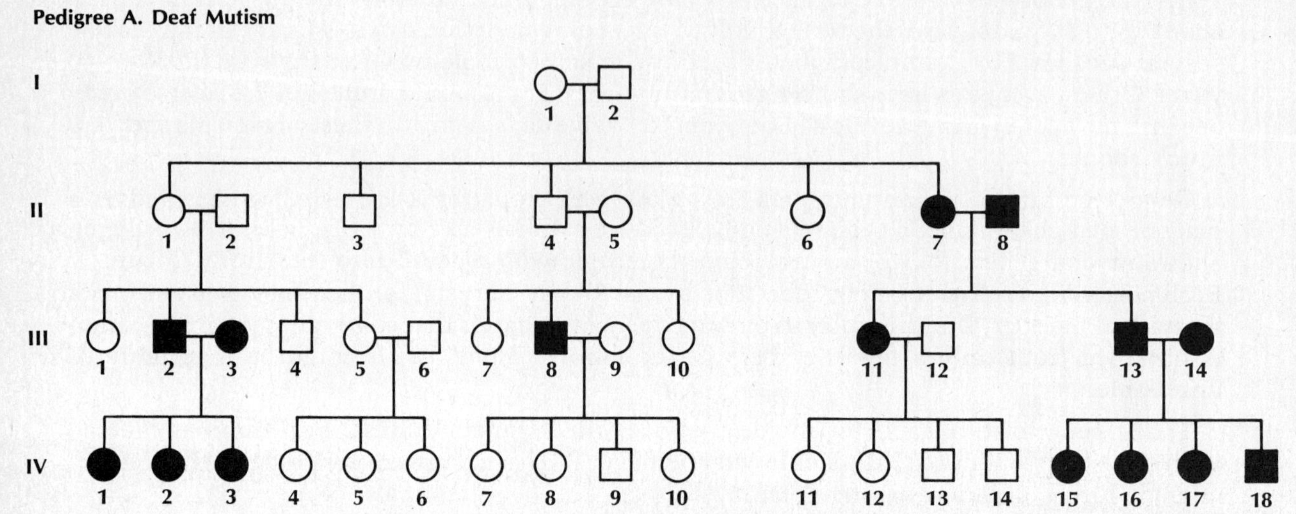

FIGURE 2

Pedigree B. Hemophilia

Hemophilia is a disease of the circulatory system. It is sometimes called bleeder's disease because persons with the disease have a very long clotting time when injured. An affected person could bleed to death from minor wounds or internal injuries. Use symbols *H* for dominant, *h* for recessive.

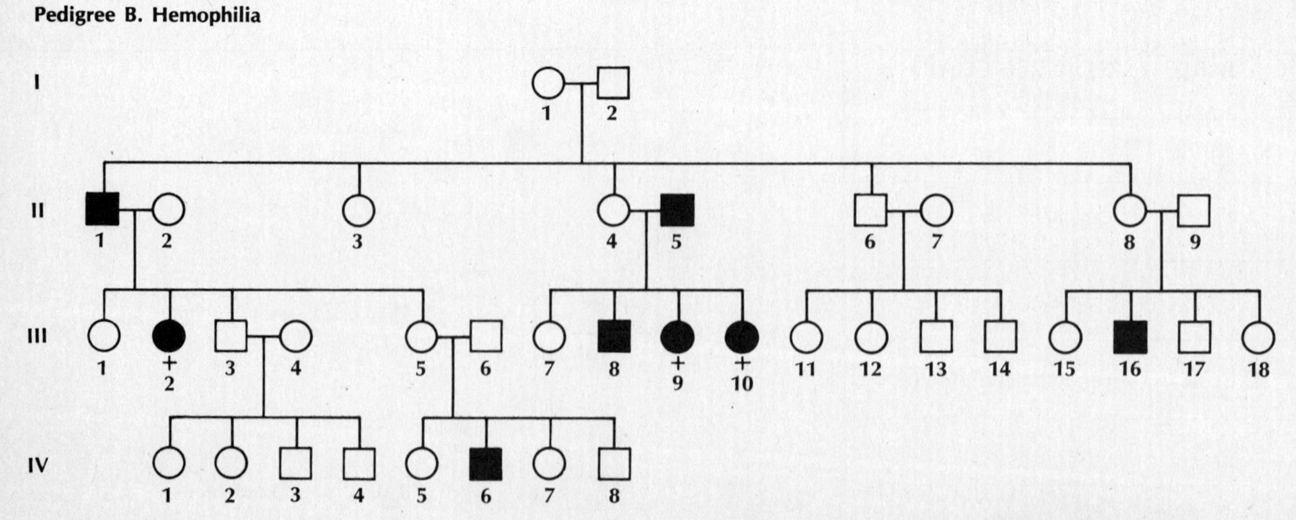

FIGURE 3

Pedigree C. Brachydactyly

Brachydactyly is a condition in which fingers are abnormally short. The last two joints of the middle finger are shortened. In the other four fingers, the last two joints are fused into one and are also shortened. Use symbols *B* for dominant, *b* for recessive.

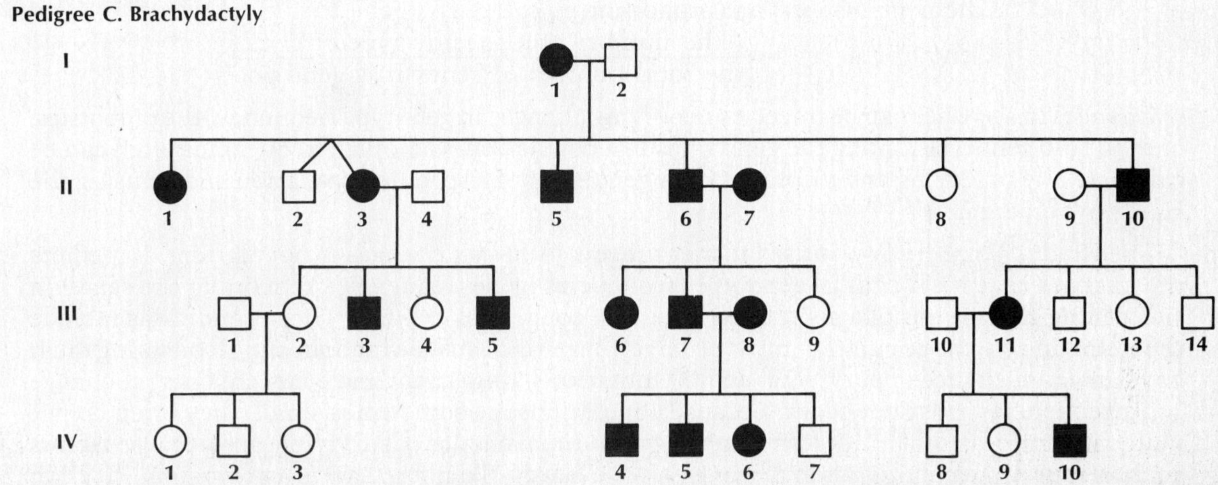

FIGURE 4

Formulating Generalizations

1. In pedigree A, why do parents 13 and 14 in generation III have four deaf children?
2. In pedigree A, how can parents 1 and 2 have a deaf child even though neither parent is deaf?
3. In pedigree A, why don't parents 8 and 9 and 11 and 12 have at least one deaf child?
4. List by number the persons in pedigree A for which you cannot determine a genotype. For example—II-1.
5. Why can't you determine the genotypes of these people?
6. In pedigree B, how can unaffected parents have an affected child?
7. What is the genotype of the mothers of all affected females in pedigree B? Explain.
8. What characteristic do all affected females in pedigree B have in common?
9. List by number the persons in pedigree B for which you cannot determine a genotype. Explain why a genotype cannot be determined.
10. Is the brachydactyly trait in pedigree C dominant or recessive? Explain.

23 Natural Selection In Populations

Evolutionary changes occur in populations rather than individuals. All the genes of a population are called the gene pool. Each gene in the gene pool is present in a certain proportion of the genes of the population. That proportion is called the gene frequency.

$$\text{Gene frequency} = \frac{\text{the number of a specific type of gene}}{\text{the total number of genes in a gene pool}}$$

Changes in a species can be traced by observing changes in genotype frequency, the proportion of a specific genotype among the genotypes of a population. Genotype frequencies often can be calculated by observing and recording the phenotypes of a specific population and by using the Hardy-Weinberg Law.

The Hardy-Weinberg Law is used to measure evolutionary changes in populations. It predicts the changes that will occur in genotype frequencies (gene frequencies remaining the same) in succeeding generations of a population if certain conditions are met. Those conditions include the following: (1) the population must be large, (2) mating must be random and all offspring must have an equal chance of surviving, and (3) mutations, migration, and other things that change gene frequencies must not occur. Because populations are sometimes small, they often do not mate randomly, all offspring often do not have an equal chance of surviving, and because factors such as mutation and migration often occur, the Hardy-Weinberg Law is an oversimplification of what really happens in natural populations. However, it has some value in studying populations, especially those that are isolated. In real populations, gene frequencies do change.

Mathematically, the Hardy-Weinberg Law states that $p^2 + 2pq + q^2 = 1$ and $p + q = 1$, where p and q represent the dominant and recessive alleles respectively for a trait with two possible alleles. The formulas can be used to determine the genotypic frequencies if the frequency of the genes or of a genotype are known. A sample problem is given at the end of this investigation.

In this investigation you are to determine the frequencies of genotypes and phenotypes in two salamander populations by using beans to represent the possible alleles. The two populations have different gene frequencies. In Population 1, $p = q = 0.5$. That is, half of the beans used are of one kind (representing one gene) and half are of another kind (representing the other gene). In Population 2, a different gene frequency will be tested by removing some of the beans for one allele. Thus, $p \neq q$. You are to calculate the genotype and phenotype frequencies and change in these frequencies for each population.

Materials *(per team of two students)*

red beans—200
white beans—200 (same size as red)
brown lunch bag

Procedure

Place 200 red beans and 200 white beans in a large jar. This jar will represent the gene pool of an isolated salamander population. The salamanders in this population have two possible spotted patterns due to one pair of genes.

Each bean is to represent a gamete. Each gamete contains one gene for skin color. Red beans represent the dominant gene (*D*) for red-spotted skin. White beans represent the recessive gene (*d*) for brown-spotted skin.

Questions

Use the formula in the introduction and the Punnett square (Figure 1) to answer the questions.

1. On the basis of the number of beans in the jar, what is the frequency of each gene (*D* and *d*) in the original population?
2. Assuming random mating, calculate the expected frequency of red- and brown-spotted salamanders.
3. How many of the red-spotted salamanders will be homozygous dominant?
4. How many will be heterozygous?

	p	q
p	p^2	pq
q	pq	q^2

FIGURE 1

Part A. Population 1 (p = q)

Mix the beans thoroughly in the paper bag. One student (student A) is to remove two beans while the other student (student B) will record these two as zygote 1. Return the two beans to the paper bag and mix the beans. The combinations can be recorded on scrap paper. Continue removing, recording, and returning pairs of beans until you have 25 zygotes. Be sure to mix the beans after each pair is returned. Record the total for each genetic combination in a table similar to Table 1. Multiply your results by four to indicate how many of each combination there would be in a population of 100. This number is a percentage.

Repeat the pairing of 50 beans to make 25 zygotes. This time switch jobs. Record the results in the table. Calculate the frequency of each genotype and phenotype in Population 1.

TABLE 1. INDIVIDUAL AND CLASS DATA

POPULATION 1 (OR 2)

GENOTYPE	STUDENT A			STUDENT B		
	NUMBER		PERCENTAGE	NUMBER		PERCENTAGE
DD		x4			x4	
Dd		x4			x4	
dd		x4			x4	

GENOTYPE	CLASS TOTALS	AVERAGE	PERCENTAGE
DD			
Dd			
dd			

Question

5. Why are the beans returned after each "mating"?

Part B. Population 2 ($p \neq q$)

Remove 20% (40) of the white beans from the jar. This procedure will remove 20% of the recessive (brown) genes from the population to simulate a selection pressure.

Mix the beans in the container. Student A is to remove 50 beans in pairs as before returning the beans and mixing them after each mating. Student B is to tally the 25 zygotes. Then Student B is to remove 50 beans in pairs while student A tallies the 25 zygotes. Record the total for each genetic combination on another table like that used in Part A. Again determine the numbers for a population of 100. From your data, compute the frequency of each genotype and phenotype.

Collect class data on both populations. Record the totals in the proper columns of the two tables. Add class data and compute the frequencies for each genotype.

Formulating Generalizations

1. How do your data on frequencies of genotypes and phenotypes of Population 1 compare with those of your partner? What does this comparison show about the Hardy-Weinberg Law?
2. How do your data compare with class totals?
3. Which set of data—yours, your partner's, or the class totals—most accurately represents the population? Explain.
4. How do your data on frequencies of genotypes and phenotypes of Population 2 compare with those of your partner?
5. How do your data compare with class totals?
6. Does any set of data—yours, your partner's, or class totals—accurately represent the population? Explain.
7. From the two sets of data—Population 1 and Population 2—is it evident that natural selection can be a guiding mechanism of evolution? Explain.

Problems Applying the Hardy-Weinberg Law

Sample Problem

Suppose that in a population of frogs, a dominant allele is for red-spotted skin and a recessive allele is for brown-spotted skin. Nine out of every 100 frogs have brown-spotted skin. How many of the 100 frogs are heterozygous for that trait?

Solution

Use p and q as symbols for the dominant and recessive alleles respectively and the equations $p^2 + 2pq + q^2 = 1$ and $p + q = 1$.

According to the information given, 9 out of every 100, or 0.09 (q^2), are pure recessive. Because 0.09 is the value of q^2, the value of q is $\sqrt{0.09}$ which equals 0.3. Because $p + q = 1$, $p = 1 - 0.3 = 0.7$.

The frequency of the homozygous dominant frogs would be p^2 or $0.7 \times 0.7 = 0.49$. Thus, out of 100 frogs, 49 are homozygous dominant. The frequency of the heterozygotes would be 2pq or $2 \times 0.7 \times 0.3 = 0.42$. Thus, 42 out of each 100 frogs would be heterozygous for the trait.

You can check your work by adding the frequencies of each genotype. Their total must equal 1. Thus,

$$\begin{array}{rcl} p^2 & = & 0.49 \\ 2pq & = & 0.42 \\ + \; q^2 & = & 0.09 \\ \hline 1 & & 1.00 \end{array}$$

	p (0.7)	q (0.3)
p (0.7)	p^2 (0.49)	pq (0.21)
q (0.3)	pq (0.21)	q^2 (0.09)

FIGURE 3

Additional Problems

1. Screech owls are found in two different color patterns, red and gray. Scientists have raised and bred these owls in captivity. The scientists mated red to red, red to gray, and gray to gray. The red to gray matings usually gave equal numbers of red and gray offspring, but sometimes gave only red offspring. A population survey done in Pennsylvania showed the population to be composed of 51% red and 49% gray owls. Use the formula $p^2 + 2pq + q^2 = 1$ and Figure 3A to help you answer the questions below.

(a) Which gene is dominant?
(b) Which gene is recessive?
(c) Calculate the frequency of each gene.
(d) Suppose the frequency of the gene for red feathers is 0.42 ten years later in the same population. What could have caused the change in the gene frequency?

2. The ability to taste a chemical substance called PTC is the result of inheriting a dominant gene (P). Humans that are hybrid (Pp) for the gene are also tasters. Humans that are pure recessive (pp) cannot taste PTC. A population sample was taken in a small town and of 1092 people tested 64% were found to be tasters.

(a) What is the frequency of each gene? (Use Figure 3B.)
(b) How many people in the sample can taste PTC?
(c) How many people cannot taste PTC?
(d) A sample was taken in the same town 15 years later and the gene frequency was found to be the same as in the earlier sample. How can you account for this result?

	p ( )	q ( )
p ( )	p^2 ( )	pq ( )
q ( )	pq ( )	q^2 (0.49)

A

	p ( )	q ( )
p ( )	p^2 ( )	pq ( )
q ( )	pq ( )	q^2 (0.36)

B

FIGURE 3

24 Coacervates—A Model of Life's Origin

For centuries people have wondered if life came from preexisting life or if it arose spontaneously. From the time of the first controversy over spontaneous generation (1780) until spontaneous generation was disproven in 1864, some scientists favored spontaneous generation over biogenesis. Biogenesis is the theory that life comes from preexisting life.

In 1931, a Dutch biochemist, H. B. Bungenberg de Jong conducted experiments with materials that formed organic colloids when mixed together. Colloids are composed of particles that range from 0.001 to 0.1 μm in diameter. The particles are dispersed in a medium. Being so small, they can collide with moving molecules of the medium. The particles do not settle out. Colloidal particles have electric charges. Those of like charges repel each other, enabling them to stay suspended. De Jong mixed organic colloids of opposite charges. They attracted each other and formed large droplets (they coalesced). He called these large droplets coacervates (Figure 1).

A Russian biochemist, Oparin, investigated the coacervate system. In 1936 he proposed that proteins and carbohydrates could come together and form a "life unit." Oparin further proposed that coacervates are similar to cells. They react to the physical and chemical conditions of the environment in which they are formed. Coacervates can become complex, large globules or they can dissolve into the media from which they are formed. From the large, complex coacervates the true life forms of the earth may have evolved.

Sidney Fox showed that heat caused a dry mixture of amino acids to form long chainlike masses called proteinoids. These proteinoids appeared to be osmotic because they shrank when placed in salt water and swelled when placed in distilled water. Proteinoids may be another type of "precell."

In this investigation you are to form coacervates. Also you are to identify the pH at which coacervates form and decompose.

Materials *(per student)*

1% gelatin solution—5 mL
1% gum arabic solution—3 mL
0.1 *M* hydrochloric acid—5 mL
droppers—2
test tube
stopper to fit test tube
pH paper—1 roll
glass slide
coverslip
microscope

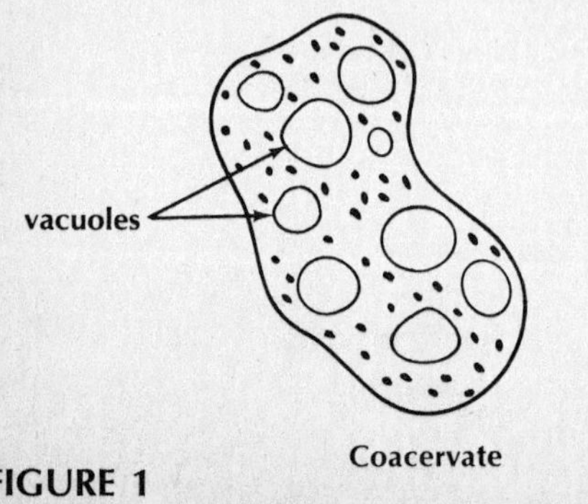

FIGURE 1

Procedure

Add 3 mL of gum arabic solution and 5 mL of gelatin solution to a test tube. Insert a stopper into the test tube. Invert the test tube to mix the solutions. Determine the pH of the medium by dipping a piece of pH paper into the gelatin-gum arabic solution. Compare the color of the pH paper with the standard color chart and record the pH. Also record the clarity or cloudiness of the solution. Record the data in a table in your notebook similar to Table 1.

Make a wet mount of the gelatin-gum arabic solution by adding 2 drops of solution to a clean slide. Add a coverslip. Observe the slide with low power of a compound microscope. If coacervates are present, they will appear as viscous droplets containing vacuoles. The droplets will come together to form larger droplets.

Continue searching for coacervates by doing the following: Using a dropper, add one drop of 0.1 *M* hydrochloric acid to the solution in the test tube. **CAUTION:** *Hydrochloric acid burns skin and ruins clothes. If spillage occurs, rinse with water and call your teacher immediately.* Replace the stopper and shake gently. Determine the pH and observe the clarity or cloudiness of the solution. Make a wet mount and look for coacervates. Keep adding a drop of hydrochloric acid and making other wet mounts until coacervates form. Record the pH, clarity of medium, and presence or absence of coacervates for each trial.

After you locate coacervates, continue to add 1 drop of 0.1 *M* hydrochloric acid, determine the pH and cloudiness, and make wet mounts until coacervates disappear. Record data in the table for each additional trial.

Formulating Generalizations

1. At what pH is coacervation most evident?
2. Did the gelatin-gum arabic solution appear cloudy or clear at the height of coacervate formation? Why?
3. What organism does a coacervate resemble?
4. Describe the possible role of coacervates in evolution of life forms.
5. What physical and chemical factors would have had to be present on the earth for coacervate formation?

TABLE 1. APPEARANCE AND DISAPPEARANCE OF COACERVATES

		MEDIUM	COACERVATES
	pH OF MEDIUM	CLEAR OR CLOUDY	PRESENT OR ABSENT
trial 1			
trial 2			
trial 3			
trial 4			
trial 5			
trial 6			

25 Adaptation

Adaptations are necessary for the survival of a species. An adaptation is an inherited structure, physiological reaction, or behavioral mechanism that better allows an organism to survive and reproduce in its environment. An adaptation allows an organism to exist under a specific set of conditions. The mechanism for producing an adaptation is natural selection. An adaptation results from many evolutionary changes over a long period of time. Genes for favorable adaptations are in the gene pool of a species. These often get passed on to offspring. A poorly adapted organism may not survive to reproduce.

Adaptation causes degrees of specialization in specific groups of plants and animals. The specializations in one biological group (class, order, etc.) may not be found in another closely related group. The distribution of living things in the world depends on the adaptations of the living things.

Structural and behavioral adaptations are easy to observe in nature. Physiological adaptations are not as easy to observe. For example, it is easy to see the mouthparts of insects, but it is more difficult to determine enzymes that digest blood ingested by a mosquito.

In this investigation, you are to identify, compare, and describe specific adaptations in living and preserved specimens of plants and animals.

Materials *(per class)*

various living and preserved organisms placed throughout the lab

Procedure

Observe certain specimens for specific adaptations as directed by your teacher. The organisms are grouped by types of adaptations. Record your observations in your lab notebook and answer the questions for each group.

Station A. Observe, compare, and describe the organs of locomotion in the animal specimens.

1. List the organs of locomotion of each specimen.

2. Describe the adaptations of the specific organs for movement of each specimen.

3. Describe the similarities and differences in the organs of locomotion of all specimens.

4. How are the specific differences of each organism adaptations to particular environments?

Station B. Observe the front and rear limbs of the animal specimens. Compare and describe the differences in the front and rear limbs of each specimen.

5. How are the limbs of each organism adaptive?

6. Are there any differences between front and rear limbs of any specimen? Explain.

Station C. Observe the mouthparts of various preserved insect specimens. Compare and describe the differences and similarities in the mouthparts.

7. Which insects have mouthparts that are adaptations for biting? For sucking and piercing? For catching and holding prey? For obtaining nectar?

Station D. Observe the layers of tissue in a prepared microscope slide of an *Elodea* leaf cross section.

8. How is the leaf adapted for photosynthesis?
9. What adaptations prevent the leaf from "drowning"?
10. How is the leaf adapted to float in water? What is the adaptive advantage of floating?

Station E. Observe the leaves and stem of a potted cactus plant.

11. How are the leaves of a cactus plant an adaptation to a dry environment?
12. How is the stem adapted for water storage?

Station F. Observe a prepared slide of a tapeworm. Observe the shape of the head and the segments of the tapeworm's body.

13. How is the tapeworm's shape an adaptation for life in the human intestine?

Station G. Observe the "specialized" leaves of a Venus's-flytrap and a pea plant.

14. How is the color of the interior of a Venus's-flytrap leaf an adaptation for catching insects?
15. What other adaptations are found on a Venus's-flytrap plant that aid catching insects?
16. What is the function of the specialized leaves (tendrils) of the pea plant?
17. How do tendrils aid the plant in competing with other plants for sunlight?

Station H. Compare the skin of the animals and describe differences and similarities in the skins.

18. How is the skin of each animal an adaptation to the animal's environment?

Station I. Observe the dentition (pattern of teeth) in the skulls of various animals. List the differences in the size, shape, and number of incisor (biter), canine (flesh-tearer), and molar (grinder) teeth.

19. How does the dentition pattern of each animal aid its survival in its environment?

Station J. Observe prepared microscope slides of *Ulothrix* and *Spirogyra.* Record differences in the two ends of each type of alga filament.

20. Which alga is adapted to fast-moving water?
21. Which alga is adapted to slow-moving or still water?
22. What structure is present or absent in the alga that lives in fast-moving water compared to the alga that lives in slow-moving water?

Station K. Observe the structure of the seeds and fruits in the plants. Compare the structures that aid in seed dispersal.

23. How are the seeds adapted for dispersal over a wide area?

Station L. Observe the parts of the specialized "underground" stems. Compare the size and shape of each underground stem.

24. How is each underground stem adapted for food storage and reproduction?

Station M. Observe the movement of an earthworm as it moves across a wet paper towel. Gently rub your fingers along the earthworm from the posterior to the anterior end. Rub your fingers on both the ventral and dorsal surfaces.

25. How are the ventral and dorsal surfaces different?

26. How is the earthworm adapted to move through the soil?

Formulating Generalizations

1. Can an organism's behavior be adaptive? Give specific examples.
2. Of the organisms that you observed, list any that could not live in any other environment except the one for which they are adapted. Explain.
3. Of the organisms that you observed, list those that could live in several environments. Explain.
4. What advantage do organisms that can exist in several environments have over those that can exist in only one environment?
5. What adaptive advantage do organisms capable of locomotion have over those that do not have locomotive adaptations?
6. A horse eats mostly grasses. Bobcats eat mostly meat. How do you think the teeth of horses and bobcats differ?

Variation Within A Species And Between Species

26

A species is a group of organisms that can interbreed to produce fertile offspring. All members of a species do not look exactly alike. For example, the size and shape of the parts of the organisms of the same species may show slight differences. These differences are called variations.

Variation is present in all types of organisms. Rabbits of the same species can have fur of different colors and color patterns. Plants of the same species can be found with flowers of different colors. Variation is also present in traits other than color. Some organisms can be taller or shorter than other members of the same species. Some may have more or less hair than other members of the same species. These variations could be related to the physiology of the organisms, to the environments in which the organisms live, or to gene expression.

In this investigation, you are to describe variation in leaves from different trees of the same species and from two closely related species.

Materials *(per student)*

pressed and dried leaves of species 1—package of 10
pressed and dried leaves of species 2—package of 10
graph paper (mm type)—2 sheets
metric ruler
colored pencils

Procedure

Obtain a package of leaves of species 1 from your teacher. Remove the leaves from the package. Handle the leaves carefully because they are dry and brittle.

Measure the length and width of each leaf blade and the length of each petiole (Figure 1). Count the number of lobes on each leaf. Record data in a table in your lab notebook similar to Table 1.

TABLE 1. LEAF MEASUREMENTS

SPECIES 1	BLADE		LOBES	PETIOLE
LEAF NO.	LENGTH	WIDTH	NUMBER	LENGTH
1				
2				
10				

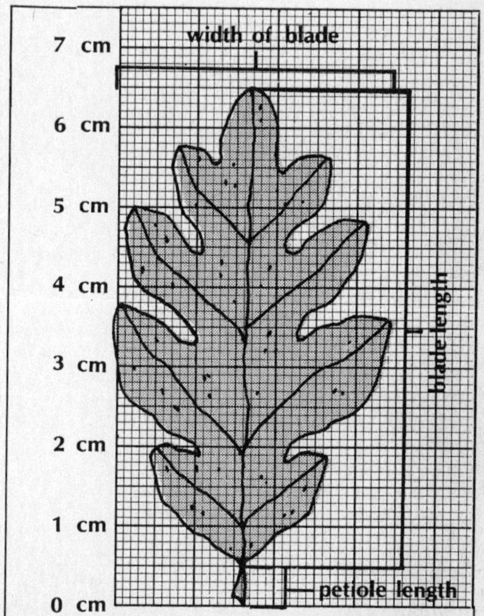

FIGURE 1

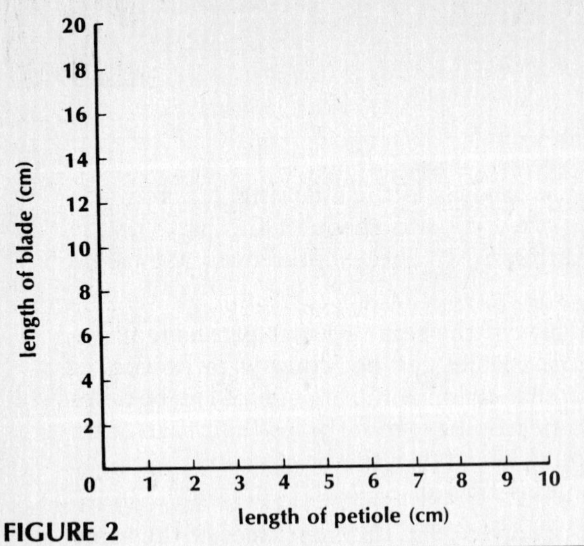

FIGURE 2

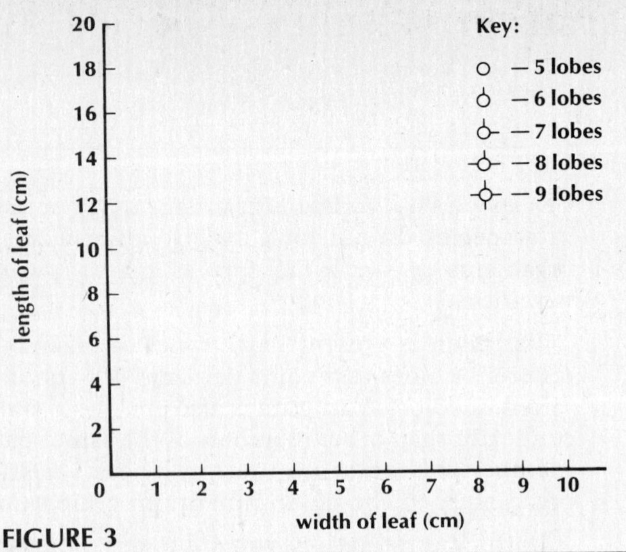

FIGURE 3

Repeat the measurements with each leaf of species 2. Record the measurements in another table similar to Table 1.

Construct a separate graph for each species of leaf by using data from your tables. Use one graph to show petiole length versus blade length (Figure 2). Where length of petiole and blade intersect, make a dot with a pencil to mark the data point. Repeat this procedure for each set of data. On the other graph, show width versus length of the leaf blade (Figure 3). Use the Key in Figure 3 to indicate the number of lobes on the leaves represented by each data point. On each graph, use a colored pencil to draw a straight line from the data point representing the leaf blade with the shortest length to the data point representing the longest leaf blade. Assume that any data points that fall on this line represent leaves growing at a constant rate and show no variance. Those data points that do not fall on the line show variations in growth.

Formulating Generalizations

1. How are the leaves of species 1 similar to species 2?
2. How do the leaves of these two species differ?
3. What name is given to these differences?
4. How many leaves of species 1 show constant growth? How many leaves of species 2 show constant growth?
5. How do the leaves of both species show variations in length and width?
6. Is there a relationship between the length and width of a leaf and the number of lobes present? Explain.
7. Would the differences in leaf lengths on the same tree be an ecological or a genetic variation? Explain.
8. Would the presence of rounded lobes on one species and pointed lobes on another species be an ecological or a genetic variation? Explain.

Evolutionary Changes In Primates

27

When paleontologists discover fossils, they determine whether they have discovered fossils of recent or ancestral organisms. They then determine to what kinds of organisms the fossils belong. If a skull were discovered and determined to be a primate skull, the next step would be to determine whether it is of an ape or a human. Because evolutionary change has occurred in both groups, the skull could be of ancestral or modern ape or ancestral or modern human. Because humans and apes evolved along separate lines, certain physical characteristics can be used in an attempt to classify the fossil skull as belonging to either ape (early or modern), early human, or modern human. Techniques similar to the ones used in this investigation are used by anthropologists, paleontologists, and archaeologists.

In this investigation, you are to examine skull diagrams of a gorilla, an early human (*Australopithecus*), and a modern human. You are to measure or observe and record specific structures and features of each skull. Then you are to evaluate evolutionary changes that have occurred in the organisms.

Materials *(per student)*

metric ruler
protractor

Procedure

Part A. Skull Characteristics and Relationships

Ratio of Brain Area to Face Area

Rectangles over the skulls in Figure 1 represent the area of the brain (upper rectangle) and face area (lower rectangle) of each skull. Determine the area of each rectangle by measuring the length and width in centimeters and multiplying the two measurements together. In your notebook in a table similar to Table 1, record the brain and face areas of the three skulls.

Determine the ratio of brain area to face area of each skull by dividing the brain area by the face area. Carry the divisions to two decimal places. Always use face area as one in the ratio. For example, a skull with a face area of 120 and a brain area of 50 has a face area to brain area ratio of 1 to 0.41. Record the ratios in the proper column of the table.

Cranial Capacity

Measure the diameter of the circle in each skull in centimeters. Multiply the cranial diameters by 200 cm^2. This calculation gives a value equivalent to the cranial capacity (brain volume) in cubic centimeters. Record the cranial capacity of each skull in the table.

NOTE: This method of measuring cranial capacity differs from the method used when an intact skull is available.

Jaw Angle (Prognathism)

In front of each skull are two heavy lines, one running parallel to the slope of the upper jaw and one running through the nose. These two lines are to be used for measuring how far the jaw protrudes forward.

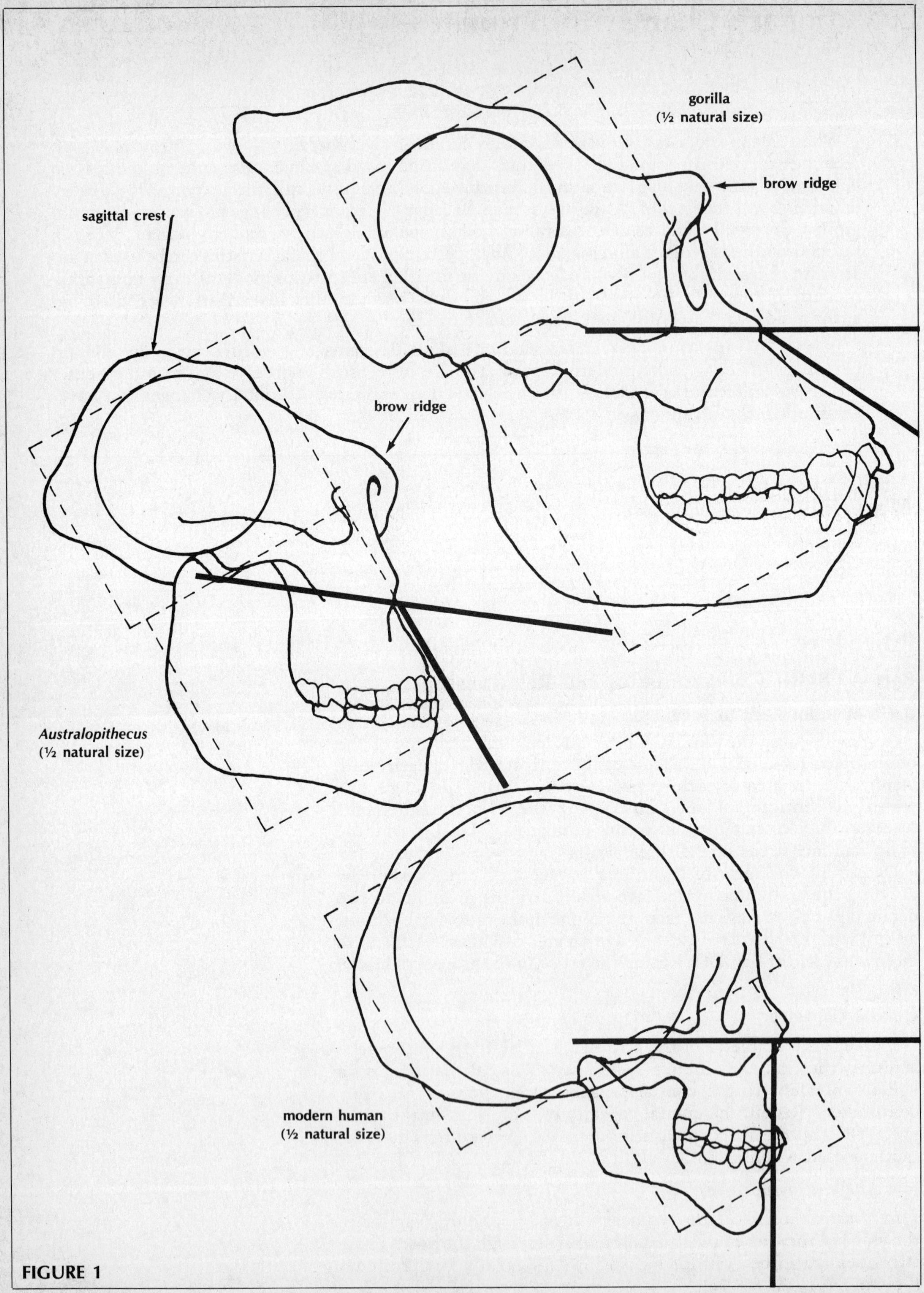
gorilla
(½ natural size)
brow ridge
sagittal crest
brow ridge
Australopithecus
(½ natural size)
modern human
(½ natural size)

FIGURE 1

With a protractor, measure the outside angle formed by the two lines in each skull (the angle toward the right).

Place the protractor onto each skull as shown in Figure 2. Read the angle by using the outside scale on the protractor. The angle is read where the lower skull line crosses the protractor. Record the angles in the proper column of the table.

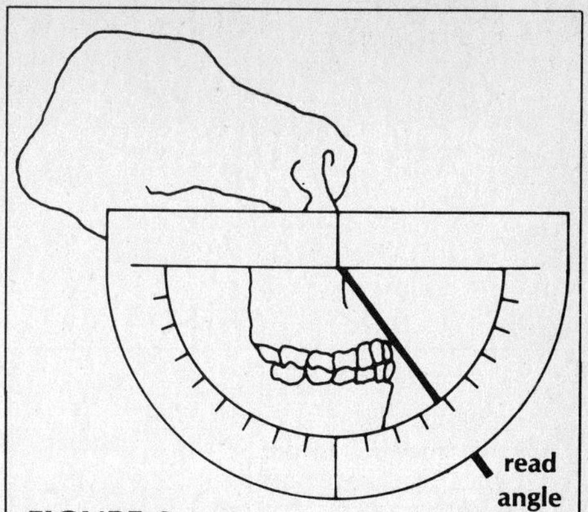

FIGURE 2

Lower Jaw Shape

The ratio between the distance across the jaw backs compared to the distance across the jaw fronts can be used to compare jaw shapes of the three jaws in Figure 3. Measure the distance across each jaw from one dot to the other on the back teeth. Measure the distance across each jaw using the dots on the front teeth. Record in the table the distances (in cm) for each jaw.

TABLE 1. COMPARISON OF GORILLA, *AUSTRALOPITHECUS,* AND MODERN HUMAN SKULLS

	GORILLA	*AUSTRALO-PITHECUS*	MODERN HUMAN
face area			
brain area			
ratio of face area to brain area			
cranial capacity			
jaw angle			
distance across back of jaw			
distance across front of jaw			
ratio of back to front distances			
number of teeth in lower jaw			
number of each type of tooth	M = P = C = I =	M = P = C = I =	M = P = C = I =
sagittal crest			
brow ridge			

Determine the ratio between the distance across the back of the jaw to the distance across the front of the jaw for each skull. Use the distance across the back of the jaw as one in the ratios. Record the ratios in the proper column of the table.

Numbers and Types of Teeth

Count the number of teeth in each lower jaw in Figure 3. Count the number of each tooth type in each lower jaw. Record in the table the total number of teeth in each lower jaw and the number of each type. Use "M" for molar, "P" for premolar, "C" for canine, and "I" for incisor.

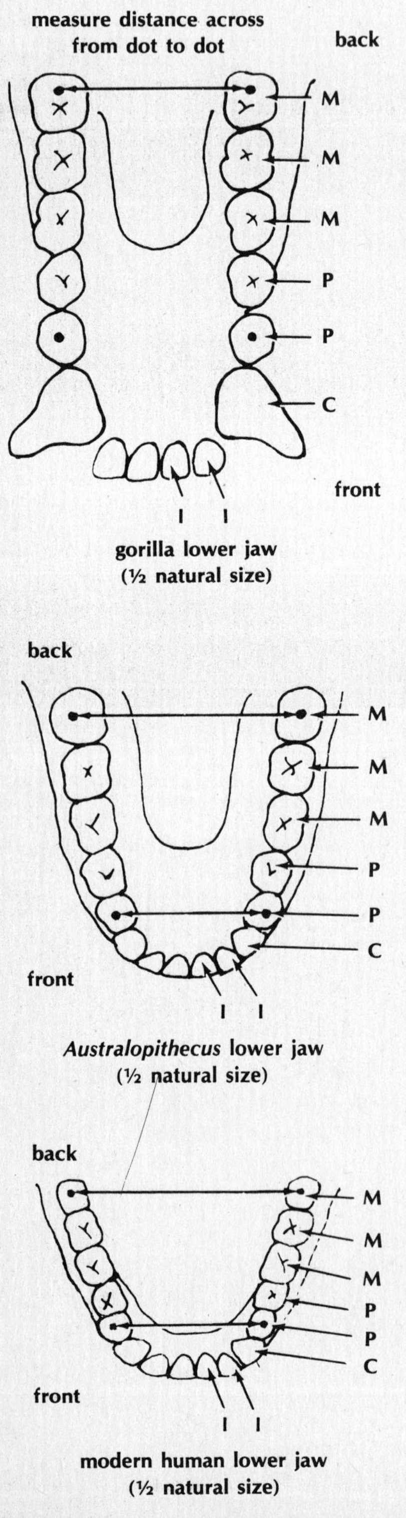

FIGURE 3

Sagittal Crest

A bony ridge running across the top of a skull for muscle attachment is called a sagittal crest. Indicate in the table whether a sagittal crest is absent or present in each skull.

Brow Ridge (Supraorbital Ridge)

Directly above the eye sockets is a thick bony ridge. This ridge may be absent or present in a skull. Indicate in the table whether or not a brow ridge is present in each skull.

Part B. Interpretation of Data

Use the following information to help you evaluate your recorded data and answer the questions in **Formulating Generalizations.**

Ratio of Face Area to Brain Area

A reduction in face area compared to brain area is a trait of modern humans.

Cranial Capacity

An increase in brain size as measured by cranial capacity is characteristic of more complex organisms. Modern humans have the largest cranial capacity of all closely related primates.

Jaw Angle

Jaw angle increase toward 90° is a trait of modern humans. Less of a protruding jaw is characteristic of more complex organisms.

Lower Jaw Shape

Gorillas have a jaw in which both sides are parallel to one another. They have a ratio of 1:1 for back to front distance. Modern humans have a more V-shaped jaw with a ratio of back to front distance of greater than 1:1.

Numbers and Types of Teeth

Adult modern humans, *Australopithecus,* and gorillas all have similar patterns in terms of numbers and types of teeth.

Sagittal Crest

This bony ridge is associated with heavy temporal muscles used to move the lower jaws. Reduction in size of the lower jaw in modern humans has resulted in a corresponding reduction in the size of this ridge.

Brow Ridge

Loss of this ridge is a trait of modern humans.

NOTE: Most anthropologists believe that *Australopithecus* evolved along with gorillas and humans. It cannot and should not be assumed that the progression of evolutionary change was from gorilla to *Australopithecus* to modern human. *Australopithecus* is used here to illustrate many traits believed to have been associated with early humans. All three animals probably evolved from some common primate ancestor. Use *Australopithecus* traits only as a means of distinguishing among modern humans, early humans, and gorillas.

Formulating Generalizations

1. How do *Australopithecus* and gorilla compare in terms of (a) cranial capacity, (b) lower jaw shape, and (c) jaw angle?
2. Which of the traits in question 1 does *Australopithecus* seem to share with modern humans?
3. Using face area to brain area ratios, does *Australopithecus* more closely resemble gorilla or modern human?
4. List the traits used in this investigation that are similar in modern human and gorilla.
5. List the traits used in this investigation that are similar in *Australopithecus* and modern human.
6. List the traits used in this investigation not mentioned in question 1 that are similar in gorilla and *Australopithecus*.
7. Explain the differences in face area to brain area ratios in gorilla, *Australopithecus*, and modern human.
8. Explain the differences in jaw angles in the three skulls.
9. Explain the differences in lower jaw shapes in the three skulls.
10. Suppose you find a distorted jawbone and note that there are 16 teeth in it. Explain why this information may or may not be helpful in determining whether the fossil is from a recent or early human or gorilla.
11. Suppose you find a distorted jawbone with most of the teeth missing. The canine teeth, however, are present and appear to be quite large. Which animal might this jaw be from?
12. Suppose you find only the top portion of a skull. No sagittal crest seems to be present, nor is there any evidence that one may have ever been present. Which animal might this skull be from?
13. Suppose you find a skull with 22 teeth. Might this skull be from a primate?

28 Construction And Use Of A Dichotomous Key

Aristotle (384-322 B.C.) classified plants and animals in subdivisions. Plants were grouped as trees, shrubs, or herbs. Animals were grouped as land, air, or sea dwellers. As humans explored the world, new living things were discovered. Scientists began to see a need for standard names and descriptions of living things.

Carolus Linnaeus (1707-1778) devised a standard system using Latin names for all organisms. He described the organisms by specific criteria. These criteria were based on structure. He gave each living thing two names, a genus and a species name. This system is called binomial nomenclature. Many closely related species made up one genus.

Today, biologists use dichotomous keys to identify plants and animals. Dichotomous means to branch into two divisions. A key will list the similarities and differences among living things. By using the process of elimination, you may arrive at the name of an organism on the basis of opposing characteristics. Use of a dichotomous key enables you to eliminate groups of organisms in order to narrow your choices to one organism.

In this investigation, you are to arrange a set of geometric figures into groups according to like characteristics. Then you are to write a dichotomous key that will classify each geometric figure.

Materials (*per student*)

typing paper
paste or tape
scissors

Procedure

At each step in a dichotomous key you are given two alternatives. On the basis of the object you are trying to identify, choose the more appropriate description. If you choose the correct one, it will lead you to identify the object. One error will bring you to the wrong classification, so each choice must be made after careful examination of the object.

A simple dichotomous key can be used to distinguish between a nail, a bolt, a nut, and a washer (Table 1). To use the key, begin at step 1. Decide whether the object you wish to classify is "cylindrical" or "other than cylindrical." If your object is cylindrical, you would choose "1-a." At "1-a" you are directed to "Go to 2." This means to proceed to the set of choices numbered "2." Here you would determine which of the two choices, "2-a" or "2-b," best describes your object. If the object were not cylindrical, you would choose "1-b," then proceed to the set of choices numbered "3." There you would choose between "3-a" or "3-b."

In this key, you are directed to proceed to only one other set of choices. However, many biological dichotomous keys have many steps in which you would be directed to go to several sets of choices before arriving at the name of the organism.

TABLE 1. A SIMPLE DICHOTOMOUS KEY OF METAL OBJECTS

1a.	Cylindrical	Go to 2
1b.	Other than cylindrical	Go to 3
2a.	With threads	Bolt
2b.	Without threads	Nail
3a.	Rectangular, with threads and hole	Nut
3b.	Circular, without threads, with hole	Washer

FIGURE 1

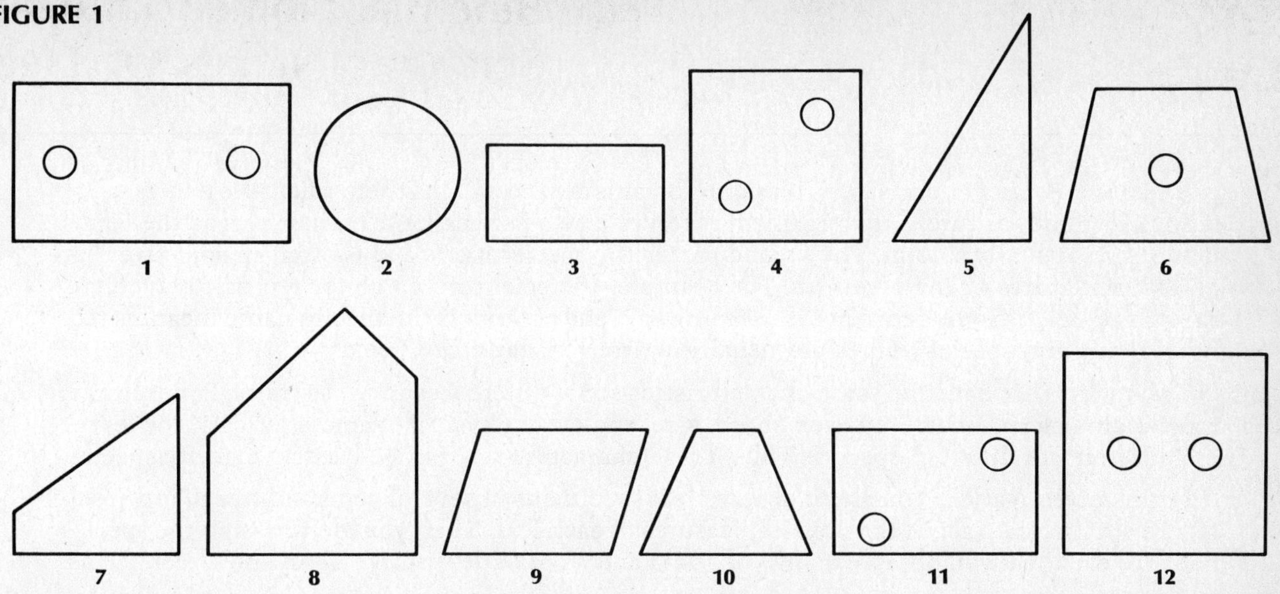

FIGURE 2

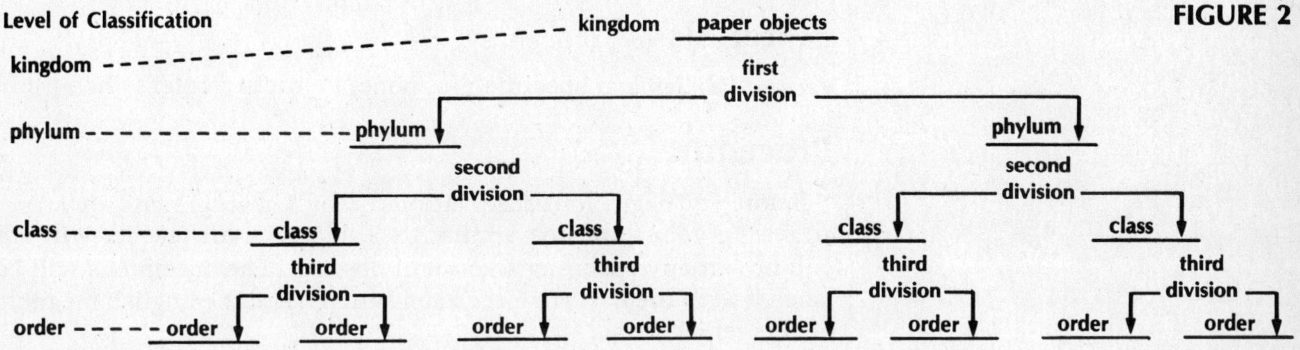

Using typing paper, trace and cut out each geometric figure in Figure 1. Make a chart similar to Figure 2 in your lab notebook. Arrange the geometric figures into two phyla according to like characteristics. Give names to the two phyla based on their physical features. Record the names on the chart in your lab notebook. Divide each phylum into two classes for a total of four classes. Divide each class into two orders for a total of eight orders. Some orders may have only one specimen. Give and record a name for each class and order.

Using paste or tape, place your figures in your notebook in eight orders. Write a dichotomous key for classifying these figures similar to the dichotomous key for the metal objects. Keep in mind that anyone in your class should be able to use your key. Use the number of each object rather than its name.

Formulating Generalizations

1. At what classification level were all of the objects most alike?
2. At what classification level were all of the objects least alike?
3. Do all paper objects in the same class belong to the same phylum? Explain.
4. Do all paper objects in the same class belong to the same order? Explain.
5. What features could a person use to build a dichotomous key for cars or for objects on a pantry shelf?

29 Binomial Nomenclature—Scientific Names Of Trees

A taxonomist is a scientist who classifies organisms and assigns them scientific names using binomial nomenclature. Each organism receives a two-part name. The first part is the genus name and is usually a noun. The second part is the species name and is often an adjective that describes features of the organism. For example, the scientific name for red oak is *Quercus rubrum. Quercus* is the genus name meaning oak, and *rubrum* is the species name meaning red. Both genus and species names are usually written in Latin or Greek.

Organisms that have the same characteristics show differences in those traits. For example, most plants have leaves. However, shape, size, and other physical characteristics of the leaves are different for different species. Thus, these characteristics can be used to identify species.

In this investigation, you are to observe leaf specimens of several genera of trees. You are to record specific data about the physical features of each leaf. Then you are to assign the species name to each leaf you observe using your data and a list of descriptive Latin and Greek terms.

Materials *(per student)*

various labeled leaf specimens pencil metric ruler hand lens

Procedure

Before you begin your observations of the leaf specimens, construct a table in your notebook similar to Table 1. Your teacher will tell you how many specimens you will observe. The specimens will be labeled with the Latin or Greek genus name and the English meaning of the genus name.

Figure 3 shows the parts of a leaf, and Figure 2 shows different physical features of leaves. Using these figures as a guide, observe each leaf and record its blade, tip, and base shape, the type of margin present, the vein pattern, and the widest part of the leaf. After observing the leaves, use your data from Table 1 and the descriptive terms listed in Table 2 to assign a Latin or Greek *species* name to each leaf. For example, the leaf in Figure 1 could be classified as *Plantanus flabellatus,* meaning fan-shaped sycamore. It could also be classified as *Plantanus trimacrovenosus,* meaning a sycamore with three large veins. Note that the species name should describe the physical features of the leaf.

FIGURE 1

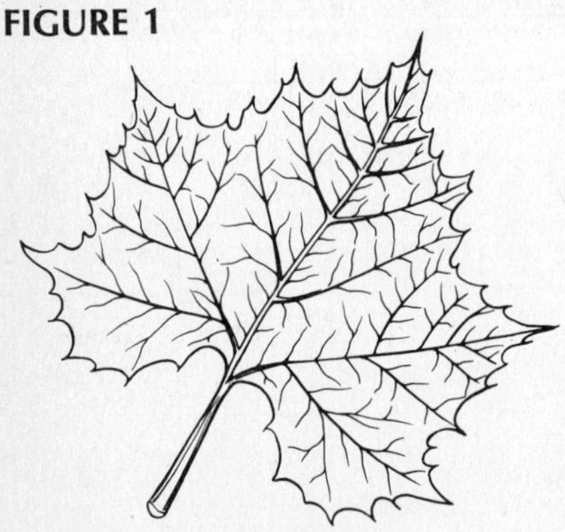

Plantanus flabellatus **or** ***Plantanus trimacrovenosus***

Formulating Generalizations

1. Give two reasons why an understanding of Latin and Greek is helpful to a taxonomist.
2. Which two genera of leaves studied in this investigation are very similar? Explain.

TABLE 1. PHYSICAL FEATURES OF LEAVES

LEAF SPECIMEN NUMBER	MARGIN OF LEAF	BLADE SHAPE	WIDEST PART OF LEAF	SHAPE OF TIP	SHAPE OF BASE	VEIN PATTERN	COMMON NAME	GENUS NAME	SPECIES NAME
1									
2									

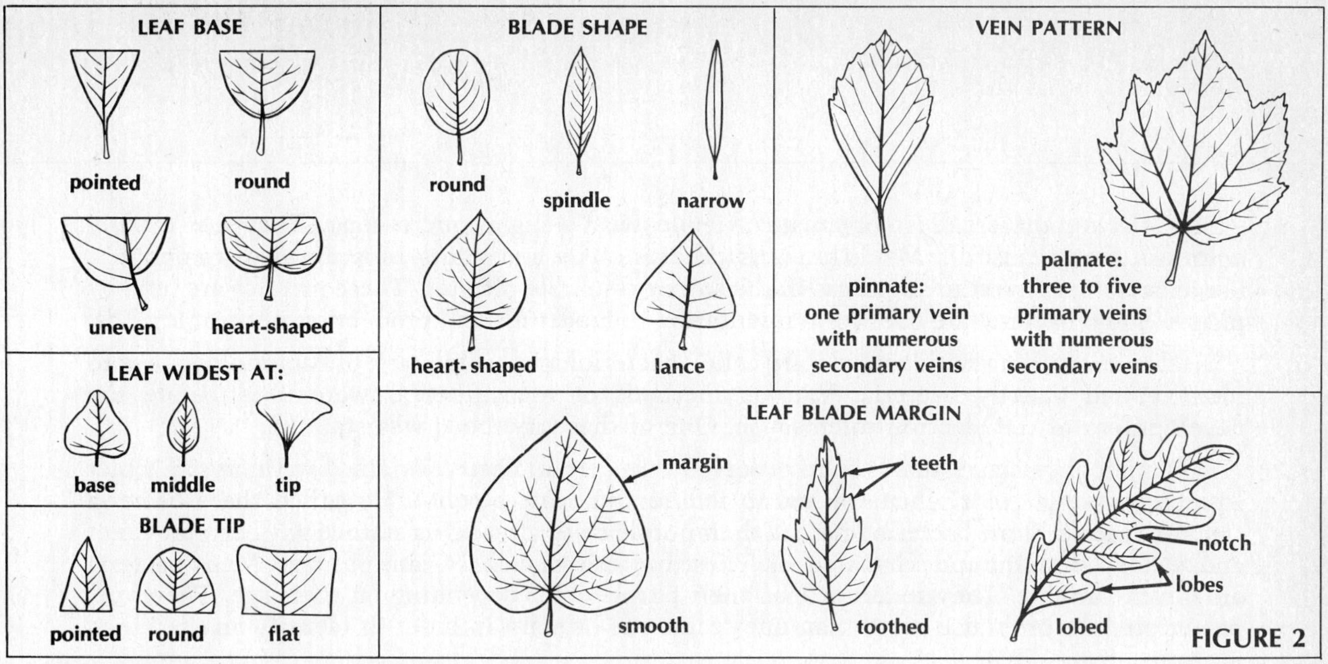

FIGURE 2

TABLE 2. ENGLISH WORDS AND LATIN OR GREEK DESCRIPTIVE WORDS					
ENGLISH WORD	LATIN OR GREEK WORD	ENGLISH WORD	LATIN OR GREEK WORD	ENGLISH WORD	LATIN OR GREEK WORD
above	hyper	many	poly	thick	pachy
base	basis	middle	medius	thin	tenuis
below	hypo	notch	incisum	tip	apex
common	vulgaris	oval	ovalis	toothed	dentatus
fanlike	flabellatus	pointed	cuspis	uneven	iniquis
feathered	pinnatus	pointed,	acumen	vein	venosus
flat	planus	sharp		wide	latus
forked	furcatus	projecting	prominens	without	a, an
hair	trichos	above		one	mono
half	hemi	round	rotundus	two	bi
hand-	palmatus	shape	figura	three	tri
shaped		short	brevis	four	quadra
heart	cor	slender	gracilis	five	quinque
lance	lancea	small	micro	six	sex
large	macros	small (very)	parvulus	seven	septem
leaf	folium	smooth	blandus	eight	octo
like	similis	spindle	fusi	nine	novem
lobe	lobus	spiny	echinatus	ten	deca
long	dolichos	stem	stirps		

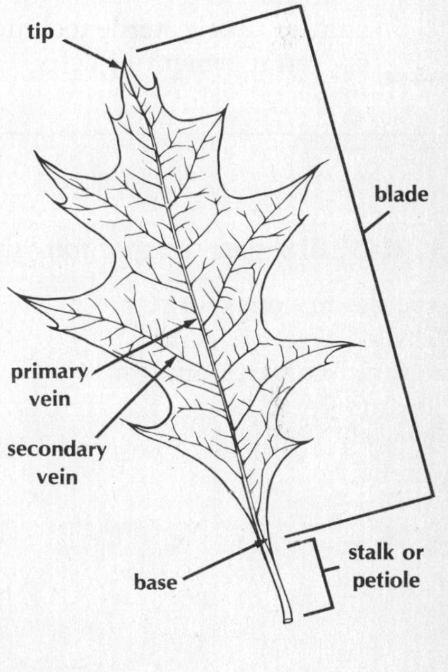

FIGURE 3

3. Why is the scientific name more important to the biologist than local names such as "swamp willow tree"?
4. From your observations of several leaves, what is the relationship between a lobe, a notch, and a tooth?
5. How could you use the physical features of the leaf to identify which trees in a forest are closely related?
6. Could you use the green color of leaves to identify species? Explain.
7. Suppose you found two trees that had leaves that were alike in all physical features except the length and width of the blades. Would you expect these two trees to be the same or different species? Explain.
8. What is the difference between a genus name and a species name?

30 Morphology And Staining Of Bacteria

Bacteria are the smallest organisms visible with a light microscope. They are usually colorless. Many cause diseases in humans, other animals, and plants. Most are also saprophytes. Some bacteria convert nitrogen gas in the soil into soluble nitrates. These nitrates are used by plants. Some bacteria are used for fermentation of foodstuffs and production of organic acids.

Scientists working with bacteria are called bacteriologists. One task of bacteriologists is to identify and classify bacteria. Various methods of identification were used before the development of the electron microscope. One of these methods was staining.

A Danish physician named Gram observed that certain bacteria stained with crystal violet lost their purple color when washed in iodine and ethyl alcohol. He called these bacteria Gram-negative. Some bacteria retained their purple color after being stained with crystal violet and washed in iodine and ethyl alcohol. These bacteria he called Gram-positive. Many bacteria are Gram-variable. They retain or lose their purple color depending on their age. Therefore, bacteriologists often use more than one technique or stain in order to identify an unknown bacteria.

In this investigation, you are to make Gram stain preparations of several known bacterial cultures using sterile techniques. You are to identify the bacteria as to their Gram stain, shape, and arrangement of cells.

Materials *(per team of four students)*

inoculating loops—4
distilled water—15 mL
bacterial cultures on agar slants (for class)
burner
water
paper towels
glass slides—4 or 5
wooden, snap-type clothespins
crystal violet stain—20 mL
Gram's iodine—20 mL
95% ethyl alcohol—20 mL
safranin—20 mL
compound microscope with oil immersion lens
immersion oil
plastic container

Procedure

Part A. Preparation of Smear

CAUTION: *Bacteria may cause infection. Keep hands away from face throughout this investigation. Do not chew gum or eat while carrying out the procedure. Wash hands immediately after finishing procedure.*

Carefully light the burner. Sterilize the end of the inoculating loop by placing it in the flame of the burner until the wire turns bright red. **CAUTION:** *Use care with the open flame of the burner. Do not touch the hot end of the inoculating loop. The loop may still be quite hot after the red glow has faded.* Place a loopful of distilled water on a clean, dry microscope slide. Resterilize the loop. Place a test tube containing a bacteria culture in your left hand (or right hand if you are left-handed). Grip the cotton plug between two fingers of the right hand (or right hand if left-handed) and remove the cotton plug from the culture tube (Figure 1). Flame the mouth of the test tube (Figure 2). **CAUTION:** *Do not touch the mouth of the hot test tube.* Hold the tube parallel to the table to prevent contamination.

FIGURE 1

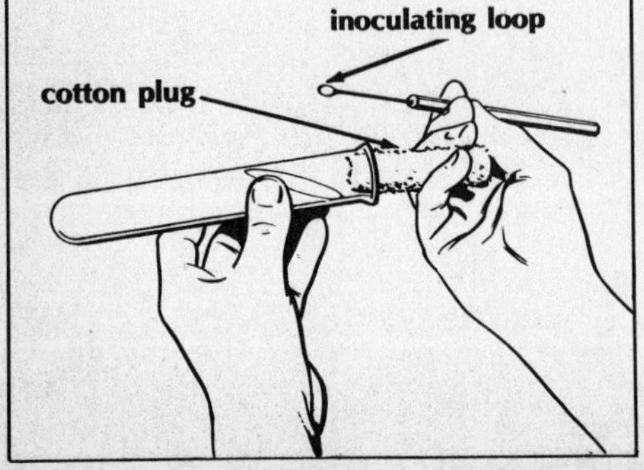

FIGURE 2

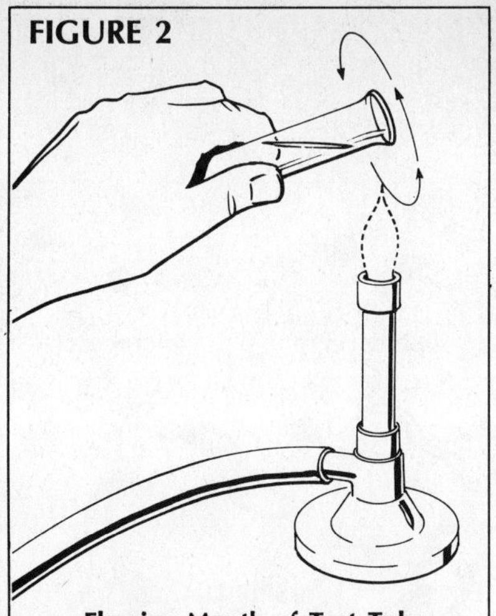

Flaming Mouth of Test Tube

FIGURE 3

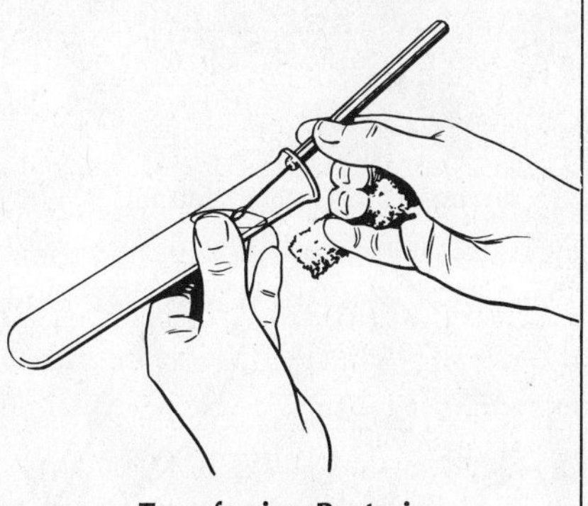

Transferring Bacteria

Insert the loop into the culture and touch the loop to the agar at the tube side to cool the loop. Then without breaking the agar surface touch the loop to the bacteria on the agar (Figure 3). Withdraw the loop. Reflame the mouth of the test tube and replace the cotton plug. Work quickly so that the tube is open only a short time. Place the loop with bacteria in the distilled water on the slide. Smear the bacteria over an area about the size of a dime.

Part B. Staining of Bacteria

Air dry the bacteria smear for about two minutes (Figure 4). Pass the slide through the flame three to five times in order to "fix" or cause the bacteria to adhere to the slide. Make sure the side of the slide containing the bacteria faces up. Extinguish your flame after this step.

Hold the fixed slide over a plastic container. Add crystal violet stain to the fixed smear until it entirely covers the area of the smear. Allow it to stand for one minute. Rinse the smear with tap water. Then flood the smear with Gram's iodine for one minute. **CAUTION:** *If iodine spillage occurs, rinse with water.* Rinse the smear in tap water. Add 95% ethyl alcohol for 30 seconds. **CAUTION:** *Alcohol is flammable. Be sure all flames in your work area are extinguished before using alcohol.* Add safranin for 30 seconds. Wash in tap water, drain off excess water, and blot the smear dry. To blot dry, touch the prepared smear lightly with a paper towel until the smear is dry.

Repeat the smearing and staining procedures using several types of bacteria.

Observe the slides using an oil immersion lens. Place a small drop of immersion oil on the center of the stained smear. Place the slide on the stage of the microscope. Locate the smear and oil droplet with the low power lens. Raise the nosepiece and rotate it to the immersion lens. Lower the immersion lens into the oil droplet and observe the smear. *Do not observe* on high power as oil can ruin the high power lens. Note the color of the bacterial colony.

Determine the Gram reaction of each culture. If the bacteria are Gram-positive, they will be purple in color. The crystal violet-Gram iodine stain was not washed out and the cells were not stained by the safranin. If the bacteria are Gram-negative, they will be pink. The crystal violet-Gram iodine stain was washed out and the cells stained pink with the safranin.

FIGURE 4

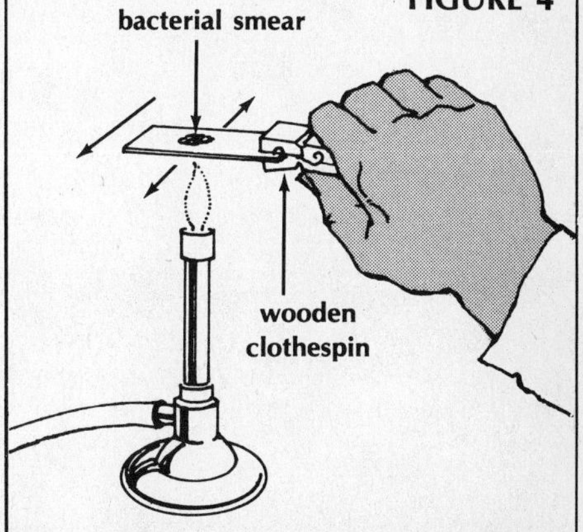

Fixing a Bacterial Smear

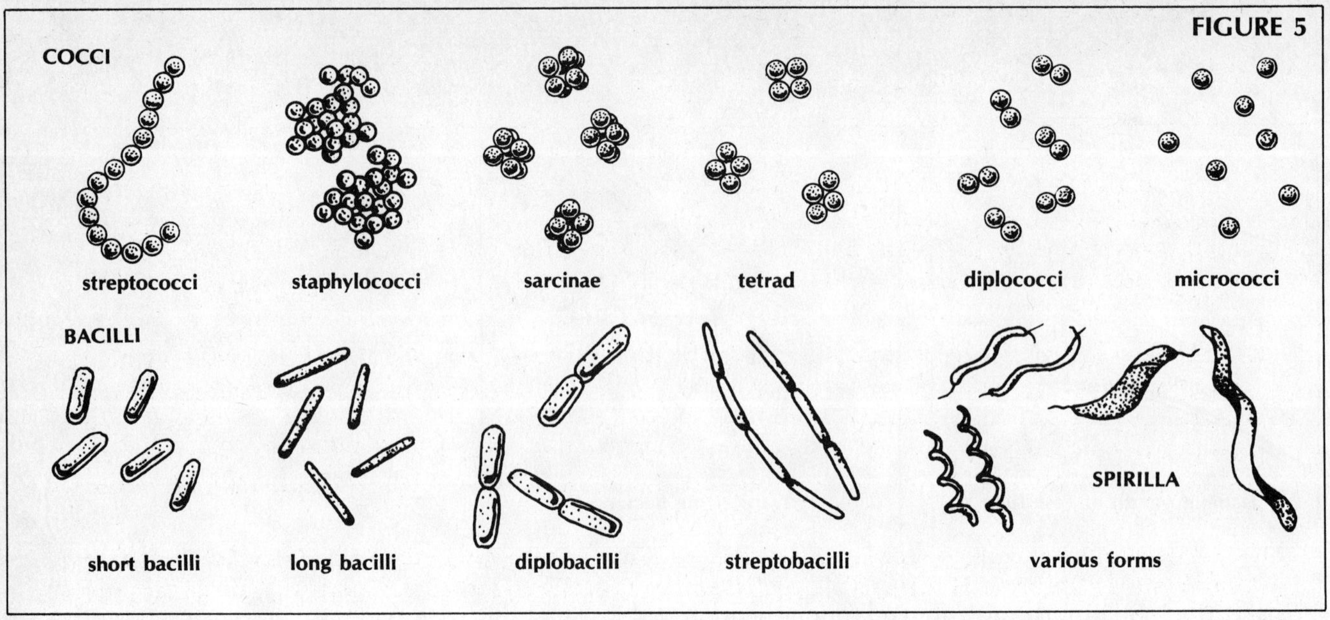

TABLE 1. OBSERVATIONS OF BACTERIA

NAME OF BACTERIA	GRAM REACTION	SHAPE/ ARRANGEMENT	LENGTH	COLONY COLOR

Calculate the size in micrometers of the bacteria cells. (See Investigation 4.)

Identify the shape of bacteria cells as round (coccus), rod (bacillus), or spiral (spirillum).

Describe the arrangement of rod-shaped cells as single, pairs, or clusters. Describe the arrangement of round cells as chains (streptococci), pairs (diplococci), single (micrococci), cubes of eight cells (sarcinae), irregular clusters (staphylococci), or packets of four cells (tetrads) (Figure 5).

Make a table similar to Table 1 and record your data on each bacterial type you observed.

Formulating Generalizations

1. What is the range in size of the bacterial cells?
2. Did all the cocci or bacilli stain the same way (either Gram-positive or Gram-negative)? Explain your answer.
3. What bearing would the arrangement of cells have in identification of bacteria?
4. Describe the sterile technique you used in this investigation. How might you use these procedures in the future?

Morphology Of Green Algae

31

Green algae are mostly multicellular organisms that make their own food by photosynthesis. However, a few algae are unicellular. Green algae range in size from microscopic to six to eight meters long. Most green algae live in fresh water, but a few live in salt water. Green algae also inhabit moist environments such as damp soil. Some green algae live on the sides of trees and rocks.

A green alga has a cell wall which appears as a clear boundary on the outside of a cell. A single nucleus is found inside each cell, and most cells contain a single, green chloroplast that varies in shape. The chloroplast can be ribbonlike, cup-shaped, round, or netlike in appearance. The chloroplasts trap energy from sunlight and make food for the cell. Inside the chloroplast are storage structures called pyrenoids. Starch is stored in the pyrenoids. A thick, jelly-like fluid called cytoplasm fills the inside of each cell.

In this investigation you are to observe five types of fresh water green algae. You are to locate and identify the various parts of the algal cells, and you are to measure the size of individual cells of each type of algae.

Materials *(per student or team)*

Cultures of algae (1 per class):
- *Closterium*
- *Hydrodictyon*
- *Spirogyra*
- *Ulothrix*
- *Zygnema*

water
dropper
probe
scissors
coverslip
glass slide
microscope
Gram's iodine solution—1 mL
paper towels

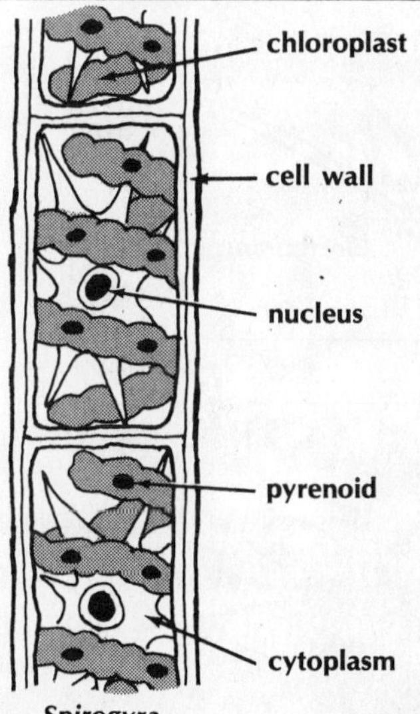

FIGURE 1

Procedure

Part A. *Spirogyra*

With a probe remove some filaments of *Spirogyra* from a culture dish. Place the filaments on a clean, dry slide. Add a drop of water, and cover with a coverslip. Observe the slide on low power, then high power under your microscope. Locate the cell wall, the spiral shaped chloroplast, and nucleus (Figure 1). To locate the pyrenoid body, add a drop of Gram's iodine solution at the edge of the coverslip. **CAUTION:** *If iodine spillage occurs, rinse with water.* Draw the iodine across the slide with a paper towel. If starch is present, the numerous pyrenoids will turn blue-black in color. Compute the size of a cell in micrometers. Make a labeled sketch of your observations.

Part B. *Hydrodictyon*

With a probe and scissors, remove a small clump of *Hydrodictyon* from a culture dish. **CAUTION:** *Always be careful with sharp instruments.* Place the clump on a clean, dry slide. Add a drop of water and a coverslip. Observe the slide with a microscope using low power, then high power. Locate the cell wall, the small dotlike chloroplasts, and the larger, single round nucleus (Figure 2).

FIGURE 2

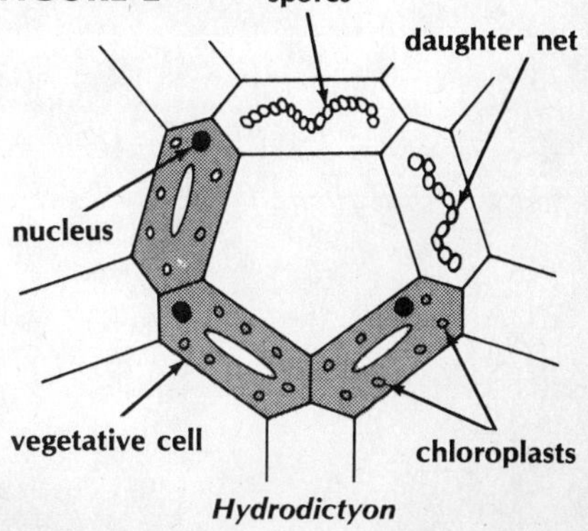

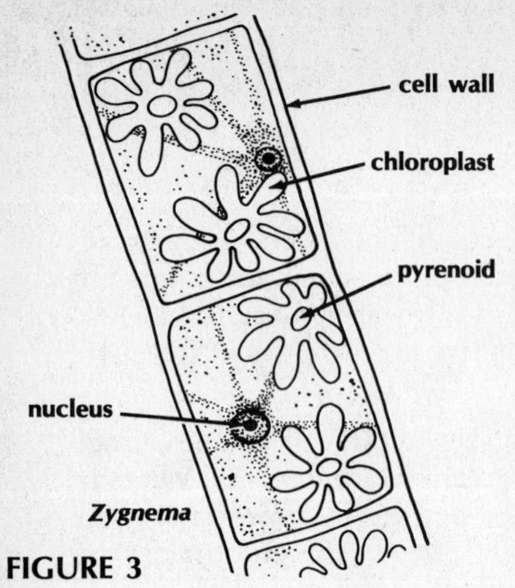

FIGURE 3

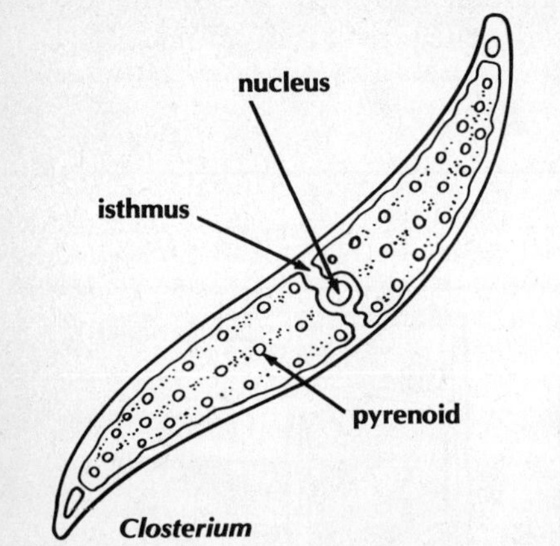

FIGURE 4

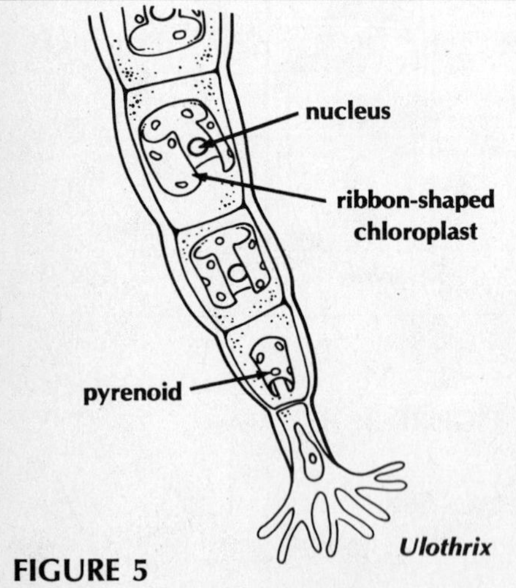

FIGURE 5

Repeat the Gram's iodine procedure as in Part A to locate the pyrenoids. Compute the size of a cell in micrometers. Make a labeled sketch of your observations.

Part C. *Zygnema*

With a probe, remove some filaments of *Zygnema* from a culture dish. Place the filaments on a clean, dry slide. Add a drop of water and a coverslip. Observe the slide on low, then high power. Locate the cell wall and the two star shaped chloroplasts (Figure 3). Locate the nucleus between the chloroplasts. Repeat the Gram's iodine procedure as in Part A to locate the pyrenoid in each chloroplast. Compute the size of a cell in micrometers. Make a labeled sketch of your observations.

Part D. *Closterium*

With a dropper remove some cells from the bottom of a culture dish. Place a drop of the culture on a clean, dry slide and add a coverslip. Observe the slide on low, then high power. Locate the two symmetrical halves of the cell (Figure 4). The cell is separated in the middle by a small passage called the isthmus. Locate the nucleus in the center of the isthmus and the two chloroplasts, one in each half of the cell. Repeat the Gram's iodine procedure to locate the pyrenoids in the chloroplasts. Compute the size of a cell in micrometers. Make a labeled sketch of your observations.

Part E. *Ulothrix*

With a dropper remove some filaments of *Ulothrix* from a culture dish. Place the filaments on a clean, dry slide and cover with a coverslip. Observe the slide on low, then high power. Locate a holdfast cell at one end of the filament (Figure 5). Locate the cell next to the holdfast cell. Locate the cell wall, collar-shaped chloroplast, and the nucleus. Repeat the Gram's iodine procedure to locate the pyrenoids in the chloroplast. Compute the size of the cell in micrometers. Make a labeled sketch of your observations.

Formulating Generalizations

1. Which type of cell is the largest? The smallest?
2. If the period at the end of this sentence is 500 micrometers in diameter, how many *Ulothrix* cells would fit end to end to cover the diameter of the period? How many *Closterium* cells could fit end to end on this period?
3. In what way is *Closterium* different from the other algae observed?
4. What feature of the chloroplast enabled you to identify it easily?
5. Describe the differences in shape you observed in the chloroplasts of the five types of algae.
6. Why are pyrenoids found in or on the chloroplasts of the algae cell?
7. In which cell did you see the most pyrenoids? The least?
8. How is the holdfast different from the other cells of *Ulothrix*?

Size And Structure Of Protozoa

32

It is estimated that there are over 45 000 species of protozoa. They occur in many habitats. Because they are associated with water, they may be found in soil water. They are also found in freshwater streams, ponds, and lakes. They also can live in a marine environment. They are both free-living and parasitic. They are protists that occur as single cells or colonies.

Protozoa range in size from 5 μm to 5 mm in diameter or length. Locomotion occurs in any of three ways. Members of phylum Rhizopoda move by means of streaming protoplasm which forms broad extensions called pseudopods. Members of phylum Zoomastigina move by means of hairlike structures called flagella. A flagellum moves from side to side producing forward movement. A flagellate usually has one or two flagella. Members of phylum Ciliophora have similar hairlike structures called cilia. However, cilia are much shorter and more numerous than flagella.

Protozoa have organelles that carry out processes such as digestion, excretion, and ingestion. These organelles are analogous to organs such as the stomach and intestines of higher animals.

In this investigation you are to determine the size of three representatives of the protozoa and observe and locate specific organelles of each of the three protozoans.

Materials *(per student)*

microscope
glass slides
coverslips
dropper
absorbent cotton
cultures of: *Chaos chaos* (amoeba)
Peranema
Blepharisma

Procedure

Part A. *Chaos chaos* (amoeba)

With a dropper, remove a sample of the amoeba culture *Chaos chaos* from the bottom of the dish. Place a drop of the culture on a clean, dry slide and gently add a coverslip. Place the slide on the stage of a microscope. Locate an amoeba with low power, then high power. Locate pseudopods, nucleus, and food and contractile vacuoles under high power (Figure 1). Observe the streaming of the cytoplasm. Calculate the size of an amoeba. Record data in your notebook. Diagram and label an amoeba.

FIGURE 1

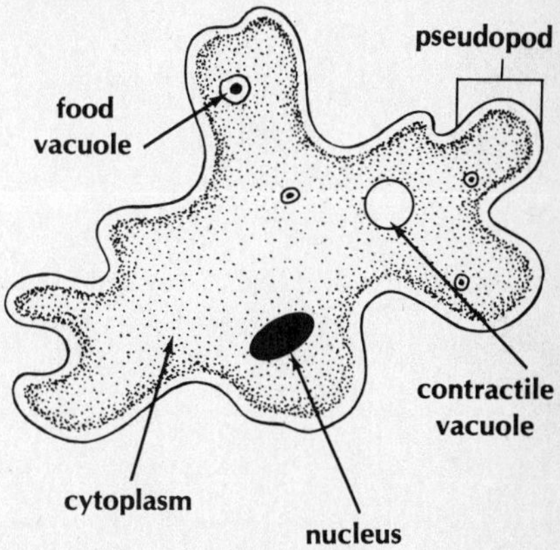

Chaos chaos

Part B. *Peranema*

Using a clean slide make a wet mount from the *Peranema* culture in the same way you did for *Chaos chaos*. Place the slide on the stage of the microscope. Locate a *Peranema* cell with low power. Using high power, locate the flagellum, nucleus, food vacuole, and gullet (Figure 2). Calculate the size of a *Peranema* cell. Make drawings and record data in your notebook.

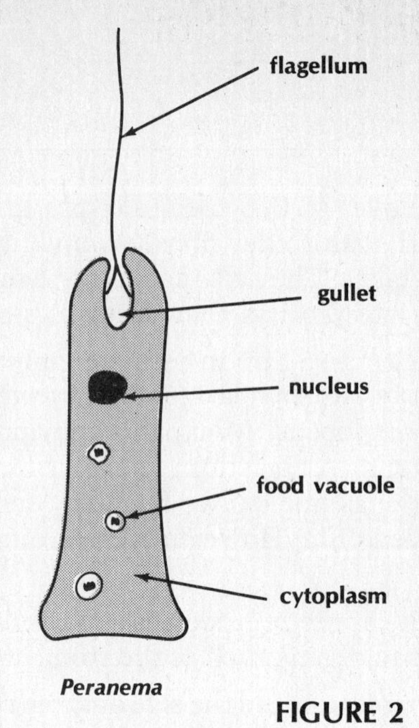

FIGURE 2

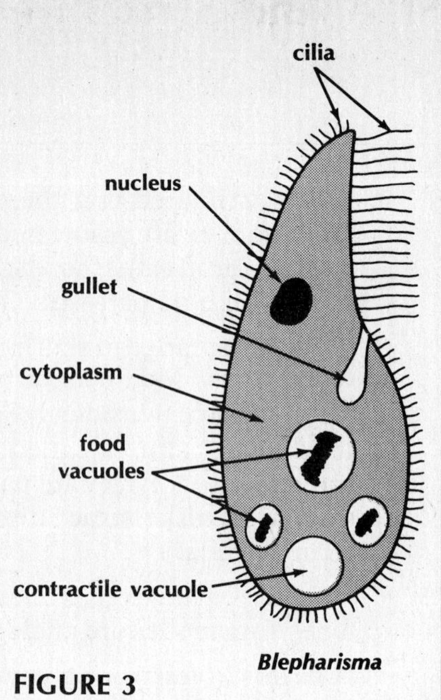

FIGURE 3

Part C. *Blepharisma*

Blepharisma may move too fast for extended observation. Therefore, use cotton fibers in your wet mount to "imprison" the *Blepharisma.* Separate a few fibers of absorbent cotton and place them on a clean, dry slide. With a dropper, remove a sample of the *Blepharisma* culture from the bottom of the dish. Place a drop of the culture on the cotton fibers. Add a coverslip. Place the slide on the stage of the microscope. Locate a *Blepharisma* with low power. Using high power, locate cilia, nucleus, and food and contractile vacuoles (Figure 3). Calculate the size of a *Blepharisma.* Make drawings and record data in your notebook.

Formulating Generalizations

1. Describe the posterior and anterior ends of *Chaos chaos*, a *Peranema*, and a *Blepharisma.*
2. Explain whether the shapes of the three protozoans change as they move.
3. Describe the length of the flagellum in *Peranema* in relationship to the cell body length.
4. What is a function of flagella other than movement?
5. How many types of cilia did you observe in *Blepharisma?*
6. Do cilia serve any function other than movement? If so, what?
7. Compare the size of the food vacuoles in the *Peranema* with those in *Blepharisma.* How are they different?
8. Describe the action of *Blepharisma* when it bumps into cotton fibers.
9. Does the shape of any of the protozoa aid rapid movement through water? Explain your answer.
10. Is speed related to capture of food? Explain.

Morphology and Growth Of Fungi

33

Fungi are universal in distribution. They are found around the world in both soil and aquatic habitats. They are found in our food and clothing. Fungi do not make their own food and thus, they are parasites, saprophytes, or mutualists. The fungi that are parasites cause many diseases of animals and plants. Not all fungi are harmful. Some fungi, such as some mushrooms, are used as food. Others, such as yeast, are used in industrial processes. Still other fungi are used in medicine, such as *Penicillium*, because of beneficial chemicals they produce.

The mycelia of a fungus have enzymes that digest food. The digested food is used by the fungi for energy, growth, and reproduction. At certain times, some of the hyphae (strands of mycelium) develop into spore-bearing structures. When spores land on a suitable food source, new fungi mycelia grow. Fungi are classified into three groups according to the kinds of spores they produce.

In this investigation, you are to grow fungi on a food source and on an agar-food source. You are to identify the basic structures of fungi. Also you are to measure the growth rate of a colony of fungi.

Materials *(per student or team)*

paper towels—5
baby food jars—2
stale bread—1 slice
aluminum foil, 6 cm × 2 cm—2
potato dextrose agar, 2 cm × 2 cm hardened block
petri dish
knife or spatula
glass slides—3 or 4
coverslips—3 or 4
inoculating loop
burner
petri dishes—3 or 4
microscope
popsicle sticks—2 for each petri dish
stereomicroscope
ruler, metric

Procedure

Part A. Fungi Culture on Bread

Place a piece of stale bread on a paper towel and lightly moisten the bread with tap water. Press the bottom half of a petri dish into and through the bread (Figure 1). Your petri dish should be completely filled with bread. Discard the remainder of the bread.

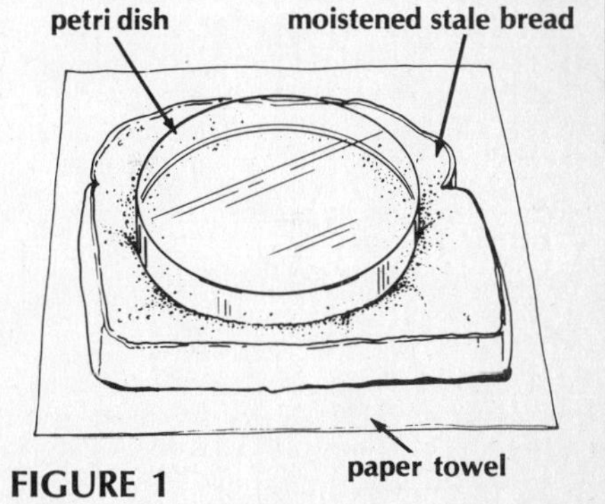

FIGURE 1

Expose the bread in the petri dish to the air for at least 30 minutes, then place the lid on the petri dish over the bread. Incubate the dish in the dark at room temperature for two days.

After two days of incubation, observe the fungal colonies on the bread. Record in your notebook the number of fungal colonies you observe. After removing the top of the petri dish, observe the fungal colonies under the stereomicroscope. The fungal mycelium should appear as a cottonlike growth on the bread (Figure 2).

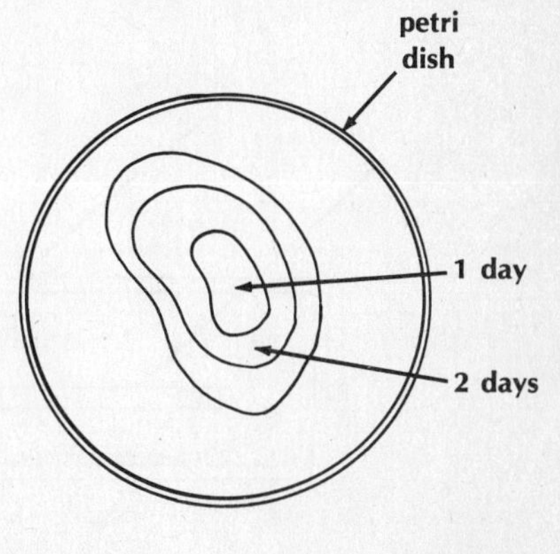

Growth of Bread Mold
FIGURE 2

Calculate the rate of growth on one fungal colony on the bread. Using a centimeter ruler, measure the diameter of a specific colony at its widest point. Record your measurement. Repeat this procedure each day for three days. Make drawings in your lab notebook recording the changes which occur to your colony. Be sure to note any color changes.

FIGURE 3

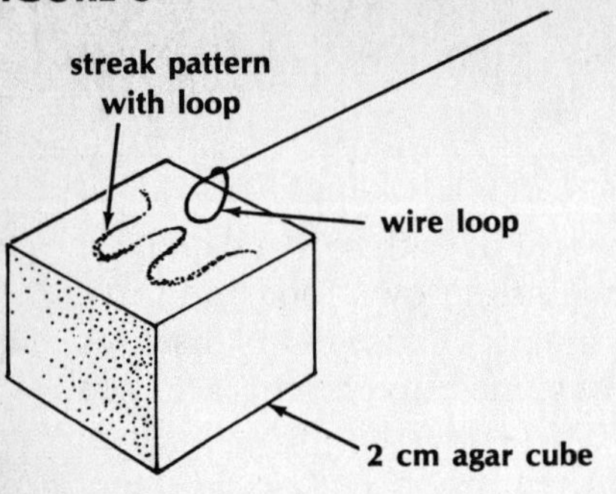

Part B. Petri Dish Chamber

To a clean, dry slide add a 2 cm × 2 cm block of potato dextrose agar and inoculate the agar with spores of a well-formed colony of fungi from the bread or agar plate. Sterilize an inoculating loop with the flame of a burner. **CAUTION:** *Be extremely careful around open flames. Secure all loose clothing and hair before proceeding.* Cool the loop by touching it to the bread or agar. Then rub the loop through the spore-bearing structures of a single colony on the bread or the agar plate. Gently rub the surface of the agar block with the loop to transfer the spores. See Figure 3.

Add a clean, dry coverslip to the top of the agar block. Construct a petri dish chamber by placing a damp paper towel in the bottom half of a petri dish. Cut two popsicle sticks in half. Stack two of the halves on top of each other on one side of the petri dish (Figure 4). Place the other two halves on top of each other on the other side of the petri dish. Place the slide on top of the popsicle sticks. Cover the chamber with the top half of the petri dish. Incubate the petri dish chamber in the dark for 2 or 3 days at room temperature.

Make several slides and petri dish chambers using agar and fungi from your bread blocks and agar plate.

After the 2 to 3 days of incubation, remove the slides from the petri dish chambers. Observe the slides on low power, then on high power. You may have to open the diaphragm slightly to allow more light to penetrate the agar. Locate the hyphae and spore-bearing structures for each slide. Record the presence or absence of septae and nuclei. Make sketches of your observations in your notebook.

Formulating Generalizations

1. What part of a growing fungus may give rise to a new fungal colony?
2. What is one way to tell if different types of fungi are growing on the same piece of bread?
3. Which showed more detail under observation, the bread mold culture or the agar block? Why?
4. Describe the appearance of mycelia as seen on the agar block.
5. Why were both cultures incubated in the dark?
6. What factor besides food is needed for fungal growth?
7. From what source did the colonies on your bread mold come?

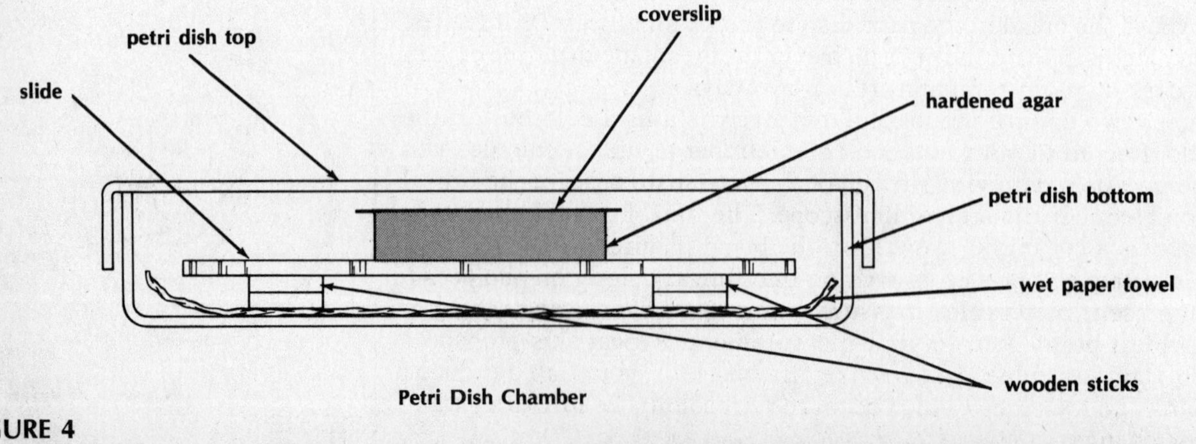

Petri Dish Chamber

FIGURE 4

Mosses, Club Mosses, And Horsetails

35

Mosses are land plants that require a moist environment during at least a portion of their life spans. Most mosses grow in damp areas such as in forest soils, among rocks, and on the branches and trunks of trees. These plants cannot transport water long distances internally because they do not have vascular tissues; they lack true roots, stems, and leaves.

Club mosses are land plants that often grow in damp forest soils. Club mosses have vascular tissues; they have roots, stems, and leaves. Vascular tissue is an adaptation for a drier environment and larger plant size.

Horsetails live in a variety of environments ranging from very wet areas (swamps, ponds, and streams) to drier areas (along river banks and in open fields). These plants also are adapted to drier areas because of the presence of vascular tissue.

Mosses, club mosses, and horsetails all produce spores in specialized structures. A moss bears spores in a capsule which is part of the sporophyte generation of the plant. The sporophyte generation is a multicellular diploid stage that produces spores and reproduces asexually. Club mosses and horsetails form structures called strobili which bear the spores.

In this investigation, you are to identify the various parts of mosses, club mosses, and horsetails. Also, you are to observe and compare the spores and the spore-bearing structures of these plants.

Materials *(per team of four students)*

moss protonema growing on agar
live moss gametophyte—1 clump
probes—2
forceps—2
microscope—2
droppers—2
club moss—1
horsetail—1
glass slide—2
coverslip—2
hand lens—2

Procedure

Part A. Moss

With a probe, remove a moss protonema from the agar. Using two probes, carefully pull any agar from the protonema. **CAUTION:** *Always be careful when using probes or other sharp instruments.*

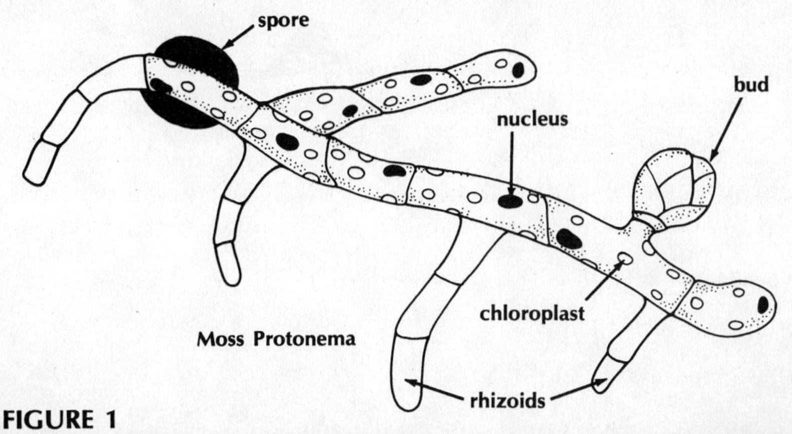

FIGURE 1

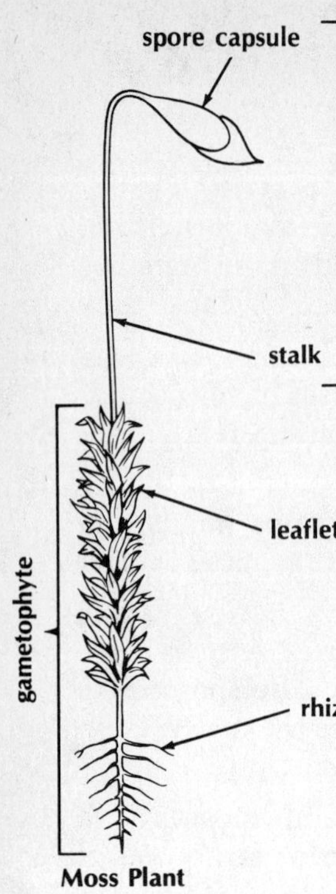

FIGURE 2

Take care not to crush the protonema. Place the protonema on a clean, dry slide. With a dropper, add a drop of water. Then add a coverslip. Observe the slide under low and high powers. Locate and identify the spores (if present), bud, nuclei, chloroplasts, and rhizoids (Figure 1).

Remove the soil from the base of a "leafy" moss plant. Using a hand lens, locate and identify rhizoids and leaflets. These two structures are part of the gametophyte. The gametophyte generation is a multicellular haploid stage that produces gametes and reproduces sexually. Remove a single leaflet from the gametophyte and make a wet mount. Observe under low and high powers. Locate the leaf cells and chloroplasts. Make a labeled drawing of these structures in your notebook.

The sporophyte generation consists of a stalk and terminal capsule. The sporophyte grows from the tip of the female gametophyte (Figure 2). Remove the terminal capsule from the stalk of the sporophyte. Remove spores from the terminal capsule and make a wet mount of them. Observe under low and high powers. Compute the size of the moss spores in micrometers. Make a sketch of one spore in your notebook.

Part B. Club Moss

Using a hand lens, locate and identify the branching stems, leaves, and strobilus of a club moss (Figure 3). Make a labeled sketch in your lab notebook showing these parts.

Using forceps and a probe, remove a section of a sporangium from the strobilus and place the sporangium on a clean, dry slide. Add a drop of water and open the sporangium with the forceps and probe. Add a coverslip and observe the spores on low power, and then on high power. Record the color, shape, and size in micrometers of the spores. Make a sketch of one spore in your notebook.

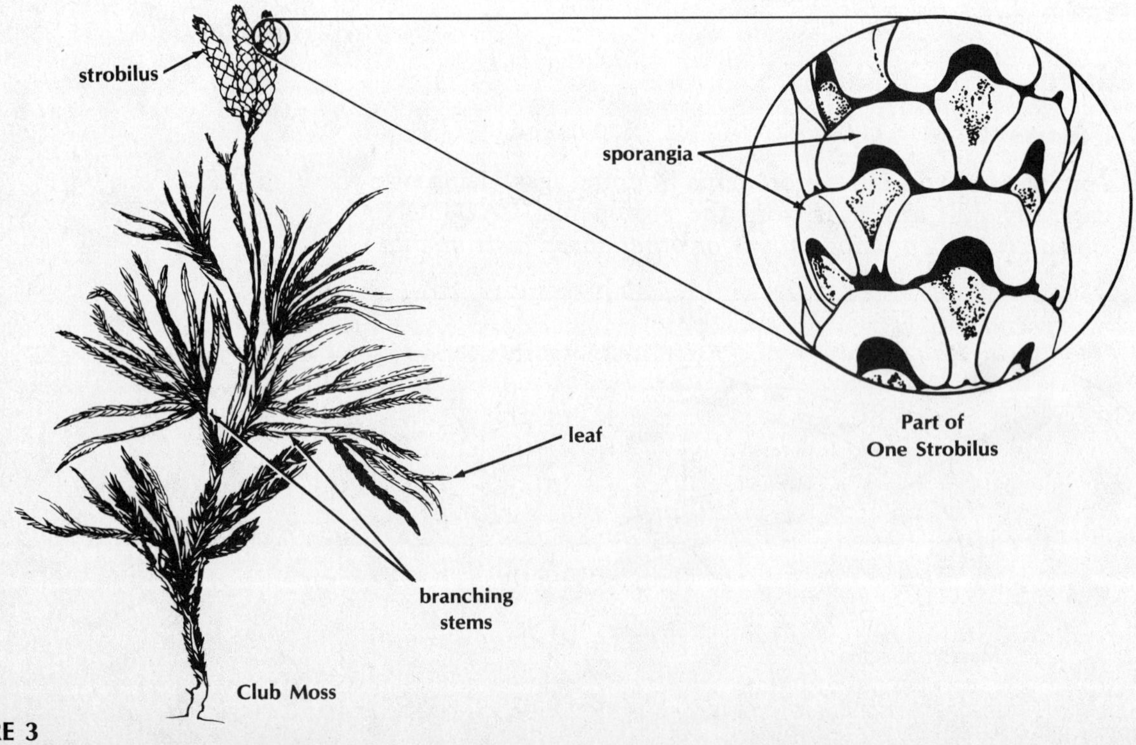

FIGURE 3

Part C. Horsetail

Using a hand lens, locate and identify the leaves, stem, and strobilus of the horsetail (Figure 4). Make a sketch in your notebook showing these structures. Using forceps and a probe, remove a section of a sporangium from the strobilus. Place the sporangium on a clean, dry slide and add a drop of water. Open the sporangium with a probe and forceps. Add a coverslip and observe the spore on low power, and then high power. Record the color, shape, and size in micrometers of the horsetail spores. Make a sketch of a horsetail spore in your notebook.

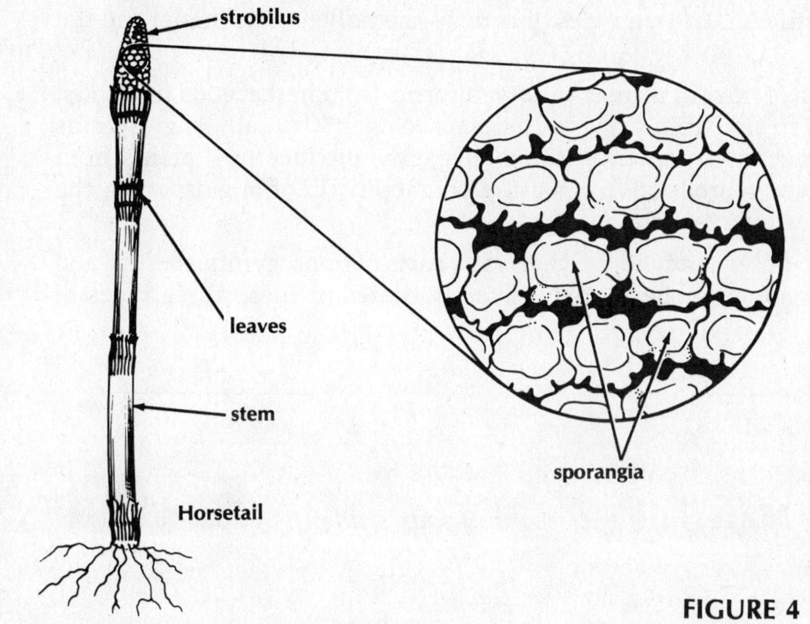

FIGURE 4

Formulating Generalizations

1. How does a moss protonema resemble the filamentous type of algae?
2. How can you distinguish between the rhizoids and the rest of the moss protonema?
3. What is the shape, color, and size in micrometers of a moss spore?
4. Describe the stem and leaves of a club moss.
5. How do the shapes of the strobilus and leaves explain the name given to the club moss?
6. What is the shape, color, and size in micrometers of a club moss spore?
7. How are the leaves of a horsetail arranged on the stem?
8. Which part of the horsetail plant appears to make food for the rest of the plant? Explain your answer.
9. What is the shape, color, and size in micrometers of a horsetail spore?
10. How is the location of the spore-bearing parts of the mosses, club mosses, and horsetails similar?
11. What observable feature of the spores do all three plants share?
12. What part of the "leaf" is present in horsetails and club mosses but absent in mosses?

36 Ferns, Gymnosperms, And Angiosperms

Ferns are herbaceous land plants ranging in size from four to six millimeters to two meters tall. Most ferns live in moist, shaded environments such as forest floors, but some ferns live in dry, sunny areas such as open fields. Ferns produce new plants from spores.

Gymnosperms are woody land plants ranging in size from 0.5 m to over 85 m tall. Most of the gymnosperms you are familiar with are evergreen trees called conifers. Conifers grow in sunny environments ranging from wet swamps to dry mountain regions. Conifers produce new plants from seeds formed in cones. Conifers bear two types of cones—the pollen cone (male) and the seed cone (female).

Angiosperms are land plants that exist in a great variety of forms from herbaceous to woody. This large group of plants ranges in size from a few millimeters to over 50 m tall. Angiosperms are widespread and inhabit diverse environments. All angiosperms produce new plants from seeds. Eggs and pollen form in the reproductive structure characteristic of angiosperms, the flower. Seeds form in the former ovary of the flower.

In this investigation, you are to observe and identify specific parts of ferns, gymnosperms, and angiosperms. You will compare some of the reproductive structures of these three types of plants.

Materials *(per team of four students)*

probes—2
forceps—2
droppers—2
fresh fern frond—1
culture dish of fern prothallia growing on agar
glass slides—2
coverslips—2
microscopes—2
water
hand lenses—2
gymnosperm, woody stem with leaves
gymnosperm cone, male
gymnosperm cone, female
angiosperm leaf
flower

FIGURE 1

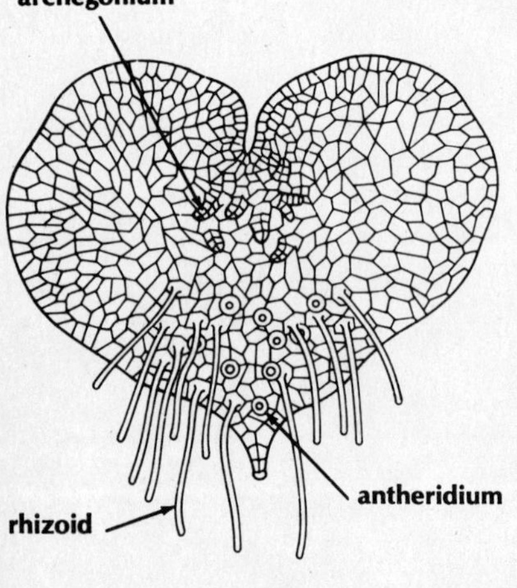

Fern Prothallium

Procedure

Part A. Ferns

Remove a fern prothallium (the gametophyte of the fern) from the agar medium using a probe and forceps. **CAUTION:** *Always be careful when using a probe or other sharp instruments.* Place the prothallium on the slide with the rhizoid side facing up. Make a wet mount. Observe the prothallium on low and high powers. Locate the archegonium (female), antheridium (male), and rhizoids (Figure 1). Make a labeled sketch of the prothallium in your notebook.

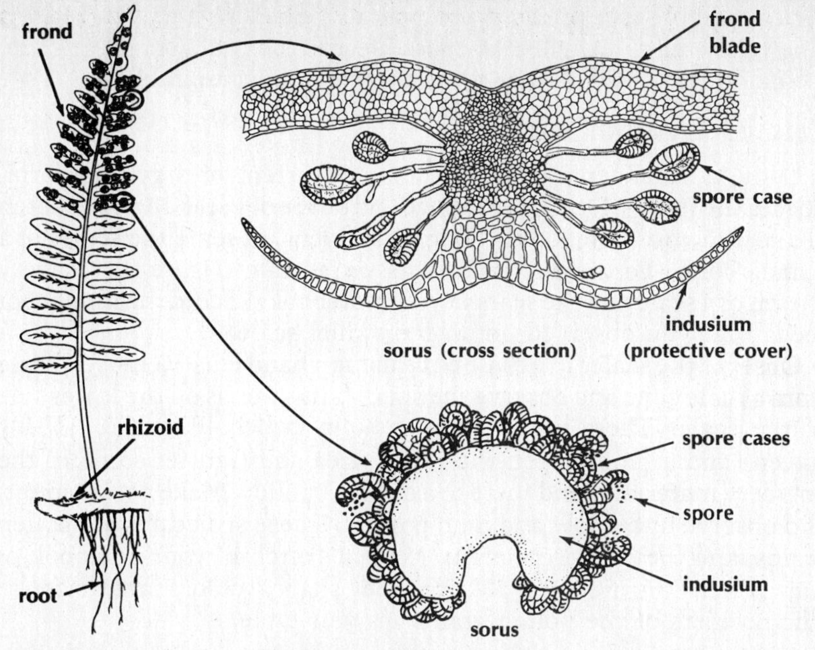

FIGURE 2 Fern Reproductive Structures

Using a hand lens, observe the top and then the bottom side of a fern frond. Make a labeled sketch of the fern frond. Locate the dark colored sori and carefully remove a spore case using a probe and forceps (Figure 2). Place the spore case on a clean, dry slide. Make a wet

TABLE 1. OBSERVATIONS OF SPECIMENS

SPECIMEN	COLOR	SHAPE	SIZE
fern spore			
gymnosperm pollen grain			
angiosperm pollen grain			

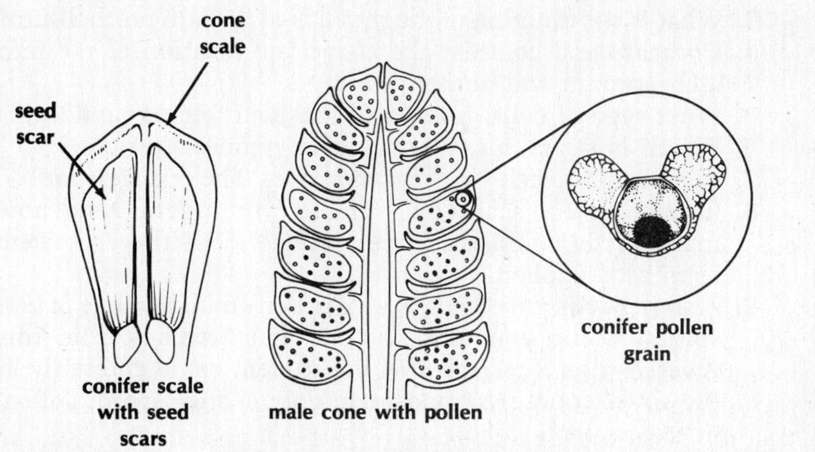

FIGURE 3 Gymnosperm Reproductive Structures

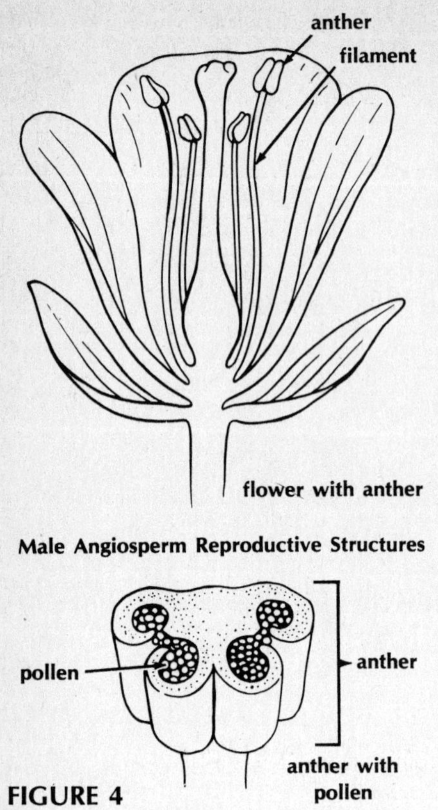

FIGURE 4

mount and observe the spore case on low, then high power. Make a labeled sketch of a single fern spore. Record the color, shape, and size in micrometers of a fern spore in a table similar to Table 1.

Part B. Gymnosperms

Using a hand lens, observe the woody stem of a gymnosperm. Locate the leaves. Describe the size and shape of a leaf. Make a sketch of a leaf in your notebook. Using a hand lens, observe the scales of a female cone. Locate the seed scars on a scale (Figure 3). Make a sketch of a scale and the scars in your notebook. Record the number of seeds that you observed on an individual scale.

Observe the scales of a male cone using a hand lens. Remove a scale from a male cone and observe the small, raised areas on the lower side of the scale. These raised areas contain pollen (Figure 3). Using forceps and a probe, open the raised area and transfer some of the powdery material found there to a clean, dry slide. Make a wet mount, and observe under low and high powers. These structures are pollen grains, and they contain sperm. Make a sketch in your notebook of the pollen (Figure 3). Record the shape, color, and size in micrometers of the pollen grains in your table.

Part C. Angiosperms

Using a hand lens, observe the upper and lower surfaces of an angiosperm leaf. Describe any differences you observe between the upper and lower surfaces of the leaf in your notebook. Make sketches of the upper and lower leaf surfaces.

Obtain a flower, and remove its petals. Locate the balloon-shaped anther of the flower (Figure 4). The anther is the male reproductive organ of angiosperms. Describe the shape and make a sketch of the anther in your notebook. Using forceps, remove an anther from the flower and place it on a clean, dry slide. Open the top of the anther using probe and forceps. Observe the fine, powdery pollen. Add a drop of water to the anther on the slide, and then remove the anther itself. Observe the pollen grains remaining on the slide under low and high powers. Sketch the pollen grains, and record their shape, color, and size in micrometers in your table.

Formulating Generalizations

1. Describe the shape of the fern prothallium.
2. What is the function of the green cells of the fern prothallium?
3. What is the function of the rhizoids of the fern prothallium?
4. Compare and contrast the shape and location of the fern archegonium and antheridium.
5. What type of cells do each of these structures produce?
6. Which is larger, a male or female gymnosperm cone?
7. What is produced by the male cone? The female cone?
8. If there are 100 scales on a female gymnosperm cone, how many seeds could the cone produce if all the eggs were fertilized? Explain.
9. A student has two slides, one of pollen grains and one of fern spores. Using your observations and sketches from this investigation, describe how the student could determine if the slides contain gymnosperm pollen, angiosperm pollen, or fern spores.
10. Why do you suppose gymnosperm pollen has "wings"? Why didn't the angiosperm pollen you observed have "wings"?

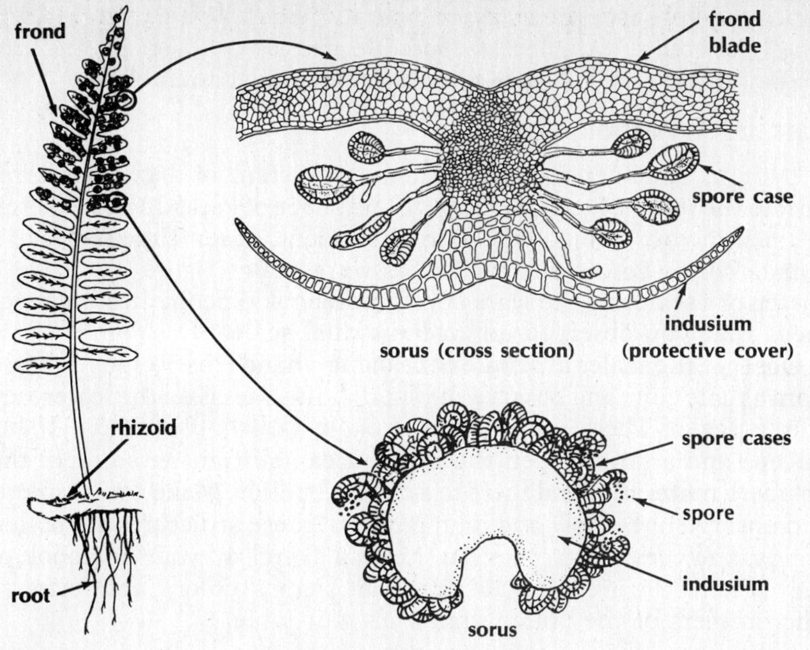

FIGURE 2 Fern Reproductive Structures

Using a hand lens, observe the top and then the bottom side of a fern frond. Make a labeled sketch of the fern frond. Locate the dark colored sori and carefully remove a spore case using a probe and forceps (Figure 2). Place the spore case on a clean, dry slide. Make a wet

TABLE 1. OBSERVATIONS OF SPECIMENS

SPECIMEN	COLOR	SHAPE	SIZE
fern spore			
gymnosperm pollen grain			
angiosperm pollen grain			

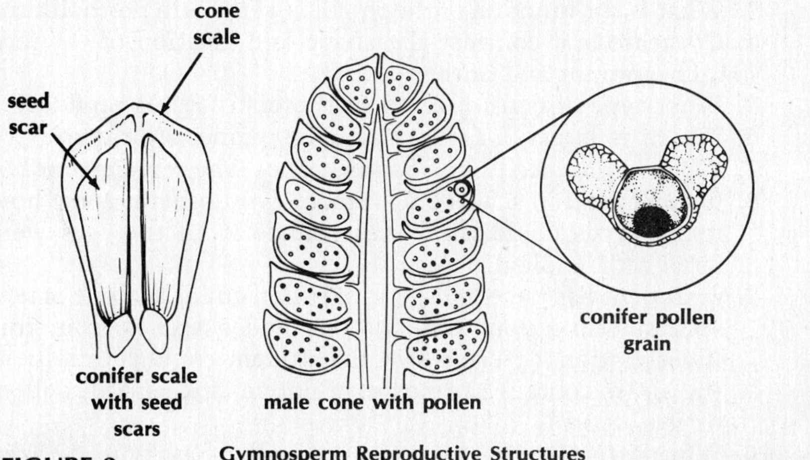

FIGURE 3 Gymnosperm Reproductive Structures

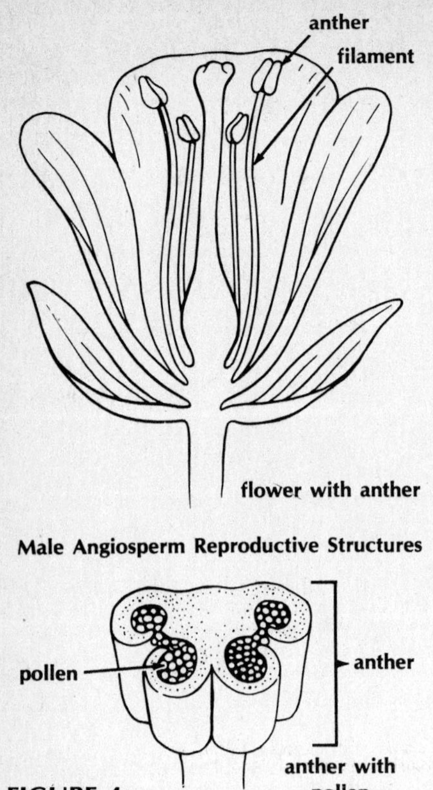

FIGURE 4

mount and observe the spore case on low, then high power. Make a labeled sketch of a single fern spore. Record the color, shape, and size in micrometers of a fern spore in a table similar to Table 1.

Part B. Gymnosperms

Using a hand lens, observe the woody stem of a gymnosperm. Locate the leaves. Describe the size and shape of a leaf. Make a sketch of a leaf in your notebook. Using a hand lens, observe the scales of a female cone. Locate the seed scars on a scale (Figure 3). Make a sketch of a scale and the scars in your notebook. Record the number of seeds that you observed on an individual scale.

Observe the scales of a male cone using a hand lens. Remove a scale from a male cone and observe the small, raised areas on the lower side of the scale. These raised areas contain pollen (Figure 3). Using forceps and a probe, open the raised area and transfer some of the powdery material found there to a clean, dry slide. Make a wet mount, and observe under low and high powers. These structures are pollen grains, and they contain sperm. Make a sketch in your notebook of the pollen (Figure 3). Record the shape, color, and size in micrometers of the pollen grains in your table.

Part C. Angiosperms

Using a hand lens, observe the upper and lower surfaces of an angiosperm leaf. Describe any differences you observe between the upper and lower surfaces of the leaf in your notebook. Make sketches of the upper and lower leaf surfaces.

Obtain a flower, and remove its petals. Locate the balloon-shaped anther of the flower (Figure 4). The anther is the male reproductive organ of angiosperms. Describe the shape and make a sketch of the anther in your notebook. Using forceps, remove an anther from the flower and place it on a clean, dry slide. Open the top of the anther using probe and forceps. Observe the fine, powdery pollen. Add a drop of water to the anther on the slide, and then remove the anther itself. Observe the pollen grains remaining on the slide under low and high powers. Sketch the pollen grains, and record their shape, color, and size in micrometers in your table.

Formulating Generalizations

1. Describe the shape of the fern prothallium.
2. What is the function of the green cells of the fern prothallium?
3. What is the function of the rhizoids of the fern prothallium?
4. Compare and contrast the shape and location of the fern archegonium and antheridium.
5. What type of cells do each of these structures produce?
6. Which is larger, a male or female gymnosperm cone?
7. What is produced by the male cone? The female cone?
8. If there are 100 scales on a female gymnosperm cone, how many seeds could the cone produce if all the eggs were fertilized? Explain.
9. A student has two slides, one of pollen grains and one of fern spores. Using your observations and sketches from this investigation, describe how the student could determine if the slides contain gymnosperm pollen, angiosperm pollen, or fern spores.
10. Why do you suppose gymnosperm pollen has "wings"? Why didn't the angiosperm pollen you observed have "wings"?

Diversity Of Lower Invertebrates

38

The Animal Kingdom can be divided into two groups: invertebrates and vertebrates. Invertebrates are animals that do not have backbones. Invertebrates are diverse in size, shape, and structure. The body plan of most invertebrates is either bilaterally or radially symmetrical. In bilateral symmetry, the body parts are usually in pairs. One line drawn through the organism from one end to the other equally divides the organism into left and right halves (Figure 1). In radial symmetry, body parts are arranged in a circular pattern. Many lines drawn through the center of the organism end to end produce two identical halves.

As you observe examples of invertebrates, you should notice that some structures, such as many body openings, are found in only one phylum. Other structures such as testes and ovaries are found in several phyla. Invertebrates are cold blooded. Their body temperatures are a few degrees Celsius different from the environments in which they live. Twenty-five invertebrate phyla are known; however, you only will be observing and studying about a dozen.

In this investigation you are to observe the invertebrates displayed on the laboratory tables. You are to describe and distinguish those characteristics which may be used to separate the invertebrates into their respective phyla.

Materials *(per class)*

various labeled invertebrates

Procedure

Before beginning your observations of the specimens, construct a table similar to Table 1 for the number of specimens indicated by your teacher. Numbered specimens of invertebrates are displayed in containers throughout the laboratory. The specimens displayed will be labeled with their common name, biological name, and the phylum to which they belong.

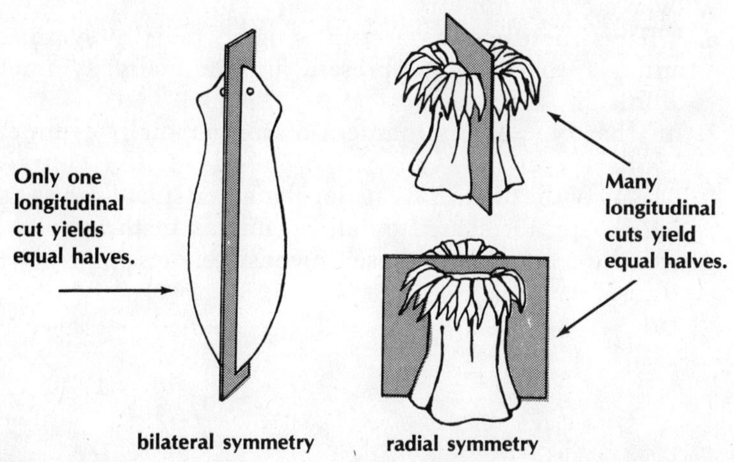

FIGURE 1

Move from station to station on a signal given by your teacher. Observe each specimen for a short period of time (two to five minutes) then move to the next station. Record specific information about each organism in the appropriate place in your table. The parts of some specimens are labeled in order to help you differentiate between complicated structures.

TABLE 1. CHARACTERISTICS OF LOWER INVERTEBRATES

NAME AND PHYLUM OF ORGANISM	BILATERAL OR RADIAL SYMMETRY	NUMBER OF APPENDAGES PRESENT	EYES	OTHER FEATURES

Formulating Generalizations

1. Are there any phyla that have no distinctive characteristics?
2. Arrange the phyla in order from the least complex to the most complex. What structures or features aid you in arranging the phyla in complexity?
3. Which phyla seem to be closely related to each other?
4. What characteristics are essential in the classification of invertebrates?
5. What is a possible adaptive advantage of bilateral symmetry over radial symmetry?
6. What structure(s) is (are) missing in radially symmetrical animals that (is) are present in bilaterally symmetrical animals?
7. In what type of environment do most radially symmetrical animals live?
8. Do any of the phyla have major characteristics (such as a shell) which are not shared by all organisms in the phyla? Give specific examples of these "inconsistencies."

Classification Of Fruits

37

After a flower has been pollinated, fertilization usually occurs. After fertilization, the ovary develops into a fruit. Ovules develop into seeds within the fruit. As a fruit develops, sugars, amino acids, proteins, and fats and oils accumulate in the ovary and ovule tissue.

Some of the plants we call vegetables are misnamed because they are actually fruits. A fruit is a ripened ovary; hence, any "vegetable" that is a ripened ovary is really a fruit. Tomatoes, cucumbers, and squash are fruits which are commonly misnamed "vegetables."

As the ovary develops into a fruit, the ovary wall thickens and develops into three layers: exocarp, mesocarp, and endocarp (Figure 1). The exocarp is the outermost layer of the fruit. It is composed of one layer of epidermal cells. The mesocarp is the middle layer and contains from one to several layers of cells. This layer sometimes becomes the pulp, or meat, of the fruit. It contains the stored food of the fruit. It is usually several centimeters thick. The endocarp is the innermost layer of cells. It varies in thickness and texture. In some fruits, the ovary wall is fleshy throughout, while in others, one or two layers are fleshy while the others are hard (Figure 2).

In this investigation you are to observe the various fruits on display. Classify the fruits by using a classification key. Answer all questions which appear on the cards at each fruit sample.

Materials *(per class)*

various labeled fruits
hand lenses

Procedure

Several numbered fruits are displayed in pans and culture dishes. Proceed from station to station. Answer the questions which appear on the cards at each station and classify the fruits. Prior to answering the questions, study the classification key of fruits.

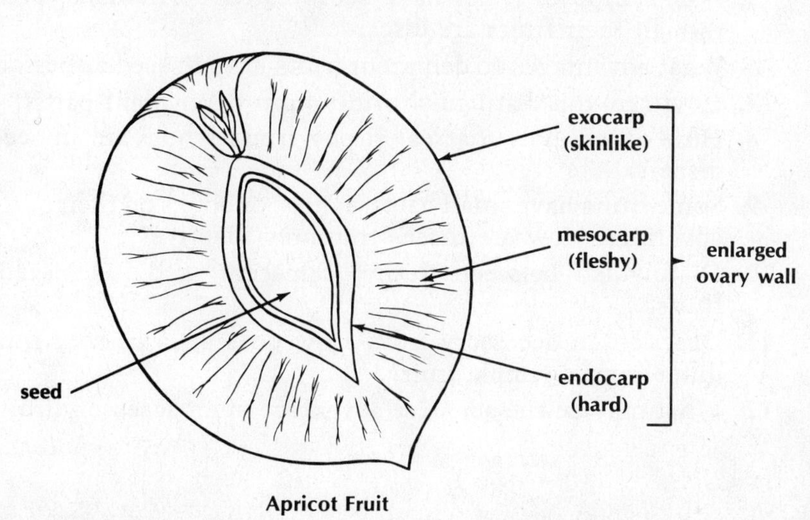

FIGURE 1

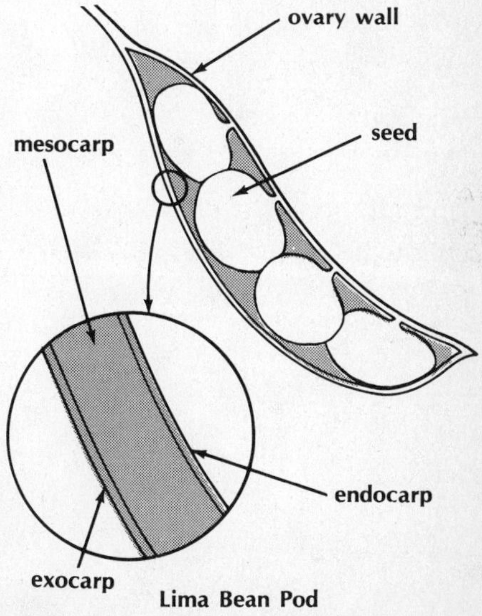

FIGURE 2

Classification Key of Fruits

I. Simple Fruits—Fruits consist of a single ripened ovary.
  A. Fleshy—The ovary wall is soft and fleshy when ripe.
    1. Berry—The entire ovary is soft. Contains many seeds.
    2. Drupe—The exocarp is covered with a skin. Exocarp and mesocarp are fleshy while the endocarp is very hard. The endocarp encloses the seed.
  B. Dry Fruits—Entire ovary is dry and brittle when ripe.
    1. Indehiscent—Fruit does not split along a definite seam when ripe.
      a. Achene—Fruit contains one seed. The seed is separate from the ovary wall except at point of attachment.
      b. Samara—Ovary is flat and wing-shaped. It bears one or two seeds.
      c. Nut—Entire ovary wall is hard and thick. Fruit contains one seed.
      d. Grain—Ovary and seed wall are fused together. One seed present.
    2. Dehiscent—Fruit splits along a definite seam when ripe. Contains many seeds.
      a. Follicle—Seed-bearing organ splits along one seam.
      b. Legume—Seed-bearing organ splits along two seams.
      c. Capsule—Seed-bearing organ splits along three or more seams.

II. Accessory fruits—Parts other than the ovary become fleshy and develop into fruit tissue. The ovary then becomes harder and is encased by or is found outside of the accessory parts. For example, the receptacle in some fruits develops into a fleshy substance and the ovary is brittle.

Formulating Generalizations

1. What part of the flower becomes the fruit?
2. What part of the flower becomes the seed?
3. List five seeds that humans eat for food.
4. From what specific types of fruits do these seeds come?
5. Which type of fruits have seeds eaten by humans, even though their fruits are discarded?
6. What advantages do dehiscent fruits have in seed dispersal?
7. How can you distinguish fruits from other plant parts?
8. How do animals that eat fleshy fruits whole aid in seed dispersal?
9. Some fruits have small barbs, spines, or hooks on their outer coverings. How are these structures adaptive?
10. Distinguish between fleshy, dehiscent, and indehiscent fruits.
11. Describe an accessory fruit. How does an accessory fruit differ from a simple fruit?
12. What may be the adaptive advantage of an accessory fruit?

Development Of Seeds Into New Plants

45

Living things show specific patterns of growth. The seed of a true flowering plant develops from an ovule of a flower. During fertilization, one sperm cell from the pollen tube unites with the egg to form the new sporophyte embryo in the forming seed. The other sperm cell unites with two polar nuclei of the ovule to form endosperm tissue in the seed. The sporophyte embryo will give rise to a new plant. The endosperm tissue provides food for the embryo before and during germination.

A seed also contains one or more "seed leaves" called cotyledons. Cotyledons store and digest food. Plants which have seeds with one cotyledon are called monocots. Those with two cotyledons are called dicots. A small pore called the hilum is found on some dicot seeds. This pore is a scar that shows where the seed was attached to the ovary wall. The small scar found on some monocot seeds is called the stalk. An embryo is composed of an epicotyl, hypocotyl, and radicle. The hypocotyl is located below the attachment point of the cotyledons. The radicle is the lower portion of the hypocotyl. The epicotyl is the part of the embryo above the point of attachment of the cotyledons.

In seeds of corn, wheat, and oats, digestion and absorption of food stored in the endosperm occur after the seeds are planted in the ground and absorb water. Bean and pea embryos absorb the food from the endosperm while still in the ovary. Thus, these seeds do not have endosperm tissue. When planted they will germinate more quickly than corn, wheat, or oats.

After a seed is mature, it may remain dormant for a long period of time. In some cases this may be several years. Dormancy is a period of inactivity in a seed. No new cells are formed in the seed. However, the embryonic plant is carrying on respiration at a slow rate. Germination is the process in which the dormant period is broken and growth is resumed.

In this investigation you are to observe two types of seeds, monocot and dicot; locate the various parts of the seeds; and observe changes in seeds and embryos in various stages of germination.

Materials *(per student or team)*

forceps
dropper
paper towels
petri dish
scalpel
probe
Gram's iodine solution — 3 mL
stereomicroscope
bean seed soaked for 24 hours
corn seed soaked for 24 hours
germinating seeds in vermiculite—
1 corn and 1 bean at:
3 days old 9 days old
6 days old 12 days old

FIGURE 1

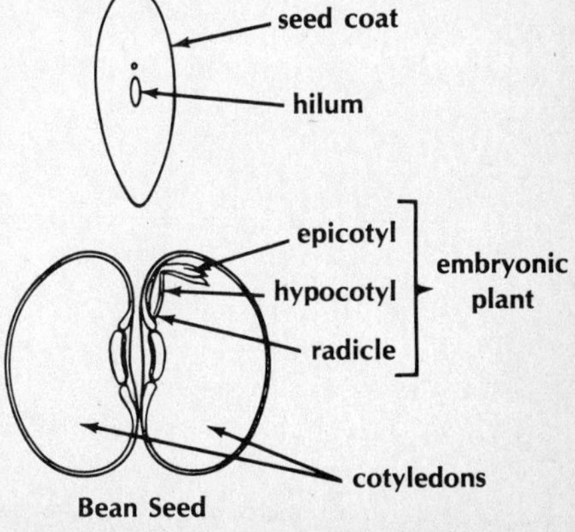

Procedure

Part A. Observation of Dicot Seed—Bean

Remove a bean seed that has been soaking in water for 24 hours and place it on a dry paper towel. Locate the hilum and seed coat (Figure 1). Remove the seed coat and test it for starch by adding a drop of iodine solution to it. **CAUTION:** *If iodine spillage occurs, rinse with water.* Separate the two cotyledons from each other with a gentle pulling motion. Remove the embryonic plant from the cotyledon. Make a scratch in a cotyledon with a probe and test it for starch.

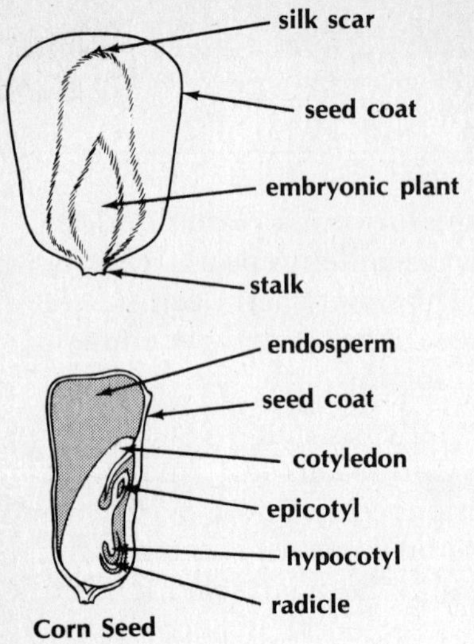

FIGURE 2

CAUTION: *Always be careful when using probes or other sharp instruments.* Locate the epicotyl, hypocotyl, and radicle on the embryonic plant (Figure 1). Observe the structures with a stereomicroscope. Place the embryonic plant in a petri dish. Puncture the epicotyl, hypocotyl, and radicle with a probe. Test them for starch.

Observe germinating beans growing in vermiculite. Locate the epicotyl, hypocotyl, radicle, seed coat, and cotyledons. Record in your lab notebook the changes in these parts as the plant develops from a soaking seed to a 12-day-old seedling.

Part B. Observation of Monocot Seed—Corn

Remove a corn seed that has been soaking for 24 hours and place it on a dry paper towel. Locate the seed coat, silk scar, and stalk (Figure 2). Cut the corn seed in half. **CAUTION:** *Always be careful when cutting with the scalpel. Cut away from hands and fingers.* Locate the seed coat, hypocotyl, epicotyl, radicle, cotyledon, and endosperm (Figure 2). Test the seed for starch by adding one to two drops of iodine directly to one of the cut halves. Puncture the epicotyl, hypocotyl, radicle, and cotyledon to help the iodine penetrate into the seed. Remove the seed coat from the unstained half of the seed and test it for starch.

Observe germinating corn seeds growing in vermiculite. Locate the hypocotyl, epicotyl, radicle, seed coat, and cotyledon. Record in your lab notebook the changes in these parts as the plant develops from a soaking seed to a 12-day-old seedling.

Formulating Generalizations

1. List the probable function of the seed coat, hypocotyl, epicotyl, radicle, cotyledon, and hilum of a bean seed. Do they have the same functions in the corn seed?
2. To what in the corn seed is the hilum of the bean seed similar?
3. Which parts of the bean seed contained the most starch? Why?
4. Which parts of the corn seed contained the most starch? Why?
5. What changes did you notice in the parts of the bean seed as it developed to a 12-day-old seedling?
6. What changes did you notice in the parts of the corn seed as it developed to a 12-day-old seedling?
7. What might cause a seed to remain dormant?
8. What adaptive advantage would seeds capable of a dormant period have over those which cannot remain dormant?

Effects Of Salt Concentration On Development Of Brine Shrimp

46

Brine shrimp, *Artemia salina,* live in a saltwater environment. They are able to live in a wide range of salinity. They live either in the open ocean or in small tidewater pools, hatching from eggs. Juvenile brine shrimp have three pairs of leaflike appendages. Each pair of appendages is a different size. When sexually mature, they have eleven pairs of leaflike appendages.

As a brine shrimp grows and develops, it sheds its outer covering approximately twelve times. During development, the number of body segments and the number of hairs on the appendages increase. The concentration of the salt solution in which brine shrimp grow affects the rate of development.

In this investigation, you are to compare the effects of various concentrations of salt solution on the development of brine shrimp larvae.

Materials *(per student or team)*

methyl cellulose—3 mL
glass slide
coverslip
microscope
flat toothpicks—3 or 4
brine shrimp culture (1 per class)
brine shrimp eggs, dried
yeast suspension (25 mL per class)
baby food jars—6
glass marking pencil
various sodium chloride solutions—100 mL each
    0.1% concentration
    0.5% concentration
    1.0% concentration
    2.0% concentration
    4.0% concentration
    8.0% concentration
dropper

Procedure

Place 100 mL of each salt solution into separate baby food jars. Label the salt concentration of each jar. Place 0.1 cm^3 of dry brine shrimp eggs into each jar. The volume 0.1 cm^3 is equivalent to the number of eggs that will cling to the narrow end of a flat toothpick. Place the jars on a shelf in the classroom. Make sure there are no eggs on the side of the jar above the water level.

Observe your brine shrimp cultures for the next two days for signs of hatching. Brine shrimp larvae will appear as small peach-colored organisms swimming in a jerky manner. After hatching, feed the organisms one drop of yeast suspension daily.

Observe several specimens daily for eight to ten days. Use the methyl cellulose technique to mount the brine shrimp. Place a drop of methyl cellulose on a clean, dry slide. With a toothpick, spread the methyl cellulose to form a ring with a diameter no larger than 1 cm (Figure 1). Place a few brine shrimp larvae from the culture inside

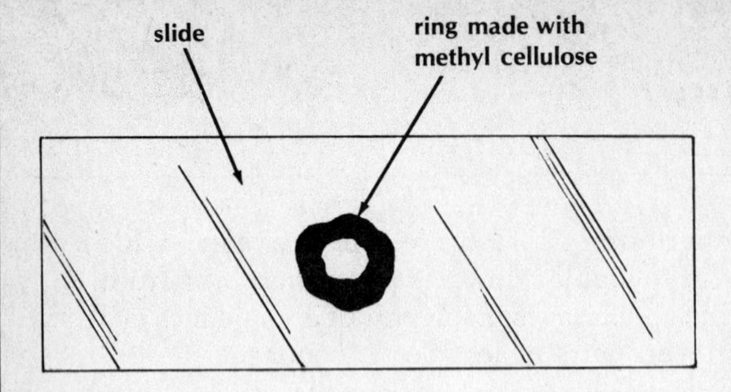

FIGURE 1

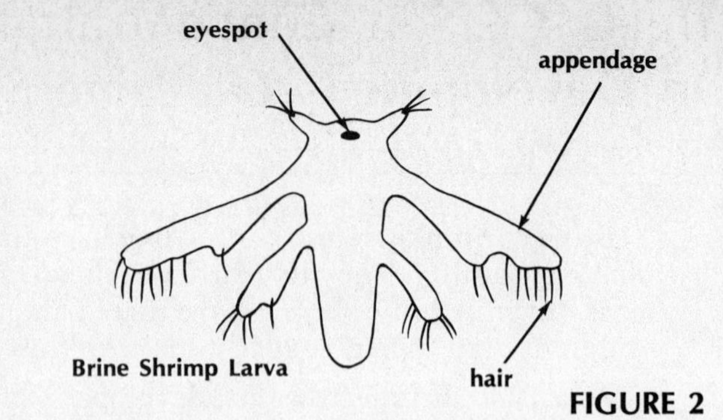

FIGURE 2

the methyl cellulose ring using a dropper. Place a clean, dry coverslip over the ring and the brine shrimp. Place the slide on the stage of a microscope and observe the brine shrimp with the low power lens. Locate the eye spot, appendages, and hairs of a brine shrimp. Use Figure 2 as a guide.

Compare the length in millimeters of the organisms in each salt solution. Record daily data in your lab notebook in a table similar to Table 1. Do not return the brine shrimp to the cultures after observing them.

After all observations are complete, record your data on the chalkboard. Record daily class averages in another table in your notebook similar to Table 1.

TABLE 1. LENGTH OF BRINE SHRIMP (mm)

DAY	SALT CONCENTRATION					
	0.1%	0.5%	1.0%	2.0%	4.0%	8.0%
1						
2						
8						

Formulating Generalizations

1. What is the difference between growth and development?
2. What changes take place in a brine shrimp after it hatches?
3. Why is the outer covering of shrimp shed during the development period?
4. In which solution did the shrimp develop most rapidly? Explain.
5. In which solution did the slowest development occur? Explain.
6. Compare your data to the class data. Explain any differences that occur between the two sets of data.
7. On the basis of your observations, what do you think the concentrations of salt is in ocean tidal pools where brine shrimp normally develop?
8. Why was salt water used rather than fresh water to mount the shrimp on the microscope slides?

Development Of A Chicken Embryo

47

In 1672, Malpighi described the growth and development of a chicken embryo. Since that time, the chicken embryo has become a very important organism in biological research. Today it is used as a culture medium to develop certain vaccines that protect humans and other animals from diseases.

In the process of embryonic development, life starts as a single, fertilized egg. A fertilized egg goes through several mitotic divisions which increase the number of cells. As the cells increase in number, they begin to differentiate into various tissues. As these tissues develop into specific organs, the organism begins to take on definite characteristics. The characteristics and size of the organism are controlled by genes.

In this investigation, you are to identify and compare the various structures found in developing chicken embryos of incubated eggs.

Materials *(per team of four students)*

incubated eggs—1 each
- 1 day
- 2 days
- 5 days
- 9 days
- 15 days
- 19 days

fertilized unincubated egg—0 days
culture dish
stereomicroscope
physiological saline solution, 37°C—100 mL/egg
scissors
forceps
paper towels—3
dropper
fire polished glass stirring rod
metric ruler
jars with lids—3
70% alcohol solution

Procedure

Part A. Fertilized, Unincubated Egg

Crack the larger (blunt) end of an unincubated fertilized egg and empty the contents into a small culture dish (Figure 1). Be sure that you do not break the yolk. Place the culture dish on the stage of a stereomicroscope. Locate the clear liquid albumen, yolk, chalaza, and blastoderm (Figure 2). The albumen is a clear liquid that occupies most of the egg. It is composed of proteins. The yolk is the large, yellow sphere near the center of the egg. It is composed of fats. The chalaza is a white, twisted cord attached to both sides of the yolk. It helps hold the yolk in place. The blastoderm is a small white spot on the surface of the yolk. It will give rise to the developing embryo. A slight turning of the yolk may be necessary to see the blastoderm. Use the stirring rod to gently turn the yolk. Make a sketch of your observations.

Part B. One-Day Incubated Egg

Crack the larger end of a 1-day incubated egg. Empty the contents of the egg gently into a small culture dish one half full of physiological

FIGURE 1

FIGURE 2

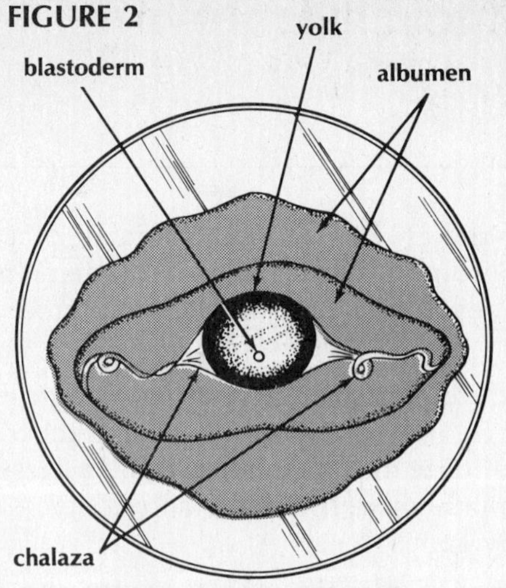

Unincubated Fertilized Egg

FIGURE 3

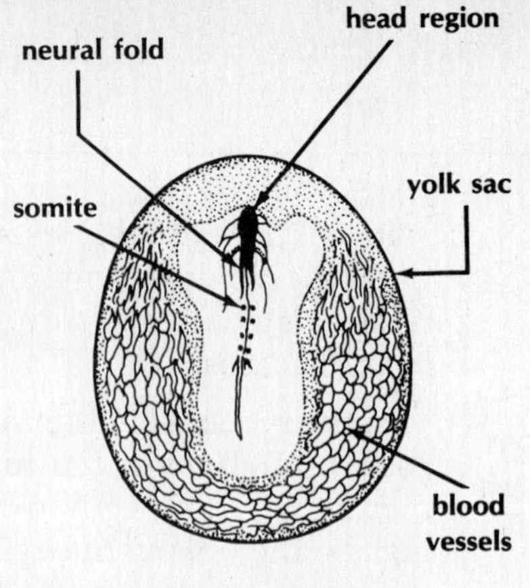

1-Day Incubated Egg

saline solution that has been heated to 37°C. Place the culture dish on the stage of the stereomicroscope. Locate the head region, neural fold, somites, yolk sac, and blood vessels (Figure 3). You may need to turn the yolk with a probe to see the embryo. Be careful not to puncture the yolk. Measure the length of the embryo in millimeters. Make a sketch of your observations.

Part C. Two-Day Incubated Egg

Place a 2-day incubated egg on its side in a culture dish that contains crumpled wet paper towels. Insert the point of a pair of scissors beneath the surface of the shell at one end of the egg (Figure 4). **CAUTION:** *Always be careful when using scissors.* Begin to cut the shell around its top. When the circle is completely cut, remove the shell with a pair of forceps. The embryo should be exposed and covered with albumen. If you cannot locate the embryo, rotate the yolk with a dropper. Be careful not to puncture the yolk. When the embryo is in view, remove the albumen with a dropper until the embryo is no longer covered with albumen. Place the culture dish on the stage of the stereomicroscope and observe. Locate the head, developing brain, eye, heart, spinal cord, blood vessels, somites, and yolk sac. Measure the length of the embryo in millimeters. Make a sketch of your observations in your lab notebook.

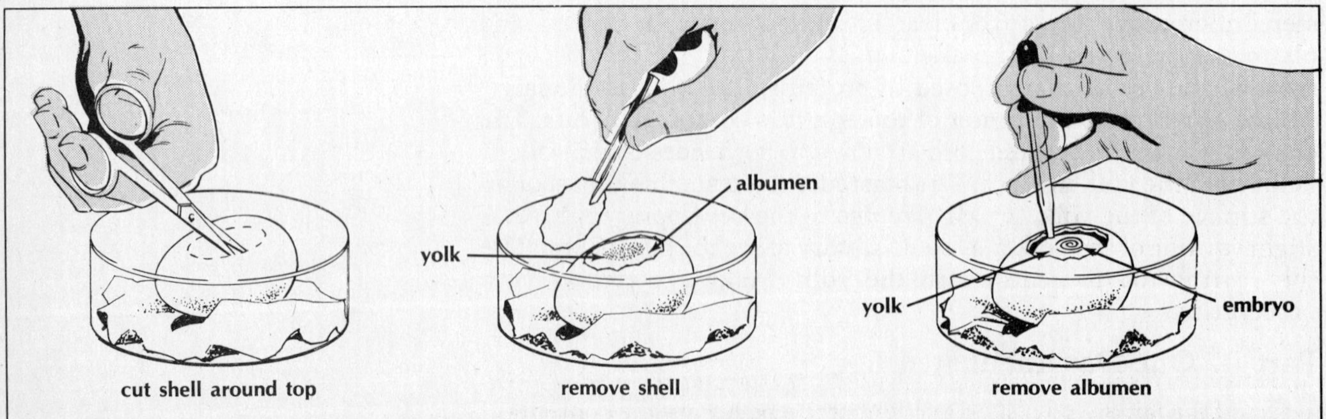

FIGURE 4

FIGURE 5

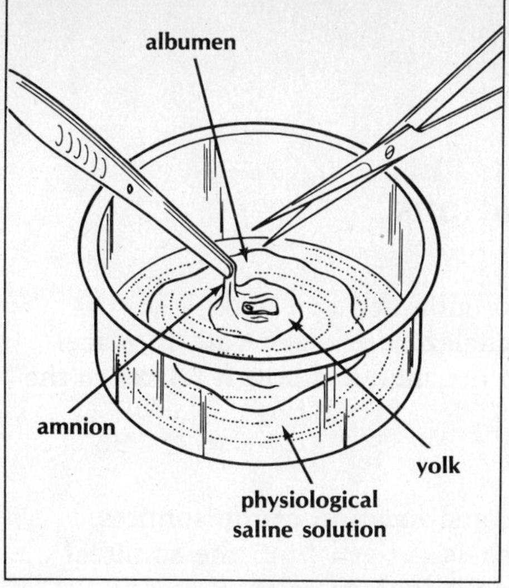

FIGURE 6

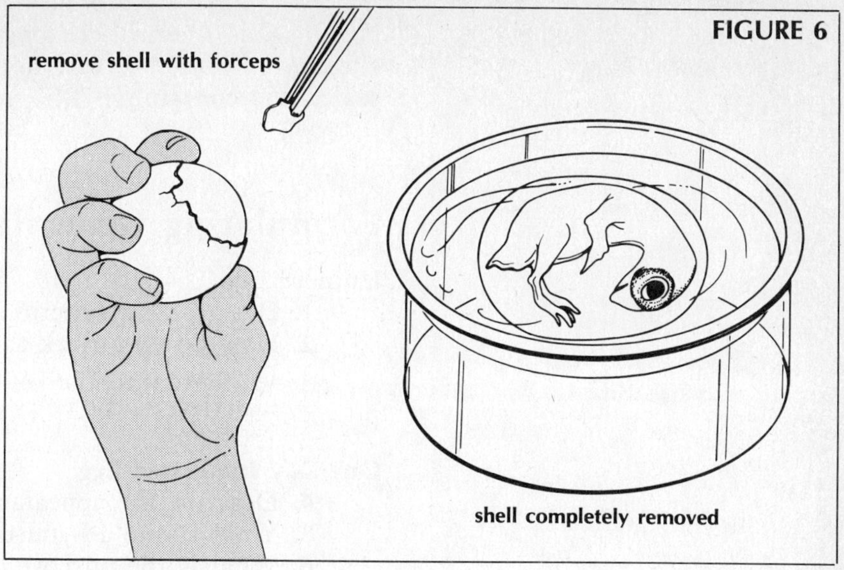

Part D. Five-Day Incubated Egg

Remove the end of the shell from a 5-day incubated egg as you did the two-day egg. Place the contents of the egg in a culture dish containing 50 to 70 mL of warm physiological saline solution. Place the culture dish on the stage of the stereomicroscope. Locate the yolk sac, allantois, and amnion. The allantois is a small, round membrane at the posterior end of the embryo. The amnion is a thin membrane surrounding the embryo.

With scissors and forceps, remove the amnion without injuring the embryo (Figure 5). Measure the length of the embryo in millimeters. Compare the size of the eyes with the size of the head. Locate the limb buds. Make a sketch of your observations.

Part E. Nine-, Fifteen-, and Nineteen-Day Incubated Eggs

Open the eggs which have been incubated for 9, 15, and 19 days by first cracking the enlarged end of the egg. Be careful not to rupture any of the membranes directly beneath the shell. With forceps, remove the shell piece by piece (Figure 6). When part of the shell has been removed, place the egg in a culture dish, containing 50 to 70 mL physiological saline solution at 37°C. Continue to remove the shell. Observe each egg by placing the dish on the stage of the stereomicroscope.

Nine-Day Egg

Locate the clear membrane that was attached to the shell. Remove the allantois. Locate the yolk sac and amnion. Remove the amnion with scissors and forceps. Examine the embryo carefully. Measure the length of the embryo in millimeters. Make a sketch of your observations. Place the embryo in a sealed jar containing 70% alcohol.

Fifteen- and Nineteen-Day Eggs

Locate the translucent membrane that was attached to the shell. Locate the yolk sac or its remnants. Locate the amnion and the amniotic cavity. The amniotic cavity is the fluid filled space. Locate the allantois. Measure the length of the embryo in millimeters. Make sketches of your observations of both embryos. Place the embryos in sealed jars containing 70% alcohol.

Formulating Generalizations

Unincubated Egg

1. Describe the functions of albumen and yolk.
2. How do you think the chalaza keeps the yolk in place?
3. Describe the structure of the shell and how it relates to the function of the cell.

One-Day Incubated Egg

4. Describe the appearance and location of the somites.
5. What tissue do you think is derived from the somites?
6. What is the purpose of the blood vessels?

Two-Day Incubated Egg

7. What differences can be noted in the size or number of blood vessels in comparison to those of a one-day egg?
8. How much larger is the day two embryo than the day one embryo?

Five-Day Incubated Egg

9. From the location of the amnion and allantois, suggest a function of each.
10. What are limb buds?

Nine-Day Incubated Egg

11. What changes do you notice in the allantois?
12. Has the yolk sac changed in size? Why?
13. List the structures visible in this embryo that were not present before.

Fifteen-Day Incubated Egg

14. What has happened to the structure of the beak as compared to a nine-day embryo?
15. Compared to day nine, which part of the body appears to be growing faster, the head or trunk?
16. Has the allantois cavity increased or decreased in size? Why?

Nineteen-Day Incubated Egg

17. Are the allantois and amnion still present? Explain.
18. Which has enlarged the most since the second day, the embryo, yolk sac, allantois, or amnion? Explain.
19. From day zero (unincubated, fertilized egg) to day nineteen, what was the overall increase in body length in millimeters?
20. What were the first and last systems to appear in the developing embryo?

Ingestion And Digestion In Protists

48

Protists have many ways of obtaining food. Some protists contain chlorophyll and thus can convert carbon dioxide and water to sugar. This sugar then is converted into more complex organic molecules. Some protists can capture and ingest particles of food in the water. The food may be bacteria, algae, microscopic invertebrates, or other protists. This food is digested in a food vacuole inside the organism. After being digested, it is converted into complex molecules. These molecules are used either as basic building blocks for cell parts or they enter various biochemical cycles.

Another type of nutrition occurs in protists. Some protists can absorb salts, minerals, and organic compounds from the surrounding media. They convert these materials into useful materials and chemicals.

In this investigation, you are to locate and identify food vacuoles and gullets of *Paramecium* and *Blepharisma*. You are to observe the formation and breakdown of food vacuoles. You are to contrast the food vacuoles of *Paramecium* and those of *Blepharisma* according to size, location, color, shape, and number.

Materials

Per student
- absorbent cotton
- glass slide
- dropper
- coverslip
- microscope
- alum carmine crystals
- flat toothpick

Per class
- *Paramecium* culture
- *Blepharisma* culture

Procedure

Part A. *Paramecium*

Pull apart some fibers of a piece of absorbent cotton and place them on a clean, dry slide. With a dropper, add a drop of *Paramecium* culture to the cotton fibers. Paramecia will become trapped between the fibers and will not move out of the field of view too easily (Figure 1). Place some alum carmine crystals on the end of a flat toothpick. Add the crystals to the paramecia and cotton fibers. Stir gently on the surface of the drop to break apart large particles of carmine. During active feeding, a *Paramecium* will ingest some carmine particles along with its food. Add a coverslip to the slide. Place the slide on the stage of a compound microscope.

Observe the slide on low power. Locate a *Paramecium*. Locate a food vacuole and the gullet (Figure 2). Observe the *Paramecium* on high power. Make a sketch of a food vacuole in relationship to other structures of the *Paramecium*.

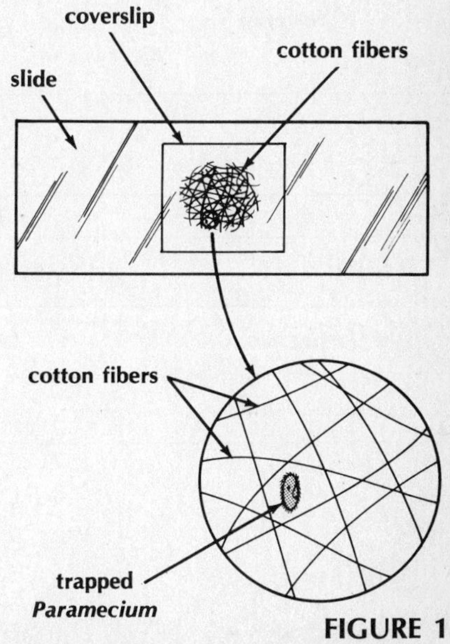

FIGURE 1

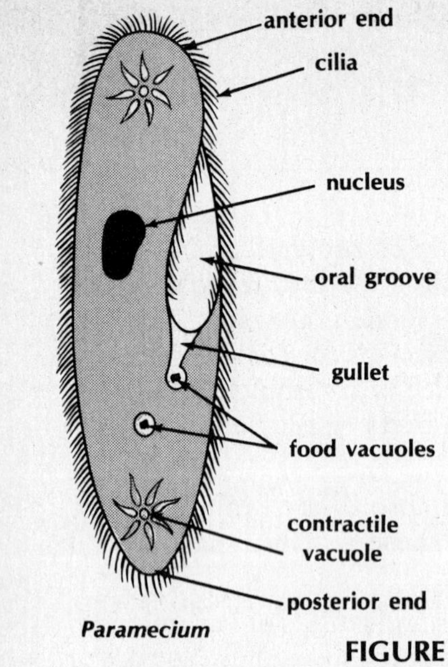

FIGURE 2

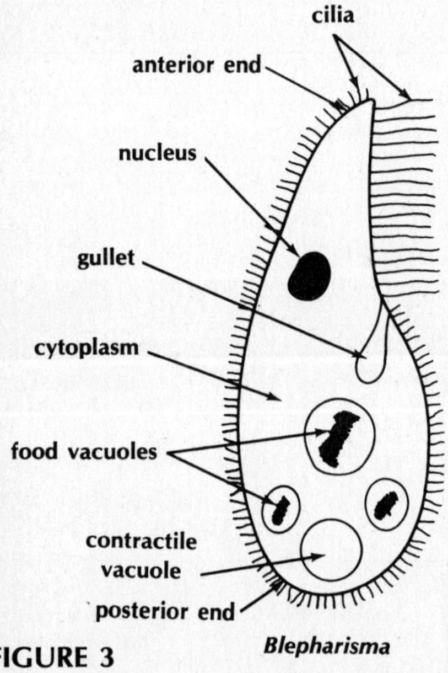

FIGURE 3

Compute the length and width of a *Paramecium* in micrometers. Compute the diameter of a food vacuole in micrometers and record it in a chart similar to Table 1. Record any differences in size, shape, color, and number of food vacuoles observed. Trace the path of one food vacuole as it moves through a *Paramecium* from the time of formation to egestion (removal of non-digestible food).

Part B. *Blepharisma*

Pull apart some fibers of a piece of absorbent cotton and place them on a clean, dry slide. With a dropper, add a drop of *Blepharisma* culture to the cotton fibers. Add some alum carmine crystals as you did in Part A. Add a coverslip to the slide and place the slide on the stage of the microscope.

Observe the slide on low power of the microscope. Locate the gullet and food vacuoles of a *Blepharisma* (Figure 3). Observe the *Blepharisma* on high power. Make a sketch of the food vacuoles in relationship to the other structures of the *Blepharisma.*

Compute the length and width of the *Blepharisma* in micrometers. Compute the diameter of the food vacuoles in micrometers. Record any differences in size, shape, color, and number of food vacuoles observed.

Compare the size, number, color, and shape of the food vacuoles in *Blepharisma* and *Paramecium.*

Formulating Generalizations

1. How can you tell which food vacuoles contain the most recently ingested food particles in a *Paramecium*?
2. Why do the food vacuoles vary in color?
3. Do you have any evidence that either *Paramecium* or *Blepharisma* can digest carmine particles? Explain.
4. What structures in *Paramecium* and *Belpharisma* aid in the process of ingestion? How do they help?
5. Describe the difference in location of the food vacuoles in *Paramecium* compared with the food vacuoles in *Blepharisma.*
6. How does the size of the food vacuole compare with the width of each protist?
7. What is the function of a gullet in protozoa?
8. What happens when a food vacuole becomes filled?

TABLE 1. OBSERVATIONS OF VACUOLES

PROTIST	DIAMETER	LENGTH	WIDTH	SHAPE	NUMBER PRESENT
Paramecium					
Blepharisma					

Constructing A Key To The Lower Invertebrates

39

Classification is a way of separating a large group of closely related organisms into smaller subgroups. With a classification system, identification of an organism is easy. The scientific names of organisms are based on the classification systems of living organisms. To classify an organism, scientists often use a key such as the one you constructed in Investigation 28. A key is a listing of specific characteristics, such as structure and behavior, in such a way that an organism can be identified through a process of elimination.

In this investigation, you are to use the data you collected in Investigation 38 to construct a dichotomous key of the lower invertebrate phyla that you observed.

Procedure

To construct your dichotomous key of lower invertebrates, refer to your data table from Investigation 38. The key you construct should be similar to the key of Investigation 28. Some of the characteristics which should be included in your key are radial or bilateral symmetry, number of appendages present, and presence or absence of eyes. You may think of other characteristics you wish to include in your key. To help you get started, two sample statements have been provided. You may begin with other statements if you wish.

1a. Body covered with many openings......................... Go to 2
1b. Body has only one or two openings....................... Go to 3

After you have completed your key, exchange keys with a classmate. Try to use each other's keys to identify organisms.

Formulating Generalizations

1. Why do dichotomous keys make identification of organisms easier?
2. What procedure would a scientist have to follow to identify an organism if dichotomous keys were not available?
3. What features or characteristics of the lower invertebrates did you include in your key?
4. Why did you pick these features?
5. Was your key exactly like your classmate's key? Explain.
6. Why is it possible to construct several different keys for the same group of animals?
7. Are there any characteristics which are essential to an invertebrate classification key?
8. A scientist discovers a new life form at the bottom of the ocean. How could a dichotomous key help the scientist determine to which types of known organisms the new organism is similar?

40 Identification Of Aquatic Insect Larvae And Juveniles

Insects are one of the more successful groups of living things in terms of diversity of habitat and total number of species. Some insects inhabit different habitats during the different stages of their life cycles. For example, one species may spend the egg and larva stage in the water, while the pupa and adult stage are spent on land. Other species may spend their entire life cycles either in water or on land.

Aquatic insects are an important food source for larger organisms such as fish and frogs. Aquatic insects are also indicators of pollution. Relative numbers of certain orders of insects can be predicted for a stream having a certain physical and biological structure. Absence of this order of insect (or reduced numbers) indicates that some physical or biological factor is not present in the ideal amount.

In this investigation, you are to identify insect specimens by using a key to aquatic insects. You are to identify the insects at the order level of classification.

Materials (*per student*)

numbered specimens of aquatic insect larvae and juveniles
stereomicroscope

Procedure

Observe the insect larvae specimens with a stereomicroscope. Note especially the mouthparts and other appendages. Using the key to aquatic insects, identify the insects as to order.

Construct in your lab notebook a table similar to Table 1. As you go through the key for each specimen, record in the table the characteristics of the specimen as indicated. Record the order of the insect in the last column.

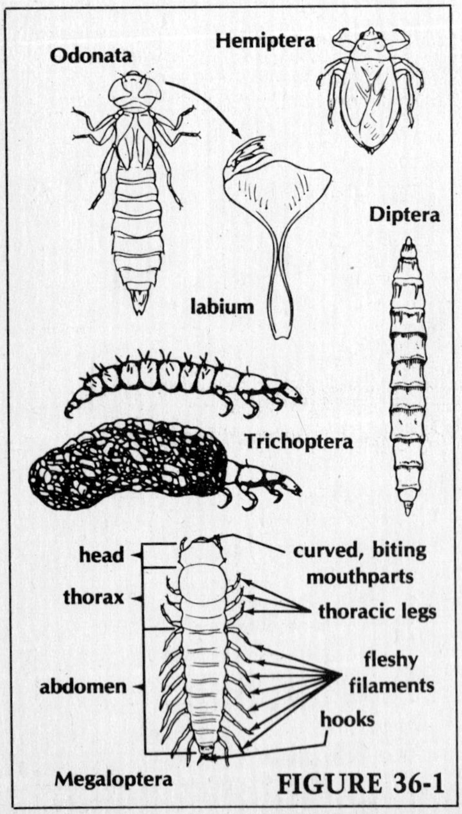

FIGURE 36-1

Key to Orders of Aquatic Insects

1a. Mouthparts resemble a long straight tube folded back between the legs.............................. Hemiptera (true bugs)

1b. Mouthparts not as above.. 2

2a. Thoracic legs absent.............................. Diptera (flies)

2b. Thoracic legs present.. 3

3a. Lower lip (labium) long and shovellike; folded similar to a hinge. Labium protrudes backward between legs and covers other mouthparts..... Odonata (dragonflies and damselflies)

3b. Labium not long and shovellike; labium does not protrude between legs, not hinged.. 4

4a. Long, curved biting mouthparts present; when present, gill filaments are on each abdominal segment.......... 5

4b. Flattened, biting mouthparts present; feathery gills present on thorax or abdomen.................................. 7

5a. **Pair of prolegs with hooks on tip of abdomen, usually minute fingerlike gill filaments on thorax and abdomen; mouthparts short and stout and crossing each other. Usually found in cases made of vegetation or stones .... Trichoptera (caddis flies)**

5b. **Prolegs, gills, and mouthparts not as above...................... 6**

6a. **One pair of lateral fleshy filaments on each abdominal segment; last abdominal segment contains a pair of hooks or long fleshy filament .... Megaloptera (dobsonflies, alderflies)**

6b. **Abdomen usually lacking fleshy filaments; last abdominal segment always lacking a pair of hooks............. Coleoptera (beetles)**

7a. **Gills on thorax when present; two cerci (lateral anal appendages) present; two claws on each end of leg.... Plecoptera (stoneflies)**

7b. **Gills on abdomen when present; three cerci present; one claw on end of each leg............. Ephemeroptera (mayflies)**

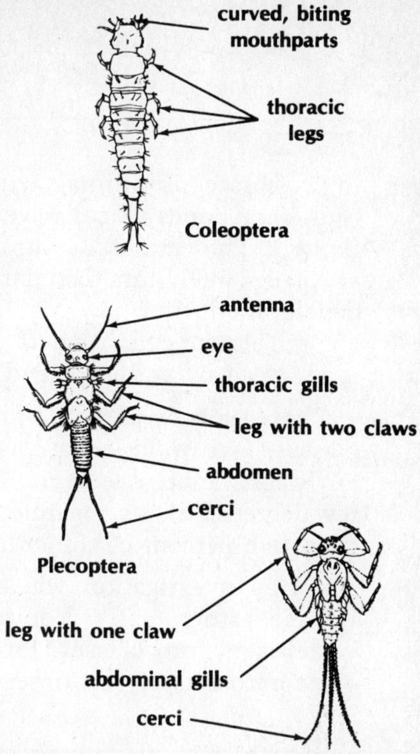

FIGURE 2

Formulating Generalizations

1. Which order(s) is (are) less insectlike? Explain.
2. What characteristics did all the insect specimens have in common?
3. Of the eight insect orders represented, list several orders of insects which appear to be very closely related. Explain why you think these orders are related.
4. How does the key indicate closely related insect orders?
5. Which order of insects appears to be more adult-like? Why?

TABLE 1. INSECT LARVAE AND JUVENILE CHARACTERISTICS

SPECIMEN NUMBER	NUMBER OF LEGS PRESENT	NUMBER OF ANTENNAE PRESENT	TYPE OF MOUTHPARTS	LOCATION OF GILLS

TYPE OF GILLS— FEATHERY OR CYLINDRICAL	BODY SHAPE	OTHER CHARACTERISTICS	LEVEL OF CLASSIFICATION: ORDER

41 Diversity Of Vertebrates

Vertebrates are animals with a dorsal row of bones or cartilage surrounding a nerve cord. The individual bones are called vertebrae. Vertebrae are connected by joints so they are movable and flexible. The vertebral column, or backbone, functions in movement and support. Vertebrates are placed in Phylum Chordata. All chordates are bilaterally symmetrical. At some stage in their development they have a hollow dorsal nerve cord, a stiff rodlike notochord made of cartilage, and gill slits or pouches in the region of the pharynx. In more complex chordates, the notochord is replaced by vertebrae and the slits are found only in embryos.

Chordata is divided into four subphyla. Subphylum Vertebrata is further divided into seven classes. Two of the seven classes are endotherms. Their body temperatures are maintained at a fairly constant temperature. The temperature of a specific warm-blooded animal will vary only a few degrees Celsius, regardless of the temperature of its environment. Vertebrates make up less than five percent of the animal kingdom—about 55 000 species.

In this investigation, you are to observe examples of the subphylum Vertebrata displayed on the laboratory tables. You are to describe and distinguish those traits which separate the vertebrates into classes. From your data, you are to construct a dichotomous key of the vertebrate classes you observed.

Materials *(per class)*

various labeled vertebrates

Procedure

Before beginning your observations of the specimens, construct a table similar to Table 1 for the number of specimens indicated by your teacher. Numbered specimens of vertebrates are displayed in containers throughout the laboratory. The specimens will be labeled with their common name, biological name, and the class to which they belong.

Move from station to station on a signal given by your teacher. Observe each specimen for a short period of time (two to five minutes) then move to the next station. Record specific information about each organism in the appropriate place in your table. The parts of some specimens are labeled to help you differentiate between complicated structures.

From the data in the table, construct a dichotomous key of the vertebrate classes. This key should be similar to the key of Investigation 39. Use characteristics of a class that will separate it from all other vertebrate classes. To help you get started, two sample statements have been provided. You may begin with other statements if you wish.

1a. Fins present.. Go to 2
1b. Fins absent.. Go to 3

TABLE 1. CHARACTERISTICS OF VERTEBRATE SPECIMENS					
NAME AND CLASS OF ORGANISM	TEETH	TAIL	NUMBER OF APPENDAGES PRESENT	EYES	OTHER FEATURES

After you have completed your key, exchange keys with a classmate. Try to use each other's keys to identify the organisms.

Formulating Generalizations

1. Are there any classes that have no distinctive characteristics that separate them from other classes?
2. Arrange the classes in order from the least complex to the most complex. What structures or features aid you in arranging the classes in complexity?
3. Which classes seem to be closely related to each other?
4. What features other than a vertebral column are found in all vertebrate classes?
5. Are the same features found in any of the invertebrates?
6. In what way is Class Agnatha different from all other vertebrate classes?
7. How is a salamander similar to a lizard? How do they differ?
8. How does the scaly skin of fishes and reptiles differ?
9. What features are common to all vertebrates?
10. What feature do all chordates share?
11. What features of vertebrates did you include in your key?
12. Why did you pick these features?
13. Is your key exactly like the key your classmate constructed? Explain.
14. How would you go about devising a key that separates a class of animals into families?
15. How would a key like the one described in question 14 differ from a key that separates a phylum (or subphylum) into classes?

42 Reproduction In Yeasts

Budding is a form of asexual (vegetative) reproduction found in simpler organisms such as yeasts. A new cell, the bud, develops as a small, swollen area on a parent yeast cell. Several buds may grow on a single parent cell. Each bud separates from the parent cell and leads an independent life. Because buds are produced by mitosis, they are genetically the same as the parent yeast cell.

Yeasts can reproduce by forming spores. Monoploid spores form by meiosis within a saclike structure called the ascus. The spores break free from the ascus and act as "resting stages" within the life cycle of yeast. When the spores land in a favorable environment, the spores germinate and the yeast can bud. The environment must have a sugar source such as fruit. The buds become independent yeast organisms and break down the sugar. When the sugar supply is depleted, a pair of yeast cells will fuse to form a diploid cell. This diploid cell undergoes meiosis forming spores within an ascus. The spores can again "rest" until conditions for growth are favorable.

In this investigation, you are to locate the structures of yeast cells. You are also to identify and count the cells with buds and the asci containing spores.

Materials *(per team of two students)*

- test tubes, small—4 (15 mL)
- yeast suspension
- dropper—2
- 0% sugar solution
- 1% sugar solution
- 2% sugar solution
- 4% sugar solution
- budding yeast suspension
- graduated cylinder—10 mL
- microscope
- glass slides—2
- coverslips—2
- paper cup
- aluminum foil, 3 cm × 3 cm—4
- masking tape
- marking pen
- water

Procedure

Part A. Preparing a Yeast Culture

Obtain four small test tubes, four pieces of aluminum foil, and four pieces of masking tape. Place a piece of masking tape on each of the tubes and label them A, B, C, and D. Add 10 mL of the solution labeled "0% sugar" to tube A, 10 mL of 1% sugar solution to tube B, 10 mL of 2% sugar solution to tube C, and 10 mL of 4% sugar solution to tube D. Add 10 drops of yeast suspension to each tube. Wrap the aluminum foil tightly over the opening of each tube to make a seal. Stand the four tubes in the paper cup overnight. Put the names of all students in your team on the cup.

Part B. Yeast Reproduction

Use a dropper to place a drop of budding yeast suspension on a second clean, dry slide. Add a coverslip and locate a single yeast cell under low power. Observe the cell on high power and locate the cell wall, nucleus, and vacuole. Locate a yeast cell that has one or several smaller cells attached to it in a chain. These cells form a budding yeast cell (Figure 2). Make a labeled drawing of a budding yeast cell in your notebook.

Part C. Growth in Yeast Cultures

After the yeast cultures prepared in Part A have incubated for 24 hours, remove the foil covers from the tubes. Smell each tube and record the strength of the odor.

Stir the contents of tube A by drawing it into a dropper and expelling the media several times. Put a drop of yeast culture A on a clean, dry slide and add a coverslip. Locate the yeast cells under low and high powers of your microscope. Using high power, count the number of yeast cells in one field of view. Keep track of the number of single cells, and cells with buds. Also record the number of buds per cell. If the field of view contains too many cells to count, make a dilution by adding one drop of yeast suspension to a tube and adding 9 drops of water. Shake the tube gently and make a wet mount from the diluted culture. Record your results in a table similar to Table 1.

Repeat this procedure for four more fields of view of the same culture. Repeat again using the other yeast cultures (Tubes B, C, and D). You will have to make a separate table for each culture. If you have made a dilution of any of the tubes, multiply each of your counts by 10, since your sample was diluted 10 times.

FIGURE 1

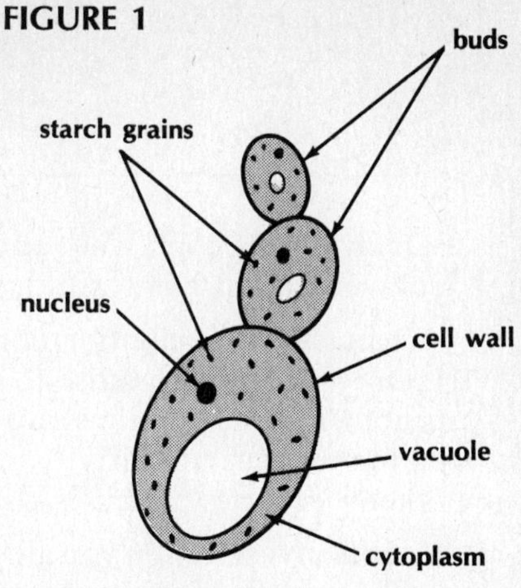

Budding Yeast

Formulating Generalizations

1. Which of the test tubes had an odor? Why was the odor present?
2. Which tubes have a weak odor or no odor at all?
3. Describe the difference between a single yeast cell and one that is budding.
4. Which of the four test tubes you examined had the greatest number of single yeast cells? Why?
5. Which tube had the greatest number of budding cells? Why?
6. What was the greatest number of buds seen on any one cell?
7. Why were sugar solutions of different concentrations used?
8. What conditions could cause the formation of spores? Where would these conditions exist in nature?

TABLE 1. TOTAL NUMBER OF CELLS IN ONE SAMPLE

TEST TUBE LETTER ________

TYPE OF YEAST CELL OBSERVED	FIELD OF VIEW OBSERVED					TOTAL
	1	2	3	4	5	
Single cell						
Cell with one bud						
Cell with many buds						

43 Vegetative Reproduction In Duckweed

Duckweed is a small aquatic plant which floats on the surface of ponds, lakes, and streams. A duckweed plant has leaflike structures called fronds.

Vegetative reproduction of this plant occurs as a frond produces new daughter fronds (Figure 1). One frond can give rise to two or three daughter fronds. As the daughter fronds increase in number, the plant divides into separate plants. If conditions such as mineral content of the water and photosynthetic activity are good, a new plant can be formed within 24 hours. The genetic makeup of a new plant is the same as that of the parent plant.

In this investigation you are to observe the vegetative reproduction of duckweed and count the number of offspring produced in various solutions over a two-week period.

Materials *(per student or team)*

duckweed plants—12
Knop's solution—100 mL
glass marking pencil
small culture dishes—4
stereomicroscope
cow manure solution—100 mL
0.1% 5-10-5 fertilizer solution—100 mL
distilled water—100 mL
petri dish

Procedure

Place a duckweed plant in a petri dish bottom and examine it with a stereomicroscope. Locate the fronds and rootlet (Figure 2). Make a sketch of the plant in your lab notebook.

Label four culture dishes 1 to 4. Fill the culture dishes ¾ full with the following: dish 1, Knop's solution; dish 2, cow manure solution; dish 3, 0.1% 5-10-5 fertilizer solution; dish 4, distilled water.

Into each culture dish place three duckweed plants. Place the dishes in a well lighted area.

Each day for the next two weeks, count the total number of plants observed in the culture dishes. Record the number of plants in a table similar to Table 1 in your lab notebook. Construct a graph of your data similar to the graph in Figure 3. Your graph should show all four solutions used. Use the key given to represent the four solutions.

FIGURE 1

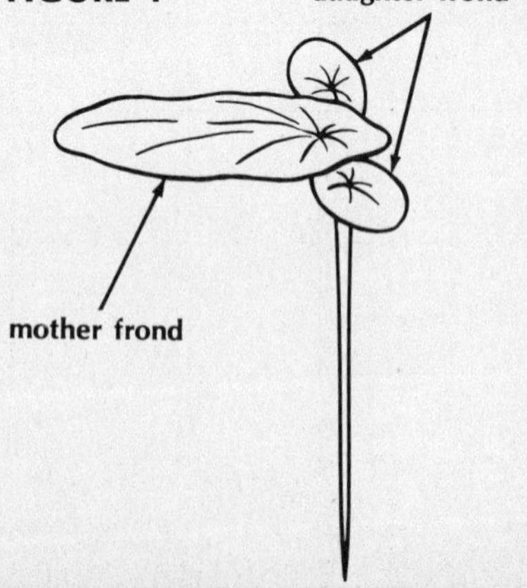

FIGURE 2

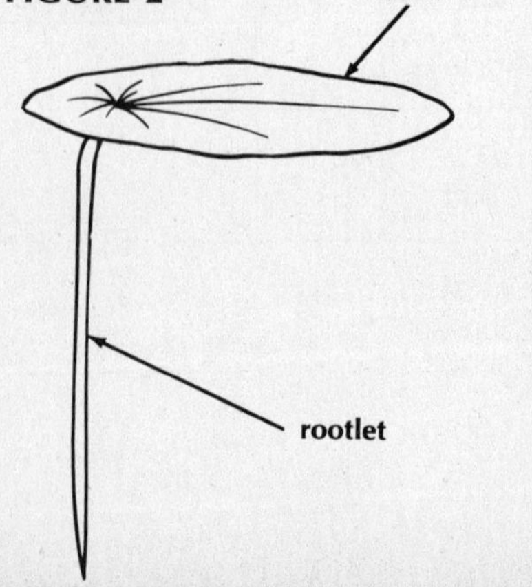

TABLE 1. NUMBER OF PLANTS EACH DAY														
	DAYS													
	1	2	3	4	5	6	7	8	9	10	11	12	13	14
dish 1														
dish 2														
dish 3														
dish 4														

Formulating Generalizations

1. How do mother and daughter fronds differ?
2. What happens to the parent plant as the number of daughter fronds increases?
3. Describe the appearance of a healthy duckweed plant.
4. Describe the appearance of an unhealthy plant.
5. Why was one culture dish set up with distilled water?
6. Which dish showed the greatest duckweed growth? Why?
7. Which dish showed the poorest growth? Why?
8. What factors besides minerals could be used in another experiment to study duckweed growth?
9. Why is the genetic makeup of a duckweed plant vegetatively produced the same as the makeup of the parent plant?

FIGURE 3

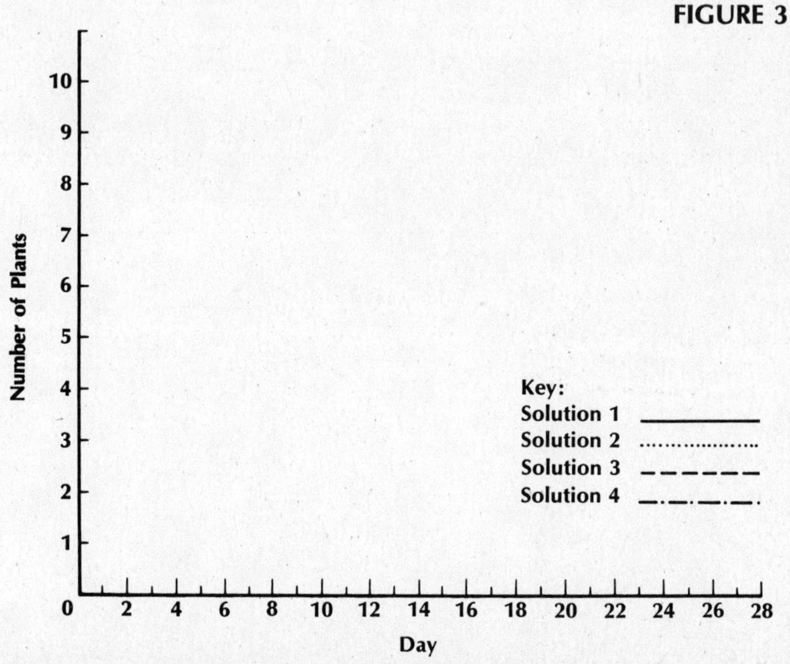

Regeneration In Planarians

44

Planaria are freshwater flatworms that live in ponds and streams. Planaria are carnivorous and scavengers; they eat smaller, slow moving animals as well as dead animals. Planaria can reproduce asexually by a process called fragmentation and regeneration. If a planarian loses part of its body, it can regenerate new tissues from the existing living tissues. If a piece of the animal tears off, this small, torn piece can regenerate into a complete organism. A new organism produced by regeneration has the same genetic makeup as the parent.

In this investigation, you are to compare and describe the regeneration of planarians when cut in four different ways.

Materials *(per student or team)*

planaria—2 or 4
9 cm petri dishes—2 or 3
razor blade or scalpel
microscope slide
water
glass marking pencil
stereomicroscope
camel's hair brush
watch glass or depression slide
pasteurized spring or pond water
paper towel

Procedure

Remove a planarian from the culture dish with a camel's hair brush and place it in a watch glass or depression slide. Observe the planarian with a stereomicroscope. Locate the eyespots, auricles, and pharynx (Figure 1).

Transfer the planarian to a clean microscope slide containing a drop of water. Allow the planarian to extend its body longitudinally. If the planarian fails to extend, remove some of the water with a corner of a paper towel. When extended, cut the planarian into sections with a razor blade or scalpel. **CAUTION:** *Always be careful with sharp instruments. Cut away from your fingers to avoid cuts.* Make one of the cuts assigned to you by your teacher. Make all cuts as you observe the planarian with the stereomicroscope. Repeat with a second planarian.

After cutting, place each section of the same type into a separate petri dish. Make a sketch of the cuts in your laboratory notebook. Label the petri dishes and place them in a cool area designated by your teacher. Do not feed the planaria during regeneration.

Cut 1

Remove the heads of two planaria immediately below the auricles (Figure 2). Place the heads in one petri dish half full of pasteurized water. Put the tails in another petri dish with the same amount of pasteurized water. Use a camel's hair brush to transfer the cut sections.

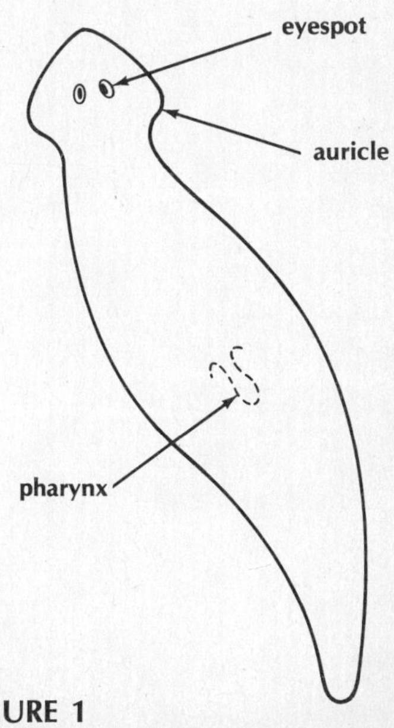

FIGURE 1

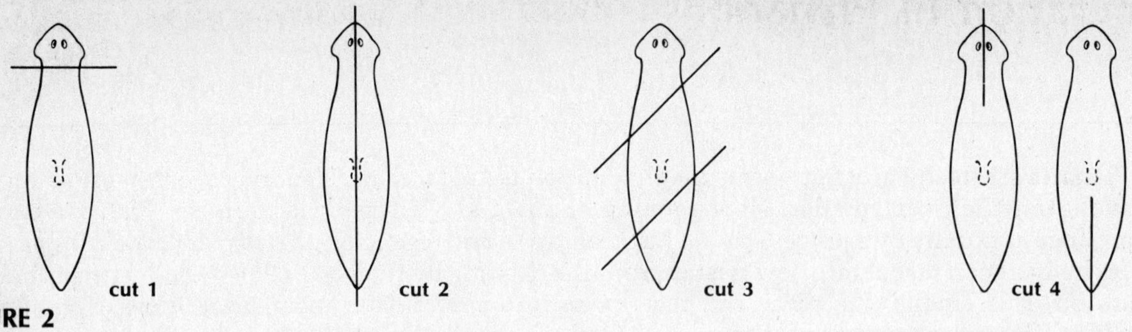

FIGURE 2

Cut 2

Divide two planaria in half longitudinally as shown in Figure 2. Place the right halves in a petri dish half full of pasteurized water. Put the left halves in another petri dish with the same amount of pasteurized water. Use a camel's hair brush to transfer the cut sections.

Cut 3

Divide two planaria into three sections as shown in Figure 2. Place the heads in one petri dish half full of pasteurized water, the midsections in another petri dish half full of pasteurized water, and the tails in a third petri dish half full of pasteurized water. Use a camel's hair brush to transfer the cut sections.

Cut 4

Starting at the anterior (head) end, make a longitudinal cut one-third down the midline of two planaria. Starting at the posterior end, make a longitudinal cut one-third down the midline of two more planaria. Place the planaria with anterior cuts in one petri dish half full of pasteurized water and the planaria with posterior cuts in another petri dish half full of pasteurized water. Because these parts are not detached it is essential to keep the cut sections apart for at least four days. The cut sections will grow together again; therefore, recut the planarians each day.

Observations

Observe the planarian sections on the first, third, seventh, and fourteenth days after the cutting. Change the water after seven days. Record any changes by giving descriptions and making diagrams. Remove any pieces that appear to be dead. Collect class data on the four different cuts.

Formulating Generalizations

1. Did you notice any differences in length, width, or color in the regenerating sections of your planaria? Explain.
2. Which sections grew into complete, new planaria?
3. Which planaria showed color changes along the margin where you cut them?
4. Which sections appeared to regenerate faster than others?
5. Are there any observable differences between the old tissue and the new regenerating tissue?
6. Why is the genetic makeup of a planarian produced by regeneration the same as that of the parent?

Ingestion And Digestion In *Hydra* And Planaria

49

Mechanical digestion is the process of breaking down food by chewing or grinding. Some simpler organisms do not have structures to mechanically grind ingested food prior to chemical digestion. *Hydra* and planaria are two such organisms.

Hydra engulf their food whole. Unlike protists, *Hydra* ingest food almost as long and wide as their body column (Figure 1). Although *Hydra* are slow moving animals and often are attached, they have little difficulty in capturing other small invertebrates. *Hydra* use stinging cells called nematocysts for capturing food. Nematocysts are located on tentacles. Following food capture, the tentacles guide the food to the mouth. Chemical digestion begins in the gastrovascular cavity after the food is ingested. Small particles are taken into the cells lining the cavity where further digestion occurs.

Planarians locate food and hover over it. They ingest living, dead, and decaying animal matter. Food is ingested through the pharynx. Cells lining the intestine are thought to ingest small particles of food and chemically digest them.

In this investigation, you are to locate and identify the ingestive and digestive organs of a *Hydra* and a planarian. After feeding the two organisms, you are to describe the processes of ingestion and digestion.

Materials *(per student or team)*

- dropper
- *Hydra*
- planarian
- brine shrimp culture
- small piece of liver
- single depression slide
- microscope
- stereomicroscope
- aquarium water
- scalpel
- forceps
- watch glass
- water

Procedure

Before class, construct a table similar to Table 1 for your observations.

Part A. *Hydra*

With a dropper, transfer a *Hydra* to a depression slide containing a drop of aquarium water. Place the slide on the stage of the stereomicroscope. Locate the mouth, column, and tentacles (Figure 1). Place the slide on the stage of a compound microscope and using low power again locate the mouth, column, and tentacles.

Wash some brine shrimp as directed by your teacher. Place the depression slide containing the *Hydra* on the stage of the stereomicroscope. While observing the *Hydra*, add five or six washed brine shrimp to the depression containing the *Hydra*. Observe the behavior of the *Hydra* from the time it makes contact with a brine shrimp until it has completely ingested the brine shrimp. You may be able to observe egestion (removal of undigested material from the organism). Repeat the feeding and observation using the low power lens of the compound microscope. Record all observations in your data table.

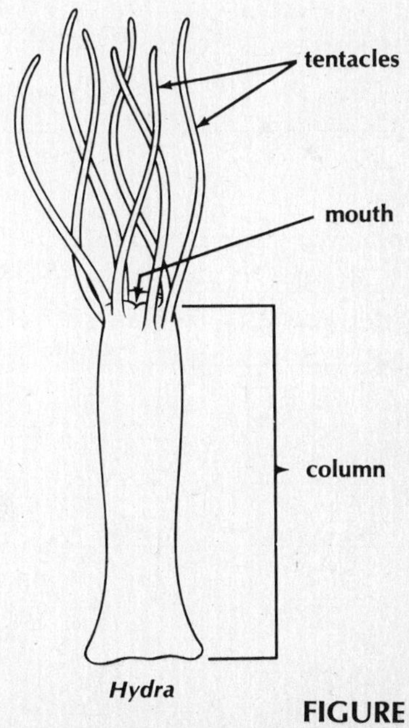

FIGURE 1

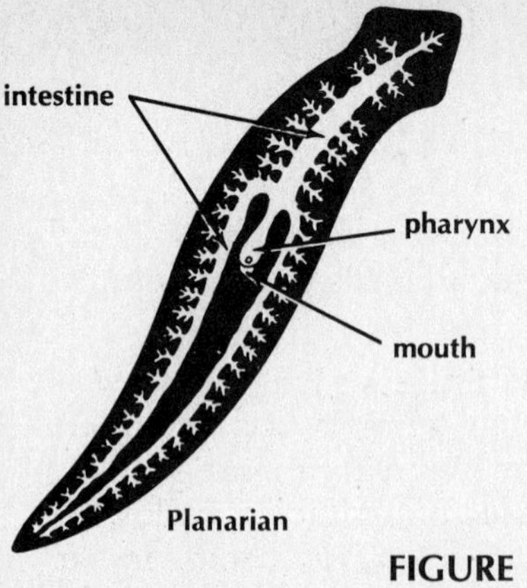

FIGURE 2

Part B. Planaria

With a dropper, transfer a planarian from the culture dish to a watch glass. Add enough aquarium water so the animal can glide freely over a small area of the dish. Place the watch glass on the stage of a stereomicroscope. Observe the planarian and locate the mouth, pharynx, and intestine (Figure 2). With a scalpel mince a piece of liver into a fine mass. **CAUTION:** *Always be careful when using a scalpel or other sharp instruments. Cut away from your fingers to avoid cuts.* Place a drop of minced liver in the watch glass near the planarian. Observe the pharynx as it is extended through the mouth. As the organism removes small particles from the liver, they will flow into the intestines. After 30 minutes of feeding, examine the intestines. Record any changes in size and color of the intestines in your data table.

Formulating Generalizations

1. Are nematocysts found on any part of *Hydra* other than the tentacles? If so, which part?
2. What happens when brine shrimp come in contact with the column of the *Hydra*?
3. Could your *Hydra* sting more than one brine shrimp at a time? If so, how many paralyzed shrimp did you observe?
4. How many brine shrimp were ingested by your *Hydra* during the lab period? Compare your data with data of other members of the class.
5. Describe extracellular digestion in the *Hydra*.
6. What response occurred when brine shrimp came in contact with *Hydra's* tentacles?
7. How did planaria respond when contacting food?
8. Describe the action of the pharynx of a planarian as it comes in contact with food.
9. Describe extracellular digestion in planaria.
10. How is digestion in *Hydra* and planaria similar?
11. Why do you think biologists call *Hydra* and planaria chunk feeders?
12. What do you think would be the advantages of a "hollow-cavity" type of digestive system?
13. What do you think would be some disadvantages of a "hollow-cavity" type of digestive system?

TABLE 1. OBSERVATIONS OF *HYDRA* AND PLANARIA

ORGANISM	OBSERVATIONS
Hydra	
Planaria	

Digestion Of Starches, Proteins, And Fats In Humans

50

Chemical digestion is the process in which large, complex molecules are chemically broken down into smaller usable compounds. In general, the substances responsible for digestion are called digestive juices. Digestive juices contain enzymes. Digestion of most substances occurs in a series of steps. Each step involves a specific enzyme.

Digestive enzymes are secreted by specialized cells in the digestive system. Other substances that aid in digestion are also secreted by specialized cells.

Digestive juices in the mouth contain a mixture of water, mucus, and an enzyme. The enzyme is amylase. It converts starch into a sugar called maltose. Digestive juices of the stomach contain mostly water, hydrochloric acid, and the enzymes pepsin and rennin. The enzymes break down proteins.

Intestinal digestive juice contains mainly water, bile salts, and lipase. They are responsible for breakdown of fats. Also in the intestines are digestive juices that break down proteins and carbohydrates.

In this investigation, you are to set up several test tubes containing artificial digestive juices and food samples containing fats, starches, and proteins. You are to describe the process of digestion of each food type and determine the materials necessary for digestion.

Materials *(per team of two students)*

Part A

- test tubes, 12 × 100 mm—9
- test tube rack
- glass marker
- mortar and pestle
- rolled oats—3 cm³
- distilled water
- dropper
- starch suspension—3 mL
- Gram's iodine solution—2 mL
- Benedict's solution—2 mL
- burner
- test tube holder
- beakers, 50 mL—2
- 0.2% diastase—7 mL
- boiling water bath

Part B

- test tubes, 12 × 100 mm—9
- cooking oil—9 mL
- test tube rack
- glass marking pencil
- 2% bile solution—3 mL
- 1% pancreatin solution—12 mL
- 1% litmus solution—1 mL

Part C

- test tubes, 12 × 100 mm—12
- test tube rack
- glass marking pencil
- hard boiled egg
- scalpel
- distilled water—4.5 mL
- 1% pepsin solution—9 mL
- 0.5% sodium bicarbonate solution—4.5 mL
- 0.5% hydrochloric acid solution—4.5 mL
- Biuret solution—24 mL

Per class

- refrigerator
- 37°C water bath

Procedure

Part A. Starch Digestion

Place nine clean, dry test tubes in a rack. Label the test tubes one to nine. Set up a table in your notebook similar to Table 1. Record the proper data in the table for each test tube. For each substance added to a test tube, record a checkmark in the proper row of the table. Indicate the test, environment, and test result. With a mortar and pestle, grind 3 cm^3 of rolled oats into a fine powder. To test tubes one and two, add 0.5 cm^3 of ground rolled oats and 2 mL of distilled water. Allow the test tubes to stand for ten minutes. Test the contents of test tube one for starch by adding four to five drops of Gram's iodine solution to the test tube. **CAUTION:** *If iodine spillage occurs, rinse with water.* If starch is present, the solution will turn blue-black in color. Test the contents of test tube two for sugar by adding eight drops of Benedict's solution to the test tube. Place the test tube in the boiling water bath for four minutes. **CAUTION:** *Always be careful around open flames. Secure all loose hair and clothing before lighting flame.* Note any color change with boiling. The presence of a green, yellow, or red color indicates the presence of sugar (Investigation 5). Record the presence or absence of sugar as − (blue), + (green), + + (yellow), + + + (orange), + + + + (brick red).

Add 2 mL of diastase to test tube three. Test the diastase for sugar. If your diastase is positive for sugar, you will have to use diastase from another container.

To test tubes four, five, and six add 0.5 cm^3 of ground rolled oats and 2 mL of diastase. Place test tube five on a shelf in the classroom. Record the temperature of the room in degrees Celsius. Place test tube six in a 37°C water bath. **CAUTION:** *Glass and water are hot. Do not touch with unprotected hands.* After ten minutes, test each test tube for the presence or absence of sugar.

To test tubes seven, eight, and nine add 1 mL of starch suspension and 2 mL of diastase. Place test tube seven in the refrigerator, test tube eight on a shelf in the classroom, and test tube nine in the 37°C water bath. After ten minutes, test each test tube for the presence or absence of sugar.

TABLE 1. TESTS FOR CARBOHYDRATE DIGESTION

TEST TUBE	OATS (0.5 cm^3)	WATER (2 mL)	DIASTASE (2 mL)	STARCH (1 mL)	TEST	ENVIRONMENT	RESULTS
1							
2							
3							
4							
8							
9							

Part B. Fat Digestion

Place nine clean, dry test tubes in a test tube rack. Label the test tubes one to nine. Set up a table in your notebook similar to Table 2. Record the proper data in the table for each test tube. For each substance added to a test tube, record the data in the proper column. Also indicate the environment and test result for each test tube. Add 1 mL of cooking oil and 0.1 mL of litmus solution to each tube. To test tubes one, two, four, five, seven, and eight add 0.5 mL of 0.5% bile solution. To test tubes two, three, five, six, eight, and nine add 2 mL of 1% pancreatin solution. Shake all tubes gently. Place test tubes one, two, and three in the refrigerator at 4°C. Place test tubes four, five, and six on a shelf in the classroom. Place test tubes seven, eight, and nine in a water bath at 37°C. Let the test tubes stand for 24 hours. Record the change in color in each test tube. If the solution turns from blue to pink, fat has been changed to fatty acid and glycerol.

TABLE 2. TESTS FOR FAT DIGESTION

TEST TUBE	COOKING OIL (1 mL)	LITMUS (0.1 mL)	BILE (0.5 mL)	PANCREATIN (2 mL)	ENVIRONMENT	RESULTS
1						
2						
3						
9						

TABLE 3. TESTS FOR PROTEIN DIGESTION

TEST TUBE	EGG WHITE (0.5 cm³)	WATER (1.5 mL)	PEPSIN (1.5 mL)	HCl (1.5 mL)	SODIUM BICARBONATE (1.5 mL)	ENVIRONMENT	RESULTS
1							
2							
9							
10							
11							
12							

Part C. Protein Digestion

Place twelve clean, dry test tubes in a test tube rack. Label the test tubes 1 to 12. Set up a table in your notebook similar to Table 3. Record the proper data in the table for each test tube. For each substance added to a test tube, record the amount in the proper column. Also indicate the environment and test results for each test tube. With a scalpel, chop the white of a hard cooked egg into small pieces. **CAUTION:** *Always be careful when using scalpels or other sharp instruments. Cut away from your fingers to avoid cuts.* Place 0.5 cm^3 of finely chopped egg white in each of the test tubes. To test tubes one, five, and nine add 1.5 mL of distilled water. To test tubes three, seven, and eleven add 1.5 mL of pepsin solution and 1.5 mL of hydrochloric acid solution. **CAUTION:** *Hydrochloric acid can cause burns. If spillage occurs, rinse with water and call your teacher.* To test tubes four, eight, and twelve add 1.5 mL of pepsin solution and 1.5 mL of sodium bicarbonate solution. Place test tubes one, two, three, and four in the refrigerator at 2°C. Place test tubes five, six, seven, and eight on a shelf in the classroom. Place test tubes nine, ten, eleven, and twelve in a water bath at 37°C. Allow the test tubes to stand for twenty-four hours.

At the end of twenty-four hours, observe the material in each test tube. Use the Biuret test to determine whether protein digestion has occurred in each test tube. Place 2 mL of Biuret solution in the twelve test tubes. If a purple color results, the intermediate compounds of protein digestion are present. Thus, protein digestion has occurred (Investigation 5).

Formulating Generalizations

1. Why was it necessary to test the diastase for sugar?
2. What role does diastase play in the process of digestion?
3. Is there a connection between temperature and the rate of digestion? Explain.
4. Why would you expect the starch to be digested more quickly in the starch suspension than in the rolled oats?
5. In which solution(s) did protein digestion appear to be more complete? Explain.
6. Did hydrochloric acid or sodium bicarbonate have any effect on the action of pepsin? If so, describe the effect and explain.
7. Why was water the only substance added to the chopped eggs in some of the tubes?
8. In which test tube did fat digestion appear to be more complete? Why?
9. What is the relationship between pancreatin and bile salts in fat digestion?
10. How would rate of digestion differ if more starches, fats, or proteins were added to the proper tubes? Explain.

Root Anatomy

51

Cells in simple plants are relatively uniform in structure. However, cells in the tracheophytes are widely diverse in size, structure, and function. Tracheophyte cells are organized into four main tissues—protective, vascular, meristematic, and fundamental. Protective tissue surrounds the outside of a root and the rest of the plant. This tissue is composed of epidermis and/or cork cells. Vascular tissue contains cells which conduct materials such as water, minerals, and food to the organs of the plant. It also provides support. Two of the major vascular tissues are xylem and phloem. Fundamental tissue includes storage areas and cells where food is manufactured. This tissue also provides support. Meristematic tissue is growth tissue. It produces new cells which develop into the other three types of tissues.

In this investigation, you are to observe and identify the various tissues in herbaceous monocot and dicot roots, the area of lateral root origin, and *Tilia* root. You are to compare the relative sizes of each cell type observed. You are also to observe and identify primary and secondary roots from different types of root systems.

Materials *(per team of two students)*

prepared slides:
- monocot root cross section
- dicot root cross section
- lateral root origin cross section
- *Tilia* root cross section

hand lens

compound microscopes—2

specimens of different types of root systems

Procedure

Part A. Herbaceous Monocot and Dicot Roots

Observe the monocot and dicot root slides on low power, then on high power of your microscope. For each root, locate and identify the

FIGURE 1

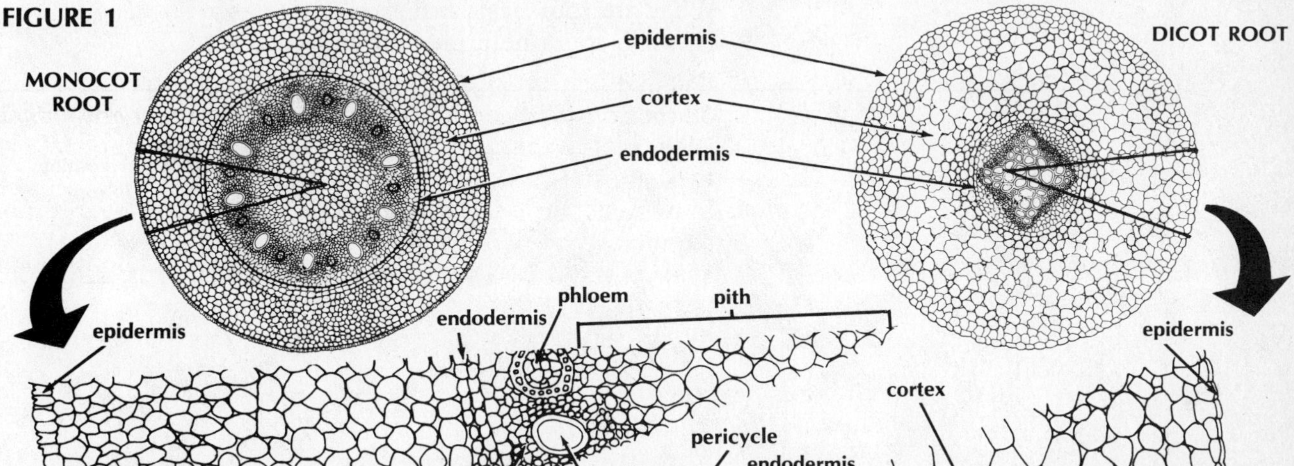

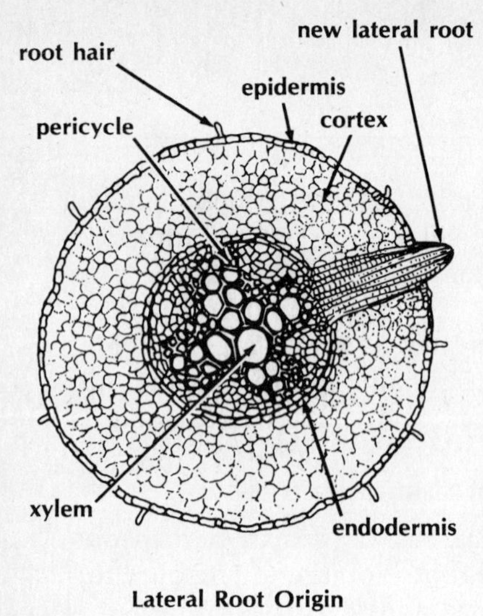

Lateral Root Origin

FIGURE 2

epidermis, cortex, endodermis, pith; xylem, pericyle, and phloem (Figure 1). Determine whether each cell type is protective, vascular, fundamental, or meristematic tissue. Compare the relative size of each type of cell. Make a sketch of each type of cell.

Part B. *Tilia* Root

Observe the *Tilia* root on low power, then on high power of your microscope. Locate and identify the cork, pericycle, phloem, xylem, cambium, vascular rays, and endodermis. Determine whether each cell type is protective, vascular, fundamental, or meristematic tissue. Compare the relative size of each cell type. Make a sketch of each type of cell.

Part C. Lateral Root Origin

Observe the slide of the area of lateral root origin on low power, then on high power. Determine the tissue from which the lateral root is growing. (See Figure 2.) Make a sketch of your observations.

Part D. Root Systems

Using a hand lens and Figure 3, observe the root systems of the specimens provided. Decide which type of root system you are observing, and locate the primary and secondary roots on each specimen.

Formulating Generalizations

1. The blue-stained material in the cortex of the dicot root is starch. Why is it found in the root and how did it get there?
2. From what specific tissue does a lateral root originate? Is it meristematic? Why?
3. What type of cells make up the larger portion of a woody root? What are the functions of these cells?
4. How do xylem patterns differ in monocot and dicot roots?
5. How do tap root systems differ from fibrous root systems?
6. Which root system, tap or fibrous, is more similar to an adventitious root system? Explain.
7. Out of what plant part do adventitious roots grow?
8. What are four basic functions of roots?
9. How do roots help prevent soil erosion?

FIGURE 3

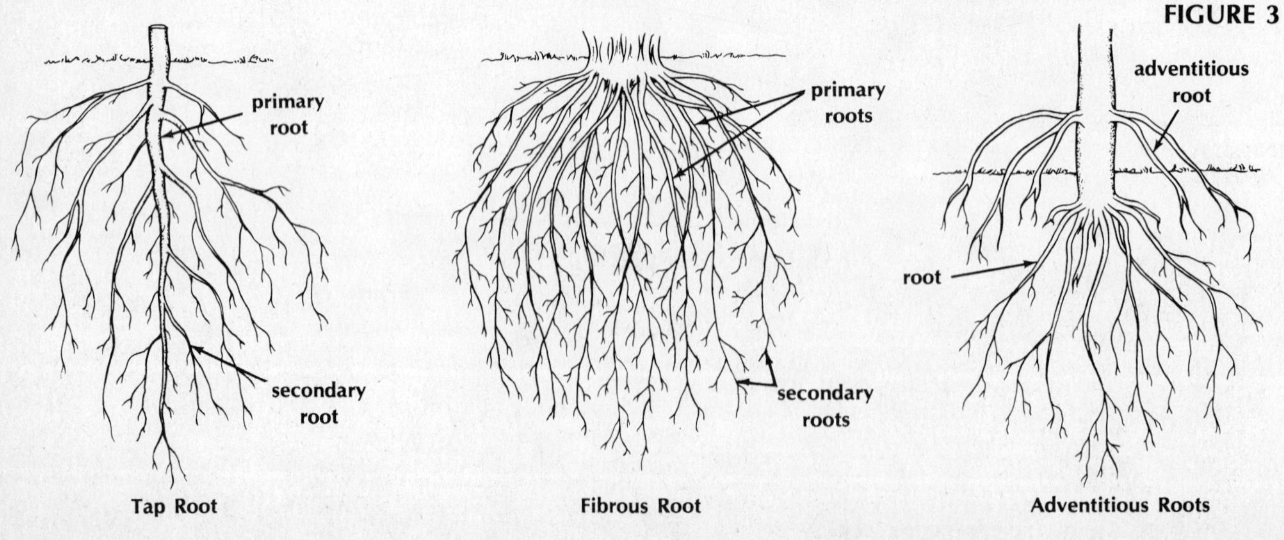

Stem Anatomy

52

As in roots, protective, vascular, fundamental, and meristematic tissues are found in stems. The difference between roots and stems may be slight or significant.

In this investigation, you are to observe and identify the tissues in a herbaceous monocot stem, a herbaceous dicot stem, and a woody stem. You are to compare the relative size of each cell to the other cells and make sketches of each. You are to observe and identify the external parts of a woody twig and determine the pattern of leaf arrangement.

Materials *(per team of two students)*

prepared slide of monocot stem cross section
hand lens
woody twigs—2
  1 alternate leaf pattern
  1 opposite leaf pattern
prepared slide of dicot stem cross section
microscope
prepared slide of three-year-old *Tilia* stem cross section

Procedure

Part A. Herbaceous Monocot and Dicot Stems

Observe the monocot and dicot slides on low power, then on high power of your microscope. For each stem, locate and identify the epidermis, cortex, fibrovascular bundles, xylem, phloem, cambium, and pith (Figure 1). List the function of each cell type. Determine

FIGURE 1

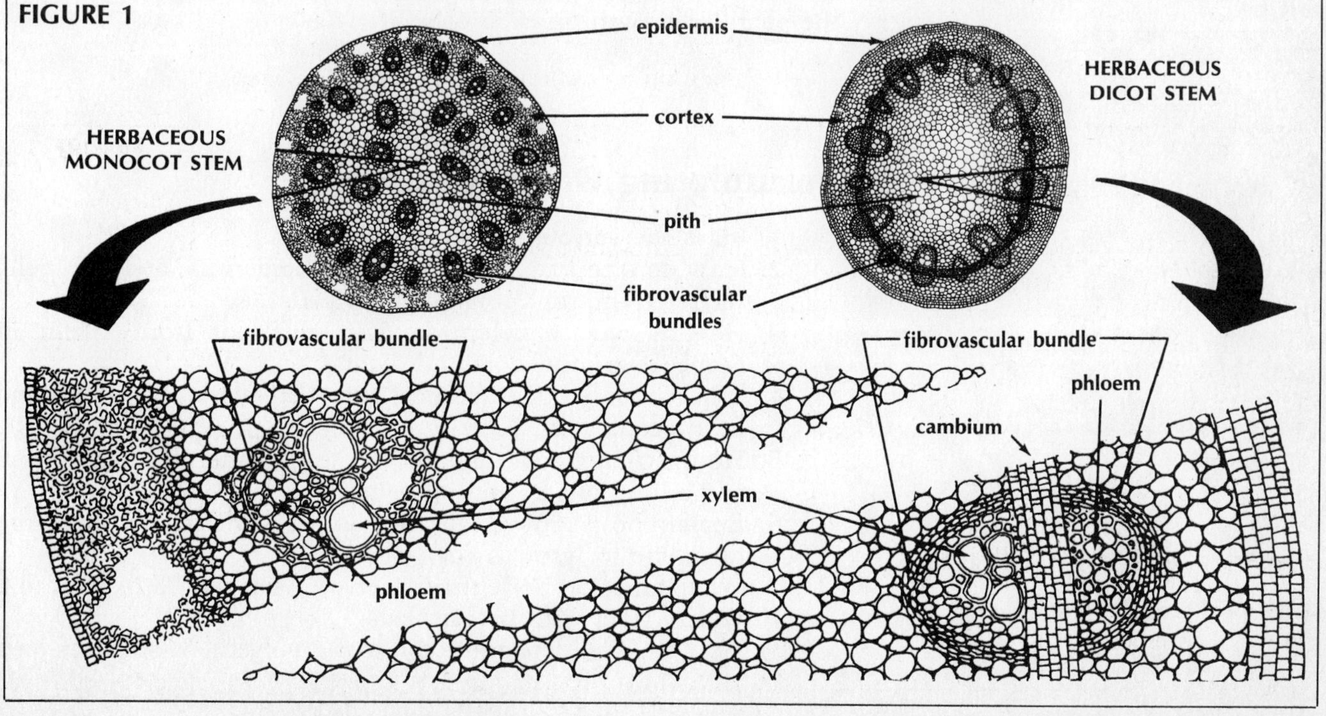

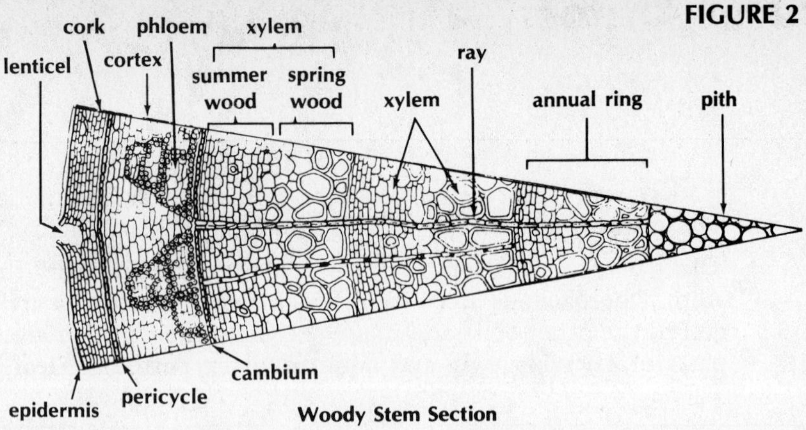

FIGURE 2

whether each cell type is protective, vascular, fundamental, or meristematic tissue. Compare the relative size of each cell to the other cells. Make a sketch of each type of cell.

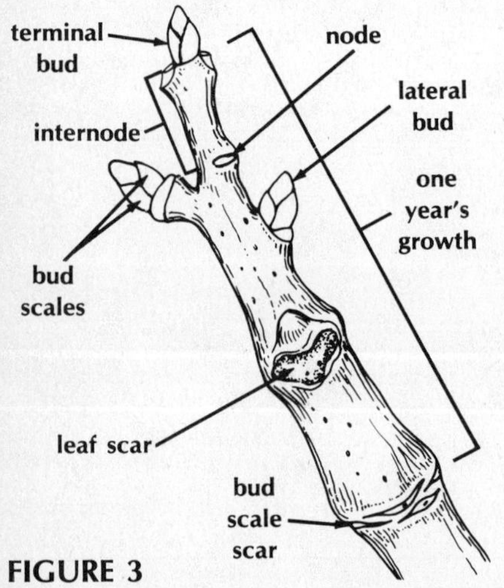

FIGURE 3

Part B. *Tilia* Stem

Observe the *Tilia* root on low power, then on high power of your microscope. Locate and identify the cork, pericycle, phloem, xylem, cambium, and vascular rays. Determine whether each cell type is protective, vascular, fundamental, or meristematic tissue. Compare the relative size of each cell type. Make a sketch of each type of cell.

Part C. Woody Twig

Observe two woody twigs with a hand lens. Locate and identify the terminal bud, lateral bud, lenticels, bud scale, bud scale scar, node, internode, and leaf scar (Figure 3). List the function of each part of a woody twig. Determine whether the stem has an alternate or opposite leaf arrangement.

The area between two bud scale scars is one year's growth. Count the years of growth on each of your twigs.

Formulating Generalizations

1. State the various functions of a stem.
2. How do size and shape of xylem, epidermis, and pith cells relate to the functions of those cells?
3. How is woody xylem in *Tilia* different from xylem in herbaceous monocots and dicots?
4. What other major differences exist between woody stems and herbaceous stems?
5. How do monocot and dicot stems differ in location of cambium, xylem, and phloem?
6. Explain how you would tell if one growing season was more favorable for growth than others.
7. What function do lenticels serve? What would happen to a woody twig with no lenticels?
8. How can you determine the past arrangement of leaves on a bare twig?

Leaf Structure And Function

53

Leaves are the main organs of food production and photosynthesis in green plants. In most plants, leaves are generally flattened. The flattened leaves have a large surface area for sun exposure. The flattened part of a leaf is called the blade (Figure 1). A leaf is attached to the stem of the plant by a petiole. The petiole contains vessels that carry water to the leaf (xylem) and carry food away from the leaf (phloem).

Leaf tissues are grouped into three types: epidermal, mesophyll, and vascular (Figure 2). Most leaves have all the tissues shown in Figure 2. However, some leaves have extra or fewer structures. Differences in leaf structures are adaptations to the type of environment in which the plant lives.

In this investigation, you are to observe prepared microscopic slides of leaf cross sections. You are to locate, identify, and distinguish the various structures. You are to describe the differences of the three types of tissues found in the seven leaf types.

Materials *(per student or team)*

microscope
prepared microscopic slides of leaf cross sections:
- *Elodea*
- alfalfa
- water lily
- corn (monocot)
- pear in sun
- pear in shade
- *Yucca*

Procedure

Prior to the laboratory period, prepare a table in your lab notebook similar to Table 1. Using low and high power of your microscope, examine the slides of the leaf cross sections. Locate cutin, epidermis, veins (xylem, phloem, and bundle sheath), palisade tissue, spongy tissue, guard cells, and stomata. Make a sketch of each cross section in your lab notebook. See Figure 2. Record your observations in the table in your notebook. Answer the specific questions for each type of leaf.

FIGURE 1

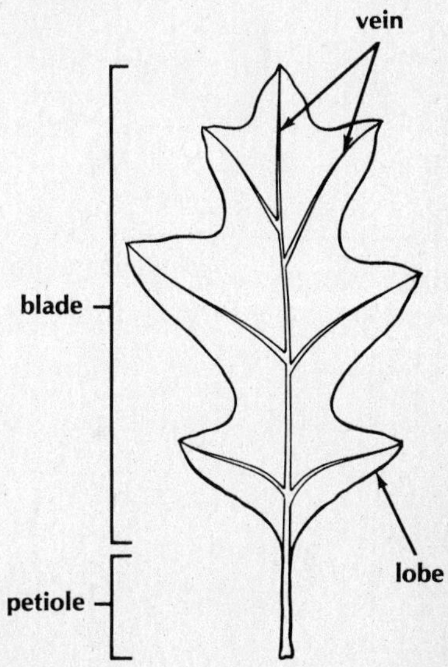

Leaf Anatomy

Part A. *Elodea*

1. How many cell layers thick is this leaf? **2.** Why are cutin, guard cells, and stomata absent? **3.** What other cells found in other leaves are not found in this leaf? **4.** What cells are responsible for photosynthesis? Give evidence for your answer.

Part B. Alfalfa

5. On which layer of epidermis are guard cells found? Why? **6.** How is the palisade tissue different from Figure 2?

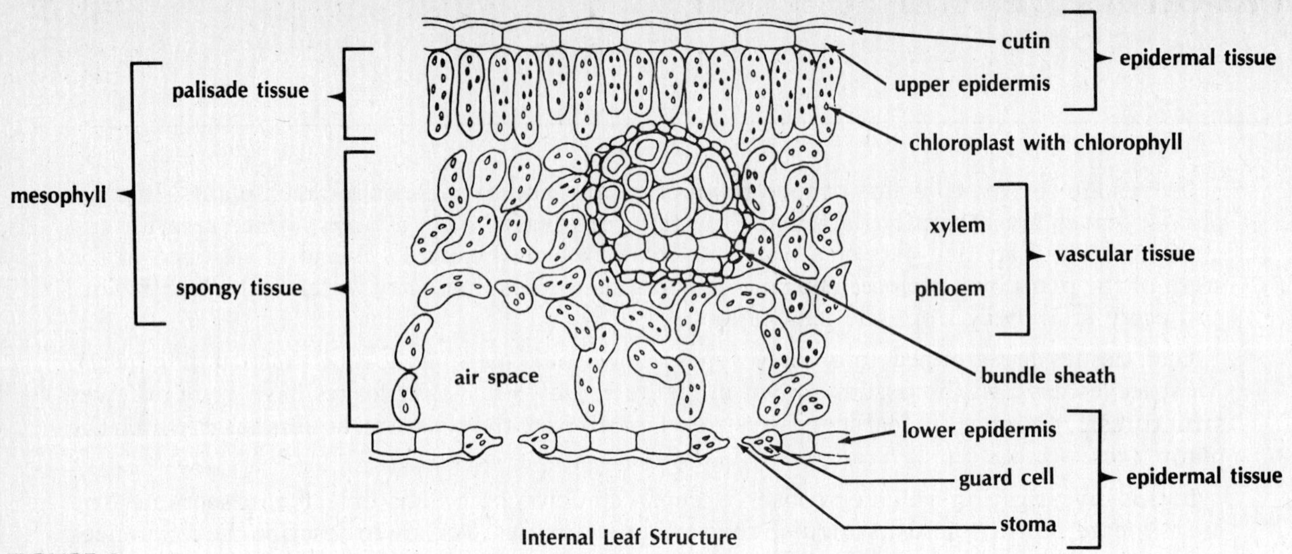

FIGURE 2

Part C. Pear in Sun and Pear in Shade

7. Compare the number of layers and length of the palisade tissue in the sun leaf and shade leaf. How are they different? **8.** Compare the number of layers and length of the spongy tissue in each leaf. How are they different?

Part D. Water lily

9. What differences did you notice between the xylem and phloem? **10.** Why are the air spaces in the spongy tissue two to four times larger than those in all other leaves? **11.** On which layer of epidermis, upper or lower, are the guard cells and stomata found? Why are stomata found here?

Part E. *Yucca* (desert plant)

12. Why do the guard cells and the stomata appear to be so small? **13.** Why are air spaces almost entirely absent?

Part F. Monocot and Dicot Leaves

14. Which leaf, monocot or dicot, appears to have veins that are more evenly spaced in cross section? Why? **15.** How are the palisade and spongy tissues of the monocot leaf different from the dicot leaf?

Formulating Generalizations

1. What determines the length of palisade cells?
2. Why are the bundle sheaths more prominent in some leaves than in others?
3. How do *Elodea* leaf veins differ from those in other leaves? Why are they different?
4. What does the thickness of the cutin have to do with the environment in which the plant lives?

TABLE 1. OBSERVATION OF LEAF CROSS SECTIONS

TYPE OF LEAF OBSERVED	STRUCTURES OF LEAF PRESENT (P) OR ABSENT (A)									FEATURES DIFFERENT FROM STRUCTURES IN FIGURE 49-2.
	CUTIN	EPI-DERMIS	XYLEM	PHLOEM	BUNDLE SHEATH	PALISADE LAYER	SPONGY LAYER	GUARD CELLS	STOMATA	
Elodea										
alfalfa										
water lily										
pear in sun										
pear in shade										
Yucca										
dicot										
monocot										

54 Transpiration In Plants

Water is absorbed through the root system of higher plants and carried upward through the stem to the leaves. Water is used chiefly in the process of photosynthesis; however, a large amount of the moved water is lost by transpiration. Transpiration is a process in which water evaporates through leaves. A corn plant transpires about 190 liters of water during a 100-day growing season. Transpiration is partially responsible for water movement from roots to leaves in a plant.

Water molecules have strong attractive forces which hold the molecules together. These forces cause water to exist as continuous columns from roots to leaves in a plant. As water evaporates from a leaf, the protoplasm begins to dry slightly. The drying protoplasm attracts water from other nearby cells that have a higher water content. These cells in turn attract water from the xylem vessels in the leaf. The leaf xylem attracts water from the stem xylem which attracts water from the root xylem. The root xylem attracts water from the surrounding cortex cells. Cortex receives water from the epidermal cells of the root.

In this investigation, you are to assemble a potometer, an instrument to determine plant water loss by transpiration, and determine the rate of transpiration in a given plant species. You are to determine the effect of certain environmental factors on transpiration rate.

Materials *(per student or team)*

burner
iron stand
test tube clamp
glass tubing—20 cm
rubber tubing—2 six-cm sections
beaker, 1000-mL
paper toweling
water
beaker large enough to hold the "U" tube
5-mL pipettes—2
cord—10 cm
razor blade or scalpel
potted plant
electric fan
spotlight or other bright light
petroleum jelly

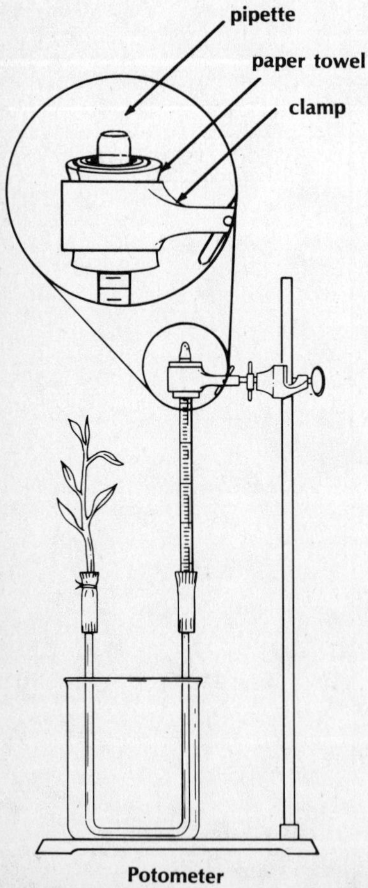

FIGURE 1

Procedure

Set up a potometer as shown in Figure 1. Make a cylinder out of a paper towel to cushion the pipette from the clamp. Insert the pipette through the cylinder, and fasten the test tube clamp firmly around the paper toweling. Mount the clamp and pipette on the iron stand. Heat a piece of glass tubing with the flame of a burner and bend it in the form of a "U." **CAUTION:** *Be careful around open flames. Secure loose hair and clothing before proceeding. Glass is hot. Do not touch with unprotected hands.* Attach the "U" tube to the 5-mL pipette with a six-centimeter length of rubber tubing. Make sure the rubber tubing fits snugly on the pipette and "U" tube. Insert another six-centimeter length of tubing on the other end of the "U" tube. Set the "U" tube in a beaker.

TABLE 1. INDIVIDUAL DATA ON AMOUNT OF WATER TRANSPIRED			
CONDITION	PLANT USED	mL OF WATER TRANSPIRED	mL OF WATER TRANSPIRED/HR
Normal			
Fan			
Spotlight			
Petroleum jelly (upper surface)			
Petroleum jelly (both surfaces)			

With a razor blade or scalpel, remove a leafy shoot from a potted plant. **CAUTION:** *Always be careful with sharp instruments. Cut away from your fingers to avoid cuts.* Place the shoot in a large beaker of water. Holding the cut end under water, cut off a 2 to 3 cm section from the cut end of the plant to remove any air in the xylem vessels. Keep the shoot submerged in the beaker.

With another pipette, fill the potometer by adding water to the pipette attached to the potometer. Add water until it overflows from the other side of the "U." When overflowing occurs, insert the leafy shoot into the rubber tubing. Tie the cord as tight as possible around the rubber tubing holding the shoot. Fill the pipette part of the potometer to the zero mark. No water should leak from around the shoot.

Allow the shoot to transpire for five minutes. At the end of five minutes, determine the volume of water that has transpired. Calculate the volume of water (mL) transpired per hour. Record your results in a table similar to Table 1.

Refill the potometer to the zero mark of the pipette. Place the leafy shoot about 1 m from an electric fan. Turn on the fan. At the end of five minutes, turn off the fan and determine the volume of water transpired. Calculate the volume of water (mL) transpired per hour. Record the data in the table.

Refill the potometer to the zero mark of the pipette. Place the leafy shoot 1 m from a spotlight or other bright light source. Turn on the light. At the end of five minutes, turn off the light and determine the volume of water transpired. Calculate the volume of water (mL) transpired per hour. Record the data in the table.

Refill the potometer to the zero mark of the pipette. Coat the upper surface of all leaves of the shoot with petroleum jelly. Place the leafy shoot 1 m from the electric fan. Turn on the fan. At the end of five minutes, turn off the fan and determine the volume of water transpired. Calculate the volume of water (mL) transpired per hour. Record the data in the table.

Refill the potometer to the zero mark of the pipette. Coat the lower surface of the leaves of the shoot with petroleum jelly. Do not remove the petroleum jelly from the upper surface of the leaves. Place the leafy shoot 1 m from the electric fan. Turn on the fan. At the end of five minutes, turn off the fan and determine the volume of water transpired. Calculate the volume of water (mL) transpired per hour. Record the data in the table.

Collect class data for each species of plant used of the volume of water transpired per hour. Record the class data in a table similar to Table 2.

Formulating Generalizations

1. What environmental factors did you use that increased the rate of transpiration?
2. What environmental factors did you not use that would increase the rate of transpiration?
3. What environmental factors did you use that decreased the rate of transpiration?
4. What effect would the size of the leaf have on the rate of transpiration?
5. What other factors affect the rate of transpiration?
6. How do the fan, spotlight, and petroleum jelly increase or decrease the transpiration rate?
7. Did any of the three conditions (fan, spotlight, or petroleum jelly) increase or decrease the rate of transpiration more than the others? Explain.
8. From the class data arrange in order from the greatest to the least the transpiration rate in the various species of plants.
9. Why do you think each species of plant transpires at a different rate?
10. Were any controls used in this investigation?
11. If you were to do this investigation again, what factors would you be certain to control?
12. How did these factors affect your results?

TABLE 2. CLASS DATA ON AMOUNT OF WATER TRANSPIRED

TYPE OF PLANT	mL OF WATER TRANSPIRED PER HOUR				
	NORMAL	FAN	SPOTLIGHT	PETROLEUM JELLY (UPPER SURFACE)	PETROLEUM JELLY (BOTH SURFACES)

Capillary Circulation

55

As complexity in animals increased, systems for respiration other than diffusion of materials into and out of cells evolved. As tissues and organs became more numerous and thicker, a better form of transport developed. This transport system is the circulatory system.

A circulatory system contains a pumplike organ called the heart. The heart is composed of muscle tissue. It forces a liquid tissue through a series of vessels. The liquid tissue is called blood.

Several invertebrates (insects and crustaceans) have open circulatory systems. Blood is pumped by a heart through a vessel which is open at the end. Blood is emptied into large, open areas within the body. After bathing the tissues, blood enters another open tube and is pumped again through the heart.

A vertebrate circulatory system consists of a heart and several vessels which carry the blood. All vertebrates have closed circulatory systems. Blood leaves the heart and is pumped through gills or lungs. At the gills or lungs, blood picks up oxygen and loses carbon dioxide. Blood leaves the heart in large vessels called arteries. Arteries branch into smaller vessels called arterioles as they enter the tissues. Arterioles branch into smaller vessels called capillaries. Capillary walls are only one cell thick. Arteriole and artery walls are composed of several layers of cells.

In the capillaries, branching allows the blood to come in contact with cells or layers of cells.Gases and other necessary materials are exchanged. Capillaries then join together to form larger vessels called venules. Venules join together to form larger vessels called veins. Veins return deoxygenated blood to the heart.

In this investigation, you are to locate and identify an arteriole, a capillary, and a venule in the tail of a goldfish. You are to determine the direction of flow of the blood and measure the diameter of each type of blood vessel.

Materials *(per student or team)*

absorbent cotton, 5 cm square—2
water
petri dish half
goldfish in aquarium
aquarium net
glass slides—2
microscope
dropper
aquarium water

Procedure

Saturate two 5-cm square pieces of absorbent cotton with water. Place one piece on the bottom of a petri dish with a small amount of aquarium water. Remove a goldfish from the aquarium and place the head of the goldfish on the wet absorbent cotton. Place the second piece of cotton over the head and gills of the fish. Place a clean microscope slide under the tail of the fish and another slide on top of

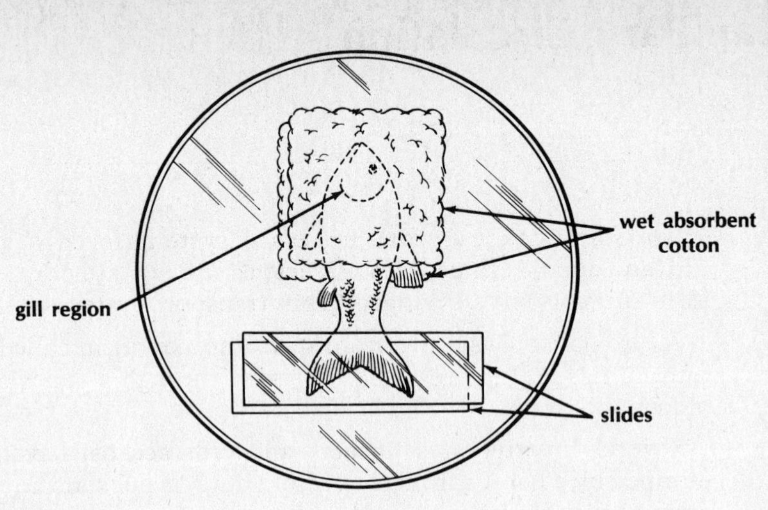

FIGURE 1

the tail (Figure 1). This will hold the tail in place for observation. Add fresh aquarium water periodically in order to add oxygen. **CAUTION:** *Work quickly. Keeping the goldfish out of water for an extended period of time will harm it. Be sure that the cotton stays wet to provide oxygen for the fish.*

Place the petri dish on the stage of your microscope. Using low power only, focus on a section of the tail that shows blood flowing through blood vessels. Locate and identify an arteriole, a capillary, and a venule. Determine whether the direction of blood flow is toward the tail, from the tail, or in both directions. Measure the diameter of each vessel in micrometers. Record the diameters in your lab notebook.

Formulating Generalizations

1. In which of the three vessels does the blood throb? Why?
2. In which of the three vessels does the blood flow at a uniform rate? Why?
3. Do arterioles carry blood to or from the tail? Give reasons for your answer.
4. Which type of blood vessel has the smallest diameter? Why?
5. Which type of blood vessel has the largest diameter? Why?
6. How can you tell the difference between an arteriole and a venule while making observations?
7. How can you tell a capillary from other vessel types while making observations?
8. Does a fish have an open or closed circulatory system? Give evidence for your answer.

Effects Of Exercise On The Heartbeat Rate

56

Your heart pumps blood to and from all cells in your body. The heart contracts rhythmically. As a result of the contractions, force is exerted on the blood. This force distributes blood to all living cells of your body. As metabolic changes occur in your body, more or less "demand" is made on your heart. Vigorous activity demands a greater than usual supply of blood and oxygen for the tissues. To increase the supply of blood and oxygen, the heart pumps more quickly. After vigorous activity, the heartbeat rate slows to its normal rate. The time it takes for the heartbeat rate to slow to its normal rate is called recovery time. If a person exercises regularly, the heart muscle becomes stronger, more blood is pumped with each beat, and recovery time is less.

The autonomic nervous system controls the heartbeat rate. Nerve impulses are constantly sent between the heart and nervous system. These impulses cause the heart to either speed up or slow down.

Heartbeat rate is influenced by many other things such as the sex of the individual, the age of the individual, and the temperature of the external and internal environment.

In this investigation, you are to locate your pulse. You are to determine your pulse rate at rest for three minutes, during vigorous exercise for 20 minutes, and at rest for 20 minutes.

Materials *(per student or team)*

clock or watch with second hand
graph paper

Procedure

Locate your pulse by placing your right index finger on the thumb side of your left wrist (Figure 1). Press lightly. You should feel a throbbing flow of blood. If you cannot find your pulse, ask your teacher for assistance.

Prepare a table in your lab notebook similar to Table 1 to record your pulse rate for each of three minutes of rest, each of 20 minutes of exercise, and each of 20 minutes of rest.

FIGURE 1

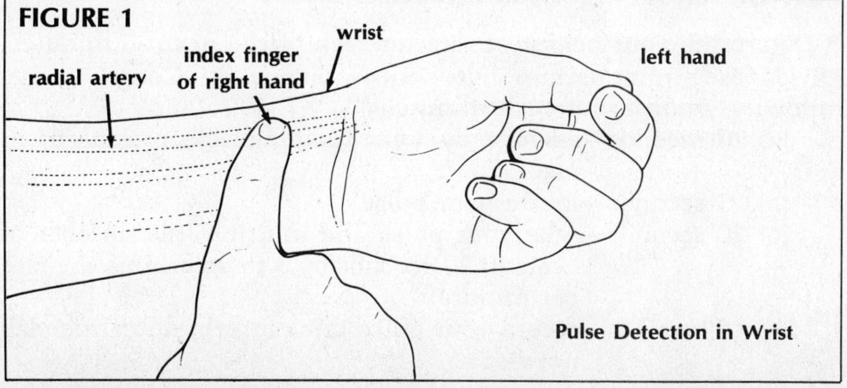

Pulse Detection in Wrist

TABLE 1. PULSE RATE			
CONDITION	MINUTES	BEATS/20 SEC	RATE/MIN
Rest	1		
	2		
	3		
Exercise	4		
	5		
Rest	24		
	25		
	43		

Part A. At Rest

Determine your heartbeat rate for each of the next three minutes. Divide each minute into four periods (Figure 2). Complete the following *in order* for each minute.

(a) 20 seconds—rest by sitting quietly at your desk
(b) 5 seconds—locate your pulse
(c) 20 seconds—take your pulse and multiply the number of beats in 20 seconds by 3 to determine rate per minute
(d) 15 seconds—record your pulse rate per minute in your lab notebook

FIGURE 2

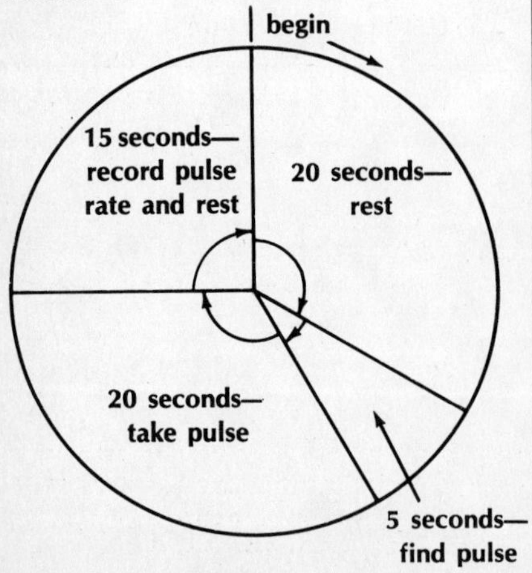

Three Minutes of Rest

Part B. After Vigorous Exercise

Determine your heartbeat rate for each of the next 20 minutes. Divide each minute into five periods (Figure 3). Complete the following *in order* for each minute.

(a) 20 seconds—exercise by doing jumping jacks or running in place
(b) 5 seconds—locate your pulse
(c) 20 seconds—take your pulse and multiply the number of beats in 20 seconds by 3 to determine the rate per minute
(d) 10 seconds—record your pulse rate per minute in your lab notebook
(e) 5 seconds—get ready to exercise for the next minute

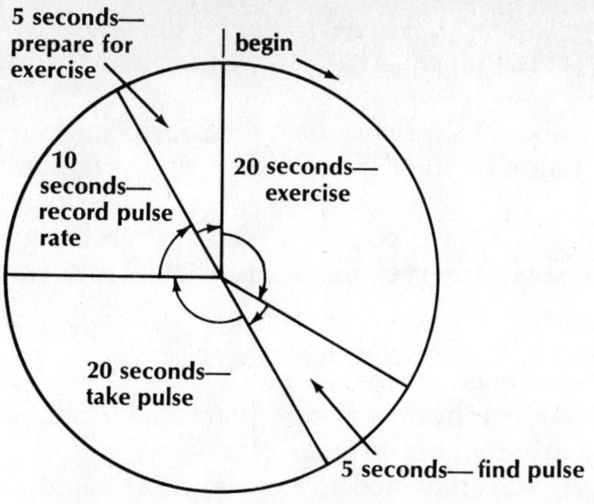

Twenty Minutes of Exercise

FIGURE 3

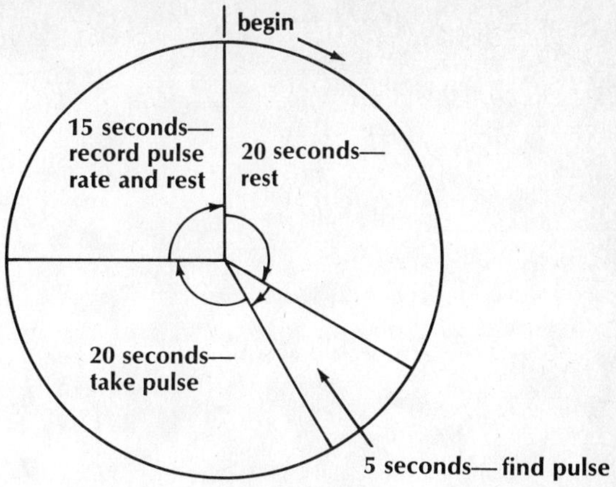

Twenty Minutes of Rest

FIGURE 4

Part C. At Rest After Vigorous Exercise

Determine your heartbeat rate for each of the next 20 minutes. Divide each minute into four periods (Figure 4). Complete the following *in order* for each minute.

(a) 20 seconds—rest by sitting quietly at your desk
(b) 5 seconds—locate your pulse
(c) 20 seconds—take your pulse and multiply the number of beats in 20 seconds by 3 to determine the rate per minute
(d) 15 seconds—record your pulse rate per minute in your lab notebook and rest

At the end of this 20-minute segment, record your pulse rates on the chalkboard as class data. Record the class data in your notebook in a table similar to Table 2. Determine the averages for each minute. Construct a graph in which you show (a) your data, (b) the average rates of all males, and (c) the average rates of all females (Figure 5).

TABLE 2. CLASS DATA AND AVERAGE PULSE RATES

MINUTE	PULSE RATES/MINUTE								AVERAGES		
	Males				Females				Male	Female	Class
	1	2	3	4	1	2	3	4			
1											
2											
3											
43											

Formulating Generalizations

Use your text or other references to help you answer questions one to three.

1. In which chamber of the heart does the heartbeat originate? What is the name of the cardiac tissue that originates the heartbeat?
2. What two sets of nerves control heartbeat rate?
3. Why are two sets of nerves necessary to control heartbeat rate?
4. What factors increase heartbeat rate in humans?
5. What factors decrease heartbeat rate?
6. What is the average heartbeat rate (Part A) for males? For females? For all students in your class?
7. After exercise, who returned to normal more rapidly than you?
8. Why do some classmates return to normal more rapidly than you?
9. Why do some classmates return to normal more slowly than you?
10. Why should all humans, especially those who sit a lot, have some physical activity each day?
11. Why do athletes usually have a shorter recovery time after exercise than nonathletes?
12. How does regular exercise affect recovery time of the heart?

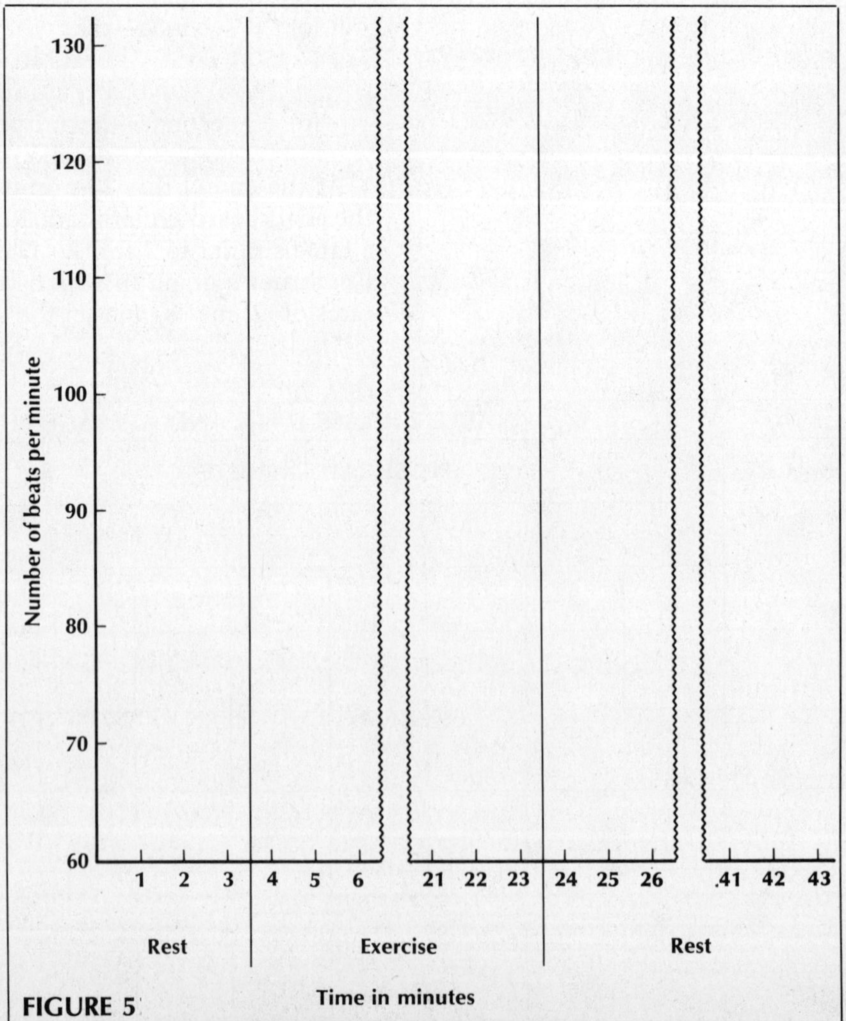

FIGURE 5

Effect Of Temperature Changes On Breathing Rate Of Fish

57

During breathing, an organism takes in oxygen from the environment. This oxygen is used for respiration. Carbon dioxide and water are by-products of respiration. They are removed from the body of the organism during respiration and breathing.

In fish, gills are the site of gas exchange. Gills are filamentous structures found beneath an operculum, a gill cover (Figure 1). A gill filament has a large surface area which allows maximum exposure to the external environment. Maximum exposure is necessary to exchange enough oxygen and carbon dioxide with the external environment.

During breathing, a fish opens its mouth and the operculum closes. As the fish closes its mouth, the pharynx contracts and forces water over the gill filaments. As water passes over the gill filaments, oxygen diffuses into the capillary net of each filament and carbon dioxide diffuses out. When the pharynx contracts, the operculum opens. After passing over the gills, water leaves the fish through the operculum. Thus, the opening and closing of the mouth can be used for measuring the breathing rate. The breathing rate in cold-blooded animals is controlled in part by the external environment.

In this investigation, you are to determine the effect of temperature variation on the breathing rate of fish.

Materials *(per student or team)*

aquarium fishnet
goldfish
beaker—1-L
thermometer
glass stirring rod

Per Class
basters—5
warm water (85°C)—1 L
crushed ice—1 L
beaker—500-mL
pond water—1 L
graph paper

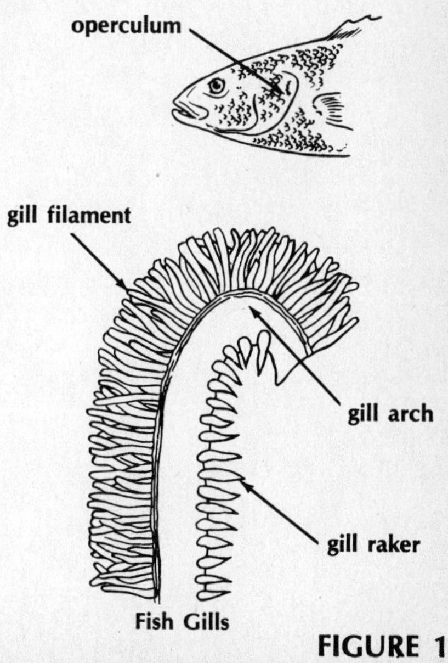

FIGURE 1

Procedure

Place a goldfish in a 500-mL beaker with enough pond water to cover the dorsal fin and allow the fish to swim. Place this beaker inside a 1-L beaker to which you have added 200 mL of water (Figure 2). Measure the temperature of the water in the beaker with a thermometer. Leave the thermometer in the beaker. Add warm water to the outside beaker until the water temperature in the inside beaker reaches 30°C. Stir the water in the outer beaker with the stirring rod so the water mixes thoroughly.

When the water in the smaller beaker reaches 30°C, allow the fish to adjust to the change in temperature for one minute. Then count the number of times the fish opens and closes its mouth for two minutes. Divide this count by two and record the per minute rate in your lab

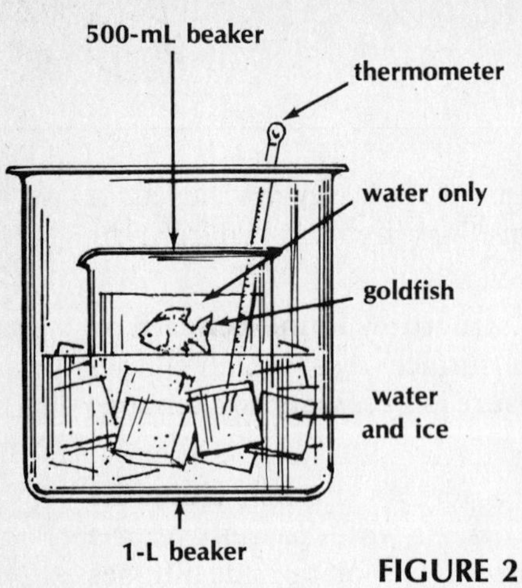

FIGURE 2

FIGURE 3
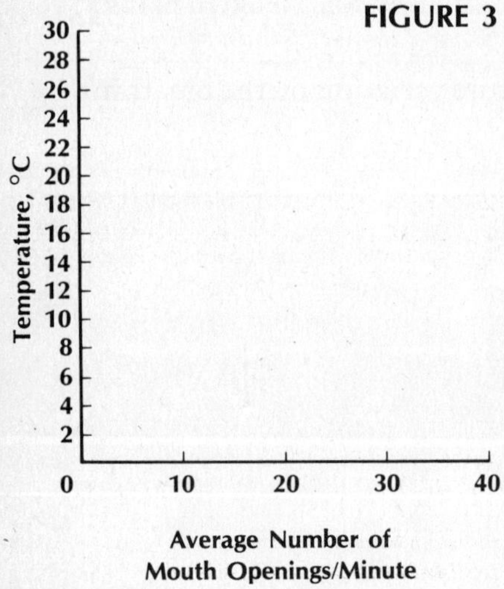

notebook in a table similar to Table 1. Lower the water temperature of the inside beaker from 30°C to 28°C by adding small pieces of ice to the outside beaker and stirring with a stirring rod. After the temperature reaches 28°C, allow the fish to adjust to the new temperature for one minute. Count the number of times the fish opens and closes its mouth for two minutes, and divide by two for the per minute rate of breathing. Record the results in your lab notebook.

Lower the temperature at 2°C intervals and count the number of mouth openings for two minutes. Record the number of mouth openings per minute. Continue lowering the temperature until you reach 2°C. As the water level in the larger beaker rises, remove some of the water to keep a constant level.

At the end of this investigation, slowly add warm water to the 1-L beaker. Add water until the temperature of the smaller beaker reaches the aquarium temperature. Then, place the fish in the aquarium.

Construct a graph showing the average respiration rate of your fish at each of the different temperatures (Figure 3). Place your data on the chalkboard. Record the class data in the table in your notebook. Using the class data, calculate the average number of mouth openings at each temperature. On the same axes as your individual data, construct a graph using the class averages and a dotted line.

TABLE 1. NUMBER OF MOUTH OPENINGS

	30°C	28°C	26°C	24°C	2°C
Your data					
Student 1					
Student 2					
Student 3					
Total					
Average					

Formulating Generalizations

1. Describe the relationship between decreasing temperature and the rate of mouth openings.
2. Why does the mouth opening rate change with changes in temperature?
3. Why must the gill filament have a large surface area?
4. Why should the fish be given a few seconds to adjust to each new temperature?
5. Compare the class data with your data. Which graph shows a smoother line? Why?

Effect Of Exercise On Carbon Dioxide Release In The Human Body

58

In mammals, carbon dioxide is a waste product of respiration. Carbon dioxide is released into the lungs as oxygen is taken into the red blood cells from the lungs. The lungs contain many small air sacs called alveoli (singular, alveolus). The walls of the alveoli are one cell thick. A small network of capillaries passes over the outer surface of the alveoli. Through the alveoli and capillaries, carbon dioxide and oxygen are exchanged. The lungs of a human contain nearly one thousand square feet of surface area. This large area is needed for exchange of the required gases.

As a warm-blooded organism becomes more active, more respiratory demands are placed on the breathing apparatus. The exchange rate of carbon dioxide and oxygen changes with this demand.

In this investigation, an indicator will be used to determine the presence of carbon dioxide in water. The indicator (phenolphthalein) turns pink in the presence of carbon dioxide. You are to determine and compare the amount of carbon dioxide released by your respiratory system after rest and after 30 seconds of exercise.

Materials *(per student)*

distilled water—600 mL
flask—125-mL
watch or clock with second hand
phenolphthalein solution —3 mL
1- or 2-mL graduated pipette
0.4% sodium hydroxide solution—20 mL
soda straw

Procedure

Add 100 mL of distilled water to a clean flask. Using a soda straw, bubble air from your lungs into the flask for one minute. Add four drops of phenolphthalein solution (indicator) to the flask. Using a graduated pipette, add 0.4% sodium hydroxide solution one drop at a time to the flask. Swirl the flask gently after you add each drop of sodium hydroxide solution. **CAUTION:** *Sodium hydroxide can cause burns. If spillage occurs, rinse with water and call your teacher immediately.* When the liquid in the flask turns pink and remains pink for one minute, record in a table similar to Table 1 the milliliters of sodium hydroxide solution added to the beaker.

Compute the parts per million (ppm) of carbon dioxide in the flask. One ppm of carbon dioxide is one part of carbon dioxide in a total of one million parts of water. Each milliliter of 0.4% sodium hydroxide solution will chemically combine with 100 ppm of carbon dioxide. To compute the ppm of carbon dioxide in the flask, multiply the milliliters of sodium hydroxide added by 100.

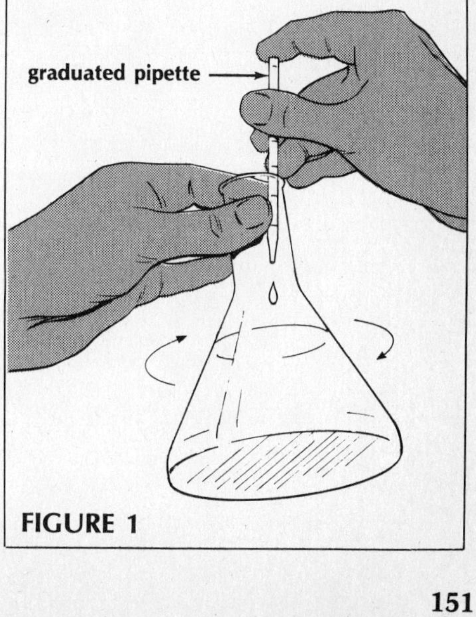

FIGURE 1

TABLE 1. INDIVIDUAL DATA							
AT REST	NaOH (mL)		PPM CO_2	AFTER EXERCISE	NaOH (mL)		PPM CO_2
Trial 1		× 100		Trial 1		× 100	
Trial 2		× 100		Trial 2		× 100	
Trial 3		× 100		Trial 3		× 100	
Average				Average			

TABLE 2. CLASS AVERAGES		
	AVERAGE PPM AT REST	AVERAGE PPM AFTER EXERCISE
your data		
student 1		
student 2		
Total		
Average		

Example:
(3.5 mL sodium hydroxide) (100) = 350 ppm of carbon dioxide

Record your computations in the table in your notebook.

Repeat the above procedure two more times. Rinse out the flask and use new distilled water for each trial. Compute the average ppm of carbon dioxide liberated in the three trials at rest. Record the averaged data in the table in your lab notebook. Place your averages on the chalkboard. Record the class data in your notebook in a table similar to Table 2. Determine class averages.

Perform three more trials as above except this time, exercise vigorously for 30 seconds before bubbling air from your lungs into the flask. Exercise by doing jumping jacks or running in place. Do the same exercise at the same level of intensity for all three trials. Record and average your results in the table. Again record the class data and determine the class average.

Formulating Generalizations

Use your text to help you answer the first four questions.

1. What three body parts cause the lungs to expand and contract during breathing?
2. **(a)** How do these three body parts function during the intake of air into the lungs (inspiration)?
   (b) How do they function during expiration?
3. What metabolic process has carbon dioxide as a waste product?
4. Write a word equation for this metabolic process.
5. Was there more or less carbon dioxide in your flask at rest than after exercise? Why?
6. How do your results compare with other members of the class?
7. How do you think constant daily exercise would change the amount of carbon dioxide released?

Assay Of Bacteriophage

59

Bacteriophages are viruses that attack bacteria. They are host specific, which means that a specific bacteriophage attacks a specific bacteria species. For example, T_2 bacteriophage attacks only *Escherichia coli (E. coli),* the bacteria found in the intestines of humans and other mammals. For convenience the name bacteriophage is often shortened to phage.

A phage attaches to the cell wall of a bacterium and the DNA of the phage enters the cytoplasm of the bacterial cell. Synthesis of molecules normally produced by the bacterial cell is stopped because the phage DNA directs the bacterial cell to synthesize phage DNA and protein. In effect, the phage "takes command" of the bacterial cell. About 20 minutes after a phage penetrates a cell, 50 to 200 new phages are formed within the bacterial cell. The cell ruptures (lyses), releasing the phages into the surrounding medium. If other bacterial cells of the specific type are present, the cycle of phage penetration is repeated.

In this investigation you are to determine the number of phages in a culture by using the agar assay technique. An assay is an examination to determine the presence and quantity of one substance in another.

Materials *(per student or team)*

sterile, 9-cm petri dishes—7
T_2 bacteriophage suspension
Escherichia coli suspension in nutrient broth
sterile, 5-mL pipettes with bulbs—2
water bath, 42°C
glass marking pencil
2% nutrient agar—100 mL
1% nutrient agar—25 mL in a flask
test tubes with 9 mL sterile sodium chloride solution—6
incubator
dropper

Procedure

CAUTION: *E. coli may cause infection. Keep hands away from face throughout this investigation. Do not chew gum or eat while carrying out the procedure. Wash hands immediately after finishing procedure.*

Pour 10 to 15 mL of 2% nutrient agar into each of seven sterile petri dishes. Cover the dishes and allow the agar to harden. Number the dishes one to seven. To dish one, add 2 to 3 mL of 1% nutrient agar. Allow the agar to harden forming a second layer of agar on the 2% nutrient agar. Add the *E. coli* suspension to the flask containing 1% nutrient agar. Place the agar in a water bath at 42°C until used to keep it from hardening.

Dilute the phage suspension to a 1:1 000 000 dilution. Using a sterile 5 mL pipette, transfer 1 mL of phage suspension to a test tube containing 9 mL of sterile 0.8% salt solution to make a 1:10 dilution

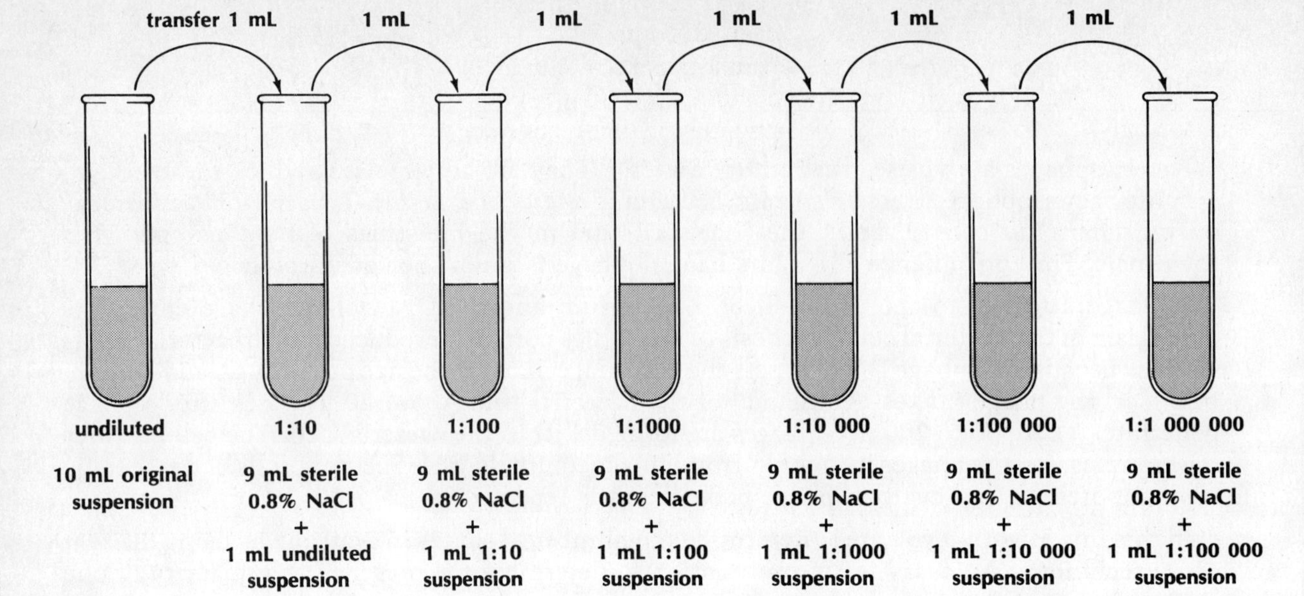

FIGURE 1

of phage suspension. **CAUTION:** *Do not mouth pipette.* Fill the same pipette to the 1 mL mark with the 1:10 dilution and discharge it back into the same 1:10 dilution tube to mix the suspension and rinse the pipette. Fill and discharge the same pipette at least two more times to ensure thorough mixing.

With the same pipette, transfer 1 mL of the 1:10 dilution of phage suspension to another test tube containing 9 mL of sterile 0.8% salt solution to make a 1:100 dilution. Mix the suspension using the pipette as you did the 1:10 dilution.

Continue this process with four more test tubes containing 1 mL of sterile 0.8% salt solution to make 1:1000; 1:10 000; 1:100 000; and 1:1 000 000 dilutions (Figure 1). Work quickly and keep tubes capped as much as possible to maintain sterility. Be sure to mix the suspension after each dilution. Label each tube as to its dilution.

After the dilutions are completed, use a sterile pipette and add *in order* 1 mL of each dilution to a petri dish. To dish two add 1:1 000 000 dilution, to dish three add 1:100 000 dilution, to dish four add 1:10 000 dilution, to dish five add 1:1000 dilution, to dish six add

TABLE 1. NUMBER OF PLAQUES AND PHAGES

PETRI DISH	DILUTION OF PHAGE SUSPENSION	NUMBER OF PLAQUES	NUMBER OF PHAGES	PHAGES/mL OF ORIGINAL SUSPENSION
1				
2				
7				

1:100 dilution, to dish seven add 1:10 dilution. Record the dilution of suspension in each petri dish in your lab notebook in a table similar to Table 1. Note that dish one contains no phage dilution.

To petri dishes one through seven use a clean dropper to add two to three mL of 1% nutrient agar containing the *E. coli* suspension. Gently swirl the agar in the flask before adding to each dish to ensure thorough mixing of the *E. coli.* After you add the agar to the dishes, swirl the dishes to ensure mixing of the phage suspension with the agar. Allow the agar to harden. Incubate the inverted petri dishes for 24 hours at 37°C. Nutrients in the bottom layer of agar will nourish the bacteria in the top layer of agar.

Phage particles will attach to bacteria cells causing lysis of the cells. Bacteria cells are killed by phages. An area where bacteria are killed becomes clear. Bacteriologists call these clear areas plaques. Each plaque represents one original phage particle (Figure 2).

Examine the dishes after 24 hours. Count the number of plaques formed in each dish and record the numbers in the table in your lab notebook. From the number of plaques, the number of phages can be determined. The number of plaques equals the number of phages. Record the number of phages in each dish.

Because you made dilutions of the original phage suspension, multiply the number of plaques found in each dish by the denominator of the dilution to determine the number of phages in the suspension. For example, 20 plaques × 1000 dilution factor = 20 000 phages per mL in suspension. Thus, 20 000 phages per mL were present in the original phage suspension. Compute and record in the table the number of phages per mL of original suspension from the number of plaques in each dish.

FIGURE 2

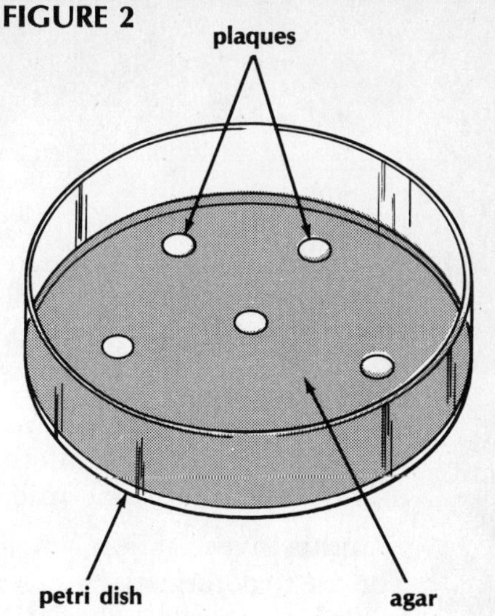

Formulating Generalizations

1. What is a plaque?
2. What is a phage?
3. What is the relationship between plaques and phages?
4. How are new phages produced?
5. What happens to the bacteria used by a phage when new phages are formed?
6. Were any of the dishes without phages? If so, why?
7. Were any dishes completely clear? If so, why?
8. Upon close examination of your data, can you establish that you made little error in your experiment? How?
9. Why was the plating of the phage particles done in reverse order of concentration?
10. Why would this viral life cycle be called the lytic cycle?
11. A student finds 15 plaques in a dish containing a 1:10 000 dilution phage suspension. How many phages per mL were in the original suspension?
12. A student is given a solution containing 1000 phages per mL. About how many plaques should be present after 24 hours in a dish containing a 1:100 phage dilution?

60

Controlling Microbial Growth

Humans are constantly exposed to microorganisms. Microorganisms are found in the air, in water, and in food. Although many microorganisms are not harmful to humans, some can cause discomfort or illness and disease.

Biologists have developed various methods of controlling the growth of microorganisms. Filtering air, sterilizing liquids and solids, and adding chemicals to food and water prevent or inhibit microbial growth. Storing materials at very low or very high temperatures can also help inhibit the growth of microorganisms. However, these methods only control the growth of microorganisms; some microorganisms still survive and reproduce.

In this investigation, you are to use yeast cells to represent a disease-causing microorganism. You are to determine by observing the yeast cells the effectiveness of one method of controlling microbial growth. Using your data you are to construct graphs showing the survival rate of cells undergoing treatment.

Materials *(per team of two students)*

yeast suspension
small test tubes—8
aluminum foil, 3 cm X 3 cm—8
thermometer
small beaker—1
large beaker—1
test tube rack
test tube holder
hot plate
glass slides—2
coverslips—2
microscope
methylene blue
droppers—2
graph paper
watch or clock with second hand
tap water
graduated cylinder
marker

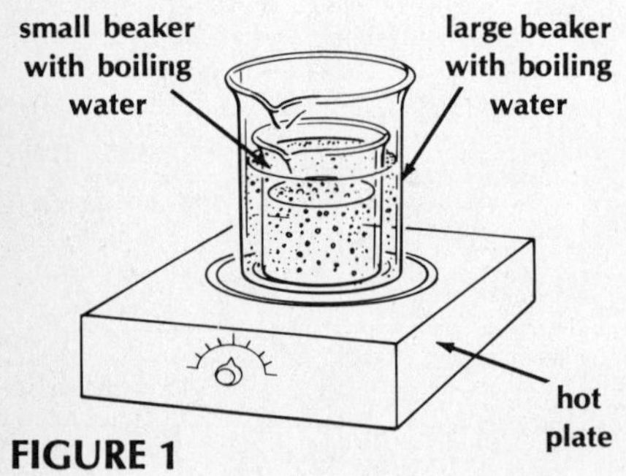

FIGURE 1

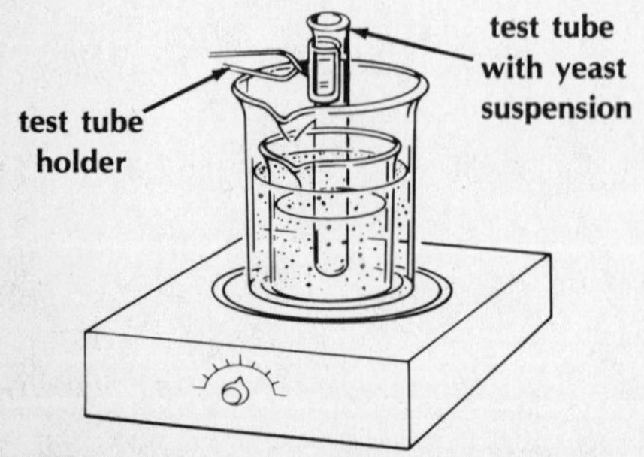

FIGURE 2

Procedure

Label eight small test tubes A through H. Add 4 mL tap water and five drops of yeast suspension to each tube. Cover each tube with a square of aluminum foil and wrap the foil around the lip of the tube. Gently swirl the contents of each tube. The water should appear cloudy. Set the tubes aside in the test tube rack.

Fill the large and small beakers half full with water. Place the small beaker inside of the large beaker, and put this assembly on a hot plate (Figure 1). Heat the water until the temperature of the water in the small beaker reaches 100°C. **CAUTION:** *Water and glass are hot. Do not touch the beakers with unprotected hands.*

Remove the foil cap from Tube B. Using a test tube holder, immerse tube B in the small beaker of water (Figure 2). Make sure that the temperature of the water in the small beaker remains constant at 100°C. Use Table 1 as a guide to the length of time to leave the tube immersed. At the end of the proper time, return tube B to the test tube rack. Repeat this procedure with tubes C through H. Remember to keep the water temperature in the small beaker constant at 100°C, and to use Table 1 as a guide to the length of time each tube should be immersed. NOTE: Tube A should not be immersed in the water.

Stir the contents of Tube A by drawing the yeast suspension into a clean dropper and squirting it out three or four times. Place one drop of yeast suspension from tube A on a clean, dry slide. Using a clean dropper, add one drop of methylene blue to the slide. Gently rotate the slide to mix the stain and the yeast suspension. Add a coverslip

TABLE 1. YEAST TREATMENT AND COUNTS						
TEST TUBE	TIME IN BOILING WATER (SECONDS)	A NUMBER OF LIVE CELLS COUNTED	B NUMBER OF DEAD CELLS COUNTED	C TOTAL NUMBER OF CELLS COUNTED (A+B)	D PERCENT ALIVE $\left(\frac{A}{C}\right)$	E PERCENT DEAD $\left(\frac{B}{C}\right)$
A	0					
B	5					
C	10					
D	20					
E	30					
F	40					
G	50					
H	60					

and observe the slide under low, then high power. Locate the yeast cells. Live cells will be clear, dead cells will be stained a dark blue.

Under low power, count the number of live and dead cells in one field of view. If the total number of cells counted is less than 100, count another field of view. Continue counting cells until the total number of cells counted is 100. Record the number of living and dead cells in a table similar to Table 1.

Repeat the staining and counting procedure with the yeast suspensions in the remaining seven test tubes. Be sure to rinse the dropper well before immersing it into the different suspensions. Calculate the percentage of live and dead cells in each tube. Plot your data using graph paper (Figure 3). Make two different graphs, one showing the percentage of live cells in each tube, and one showing the percentage of dead cells in each tube.

Formulating Generalizations

1. Why was test tube A not immersed in the hot water?
2. Which of the immersed tubes showed the smallest percentage of dead cells? How long was this tube immersed in the water?
3. Which of the immersed tubes showed the largest percentage of dead cells? How long was this tube immersed in the water?
4. Using your data and the bar graphs you drew, explain the relationship between length of immersion and the percentage of yeast cells killed.
5. A microorganism harmful to humans is found growing in the public water supply. The microorganism is known to react in ways similar to the yeast cells you have just studied. Describe a procedure that people could follow to make the water safe for drinking and explain why the procedure would work.
6. A microbiologist is called in to solve the problem described in question 5. Describe a procedure that the microbiologist could use to determine the effects of a certain chemical on the growth of the microorganism.

FIGURE 3

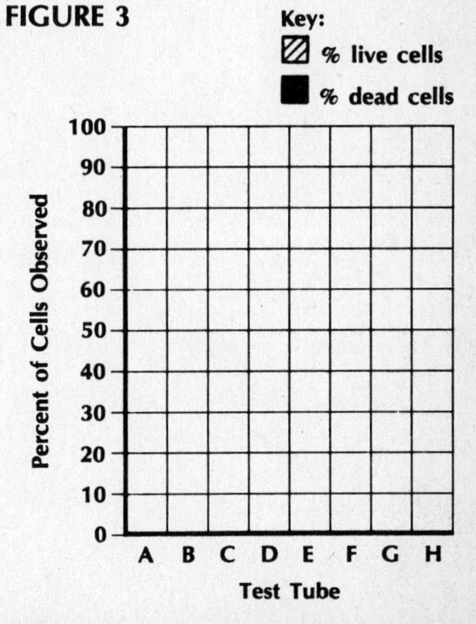

61 The Regional Spread Of Disease-Causing Protozoa

Some diseases are caused by simple organisms. These simple organisms can cause sickness or destroy the tissue of the host organism, and sometimes the disease-causing organism can kill the host organism.

Several diseases of humans and other animals are caused by protozoa. Disease-causing protozoa live in the body fluid or cells of the host. The host provides food and shelter during the growth and development of the protozoa, and also provides a protected environment in which the protozoa can reproduce. Disease-causing organisms can be spread rapidly from one organism to another as a result of unsanitary conditions or overcrowding. Disease-causing organisms may also be spread by insect bites.

In this investigation, you are to read the written report made by a biologist and study the data chart compiled by biologists in the field. From this data, you are to construct a map showing the spread of the disease. Then you are to decide where the disease originated and the pattern by which the disease spread.

Materials *(per student or team)*

metric ruler　　colored pencils　　graph paper

Procedure

Read the following report made by a biologist describing the spread of a disease in a pheasant population.

Biologist's Report: Spread of *Plasmodium gallinaceum* in a Pheasant Population (April 1986 to August 1987)

In early April, 1986, a protozoan parasite identified as *Plasmodium gallinaceum* was first isolated in salivary gland cells of a *Culex* mosquito. This parasite causes a disease in birds commonly called bird malaria. The mosquito was found in a roadside ditch in Region V Game District. In late April, 1986, a blood sample was taken from several pheasants in the same game district. One pheasant was found to be carrying a stage in the life cycle of *P. gallinaceum* in several red blood cells.

The presence or absence of the parasite in birds was determined by blood tests done during the warm months of 1986 and 1987. All pheasants tested were live-trapped, tagged, and released. At least three pheasants from each quarter kilometer area of the Region V game district were tested during each of the sample periods. Areas newly infected with bird malaria were recorded in a data chart similar to Table 1.

The life cycle of *P. gallinaceum* is as follows. A *Culex* mosquito bites a bird with malaria. (Chickens, turkeys, pheasants, and grouse are some of the species that may be affected by this disease.) Some protozoa are sucked up in the bird's blood cells that the mosquito takes in. These protozoa then pass along with blood into the mosquito's stomach where they grow and reproduce. Some of them pass into the mosquito's bloodstream and eventually reach the salivary glands.

When the mosquito bites a healthy bird, some protozoa enter the bird's blood. These protozoa travel through the blood to the brain,

TABLE 1. SAMPLE DATA		
SAMPLE TIME	AREAS REPORTING MALARIA CASES FOR THE FIRST TIME	COLOR OF SYMBOL
A	D-3, D-4, E-3, E-4, E-5, F-3	blue
B	A-6, A-7, A-8, B-8, B-9, C-9, D-9, E-9, F-9, F-10, G-7, G-8, G-9	red
C	A-1, A-2, A-3, G-1, G-2, H-1, H-2, H-3, H-5 I-2, I-3, I-4, I-5	orange
D	F-4	yellow
E	D-2, D-5, D-6, D-7, E-2, E-6, F-5, C-2, C-3, C-4, C-5	purple
F	B-1, B-2, B-3, B-4, B-6, B-7, C-1, C-6, C-7, C-8, D-1, E-1, E-7, E-8, F-1, F-2, F-6, F-7, F-8, G-3, G-4, G-5, G-6, H-4	brown

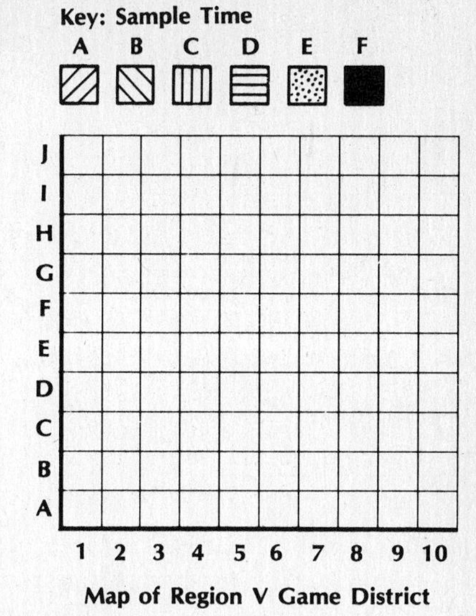

FIGURE 1

spleen, lungs, and liver where they grow and reproduce. The symptoms that the bird suffers as growth and reproduction of the protozoa occur are called malaria.

Construct a map similar to Figure 1 using a sheet of graph paper. Label the vertical scale A through J and the horizontal scale 1 through 10. The map represents Region V Game District, an area that measures five kilometers square. Each large block on the map equals one-fourth of a square kilometer.

Table 1 shows six data samples taken at different times (A through F). These samples are not listed in the order in which they were taken. A is not necessarily the first sample taken, and F is not necessarily the last. Using colored pencils, shade in the areas on the map according to the information given in Table 1. Each color represents the area where new malaria cases were found during each sample. When you are finished, your map should have six different color areas.

Formulating Generalizations

1. In what area of Region V Game District do you think that the protozoan disease bird malaria started? Explain.
2. Into which area did the disease spread next? Explain.
3. List in order the next two areas into which the disease spread. Explain.
4. Can you tell the exact order of areas into which the disease spread after the fourth area was infected? Why or why not?
5. Predict the sectors of the map that will probably be affected next. Explain why you picked the sectors that you did.
6. Why were the pheasants tagged and all of the areas sampled each time a sample was taken?
7. Why were no samples taken during the winter months?
8. You are given the job of controlling bird malaria in Region V Game District. How would you go about controlling the disease?
9. Should the game biologist also examine farm livestock in the district for bird malaria? Explain.

Tropisms in Plants

62

Certain plant responses are called tropisms. Two tropisms are phototropism, a response to light, and geotropism, a response to gravity. Phototropism and geotropism cause plant parts to bend in certain directions.

Bending in certain directions is caused by unequal growth of cells of stems or roots. If cells along one side of a stem or root grow faster than cells along the opposite side, the stem or root will bend. Auxins, hormones in plants, are responsible for unequal growth rates of cells. Some cells grow faster in the presence of auxins; other cells fail to grow when auxins are present. Concentrations of auxins in plant parts is influenced by light and gravity. Auxins move away from light and are "pulled" by gravity.

Plant parts that grow toward light are positively phototropic. Parts that grow away from light are negatively phototropic. Parts which grow downward are positively geotropic. Parts which grow upward and away from the force of gravity are negatively geotropic.

In this investigation, you are to compare the effects of the presence and absence of light on the phototropic response in plants. You are to compare the effect of gravity on shoots and roots and on cut and uncut root tips of corn seeds.

Materials *(per student)*

corn seeds—68
soil
medium-sized flowerpots—3
light-tight box
light-tight box with opening
beaker
petri dishes—2
paper towels—2
transparent tape
wax pencil
scalpel
water

Procedure

Part A. Phototropism in Corn

Plant 20 corn seeds in each of three flowerpots. Place the seeds so they are not more than 1 cm from each other (Figure 1). Allow the corn seeds to grow until they are 6 to 8 cm high. Then place the pots in a dark area overnight. During the next lab period, put one of the pots in a light-tight box. Put a second pot in a light-tight box that has a 2 cm by 6 cm opening on one side.

Place the third pot in a well-lighted area where the plant will get light from all directions throughout the day. Do not disturb the plants for 48 hours. After 48 hours, remove the two pots from the boxes. Observe the plants in all three pots. Describe any differences in color and degree of bending. Record your observations in your lab notebook.

FIGURE 1

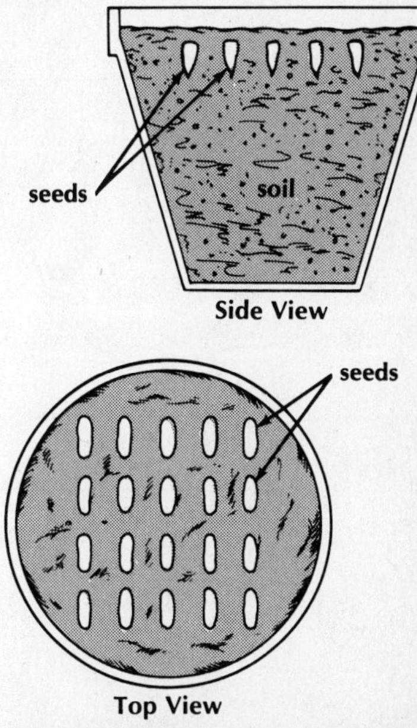

Part B. Geotropism in Germinating Corn Seeds

Soak eight corn seeds in a beaker of water overnight. Then place four seeds on the bottom half of a petri dish so the embryo side is facing up. Arrange the seeds so the points of attachment to the cob (stalks) are toward the center (Figure 2).

Moisten a paper towel and place it over the seeds. The paper towel should press the seeds and hold them in place. Add the top half of the

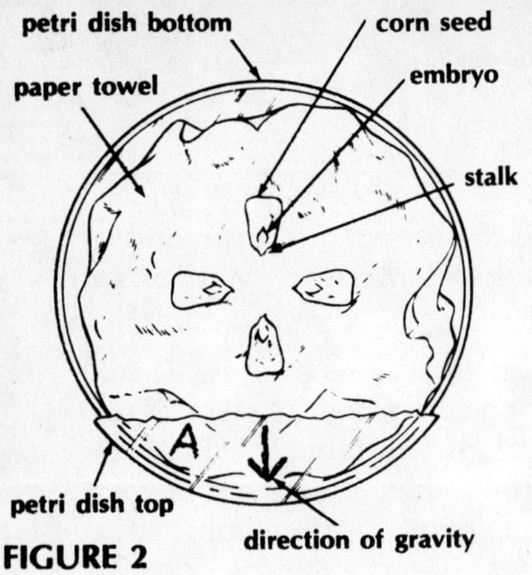

FIGURE 2

petri dish and seal it tightly with transparent tape. With a wax pencil, draw an arrow on the top of the petri dish to indicate the direction of gravity (Figure 2). Label the dish "A." Stand the petri dish on edge so the arrow points down. Put the dish in an area designated by your teacher. Observe the seeds daily for five days or until the roots appear to be growing in certain directions. Record daily observations in your notebook by making diagrams of the direction of root growth of each corn seed.

Place the other four seeds parallel to each other in the bottom half of another petri dish. Make sure the seeds are placed with the stalks down (Figure 3). Moisten a paper towel and place it over the seeds to hold the seeds in place. Add the top half of the petri dish and seal it with transparent tape. With a wax pencil, draw an arrow on the top of the petri dish to indicate the direction of gravity (Figure 3) and label the dish "B." Stand the petri dish on edge so the arrow points down. Put the dish in an area designated by your teacher.

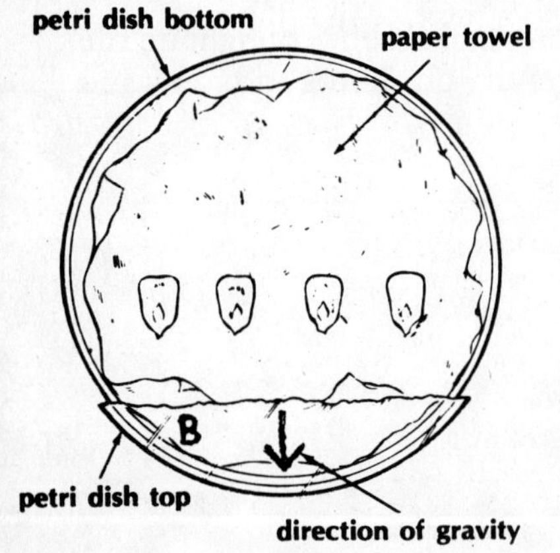

FIGURE 3

Observe the seeds daily until the roots are about 8 mm long. Then, cut off 2.5 mm of each root with a scalpel. **CAUTION:** *Always be careful when using sharp instruments. Slice away from your fingers to avoid cuts.* If necessary, arrange the seeds so they are parallel to each other again. Replace the wet paper towel and seal the dish with transparent tape. Stand the petri dish on edge so the arrow forms a 90° angle with the direction of gravity (Figure 4). Observe the roots daily for two or three days. Record your observations in your lab notebook. Make sketches to show the direction of root growth.

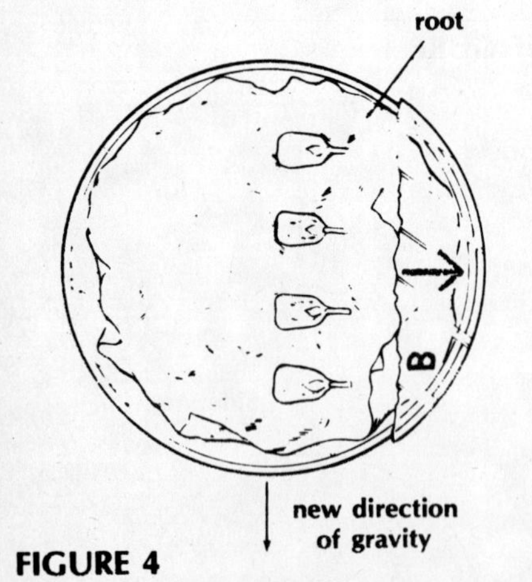

FIGURE 4

Formulating Generalizations

1. What are plant behaviors called?
2. What was the stimulus to which the corn plants responded in Part A?
3. What was the tropism shown by the plants in Part A?
4. What was the color of the plants in Part A that were grown in light? In the dark?
5. Which of the three plants in Part A showed the greatest change in the direction of growth? Explain.
6. Are the plant stems positively or negatively phototropic? Explain.
7. In responding to light, cells grow more quickly in the presence of auxins. In stems, were auxins concentrated on the side toward or away from the light? Explain.
8. What evidence do you have that verifies that auxins cause the phototropic response?
9. What is the direction of root growth in dish A after five days? Are these roots responding positively or negatively to gravity?
10. What is the direction of stem growth which you observed in dish A after five days?
11. Do the stems in dish A appear to respond positively or negatively to gravity?
12. In responding to gravity, cells grow more quickly if no auxins are present. In roots, were auxins concentrated on the side toward or away from the force of gravity?

Effects Of Iodine Compounds On Tadpole Metamorphosis

63

Metamorphosis is a process which occurs during development in some animals. During metamorphosis, the body undergoes rapid changes in structure and function. Metamorphosis sometimes brings about a change in the habitat and food of an organism. For example, a tadpole (frog larva) is aquatic and eats plants. However, an adult frog is amphibious and eats insects.

Metamorphosis of frogs and other amphibians is controlled by endocrine glands. The thyroid gland is an endocrine gland responsible for growth. It secretes a hormone called thyroxine. The thyroid gland removes iodine from the blood and uses it in making molecules of thyroxine. Thyroxine then is added to the blood.

Amphibian metamorphosis depends on the amount of thyroxine in the blood. Thyroxine speeds up the metabolic breakdown of starches and proteins. Thyroxine also regulates the rate of development in amphibians. A specific amount of thyroxine is needed in the bloodstream of a tadpole in order to bring about the development of legs and other features of adult frogs.

In this investigation, you are to compare the effects of two iodine compounds on the metamorphosis rate of tadpoles.

Materials *(per team of four students)*

aquarium fishnet
tadpoles—9
medium-sized culture dish
2-liter jars—3
glass marking pencil
boiled and cooled spring or pond water—3 liters every 3 days
iodine-potassium iodide solution—1 mL per day
thyroxine solution—50 mL per day
metric ruler
cm graph paper—4 sheets
dry baby cereal
colored pencils—3

Procedure

Working in teams of four, obtain nine tadpoles from the larger container. Place a tadpole into a medium-sized culture dish and examine it. Make a sketch of the tadpole showing the mouth, head, body, and tail. Turn the tadpole on its back and look for any limb buds on the ventral surface. Place the culture dish over a piece of cm graph paper. Using the graph paper, measure the body and tail length of the tadpole (Figure 1). Measure the body and tail lengths of each of the remaining tadpoles. Record the lengths of each tadpole in a table similar to Table 1.

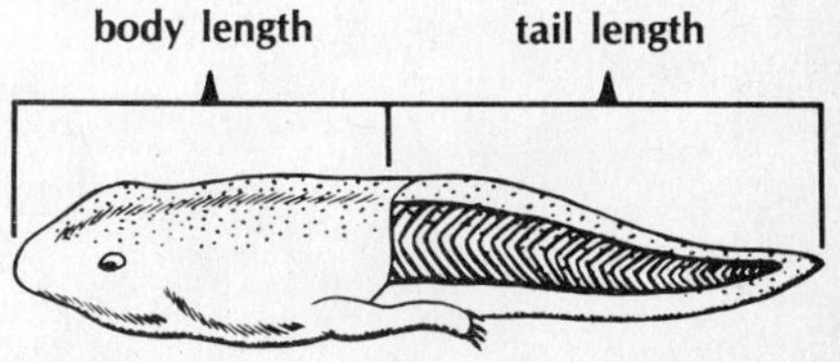

FIGURE 1

Place three of the tadpoles in each of three two-liter jars filled with a liter of boiled pond or spring water. Try to make the three groups as alike as possible with respect to tadpole size. Label one jar "I-KI." To this jar add 1 mL of iodine-potassium iodide solution (I-KI).

TABLE 1. MEASUREMENTS OF TADPOLES (cm)						
OBSERVATION	BODY LENGTH	TAIL LENGTH	HIND LIMB LENGTH	FORELIMB LENGTH	SHAPE OF	
					BODY	MOUTH
1						
2						
3						

FIGURE 2

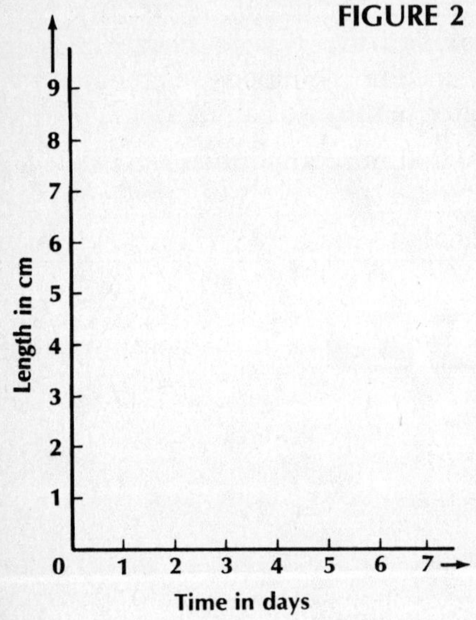

CAUTION: *If iodine spillage occurs, rinse with water.* Label another jar "thyroxine." To this jar add 50 mL of thyroxine solution.

Label the last jar "control." Do not add anything to this jar. Place the three jars on a shelf where the temperature is close to room temperature. Each day feed the tadpoles dry baby cereal. Change the water in each jar every three days. Use boiled spring or pond water. Add the iodine-potassium iodide solution and thyroxine solution to the proper jars after changing the water.

During the next several weeks, observe and record in your table the following for the tadpoles in each jar at three-day intervals:

(a) hind and forelimb lengths
(b) body and tail lengths
(c) development of joints in the feet
(d) changes in size and shape of the mouth
(e) changes in shape of the body

Use cm graph paper under the jars to measure the body, limb, and tail lengths.

At the conclusion of the experiment, construct graphs (Figure 2) showing the following data for the tadpoles in each jar. Construct four graphs—one for each measurement. For a certain measurement, put the lines for all three jars on the same graph using different colored pencils.

(a) length of the body (in cm) at three-day intervals
(b) length of the tail (in cm) at three-day intervals
(c) length of the forelimbs (in cm) at three-day intervals
(d) length of the hind limbs (in cm) at three-day intervals

Formulating Generalizations

1. Did development occur at the same rate in all tadpoles within the control jar? Explain your answer.
2. Did the tadpoles in plain water develop as fast as those in the iodine solutions? Explain your answer.
3. Describe any differences in the developments of the tadpoles in each of the three containers.
4. Explain the changes in the shape of the mouths of developing tadpoles.
5. List in order the major changes that occur during tadpole metamorphosis.
6. Which chemical substance (thyroxine or I-KI) brought about faster changes in development? Why do you think one chemical brought about faster development than the other?

Effects Of Adrenaline On *Daphnia* Heartbeat

64

Chemical control is directed most often by complex molecules called hormones. Some of the processes under hormonal control are growth, development, reproduction, and metabolism. In complex animals, hormones usually are produced by endocrine glands. Endocrine glands may produce one hormone or several hormones. Hormones are carried from endocrine glands to body organs by blood and other body fluids.

Each hormone has a specific function. Although hormones travel through many organs, each hormone usually affects only one organ or group of organs. The affected organ is called the target organ. A hormone has little or no effect on body organs other than the target organ. A specific amount of a hormone must be released in order to bring about a physiological change in the target organ. This amount is called the threshold level. If the amount of hormone released is below the threshold level, no change will be seen in the target organ.

In this investigation, you are to observe and record the effects of different concentrations of adrenaline on the heartbeat rate of *Daphnia.* You are to compare the heartbeat rate of *Daphnia* before adrenaline is added to the rate after adrenaline is added. You are to determine if the concentrations of adrenaline are above the threshold level or not.

Materials *(per team of two students)*

Daphnia—3
dropper
paper towel
microscope
plastic spoon
glass slide
culture dishes—2
adrenaline solutions
  .001%—0.1 mL
  .0001%—0.1 mL
  .000 01%—0.1 mL
clock or watch with second hand

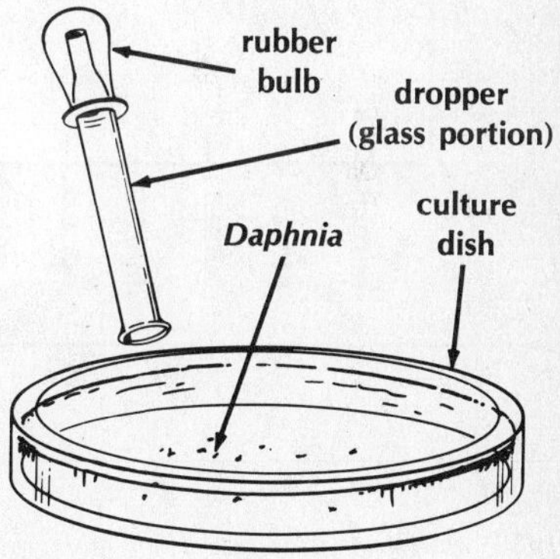

FIGURE 1

Procedure

Using a plastic spoon, place several *Daphnia* in a culture dish. Remove the rubber bulb from the large end of a dropper. Place the bulb over the small end of the dropper (Figure 1). Transfer one *Daphnia* to a clean, dry slide using the dropper. Remove some of the water with a paper towel to decrease the area in which the *Daphnia* can move.

Place the slide on the stage of a microscope and locate the *Daphnia.* Using Figure 2 as a guide, locate the heart of the *Daphnia.* Count the heartbeats of the *Daphnia* using the following method. You and your partner are to take turns being the "counter" and the "timer." After the counter locates the heart, the counter should inform the timer that he or she is ready to begin. The timer will tell the counter when to begin counting heartbeats. At the end of fifteen seconds, the

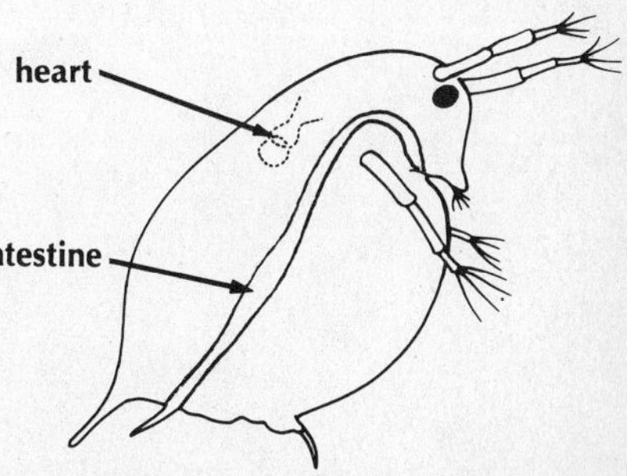

FIGURE 2

TABLE 1. TEAM DATA

TRIAL	NUMBER OF BEATS PER 15 SECONDS	NUMBER OF BEATS PER MINUTE
1		
2		
3		
4		
	Total	
	Average	

TABLE 2. CLASS DATA

TEAM	NORMAL	.000 01%	NORMAL	.0001%	NORMAL	.001%
1						
2						
3						
4						
5						
6						

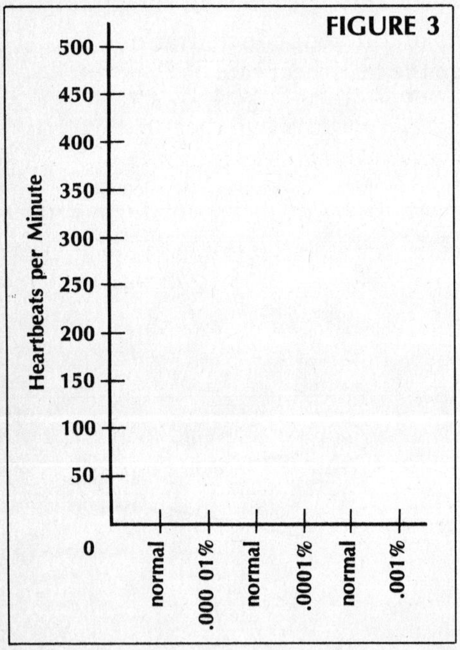

FIGURE 3

timer tells the counter to stop. Record the number of beats in a chart similar to Table 1. Count the heartbeats again for fifteen seconds and record in the data chart. Switch roles and repeat the counting and timing procedure for two more trials. Record all data in the data chart. Determine the beats per minute and the average beats per minute for your *Daphnia.*

Add a drop of .000 01% adrenaline to the *Daphnia* on the slide. Wait at least 30 seconds for the adrenaline to take effect. Remove any excess adrenaline from the slide with a paper towel. Using the procedure outlined above, count the number of heartbeats in a fifteen second period four times. Record all data in your data chart. Determine the number of beats per minute by adding the results of the four trials together.

Using a fresh *Daphnia* for each solution, repeat the above procedure. Make sure that your team determines the heartbeat rate at least four times before and after adding each adrenaline solution. After all trials have been run, plot your team data on a graph similar to the one shown in Figure 3. Collect and record class data in a chart similar to Table 2.

Formulating Generalizations

1. What was the target organ in this investigation?
2. Were any of the solutions of adrenaline at or above the threshold level? Explain.
3. What effect do threshold levels of adrenaline have on the target organ?
4. Why was the heartbeat rate taken several times before adrenaline was added to each *Daphnia*?
5. Predict what would happen if undiluted adrenaline were added to a *Daphnia.*
6. Design an investigation to determine whether different concentrations of the proper hormones could speed up the reproductive rate of *Daphnia.* (Hint: Female *Daphnia* produce eggs continually throughout their adult stage. The eggs develop into young *Daphnia* which are born alive.)
7. How could a scientist determine the target organ for a specific hormone in a group of closely related animals?
8. Predict the effect that the addition of adrenaline would have on a human heart.

The Human Menstrual Cycle

65

Usually around the age of twelve, humans begin to reach sexual maturity, and certain physical features begin to change. A deeper voice and facial hair develop in males, and both males and females begin to show changes in body shape.

These changes occur because of an increase in certain body chemicals called hormones. Hormones circulate throughout the bloodstream, but only have an effect on a certain organ or set of organs. Sex hormones control the development of the reproductive system and the processes that occur within the reproductive system once sexual maturity is reached.

The sex hormones in females control the forming of a mature egg and prepare the uterus for a possible pregnancy. It takes about twenty-eight days for these processes to occur and both processes are repeated every twenty-eight days in a cyclic manner. This pattern is called the menstrual cycle. Menstrual cycles usually begin around age twelve and continue to age forty-five or fifty.

In this investigation, you are to read the background information on the human menstrual cycle. You are to use the data in Table 1 to construct four graphs showing hormone concentrations in the blood of several females and the increase in size of the cells of the uterine lining during their menstrual cycles. From the graphs and the background information you are to formulate generalizations about the menstrual cycle.

Materials *(per student or team)*

ruler colored pencils—4 graph paper—2 sheets

Procedure

Part A. Background Information

A sexually mature female is capable of producing a mature egg, or ovum, about every 28 days. This 28-day cycle involves several different hormones. The four main hormones involved in the growth and release of the egg as well as in preparation of the uterus to receive a fertilized egg are discussed here.

There are four distinct stages in the menstrual cycle. The first stage lasts three to five days and is sometimes called menstruation. During menstruation, the thickened lining of the uterus breaks down because no fertilized egg is present. The dead cells lining the uterus as well as some blood and body fluid are released through the vagina.

The second stage of the menstrual cycle is called the follicle stage. The pituitary gland at the base of the brain releases large amounts of follicle stimulating hormone (FSH) into the bloodstream. As the level of FSH increases, it stimulates one of the ovaries to prepare an egg. This egg begins to grow and develop inside a protective group of cells called the follicle. At the same time FSH levels increase, another hormone called luteinizing hormone (LH) is released by the pituitary.

When both FSH and LH are present, the ovaries begin producing and releasing a third hormone called estrogen. Estrogen causes the cells lining the uterus to get thicker and longer. The increase in cell size occurs for several days. Estrogen also causes an increase in the blood flow to the growing uterine lining. As estrogen levels increase, the pituitary gland decreases FSH production so that a second egg does not develop.

FIGURE 1

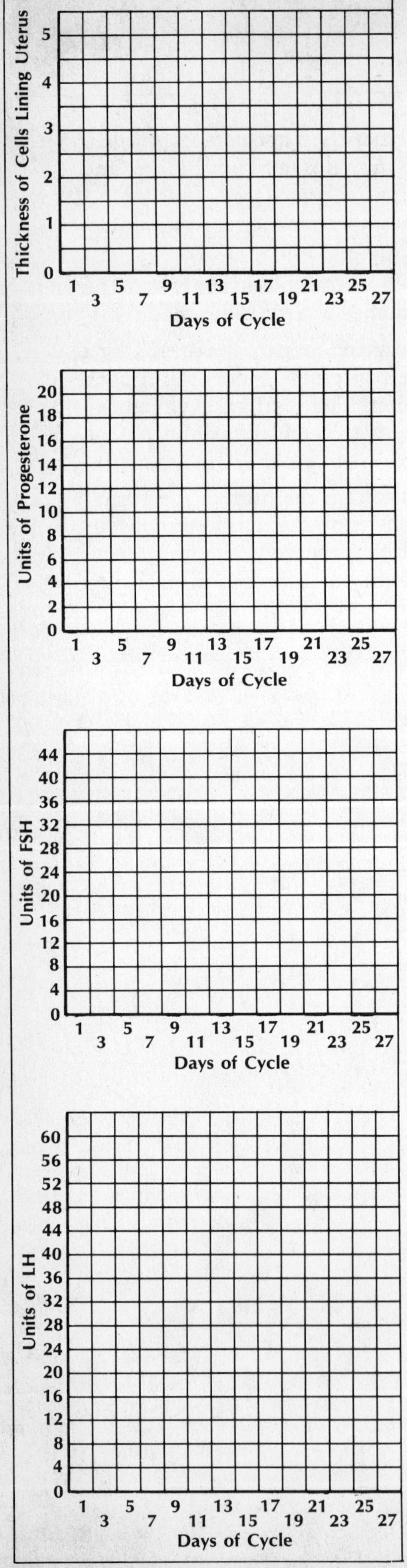

Decreasing levels of FSH stimulate the pituitary gland to release more LH. When LH levels are at their highest in the blood, the follicle breaks open and releases the egg. The release of the egg is the third and shortest stage of the menstrual cycle, ovulation.

After the egg is released, LH stimulates the follicle to become the yellow corpus luteum. This fourth stage of the menstrual cycle is called the corpus luteum stage, and it lasts for about thirteen to fifteen days. In the presence of LH, the corpus luteum produces the hormone progesterone. If fertilization does not occur, the corpus luteum stops production of progesterone, the uterine lining begins to break down, and menstruation occurs. During menstruation, the level of progesterone is low, and levels of FSH and LH begin to increase again. The uterine lining again begins to grow, and another menstrual cycle begins.

Part B. Constructing Graphs

Using centimeter graph paper, mark off axes similar to those shown in Figure 1. You should have four sets of axes. Using the data given in Table 1, construct four graphs. Each graph should show the changes that occur to either one of the hormones or to the size of the uterine lining cells during a menstrual cycle. Study the graphs and use your conclusions to answer the Formulating Generalizations questions.

TABLE 1. TRENDS OF HORMONES AND CELL THICKNESS DURING THE MENSTRUAL CYCLE

DAY	UTERUS LINING THICKNESS (mm)	LH	FSH	PROGESTERONE
1	5	8	10.5	1.0
3	2.5	12	15	1.3
5	1.1	10	14	1.0
7	1.8	13	12	1.3
9	2.1	10	13	1.0
11	2.5	11	12	1.3
13	3.0	18	12	1.3
15	3.2	58	43	3.0
17	3.2	18	12	8.5
19	3.2	10	10	13.0
21	3.3	12	9.8	18.0
23	3.5	22	9.7	14.0
25	4.0	17	9.8	8.5
27	4.8	11	9.8	3.5

Formulating Generalizations

1. How do LH, progesterone, and FSH differ in function? On what days does each hormone reach its peak? What happens when each is found in high amounts?
2. Are all three hormones ever found at their highest levels at the same time? Why or why not?
3. What would happen if progesterone levels did not increase sharply during the corpus luteum stage?
4. Why are uterine cells largest several days after FSH and LH reach their peaks?
5. How are the roles of estrogen and progesterone similar?

Response Of Protists To Chemical And Physical Stimuli

66

Behavior is an organism's response to internal or external stimuli from the environment. There are two types of behavior, unlearned or innate behavior and learned or acquired behavior.

Protists exhibit innate behavior. Innate behavior is inherited. Responses to stimuli are automatic. Mobile protists usually respond by moving away from unfavorable conditions. When protists bump into an object they stop, back up, and go forward in another direction. This type of response occurs until the organism has reached a more favorable environmental condition.

Protists have no nervous systems. Their protoplasm detects stimuli. The organism moves toward or away from the source of a stimulus in a reaction called a taxis (plural, taxes). Movement toward the source of the stimulus is called positive taxis. Movement away from the source of the stimulus is called negative taxis.

In this investigation, you are to identify and analyze the taxic responses of *Paramecium*, *Euglena*, and *Blepharisma* to touch (thigmotaxis), chemicals (chemotaxis), and electricity (galvanotaxis).

Materials

Per student

- absorbent cotton
- glass slides — 2
- coverslip
- compound microscope
- stereomicroscope
- dropper
- filter paper strips, 2 cm × 0.5 cm — 24
- 1%, 2%, 3%, and 5% sodium chloride solutions — 2 mL each
- scissors
- dry cell batteries — 2
- electrical tape — 5 cm
- distilled water
- tap water
- pencil
- paraffin wax, heated — 5 mL
- insulated copper wire — 60 cm
- 1%, 2%, 3%, and 5% acetic acid solutions — 2 mL each

Per class

- *Paramecium* cultures — 2
- *Blepharisma* cultures — 2
- *Euglena* cultures — 2

Procedure

Part A. Response to Physical Barriers

Pull apart the fibers of a piece of absorbent cotton and place them on a clean, dry slide (Figure 1). With a dropper, add a drop of *Paramecium* culture to the cotton fibers. Place a coverslip on the slide. Paramecia will become trapped between the fibers.

Observe the reaction of a specific motile *Paramecium* as it bumps into the cotton fibers. Record in your lab notebook the number of times the *Paramecium* bumps into a fiber before it changes direction.

Observe and record the reactions of *Blepharisma* and *Euglena* to physical barriers. Follow the same procedure used for *Paramecium*.

FIGURE 1

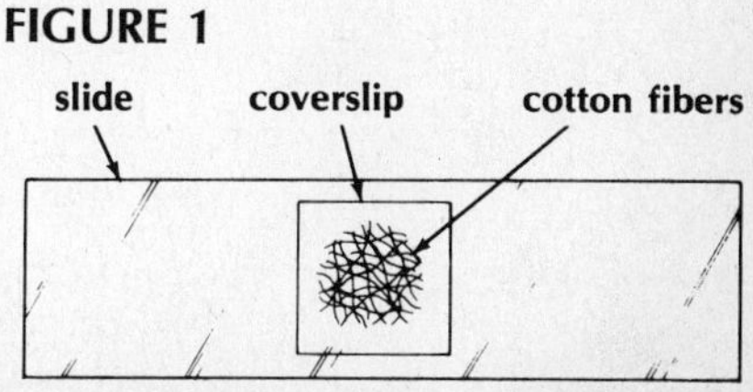

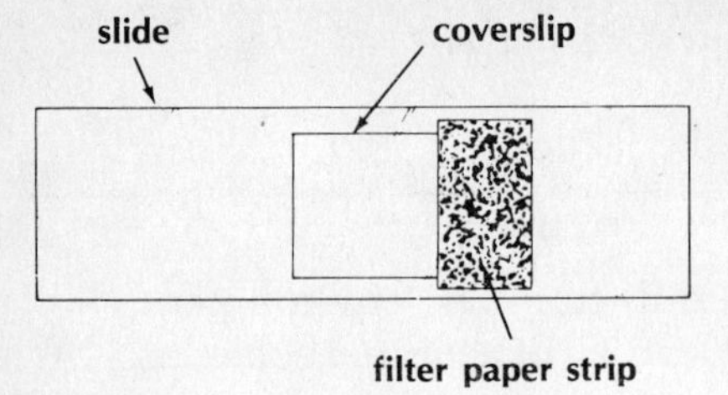

FIGURE 2

Part B. Response to Chemicals

With a dropper, add a drop of *Paramecium* culture to a clean, dry slide. Place the coverslip on the slide. With low power of your microscope, observe the pattern of movement of a *Paramecium*. Record your observations in your lab notebook.

Dip a filter paper strip in a 1% sodium chloride solution. Place the filter paper strip along one edge of the coverslip (Figure 2). Observe the slide near the filter paper strip on low power. Record the reaction of a *Paramecium* to the salt solution as it diffuses from the filter paper into the culture liquid. Note particularly any change in shape or direction of movement of the *Paramecium* relative to the salt. Record your observations in your lab notebook.

Using a fresh drop of *Paramecium* culture and a clean, dry slide each time, repeat the above procedure using a piece of filter paper dipped in 2%, 3%, and 5% sodium chloride solutions. Proceed from lower to higher concentrations. Repeat the above procedure with 1%, 2%, 3%, and 5% acetic acid solutions. **CAUTION:** *Acid causes burns. If spillage occurs, rinse with water and call your teacher.* Make a new wet mount before using the acetic acid solutions.

Using *Blepharisma* and *Euglena* cultures repeat the above procedure with all concentrations of both solutions. Proceed from lower to higher concentrations and use new wet mounts when changing to new concentrations of each solution.

Place your data on the chalkboard. Record the class data in your lab notebook. Compare your data with the class data.

Part C. Response to Electric Current

Using a microscope slide and heated paraffin, make a well 4 cm long, 1.5 cm wide, and 0.5 cm deep (Figure 3). **CAUTION:** *Paraffin is hot. Do not spill paraffin on fingers.* Add 5 to 8 drops of *Paramecium* culture to the well. Observe the specimens with a stereomicroscope. Record the behavior of the paramecia. Add an equal amount of 2% salt solution and observe the paramecia. Record any changes in their behavior. Remove the culture from the paraffin well and rinse in cool tap water.

Cut three pieces of wire long enough to fit the electrical apparatus as shown in Figure 4. Remove the insulation from both ends of each piece of wire.

Attach a long piece of wire to the positive pole of battery 1. Stick the end of the wire over one end of the wall so it extends into the well about 1 cm (Figure 5). Tape the wire to the slide to hold it in place. Connect a short piece of wire to the negative pole of battery 1. Connect the other end to the positive pole of battery 2. Attach the other long piece of wire to the negative pole of battery 2. Bend the other end of the wire over the other end of the paraffin wall so it extends into the well about 1 cm. **CAUTION:** *Make sure the two wires do not touch.* Tape the second wire to the slide. Your setup should look like Figure 5. Remove the insulation from the ends of the wires. Place the slide on the stage of a stereomicroscope.

Add 5 to 8 drops of *Paramecium* culture to the well. Add 5 to 8 drops of 2.0% salt solution to the well. Use your pencil to push the ends of the wires into the solution. Observe the movement of the paramecia with the stereomicroscope. Record any changes in their behavior.

Undo the long wires from the batteries. Reverse and reconnect them so that the wire that was connected to the positive pole is now

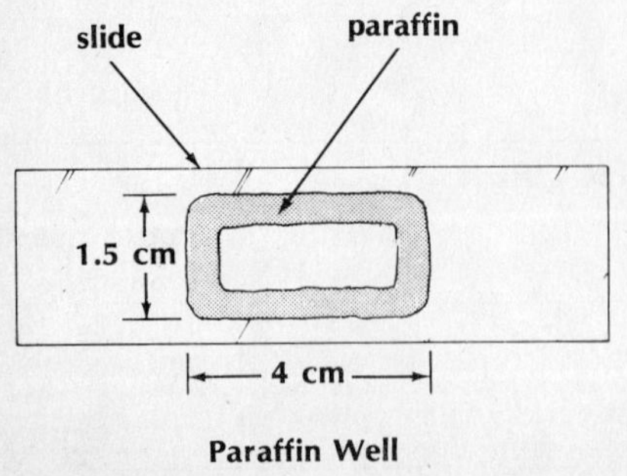

FIGURE 3

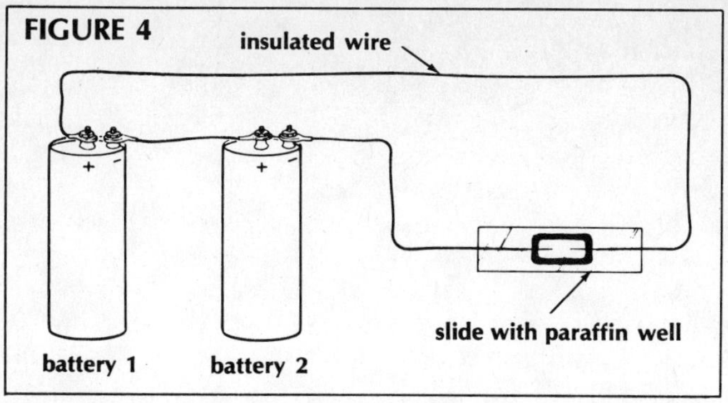

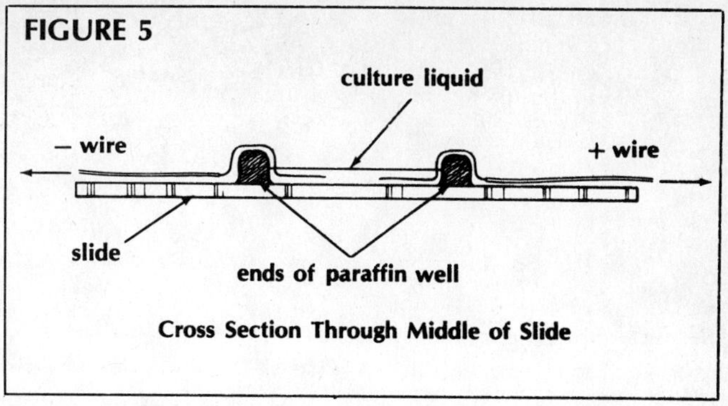

connected to the negative pole. This procedure will reverse the currents on the slide. Do not reposition the wires on the slide. Observe the movement of the paramecia. Record any changes in their behavior.

With a dropper, remove the *Paramecium* culture from the well. Rinse the well with distilled water. Repeat the above procedure using *Blepharisma* then *Euglena.* Record the movement of *Blepharisma* and *Euglena* in your lab notebook. Record any changes from their normal behavior. Record your data on the chalkboard. Compare your data with the class data.

Formulating Generalizations

1. Did the *Paramecium, Blepharisma,* and *Euglena* respond in the same manner when they bumped into cotton fibers? How do your data compare with class data? Explain any differences you observe between your data and class data.
2. Did any of the three protists move toward the salt? If so, which protist and salt concentration? Explain your answer.
3. Did any of the three protists move away from the acid? If so, which protist and acid concentration?
4. Did any of the protists respond in the same manner to the acetic acid as it did to the salt solution? If so, which protist and acetic acid concentration? How do your data compare to the class data?
5. In Part C, why was it necessary to observe each protist in the paraffin wells without the wires attached?
6. Why was it necessary to observe each protist with and without salt in the paraffin well?
7. Which protists were attracted to the positive pole in Part C?
8. Which protists were attracted to the negative pole?
9. Which protists showed no response to electric current?
10. What is the taxic response to electricity called?
11. Have you observed learned or unlearned behavior in this investigation? Explain.
12. How could you show whether or not protozoans have the ability to learn?

Response Of Multicellular Animals To Light

67

Most multicellular animals have definite nervous systems. The nervous system, along with the endocrine system, controls behavior. Multicellular animals usually have specialized cells, receptors, which detect stimuli. Multicellular animals also have effectors, cells that respond to stimuli. The eye of an animal contains receptors that perceive light. Muscles are effectors which move the organism away from or toward a light source. The movement or response toward or away from a light source is called phototaxis.

Multicellular animals exhibit innate behavior and learned behavior. Innate behavior is an inherited behavior for which the organism needs no previous experience. Different robins build similar nests, yet one robin has not learned nest building from another robin. This behavior is innate behavior. Learned behavior depends on the daily experiences of the animal. It is not inherited. Young robins peck at any moving object while feeding. Through trial and error, they learn to recognize which shapes are insects and worms and which are not. Choosing insects over other objects is a learned behavior.

Specific behavior patterns (whether innate or learned) can be adaptive. Specific behavior patterns may aid an animal's survival and reproduction. The degree of response to a stimulus depends on the strength of the stimulus and past experience of the organism.

In this investigation, you are to observe, analyze, and compare the phototaxic behavior of several multicellular animals by using beams of unfiltered and filtered light.

Materials

Per team of two or four
- flashlight
- shoe box or shirt box
- filter paper—2 pieces
- masking tape
- scissors
- thin cardboard (card stock)—20 cm × 27 cm
- thin cardboard (card stock) 4 cm × 4 cm—4
- cellophane sheets—3 cm × 3 cm in red, green, yellow, blue

Per class
- *Daphnia* cultures—6
- brine shrimp cultures—6
- planaria—12
- sowbugs—12
- guppies—12
- earthworms—12
- culture dishes

Procedure

Construct a cone from the large piece of cardboard to fit the flashlight (Figure 1). Roll the cardboard from the lower right corner to the lower left corner around the midpoint of the bottom edge. Trim the two ends so they are straight. The small end should be 1 cm or less in diameter. The large end should be large enough to fit around the flashlight. Attach the cone to the flashlight with masking tape.

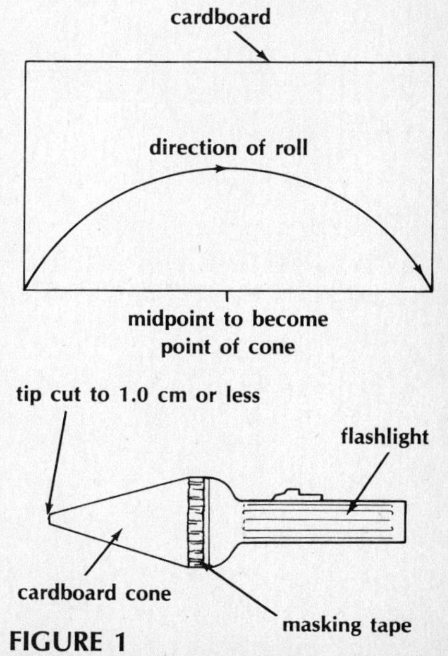

FIGURE 1

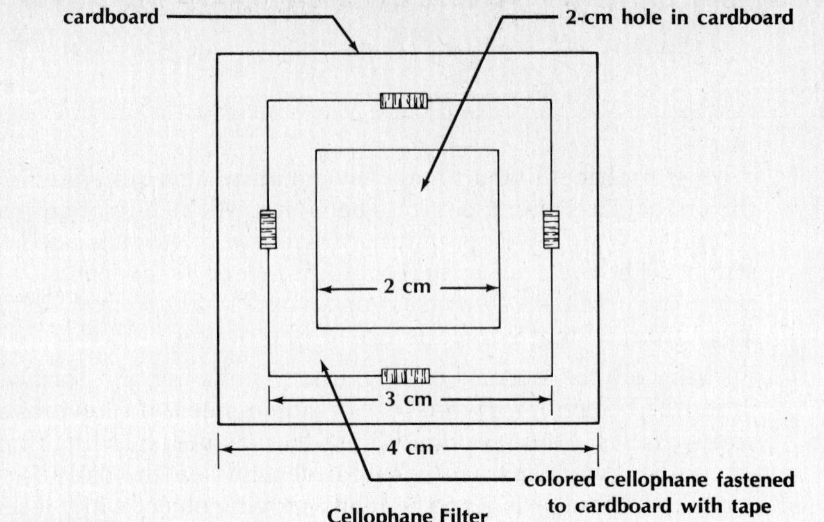

FIGURE 2

Construct four filters using the small cardboard squares and red, green, yellow, and blue cellophane (Figure 2). With scissors, cut a 2-cm square hole in the center of each piece of cardboard. **CAUTION:** *Always be careful when using scissors.* Tape one piece of cellophane over each hole. Construct a viewing box similar to Figure 3 from the bottom of a shoe box or shirt box. The viewing box is to have two openings. One opening is to be used to direct a beam of light on the specimens. Construct a table in your notebook similar to Table 1.

Daphnia

Place a culture dish containing 15 to 20 *Daphnia* on your table. Place the viewing box over the culture dish so the flashlight-beam hole is directly over the dish.

Direct the beam of light through the opening in the viewing box. Shine the beam on the middle of the culture (Figure 4). Observe the culture through the other hole. Use the holes for the same purposes in all other observations. Observe the culture for two to three minutes. Record in the table in your lab notebook the reaction of the *Daphnia* to the light.

TABLE 1. REACTIONS TO UNFILTERED AND FILTERED LIGHT

SPECIMEN	TYPE OF LIGHT				
	UNFILTERED	RED	YELLOW	GREEN	BLUE
Daphnia					
Brine shrimp					
Planarian					
Sowbug					
Guppy					
Earthworm					

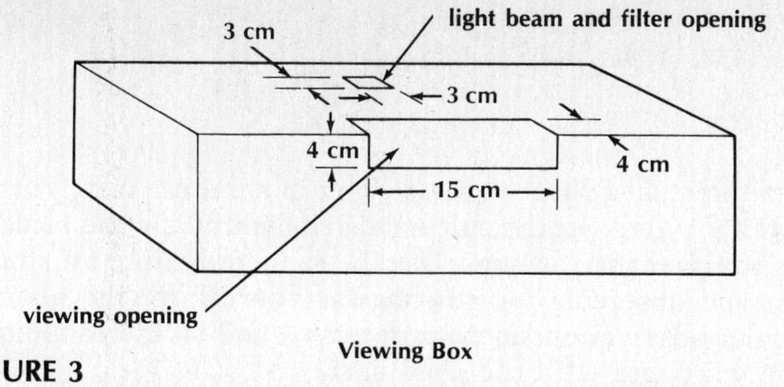

FIGURE 3

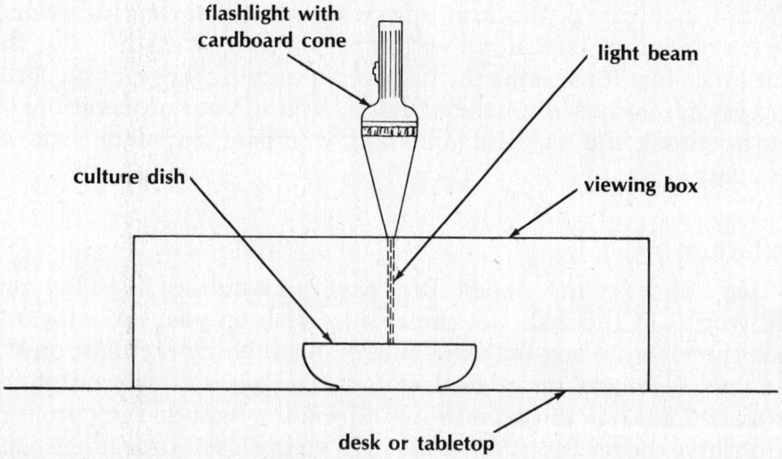

FIGURE 4

Place one of the four filters over the center opening of the viewing box. Allow one minute for the organisms to return to normal. Direct the flashlight beam through the filter onto the culture for two to three minutes. Record the reaction of the *Daphnia* to the filtered light. Repeat this procedure with the other three filters. Record your observations in your notebook. Place your data on the chalkboard. Compare your data with the class data.

Brine Shrimp

Follow the *Daphnia* procedures for a brine shrimp culture. Record all observations in your notebook and on the chalkboard. Compare your data with those of other class members.

Planarian

Obtain a culture dish with two planarians. Place the culture dish on your lab table. Place the viewing box over the culture dish with the hole over the center of the dish. Direct the flashlight beam through the opening. Shine the light in front of the anterior end of a planarian.

Observe the reaction of the planarian for one to two minutes. Keep moving the beam so it is always in front of the anterior end of the planarian. After one to two minutes, shine the light over the eyespots of the planarian. Repeat this procedure four times. Record the reaction of the planarian in your notebook. Repeat this procedure with the other planarian.

Repeat the procedure using each filter. Record your observations in your notebook. Place all your planaria data on the chalkboard. Compare your data with the class data.

Sowbug

Place a moistened sheet of filter paper in a culture dish. Put two sowbugs in the dish. Set the culture dish on your table and place the viewing box over the sowbugs. Use the same procedure for shining the light and observing the sowbugs as you did for the planaria. Record your observations in your notebook and on the chalkboard. Compare your data with the class data.

Guppy

Obtain a culture dish containing two guppies. Set the culture dish on your table and place the viewing box over the culture dish. Use the same procedure for shining the light and observing the reaction of the guppies that you used for the planaria. Record your observations in your notebook and on the chalkboard. Compare your data with the class data.

Earthworm

Place a sheet of moistened filter paper in a culture dish. Put two earthworms in the dish. Set the culture dish on your lab table and place the viewing box over the culture dish. Shine the light on the first four segments of an earthworm. Observe the reaction of the earthworm for one to two minutes. Shine the light on the clitellum and observe the reaction. Shine the light on the last four segments and observe the reaction. Record the reactions of the earthworm for each of the three body areas. Repeat the procedure with the other earthworm. Repeat this procedure using the four filters. Record all observations in your notebook and on the chalkboard. Compare your data with the class data.

Formulating Generalizations

1. Why is it important that you add a "cone" to the flashlight?
2. Which organisms responded positively to (moved toward) unfiltered light?
3. Which organisms responded negatively to unfiltered light? What does this reaction have to do with survival of an organism in its environment?
4. To which color of filtered light did most organisms respond?
5. What stimulus other than light could be causing a response in the organisms observed?
6. Why was it necessary in some instances to observe orientation of an entire culture in one dish? Describe the behavior of these organisms.
7. Why was it necessary to make observations on at least two of the larger specimens?
8. What is the difference between positive and negative phototaxis?
9. Did most organisms respond positively or negatively to the light?
10. Explain how this response might be adaptive.

Taste Perception In Humans

68

In order for an organism to survive, it must be adapted to its environment and have ways to detect stimuli from the environment. In most animals, stimuli are detected by a nervous system. The nervous system contains receptors, nerve cells or organs that detect stimuli. The organism reacts to stimuli after it interprets stimuli.

One type of receptor is the chemoreceptor. This receptor is a specialized epithelial cell which detects changes in the chemical environment of the organism. Many types of chemoreceptors are found in animals. One type, the taste chemoreceptors in humans, is located in cells of the tongue and the roof of the mouth. Chemoreceptors are nerve endings. They detect salty, sweet, bitter, or sour tastes. Many of these chemoreceptors are in taste buds. Other receptors in the body detect stimuli of pressure, pain, heat, and cold.

In this investigation, you are to locate and identify the areas of the tongue which detect salty, sweet, bitter, or sour tastes. You are to compare your data with the data of the rest of the class and determine any physiological variation that may exist.

Materials *(per team of two students)*

3% sucrose solution—5 mL
1% sodium chloride solution—5 mL
0.1% quinine sulfate—5 mL
1% vinegar—5 mL
cotton swabs—10
small beakers or vials—4
water
paper cups—2
disposable gloves

Procedure

In this investigation, you are to work in teams of two. One team member will be the "investigator" while the other team member will be the "subject." The investigator is to apply certain chemical solutions to the subject's tongue. The subject will record the responses. After completing the procedure, switch "jobs" and repeat the procedure.

Investigator

Place 5 mL of each solution into separate beakers or vials. Dip a cotton swab into the 3% sucrose solution and let excess solution drain from the cotton. While the subject's tongue is stuck out, lightly touch the cotton swab to each of the five numbered areas of the tongue (Figure 1). Allow the subject to record the response for each area before applying solution to the next area.

After applying sucrose solution to each area, use each of the other solutions in the same way. Use a new cotton swab for each solution.

Subject

Rinse out your mouth with some water. Stick out your tongue and hold it flat while the investigator applies the solutions. After the

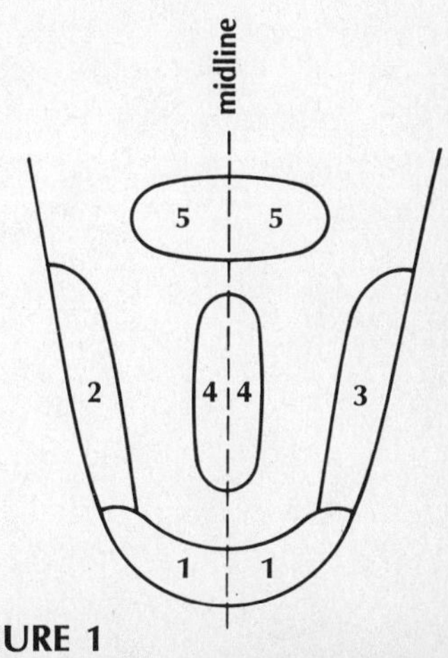

FIGURE 1

TABLE 1. RESPONSE OF TONGUE TO DIFFERENT SOLUTIONS										
TASTE	AREA OF TONGUE TESTED									
	1—Tip		2—Right side		3—Left side		4—Middle		5—Back	
	Your results	Class results	Your results	Class results	Your results	Class results	Your results	Class results	Your results	Class results
Sweet										
Sour										
Salty										
Bitter										

investigator touches the cotton swab to each area, record your response in your lab notebook in a table similar to Table 1. If you can taste the solution, place a plus sign (+) in the correct row and column of the table for the solution and tongue area. If you cannot taste the solution, place a minus sign (−) in the correct row and column. After application of each solution to all five areas, rinse out your mouth with water.

After completing the procedure twice (once as investigator and once as subject), place your team results on the chalkboard. Record a summary of the class results in your data table. Compare your data with the class results.

Formulating Generalizations

1. Why did you place the same chemical solution on all five areas of your tongue?
2. Did you taste salty, sweet, bitter, or sour in more than one of the areas of your tongue? Explain.
3. Which areas of your tongue and your partner's tongue responded in the same ways?
4. If your partner's responses are different from yours, explain what may cause the differences.
5. Assume that one area of the tongue contains only one chemoreceptor. What evidence do you have from this investigation that supports the hypothesis that a single chemoreceptor may respond to more than one chemical?
6. Why did you rinse your mouth each time you changed solutions?
7. Could any variation in taste areas be caused by physiological reasons or student error? Explain.
8. Assume that you had salty, sweet, bitter, and sour solutions of various percentage compositions. Suggest a procedure in which you could determine the threshold of taste perception in humans.
9. From this investigation, what evidence is there of receptors in the human tongue other than those for taste?
10. What other types of receptors are found on the tongue?

Muscle And Bone Tissue

69

Tissue that contracts to produce movement is called muscle or contractile tissue. Cells making up muscle tissue are usually elongated and thin. Humans and most vertebrates have three types of muscle tissue: skeletal, cardiac, and smooth.

Skeletal muscle tissue is composed of many fibers running parallel to each other (Figure 2A). Boundaries between cells are not easily distinguished. A fiber is enclosed within a membrane called a sarcolemma. Each muscle fiber is made up of contractile filaments called myofibrils. Myofibrils of skeletal muscle have small dark bands (striations) on them. Thus, skeletal muscle tissue is sometimes called striated muscle tissue.

Cardiac muscle tissue is similar to skeletal muscle tissue except that the fibers have side branches (Figure 2B). Individual cardiac muscle cells are distinguishable. The side branches of the cardiac muscle join with the long fibers on occasion. Each cell contains a nucleus and striations. Intercalary discs separate one cell from another. Cardiac muscle tissue makes up the heart.

Smooth muscle tissue is made up of individual, spindle-shaped cells (Figure 2C). Myofibrils are structures for contraction found in the cytoplasm. The myofibrils are not striated. Thus, this muscle tissue is called "smooth" as opposed to striated. Smooth muscles are found in most visceral (internal) organs.

Many animals have skeletal systems. A skeletal system supports the body. Vertebrates have endoskeletons, while many invertebrates have exoskeletons (if they have any skeletal systems).

The skeletons of most vertebrates are composed of bones. Bone-forming cells, osteoblasts, originate in cartilage. Osteoblasts are cells that produce bony material in the cartilage. After osteoblasts are surrounded by bone they are called osteocytes or bone cells. Other cells, osteoclasts, then migrate into the cartilage, making pathways for new blood vessels and nerves. Blood vessel and nerve canals are called Haversian canals. Bone cells are embedded in bony material in layers that form rings called lamellae around the Haversian canals (Figure 1). Within each lamellae layer are small canals, canaliculi, that carry fluids between blood vessels and osteocytes.

In this investigation, you are to locate and identify the structures of the three types of muscle tissues. You are to locate and identify the structures of bone tissue.

Materials *(per student or team)*

prepared slides:
- smooth muscle (longitudinal section)
- skeletal muscle (longitudinal section)
- cardiac muscle (longitudinal section)
- compact human bone cross section

microscope

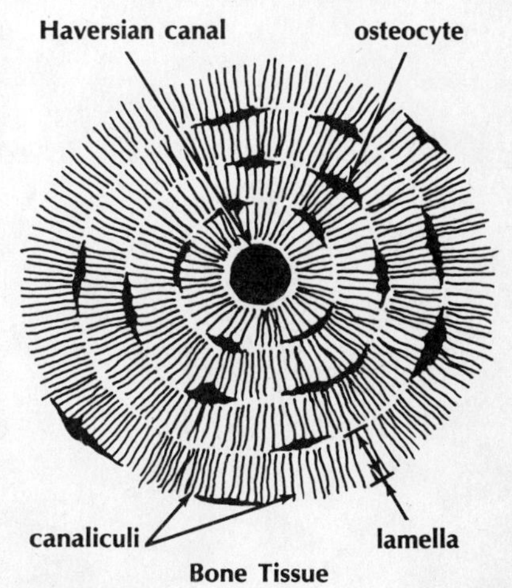

FIGURE 1

Procedure

Observe the three types of muscle cells and the compact bone cell slides with low power of your microscope. Locate and identify the structures listed below for each tissue. Count the number of nuclei

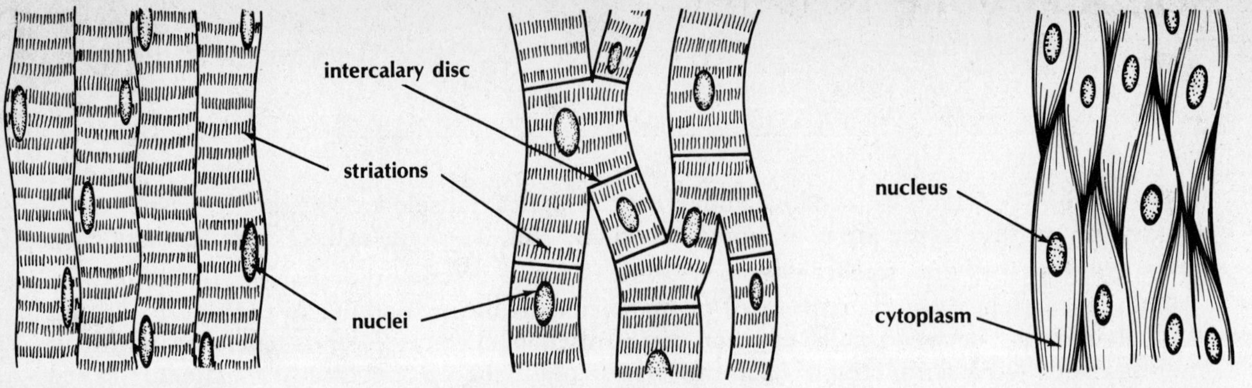

FIGURE 2

per cell in each of the muscle tissues. Make a sketch of each tissue in your lab notebook.

Smooth muscle—locate nuclei, cytoplasm, and cell membranes
Skeletal muscle—locate striations and nuclei
Cardiac muscle—locate striations and nuclei
Compact bone —locate Haversian canals, lamellae, osteocytes, and canaliculi

Formulating Generalizations

1. In what part of an organism would you expect to find **(a)** smooth muscle, **(b)** cardiac muscle, **(c)** skeletal muscle?
2. What is the basic structural difference between cardiac and skeletal muscle?
3. How does smooth muscle differ structurally from cardiac and skeletal muscle?
4. Describe the position of the nuclei in each type of muscle tissue cell.
5. What are the differences in the number of nuclei in each type of muscle tissue?
6. In what respects does muscle tissue differ from compact bone tissue?
7. What is the main function of canaliculi?
8. Why does bone tissue appear to be composed of concentric rings?
9. From what tissue do bone forming cells (osteoblasts) originate?
10. How do osteoblasts and osteocytes differ?
11. What is the function of Haversian canals?
12. How are Haversian canals and canaliculi similar in function?

Locomotion In Earthworms

70

Most tube-shaped invertebrates such as earthworms have two types of muscles—longitudinal and circular. The circular muscles are made up of short fibers which interconnect to form a series of rings. These rings do not connect directly to the skin of the animal, but fit around the animal's body in much the same way that a ring fits on a finger. Circular muscles surround the body from the anterior to the posterior end. When these muscles contract, the diameter of the animal becomes smaller. When the circular muscles relax, the diameter of the animal's body returns to a larger size.

The long, stringlike longitudinal muscle is made up of many strands that form a balloonlike shape just beneath the circular muscles. These strands are attached to the skin at the anterior end and posterior end of the animal. When the longitudinal muscle contracts, the body of the animal becomes shorter in length. When the longitudinal muscle relaxes, the animal's body lengthens.

In this investigation, you are to examine a muscle contraction model. Then you are to observe movement patterns in an earthworm. Using your observations and the model, you are to explain how the muscles work to produce movement in an earthworm.

Materials *(per student or team)*

live earthworm
hand lens
paper towel
dissecting pan
muscle model
water
dropper
small beaker

Procedure

Part A. Earthworm Muscle Model

Examine the muscle model provided by your teacher. The long, thin balloon represents a longitudinal muscle. The elastic tied around the balloon represents a few of the circular muscles. This model represents the way the two layers of muscles look inside the earthworm.

Questions:

1. If you stretched the balloon, would it get longer or shorter?
2. If the balloon were a muscle, would it be contracting or relaxing when stretched?
3. Now, suppose you were to allow the balloon to return to its original shape. Would it get longer or shorter?
4. If the balloon were a muscle, would it be contracting or relaxing when returning to its original shape?
5. If you stretched all the elastic rings, would they get longer or shorter?
6. If the elastic rings were muscles, would they be contracting or relaxing when stretched?
7. What represents the longitudinal muscle in the model?
8. What represents the circular muscles in the model?

Part B. Earthworm Observations

Place a live earthworm on a wet paper towel in a dissecting pan. Observe the movements of the earthworm for several minutes. Add water to the earthworm as needed to keep it from drying out. Observe changes in the shape and length of the anterior and posterior sections of the earthworm as it moves. Use Figure 1 as a guide to help you locate the anterior and posterior ends. Record all observations in a table similar to Table 1.

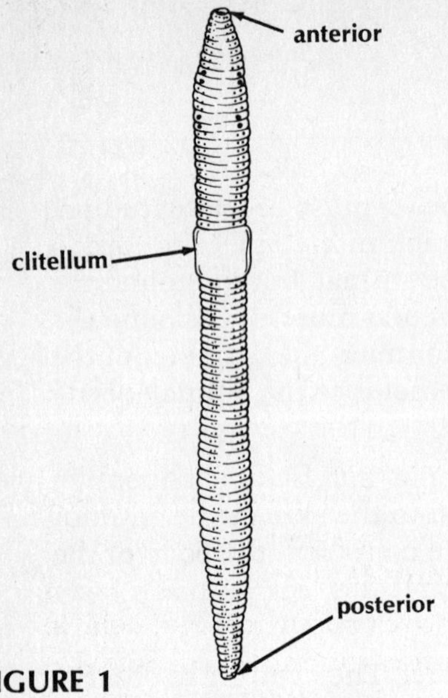

FIGURE 1

TABLE 1. EARTHWORM OBSERVATIONS

WORM PART	MOVING		AT REST	
anterior				
posterior				
	CIRCULAR	LONGITUDINAL	CIRCULAR	LONGITUDINAL
muscle contracting				
muscle relaxing				

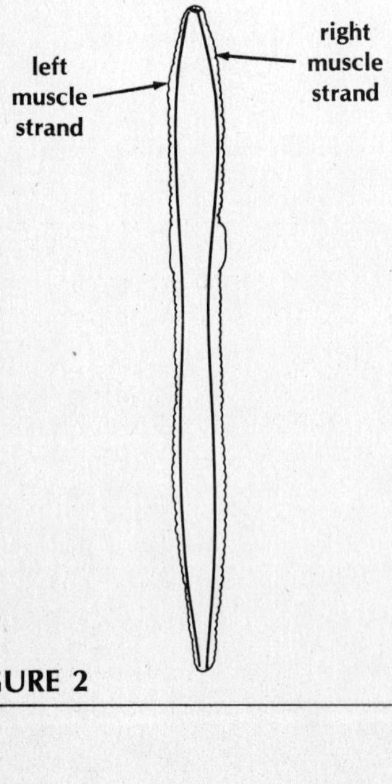

FIGURE 2

Formulating Generalizations

1. What happens to the circular and longitudinal muscles when the earthworm gets larger in diameter and shorter in length?
2. What happens to the circular and longitudinal muscles when the earthworm gets smaller in diameter and longer in length?
3. What evidence do you have to suggest that all the longitudinal muscles do not contract at the same time?
4. What evidence do you have to suggest that all the circular muscles do not contract at the same time?
5. How do the circular and longitudinal muscles work together in earthworm movement?
6. Which of the two types of muscles turn the anterior end of the earthworm to the right and left? Explain.
7. Figure 2 shows a worm with only two muscle strands. If the right muscle strand contracts as the left muscle strand relaxes, and the right muscle strand relaxes as the left muscle strand contracts, what would be the movement pattern of this worm? (You may wish to use a drawing to help explain your answer.)
8. Does a real worm move as described in question 7? Explain.

Locomotion In Protists

71

Locomotion in members of the protist kingdom is quite diverse. Some organisms are propelled by hairlike appendages. Others have pseudopods in which cytoplasm streams or flows. The type of organelle used in locomotion is a determining factor in the organism's speed through a medium.

Cilia (singular, cilium) and flagella (singular, flagellum) are similar in structure and function. Cilia and flagella are hairlike structures (Figure 1). Cilia are more numerous and shorter than flagella. They may completely cover the organism. Flagella are as long as the body of the protozoan and are located at the anterior end of some protozoans. The beating of cilia is similar to the movement of oars on a boat. A flagellum moves similarly to the action of a whip. Flagella and cilia are present on some cells of some higher plants and animals.

Cytoplasmic streaming is a process in which the cytoplasm moves about inside a cell. In protozoans, this streaming causes movement of the cell. Amoebae move by forming pseudopods. A slime mold forms a network of pseudopods extending in all directions in search of food. This branching pseudopod network of a slime mold is called a plasmodium. The plasmodium is filled with streaming cytoplasm. Pseudopods can fill and empty rapidly.

In this investigation, you are to locate and identify the organelles and structures of locomotion of several protozoans. You are to compute their speed in micrometers per second (or minute). You are to observe the flowing cytoplasm of a slime mold and compare it with the movement of an amoeba.

Materials

Per student
- dropper
- glass slide
- coverslip
- microscope
- absorbent cotton
- watch with second hand

Per class
- *Chaos chaos* culture
- *Peranema* culture
- *Blepharisma* culture
- *Paramecium* culture
- *Euglena* culture
- slime mold on agar

Procedure

Part A. Computation of Speed

In order to compute the speed of a protozoan, you need to know the diameter of the field of view of your microscope and the time it takes the protozoan to cross the field of view. To determine the time it takes a protozoan to cross the field of view of your microscope, align the slide so the organism passes from one side to the other. Several tries may be needed before a protozoan crosses the field of view in a straight line.

FIGURE 1

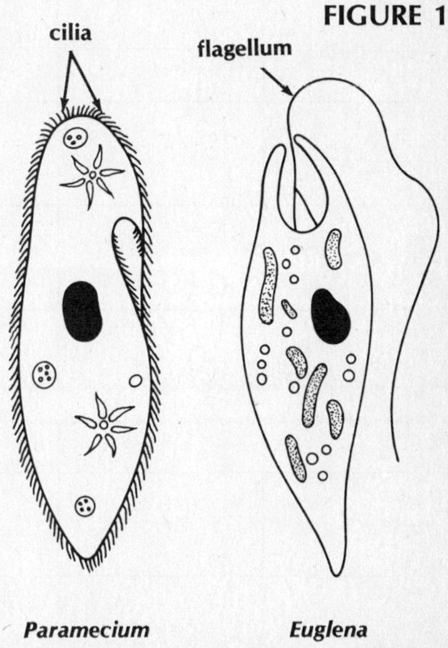

After determining the time it takes for the protozoan to cross the field of view, use the following formula to compute the speed of the protozoan:

$$\frac{\text{diameter of the low power field}}{\text{seconds to travel diameter of field}} = \text{per second (speed) } \mu\text{m}$$

Example: $\frac{1500\ \mu\text{m (diameter of field)}}{10\ \text{seconds}} = 150$ per second μm

Part B. Observations

Chaos chaos

With a dropper, remove a sample of the amoeba culture (*Chaos chaos*) from the bottom of the culture dish. Place a drop of the culture on a clean, dry slide and add a coverslip. Place the slide on the stage of a compound microscope. Locate an amoeba with the low power lens. Observe the streaming of the cytoplasm. Observe several pseudopods on the same amoeba. Make a sketch in your notebook of the amoeba showing the "direction of flow" of the cytoplasm. Note on the sketch how many other pseudopods are being formed at the same time.

Compute the speed of the amoeba in micrometers per second (or minute). Record the speed in your lab notebook in a table similar to Table 1.

Peranema

Make a wet mount from the *Peranema* culture in the same way you did with *Chaos chaos.* Place the slide on the stage of a compound microscope. Using low power, locate a *Peranema* cell. Locate and observe the motion of the flagellum. You may need to adjust the diaphragm to reduce the amount of light entering the lens. Make a sketch of a *Peranema* in your lab notebook. Describe the motion of the flagellum in your lab notebook. Also describe the motion of the rest of the organism as it moves across the field of view.

TABLE 1. INDIVIDUAL AND CLASS SPEEDS

	CHAOS	*PERANEMA*	*BLEPHARISMA*	*PARAMECIUM*	*EUGLENA*
Your data					
Student 1					
Student 2					
Student 3					
Total					
Average					

Compute the speed of a *Peranema* in micrometers per second (or minute) on either high or low power. Record the speed in the table in your lab notebook.

Blepharisma

Blepharisma may be too fast for extended observations. Therefore, use cotton fibers on your wet mount to "imprison" the organisms. Separate some fibers of absorbent cotton and place them on a clean, dry slide. With a dropper, transfer a sample of *Blepharisma* culture from the bottom of the dish to the cotton fibers and add a coverslip. Place the slide on the stage of the microscope. Locate a *Blepharisma* with low power. Use the diaphragm to adjust the amount of light for easier viewing. Using high power, locate the cilia near the gullet. Make a sketch of a *Blepharisma* in your lab notebook. Describe the movement of the cilia in your lab notebook. Observe the rows of smaller cilia that cover the rest of the organism. Describe the beating action of these cilia in your lab notebook.

On low power, move the slide until you locate a *Blepharisma* away from the cotton fibers. Compute the speed of the *Blepharisma* in micrometers per second (or minute). Record the speed in the table in your lab notebook.

Paramecium

Make a wet mount from the *Paramecium* culture in the same way you did *Blepharisma.* Locate a *Paramecium* under low power and then observe several cilia on high power. Adjust the amount of light entering your scope with the diaphragm. Make a sketch of a *Paramecium* in your lab notebook. Describe the movement of the cilia in your lab notebook. Compare their movement with that of the cilia of a *Blepharisma.*

Using low power, move the slide until you locate a *Paramecium* away from the cotton fibers. Compute the speed of the *Paramecium* in micrometers per second (or minute). Record the speed in the table in your lab notebook.

Euglena

Make a wet mount from the *Euglena* culture in the same way you did for *Chaos chaos.* Place the slide on the stage of a compound microscope. Using low power, locate a *Euglena* cell. Make a sketch of a *Euglena* in your lab notebook. Using high power, locate the flagellum. Observe the motion of a flagellum. Describe the motion of the flagellum in your lab notebook. Describe the motion of the rest of a *Euglena* cell as it moves across the field of view.

Compute the speed of a *Euglena* in micrometers per second (or minute) on either low or high power. Record the speed in the table in your lab notebook.

Record on the chalkboard the speeds in micrometers per second (or minute) of the protozoans you observed. Record the class data in the table in your notebook. Compare the class data with your data.

Part C. Observation of Slime Mold

Place a thin agar culture of slime mold with a branching plasmodium on the stage of a compound microscope. With low power, locate the plasmodium. Observe the direction of flow of the cytoplasm for several minutes. Move the slime mold culture around on the stage of the microscope in order to observe the flow of cytoplasm in the many branches of the plasmodium. Make a sketch of the plasmodium in your lab notebook.

Formulating Generalizations

1. Does the shape of any of the six protozoans change as they move? Which ones?
2. Describe the pattern of movement of each protozoan observed.
3. Does the cytoplasm of an amoeba flow in more than one pseudopod at the same time? Explain.
4. Does the cytoplasm of an amoeba flow in more than one pseudopod at the same time? Explain.
5. Compare and contrast the functions and movements of cilia and flagella.
6. Compare the beating action of cilia around the "mouth" of *Blepharisma* to the action of cilia covering the rest of the protist's body.
7. From the class averages, list the protozoans in order of decreasing speed. Also make the same type of list list using your own data. Is there any difference between your data and class data? Explain your answer.
8. Do the faster organisms have the same type of locomotion? If not, how do their locomotion patterns differ?
9. From your data, calculate how long it would take for each type of organism to travel the width of your laboratory table assuming the table is 61 cm wide.
10. Does there appear to be any coordination of the beating of each row of cilia on ciliates?
11. Describe the similarities and differences in the "flowing cytoplasm" of an amoeba and a slime mold plasmodium.
12. In the slime mold, does the "flowing" cytoplasm move from smaller branches to larger branches or vice versa? What conclusions can you draw from this motion?

Earthworm Anatomy

72

Earthworms are members of phylum Annelida. They are commonly called segmented worms because their bodies are made up of many segments. Some body parts of annelids are located in each body segment. Other body parts are only in specific segments.

In this investigation, you are to observe, locate, and identify various external parts of the earthworm. By dissection, you are to locate, identify, and distinguish various internal parts of the earthworm.

Materials *(per student or team)*

preserved earthworm	water
paper towel	hand lens or stereomicroscope
dissecting pan	scalpel
dissecting pins	forceps
scissors	prepared slide of earthworm cross section
dropper	compound microscope

Procedure

Part A. External Anatomy

Place a preserved earthworm in a dissecting pan. Locate and identify the anterior and posterior ends of the worm. Rub your fingers over the dorsal and ventral surfaces of the worm from anterior end to posterior end. Repeat the procedure going from posterior to anterior. The sharp, bristly structures you feel are setae.

Locate and identify the prostomium, mouth, anus, and clitellum (Figure 1). Hold the worm in your hand. Locate and identify the opening of the seminal receptacles (segments 9 and 10), the opening to the sperm ducts (segment 15), and the opening to the oviduct (segment 14). You may need a hand lens to see these openings.

FIGURE 1

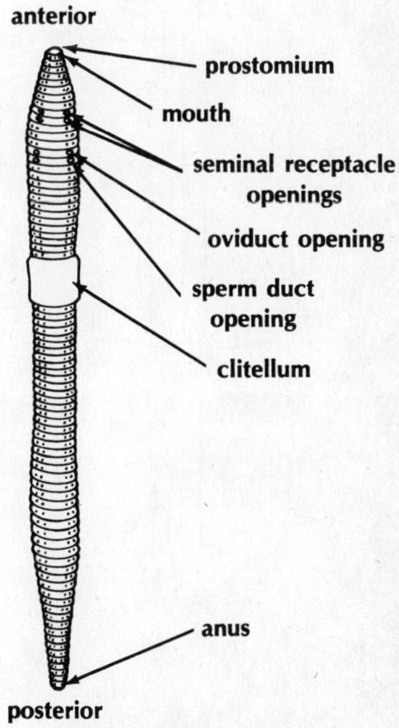

Earthworm External Features (ventral view)

Part B. Internal Anatomy

Place the preserved earthworm on its ventral side. The ventral side is lighter in color and flatter than the dorsal side. The ventral side also has several pairs of small body openings. See Figure 1.

Place a dissecting pin through the fifth segment of the worm. Stretch the worm straight and place a dissecting pin in the eighth segment from the anus.

Locate a dark-colored line running dorsally under the skin from the anterior to the posterior end of the worm. This line is the median dorsal blood vessel.

Insert a blade of a pair of scissors into the worm to the right of the blood vessel near the posterior dissecting pin. **CAUTION:** *Always be careful when using scissors.* Make a shallow incision from the posterior end all the way to the anterior end. Make sure that the cut is shallow by keeping the bottom blade of the scissors parallel to the

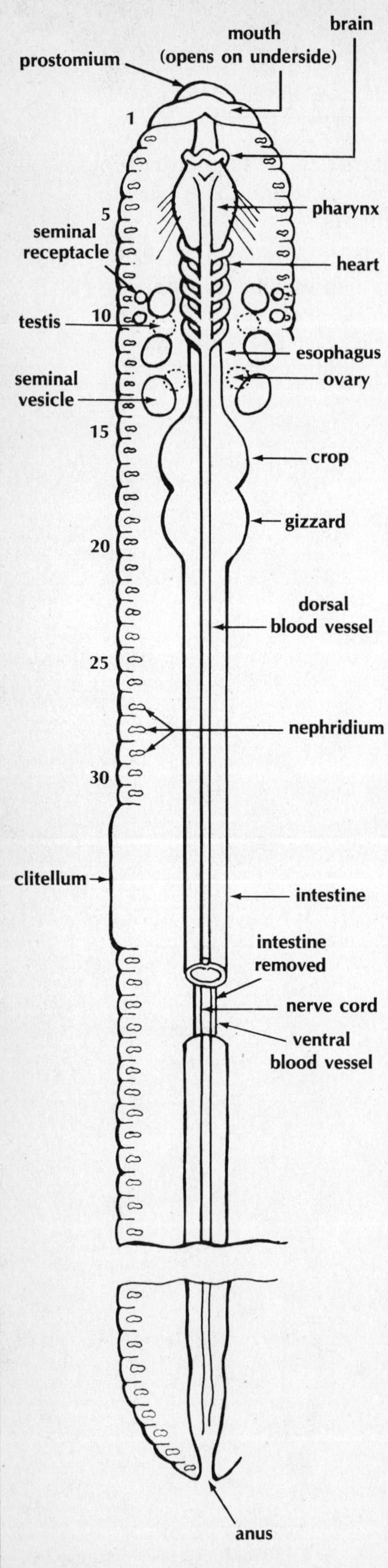

FIGURE 2

dissecting pan and near the surface of the worm. As you make your incision, you will notice thin partitions (septa) dividing each segment. Use a scalpel to cut the septa and separate the body wall from the internal organs. **CAUTION:** *Always be careful with scalpels or other sharp instruments. Slice away from your fingers to avoid cuts.* Spread the body wall open by placing dissecting pins into the body wall at intervals of every ten to twelve segments. Carefully angle the pins so they will not be in your way during observation.

Do not cut into the intestine. With a dropper, place a few drops of water on the worm periodically throughout the lab period.

Construct a table similar to Table 1. Record in the table your observations of each earthworm system you observe.

TABLE 1. SYSTEMS OF AN EARTHWORM

SYSTEM	STRUCTURES PRESENT	LOCATION BY SEGMENT
Reproductive		
Digestive		

Reproductive System

Earthworms are hermaphrodites. They have both male and female organs in the same body. However, they do not fertilize themselves. Locate the three lobes of the seminal vesicles in segments 9 to 13 (Figure 2). Sperm cells are made and stored in these lobes. Locate the two pairs of seminal receptacles in segments 9 and 10. These structures receive and store sperm cells from another earthworm during mating. Small white ovaries are located beneath the seminal vesicles in segment 13. They are very small and may not be visible without a hand lens or stereomicroscope. Testes are also present in your worm but are difficult to observe. Testes and ovaries are shown in Figure 2 with dotted lines.

Digestive System

Locate and identify the swollen pharynx in segments 2 to 6 (Figure 2). Locate and identify the esophagus which extends to segment 14. The esophagus is surrounded by the seminal vesicles and the five pairs of aortic arches (the heart). Locate and identify the crop in segments 15 through 17. Locate and identify the gizzard in segments 18 through 20. Locate the intestine which starts at segment 21 and ends at the anus.

Circulatory System

Observe the median dorsal blood vessel. Locate the five pairs of aortic arches (the heart) in segments 7 to 11. Under the intestine is the ventral blood vessel. It is small in diameter compared to the intestine. Carefully remove a portion of the intestine to observe the ventral blood vessel.

Nervous System

Locate and identify the brain in segment 3. It is a small, white mass. Beneath the ventral blood vessel is the white nerve cord.

Excretory System

Locate and identify the small coiled tubes called nephridia (singular, nephridium). There is a pair in each segment except the first

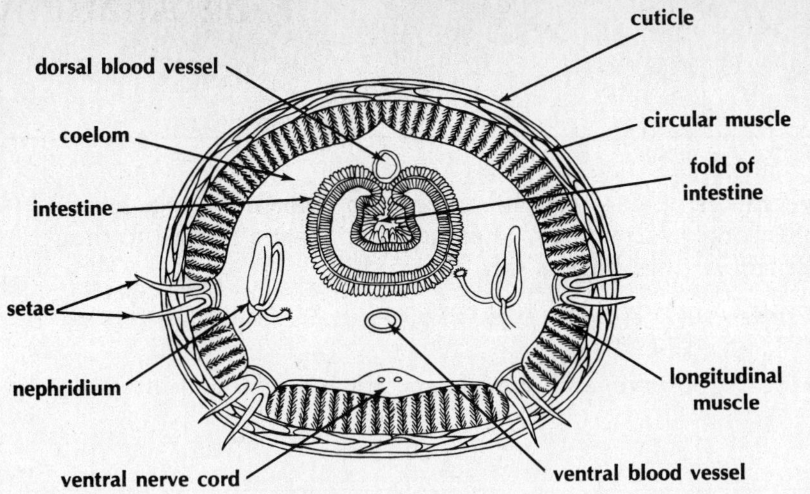

Earthworm Cross Section

FIGURE 3

three and the last segments. A nephridium is attached to the body wall on each side of the organism. It opens into the coelom body cavity and runs through the body wall forming an excretory pore.

Cross Section of an Earthworm Segment

Place the prepared microscope slide of a cross section of an earthworm on the stage of a compound microscope. Using low power, then high power, locate and identify the cuticle, circular muscle, longitudinal muscle, dorsal and ventral blood vessels, intestine, typhlosole, ventral nerve cord, setae, nephridia, and coelom. Use Figure 3 as a guide.

Formulating Generalizations

1. Describe the clitellum.
2. Which end of the earthworm (anterior or posterior) is round and pointed?
3. Which end is broad and flat?
4. In what way could the setae aid in movement of a live worm?
5. Describe the area surrounding the pores on segments 9 through 16.
6. Is there any correlation between the size of each reproductive organ and its function? Explain.
7. Why do you think an earthworm has a pair of nephridia in almost every segment?
8. Compare the function of the pharynx, esophagus, crop, gizzard, and intestine with their sizes.
9. Describe the shape and location of the aortic arches in relation to the dorsal and ventral blood vessels.
10. Because no definite respiratory apparatus is found in an earthworm, how do you think oxygen enters the body and the circulatory system?
11. How is the presence of a fold in the intestine helpful in digestion?
12. What do you think are the functions of the circular and longitudinal muscles?

73 Frog Anatomy

Frogs are vertebrates. They are members of class Amphibia, phylum Chordata. Frogs have certain adaptations not found in most other vertebrates. These adaptations are related to the frog's amphibious life. For example, most frogs have a soft, moist skin.

Frogs are carnivores. They swallow their prey whole. Their eyes, which retract into the head, help push food into the esophagus when retracted.

In this investigation, you are to locate, observe, and identify specific external and internal structures of the frog.

Materials

Per team of four
- live frog
- aquarium
- battery jar
- glass plate
- mounted frog skeleton
- paper towels
- dissecting pins
- scalpel

Per team of two
- preserved frog
- paper towels—4
- probe
- scissors
- forceps
- scalpel
- dissecting pan
- metric ruler
- stereomicroscope
- glass slide
- prepared frog skeleton

Procedure

Part A. External Anatomy

Observe the swimming movements of a frog in an aquarium. Observe both pairs of legs and feet during swimming.

Place a few wet paper towels in the bottom of a battery jar. Place a live frog in the jar and cover the jar with a glass plate but leave a small gap to allow air flow. Observe the breathing of the frog. Observe the movement of the skin below the lower jaw and over the chest.

Observe the sitting position of the frog. Tilt the battery jar at a 45° angle. Be sure to hold the glass plate in place. Observe the movements of the frog. Return the battery jar to its normal position. Slowly rotate the jar about 180°. Observe the movement of the frog.

Holding the frog in your hand, locate the head, trunk, and legs. On the head, locate the nostrils, eyes, mouth, and tympanic membrane (Figure 1). Attempt to touch the eyes with a moistened piece of paper towel. In your lab notebook, describe the action of the transparent eyelid. Determine whether the transparent eyelid is attached to the top or bottom of the socket.

On the trunk, locate the two dorsal folds and the hump in the middle of its back. Locate the anus between the rear legs. Count the number of digits on the forelegs and hind legs.

Make a table in your lab notebook similar to Table 1. Record in the table your observations of each frog system.

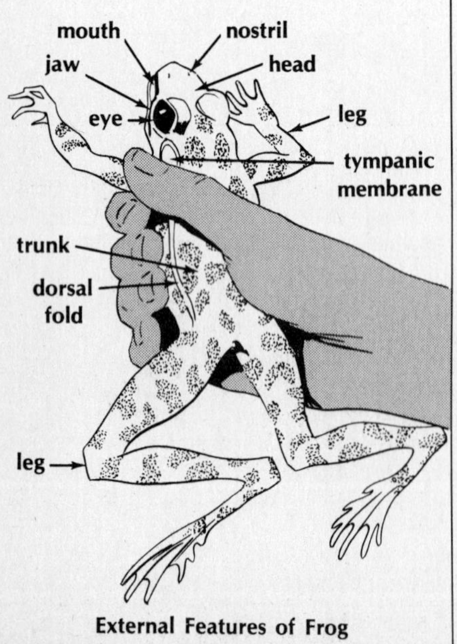

External Features of Frog

FIGURE 1

TABLE 1. SYSTEMS OF A FROG	
SYSTEM	OBSERVATIONS
Digestive	
Excretory	

Part B. Internal Anatomy

Place a preserved frog on its back. With a pair of scissors, cut the corners of the frog's jaws. **CAUTION:** *Always be careful when using scissors.* Cutting the jaw will enable you to open the mouth much wider. Open the mouth as wide as possible. Locate and identify the maxillary teeth; vomerine teeth; internal nostrils; openings of the eustachian tube and esophagus; glottis; and tongue (Figure 2). With a probe, move the tongue in order to locate its point of attachment. **CAUTION:** *Always be careful when using sharp instruments such as probes.*

Place a wet paper towel in the dissecting pan. Place the frog ventral side up in the dissecting pan. Stick a dissecting pin into each of the four appendages near the digits to hold the frog. Insert the blade of a pair of scissors through the skin just above the anus. Make a shallow incision through the skin up to the throat (Figure 3). Make two lateral incisions perpendicular to the first incision. These lateral incisions should be made near the hind legs and forelegs, forming two flaps of skin. With dissecting pins, pin the flaps open.

Locate and identify the pectoralis (chest) muscles and the abdominal muscles. The pectoralis muscles extend from the center of the chest to the forelegs. The abdominal muscles cover the abdominal cavity.

Make three shallow incisions through the muscles like the incisions in the skin. Do not cut too deeply or you will cut through the internal organs. In the mid-ventral region you will have to cut through a bone, the sternum. Pin down the two flaps of muscles like the skin.

Locate the peritoneum. The peritoneum is a thin membrane that covers the body cavity. The body cavity is called the coelom. With scissors, cut through the peritoneum while holding it away from the organs with forceps. If the frog is a female, the abdominal cavity will be filled with eggs. Remove the eggs with forceps.

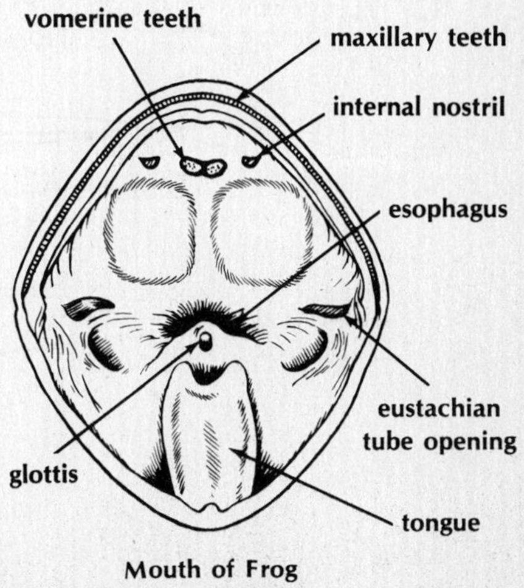

Mouth of Frog

FIGURE 2

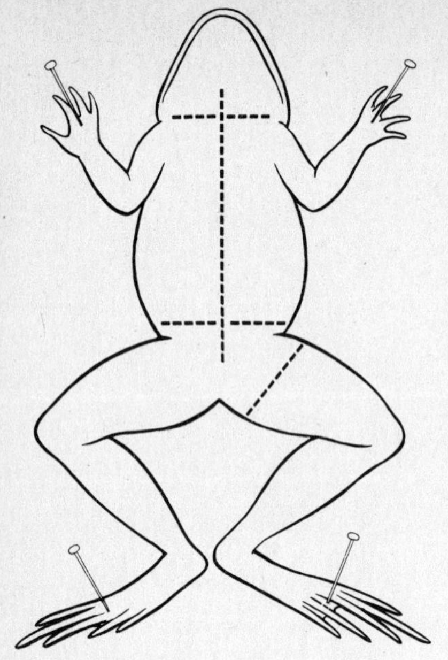

Frog Dissection Incisions

FIGURE 3

Digestive System

Using a probe to move the tissues, locate and identify the structures of the digestive system (Figure 4). The esophagus is a short, thick tube. It leads to an enlarged area called the stomach. Move the stomach with the probe. It is held in place by a thin, transparent tissue called mesentery. Locate the other part of the body to which the mesentery is attached.

At the lower part of the stomach is a small constriction. At this constriction is a valve, the pyloric valve, which is the beginning of the small intestine. Unravel the small intestine. Separate the small intestine from the mesentery with scissors. Be careful not to cut through other tissues.

Locate the short, swollen, large intestine at the end of the small intestine. Locate the cloaca and anus at the end of the large intestine. The cloaca is a narrowing of the large intestine. The anus is the terminal end of the cloaca.

Locate the three lobes of the liver. The liver lies directly over the stomach and below the heart. The left lobe is slightly larger than the other lobes. In an opening between the lobes is a small green-colored sac called the gall bladder.

Cut the esophagus near the mouth and cut the cloaca near the anus. Remove the entire digestive system and place it on the wet paper towel in the dissecting pan. Measure the total length of the esophagus, stomach, small intestine, large intestine, and cloaca in centimeters. Measure the length of the body cavity from the throat to the anus and record the length in your table.

Excretory System

Locate the two kidneys. They are dark red, oblong organs attached to the dorsal body wall. Locate yellow fat bodies connected to the ventral surface of the kidneys. Locate the urinary bladder. The urinary bladder is colorless and is connected to the ventral side of the

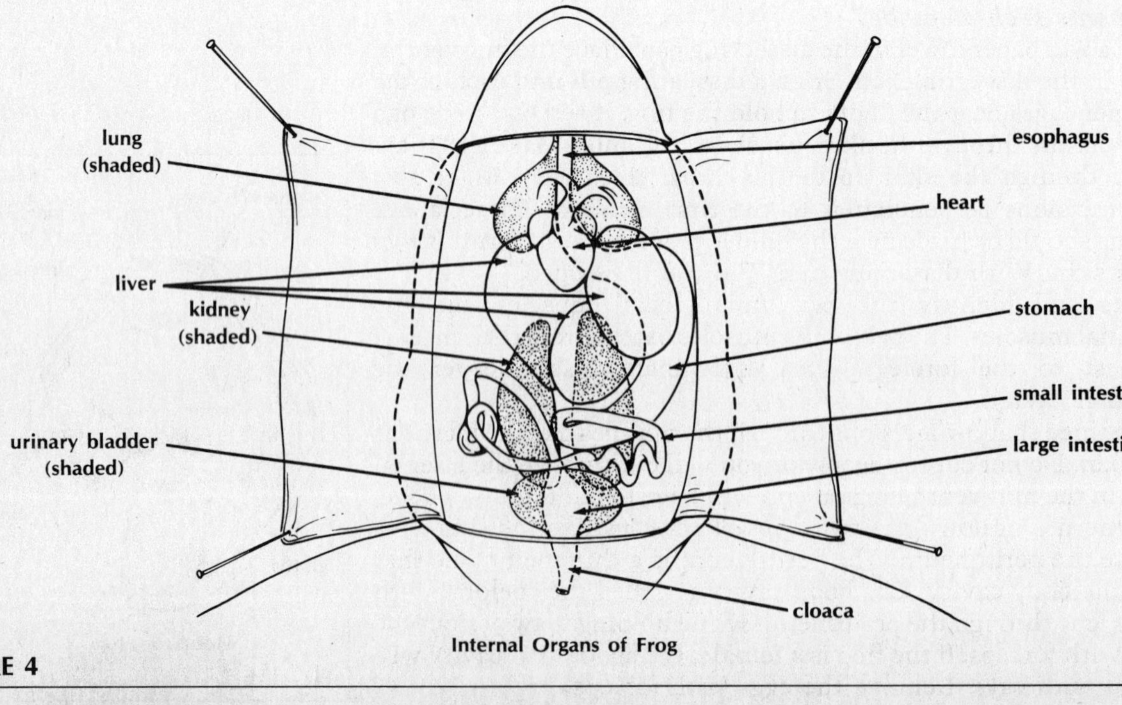

Internal Organs of Frog

FIGURE 4

cloaca. You may have removed the urinary bladder when you lifted the digestive system from the body cavity.

Reproductive System

Prominent male reproductive structures are the testes (singular, testis). They are white in color and oval in shape. They are attached to the kidneys next to the yellow fat bodies. Sperm cells form in the testes and travel through small tubes called the vasa efferentia to each kidney. Sperm cells leave the kidney through the mesonephric duct to the cloaca. From the cloaca, sperm cells leave the body of the frog through the anus. Locate the testes in your frog if it is a male.

The prominent female reproductive structures are the ovaries, oviducts, and uterus. The ovaries are organs which produce eggs. Eggs are small black and white spheres which may occupy a large part of the body cavity. Oviducts are coiled tubes running from the base of the lungs to the dorsal wall of the cloaca. The open end of the oviduct is funnel-shaped. Mature eggs break through the ovaries and enter the body cavity. They enter the open end of the oviduct and are carried to an enlarged area called the uterus. From the uterus eggs are carried to the cloaca and anus. Locate the ovaries, oviduct, and uterus if your frog is a female.

Observe a classmate's frog to be certain you see the reproductive structures of both sexes.

Respiratory and Circulatory Systems

Locate the lungs. They are small, beaded sacs in the body cavity near the forelegs. Remove the lungs from the frog with scissors. Cut a small, thin section from a lung and place it on a microscope slide. Place the slide on the stage of a stereomicroscope and observe the small sacs called alveoli (singular, alveolus).

Locate the heart, an organ between the lungs. The heart is surrounded by a thin, transparent tissue called the pericardium. A frog heart contains three chambers: left atrium, right atrium, and ventricle. Locate the blood vessels that lead to and from the heart.

With scissors and forceps, remove the pericardium. Cut the vessels leading to and from the heart. Remove the heart from the frog and place it in a dissecting pan. Locate the atria and ventricle. With a scalpel, cut a section through one of the atria and the ventricle. Compare the thickness of the walls. **CAUTION:** *Always be careful when using a scalpel. Slice away from your fingers to avoid cuts.*

Muscular System

You have already observed the pectoralis, abdominal muscles, and the heart. The digestive organs contain involuntary (smooth) muscles. Muscles attached to the skeleton are voluntary (striated) muscles.

Using scissors, cut the skin completely around the circumference of one of the upper legs where it joins the lower abdominal cavity (Figure 3). Using forceps, remove the skin of one of the legs by gently pulling the skin toward the foot. At a joint, one bone is usually stationary while the other one moves. The end of a muscle attached to the stationary bone is the origin. The end of the muscle attached to the bone that moves is the insertion. Move the leg back and forth causing the knee joint to bend. Observe the various muscles attached in the upper and lower legs. Determine the origins and insertions of the muscles that move the lower and upper legs.

Skeletal System

Observe a prepared frog skeleton. The skeleton is delicate, be careful not to break any bones.

Locate and identify the sutures of the skull. Sutures are boundaries between bones. Locate and identify the vertebrae and the pectoral (chest) and pelvic (hip) regions. Compare the bones of the forelegs with the hind legs. Compare the bones of the front feet with the hind feet. Compare the bones of the pectoral and pelvic regions.

Formulating Generalizations

1. Describe how the legs and feet of a frog are used in swimming.
2. Which pair of feet is webbed? Why?
3. What visible adaptations other than legs help the frog to swim rapidly?
4. What were the reactions of the frog when you tilted and rotated the jar?
5. Why do you think the frog has a transparent eyelid?
6. What is the adaptive value of the skin of the frog?
7. How is the point of attachment of the frog tongue different from the human tongue? How is the attachment of the tongue an important adaptation?
8. What is the function of the constriction between the stomach and the small intestine?
9. From your observations of the living frog, what evidence do you have that it breathes with lungs?
10. What differences are there in the lengths of the esophagus, stomach, small intestine, large intestine, and cloaca? What adaptive advantages are there for some organs being longer than others?
11. How does the overall length of the frog's digestive system compare with the length of the body cavity? How is this difference in length significant?
12. Which is thicker, the atrium or the ventricle? Why?
13. Describe the chief differences between the pectoralis and stomach muscles.
14. What bones are the points of origin for muscles that bend the knees?
15. What bones are the points of insertion for muscles that bend the knees?
16. Describe the digits on each foot.
17. Is there any difference in the size, shape, and number of digits on the forelegs as compared to the hind legs? Explain.
18. What causes the hump on the back of the frog?
19. A frog is considered a complex animal. List the characteristics of its internal and external anatomy that you think help justify this idea.
20. What are sutures? Why are sutures only found between bones of the skull?

Dandelion And Plantain Populations

74

A population is a group of individuals of the same species living in a specific geographical area at a specific time. Biologists can measure the size of a population by determining its density. Density is determined by counting the number of organisms of a species in a given area or volume of space. The total number of organisms is then divided by the total space. Thus, density is expressed as the number of organisms in the unit area or volume.

Suppose a biologist counted 80 cottontail rabbits in an area of 10 square kilometers (km^2). The density of rabbits would be:

$$\text{Density} = \frac{\text{total number of organisms}}{\text{total area}} = \frac{80 \text{ rabbits}}{10 \text{ km}^2} = 8 \text{ rabbits per km}^2$$

How important is this information to a biologist? From prior samplings done on the 10-km^2 plot, the biologist can determine whether the population is increasing, decreasing, or remaining the same. Further research may show that the food on the plot is decreasing or increasing in quality. It can also show that the carrying capacity (number of organisms an area can support) of the land has been reached. These population data are helpful in determining the producer-consumer structure of the plot.

Rabbits, like most consumers, are mobile. Special techniques of trapping, tagging, and releasing are used in determining the population density of mobile populations.

Plants are nonmobile. Generally, from the time a seed sprouts until it dies, the plant remains in one place. Thus, it is much easier to compute the population of a nonmobile population. Immigration and emigration do not occur on a daily basis in a nonmobile population.

In this investigation, you are to determine the dandelion and plantain (Figure 1) population densities in plots on the lawn at school and your lawn at home. You are to compare your results with other members of the class. You are to determine the average density of each plant population using class data.

Materials *(per student)*

pencil
meter stick
cord—4.5 m
large nails—4

Procedure

On your school lawn, randomly select a plot by throwing a pencil back over your head. **CAUTION:** *Be sure there is no one behind you when you throw the pencil.* Set up a square meter plot in this area by using the pencil point as one corner (Figure 2). Stick a nail in the ground at the point of the pencil. Measure off one meter and insert another nail. At a right angle to the first two nails, measure another meter and insert a third nail. After measuring, insert the fourth nail in the corner that completes the square meter. Attach the cord to one of the nails, then loop it around the other nails to enclose the square meter plot.

Starting along one edge of the plot, place a meter stick across the plot. Count the dandelion and plantain plants that touch the meter stick. Move the meter stick a little toward the opposite edge and again count the plants touching the meter stick. Keep moving the meter

FIGURE 1

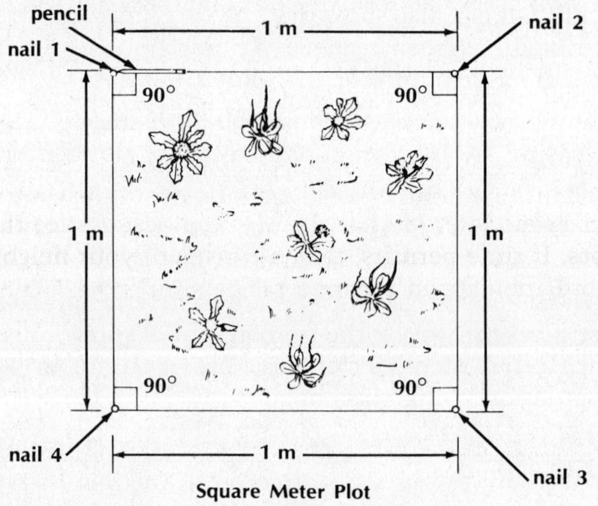

FIGURE 2 Square Meter Plot

TABLE 1. INDIVIDUAL DATA ON SCHOOL LAWN (OR STUDENT'S LAWN)		
PLOT	DANDELION	PLANTAIN
1		
2		
3		
Total		
Average		

TABLE 2. CLASS DATA ON SCHOOL LAWN (OR STUDENT'S LAWN)		
STUDENT	DANDELION AVERAGE	PLANTAIN AVERAGE
1		
2		
3		
Total		
Average		

stick and counting plants until you have covered the entire plot, counting each plant only once. This technique will enable you to locate all the plants and keep from counting some plants twice. Record the number of dandelion and plantain plants in this square meter in your notebook in a table similar to Table 1. Repeat this procedure on two other plots on the school lawn. Total and average the number of dandelions and plantains for the three plots.

On your home lawn, repeat the above procedure for three square meter plots. If time permits, take a census of your neighbor's lawn also. Record the data in separate tables similar to Table 1 in your lab notebook.

During the next class period, place your averages on the chalkboard. Compare your data with those of other members of the class. Record the class data in your notebook in a table similar to Table 2. Determine the average number of dandelion and plantain plants on the school lawn and on class members' lawns.

Formulating Generalizations

1. Did the school lawn or your home lawn have a higher population density of dandelions? Of plantains?
2. What physical and biological factors control the population density of each type of plant on the school lawn? Do the same physical and biological factors control the population density of each plant type on your home lawn?
3. If you were to return to the exact same plot one week later, would these two plant populations be the same, show an increase, or show a decrease? Explain.
4. Would the population densities of either plant change after a month? After another season? Explain.
5. Would you expect dandelion or plantain populations to be the same in other school yards in other cities? Why?
6. What factors would control the dandelion or plantain population in other school yards? In other cities?
7. How could you estimate the total number of individual dandelions and plantains on the entire school lawn?
8. What methods would you have to use to estimate animal populations? Why?

Microarthropod Populations In Leaf Litter

75

In wooded areas, leaf litter is the layer of organic debris covering the soil. Leaf litter is usually divided into two types: undecomposed organic debris that has been laid down within the past several months and partly decomposed, matted debris.

Leaf litter contains many organisms. Macroscopic organisms, such as arthropods and earthworms, physically break down leaves and other debris into smaller particles. Microscopic organisms, such as bacteria and fungi, change the small particles of organic matter into soluble nutrients.

Microarthropods are animals of the phylum Arthropoda that are usually less than 5 mm in length. Some microarthropods, such as springtails, do not grow longer than a few millimeters in length as adults. Others, such as centipedes, are only this size as juveniles. Physical and biological factors determine the number of microarthropods in leaf litter. Among these factors are moisture, temperature, food, and space.

In this investigation, you are to collect leaf litter beneath a tree in a forest. You are to determine the number of different orders of the phylum Arthropoda present in your sample.

Materials *(per team of three students)*

large plastic trash bag
cord—100 cm
large nails—4
quart bleach or cleanser container
scissors
scalpel
fiberglass window screening, 12 cm × 12 cm
metric ruler
small beaker
petri dish
glue
facial tissue
twist tie
70% ethyl alcohol—100 mL
light source
dropper
glass slide
microscope
stereomicroscope
water

Procedure

Part A. Field Collection

In a forest, locate a tree that has several centimeters of leaf litter beneath it. Set up a 20 cm by 20 cm plot using cord, four nails, and a ruler. Using your hands, remove the leaf litter and put it in a plastic bag. Be careful not to disturb the soil layer. Tie the bag shut with a twist tie.

Presence of microarthropods in leaf litter can be determined by using a Berlese funnel. A Berlese funnel is a container with fine mesh screen in the base (Figure 1). Construct a Berlese funnel. With scissors or scalpel, remove the top and bottom of powdered cleanser or household bleach container. **CAUTION:** *Always be careful when using scissors or scalpels.* The openings of the container should be at least 5 cm in diameter. Rinse the container and dry it. Cut a piece of fiberglass window screening 3 cm in diameter larger than the bottom opening of the container.

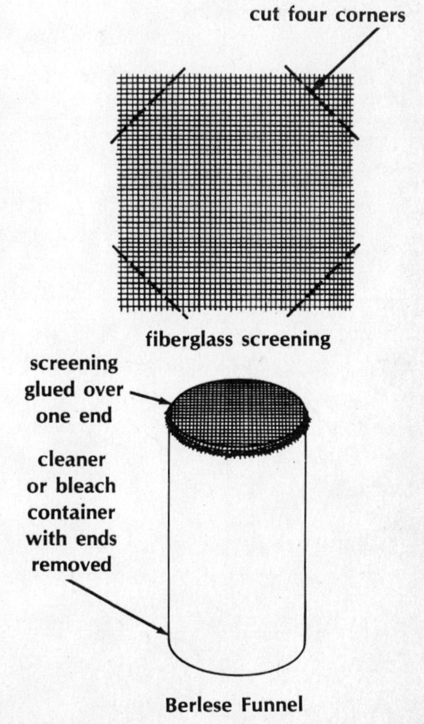

FIGURE 1

FIGURE 2

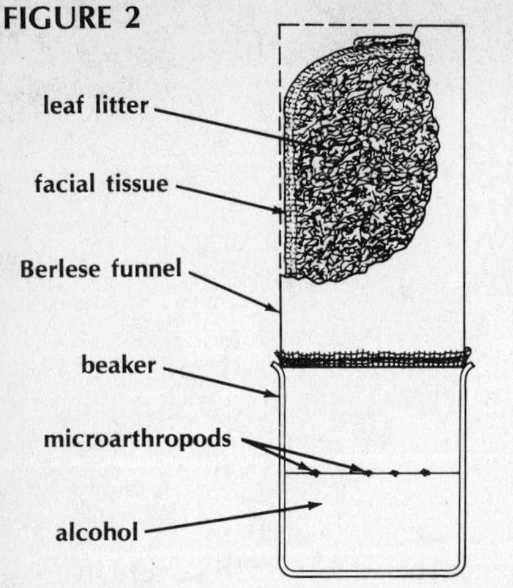

Glue the screen to the bottom of the container and allow it to dry for at least 24 hours.

Part B. Laboratory Analysis

Remove some leaf litter from the plastic bag and place it in the Berlese funnel. Do not pack the leaf litter too tightly in the funnel. Add leaf litter until the funnel is nearly full. Cover the leaf litter with a facial tissue. Thus, you will prevent any organisms from escaping.

Position the Berlese funnel beneath a light source. Place a small beaker with 50 mL of 70% ethyl alcohol beneath the opening of the Berlese funnel (Figure 2). **CAUTION:** *Alcohol is flammable. Be sure all flames are extinguished throughout the laboratory before*

TABLE 1. KEY TO THE ORDERS OF MICROARTHROPODS

1a.	Six legs; distinct head, segmented thorax and abdomen (Class Insecta)........2
1b.	More than six legs........5
2a.	Antennae, eyes, and cerci absent; 9 to 12 abdominal segments........Order Protura
2b.	Antennae present, cerci absent or present........3
3a.	Antennae with 10 to 12 segments; 2 to 3 cerci on tip of abdomen as filaments or pincers.....Order Thysanura (2 filaments, Bristletails; 3 filaments, Silverfish; 2 pincers, Slickers)
3b.	Antennae present, cerci absent........4
4a.	Antennae with 4 to 8 segments; 6 abdominal segments; forked appendage (spring) for leaping usually on fourth abdominal segment........Order Collembola (Springtails)
4b.	Antennae with 5 segments, body cylindrical, claws absent on legs........Order Thysanoptera (Thrips)
5a.	Head and thorax fused as one; 8 legs (Class Arachnida)........6
5b.	More than 8 legs on body........8
6a.	Abdomen distinctly segmented; first pair of leglike appendages (palpi) contain larger pincerlike claws; 4 pairs of true legs...... Order Pseudoscorpionida (Pseudoscorpions)
6b.	Abdomen not segmented........7
7a.	Body divided into two parts (cephalothorax and abdomen); legs on cephalothorax........Order Araneae (Spiders)
7b.	Body fused; no segments; legs on fused body........ Order Acarina (Mites)
8a.	One pair of legs on each body segment........Class Chilopoda (Centipedes)
8b.	Two pairs of legs on each body segment........Class Diplopoda (Millipedes)

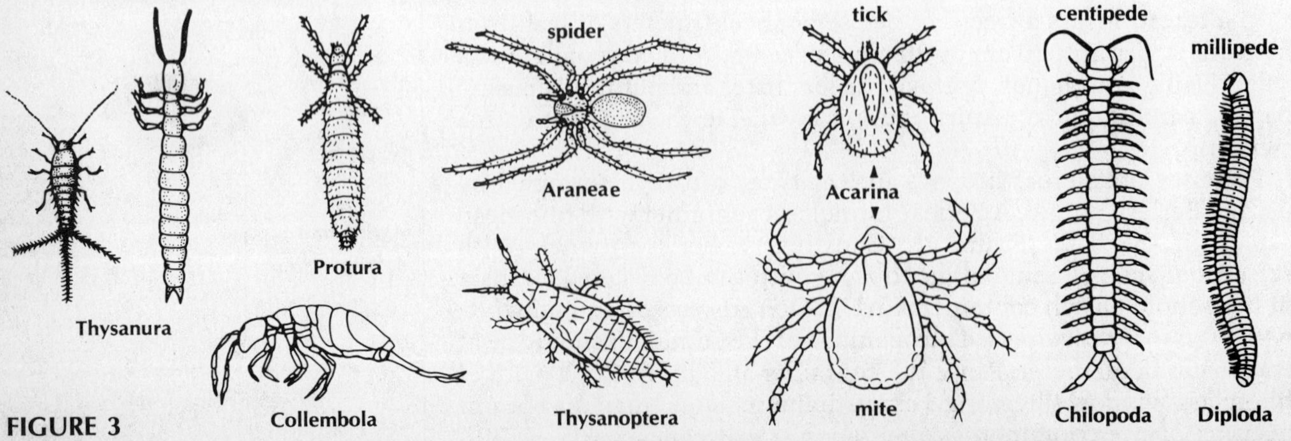

FIGURE 3

proceeding. The light will dry out the leaf litter and force any organisms to the bottom where they will fall through the screen into the beaker. Let the Berlese funnel sit for two days. The alcohol may evaporate during these two days. Add more alcohol as needed. If the leaf litter sample is fresh, microarthropods will fall into the alcohol within thirty minutes after adding leaf litter. If daily samples are desired, replace the beaker with a new beaker of alcohol every day.

After the microarthropods fall from the Berlese funnel, they will usually float on the surface of the alcohol. To examine the fallen specimens, pour the alcohol into a small petri dish. Using a dropper, place the specimens on a clean, dry slide and add a drop of water. *Do not* add a coverslip. Observe the specimens using only low power of a compound microscope. A stereomicroscope can also be used. Using the microarthropod key (Table 1) and Figure 3, classify the organisms as to order. Record the number of each order identified from the leaf litter sample in a table similar to Table 2.

Make sketches of the microarthropods observed. Place your averages on the chalkboard. Compare your data with those of other members of the class and record the class averages in a table similar to Table 2.

Formulating Generalizations

1. In what ways were the microarthropods similar?
2. In what ways were the microarthropods different?
3. Arrange the orders found in the sample from the greatest to the least in number. Does each sample have the same dominant and least dominant orders? Explain why you should or should not expect each leaf litter sample to contain the same dominant or least dominant species.
4. What physical and biological factors could have limited the size of the microarthropod population?
5. How would you compute the population density of microarthropods?
6. What factors dealing with your sample might cause an error in computing the population density of the microarthropods?
7. Do you think you have an accurate count of the microarthropods in your sample? Why or why not?
8. Would you expect your results to be similar if the leaf litter were sampled at a different time of the year? Explain.

TABLE 2. MICROARTHROPODS OBSERVED IN LEAF LITTER

ORDER	MY SAMPLE	STUDENT 1	STUDENT 2	STUDENT 3	TOTAL OF EACH ORDER OBSERVED
Protura					
Thysanura					
Acarina					
Other Animals					
Total Observed By Each Student					

76 Predation—A Limiting Factor In Population Growth

Population growth and population size are dependent upon many factors. Factors that limit the rate of population growth are called limiting factors. Limiting factors can be either biological or physical. Food, space, and interactions between organisms are examples of biological factors. Environmental factors such as rain, wind, and light are physical factors.

One biological factor that is an important limiting factor is predation. In predation, one organism eats another; the organism doing the eating is called a predator, while the one being eaten is called the prey. If there is a large number of predators in an area, they can greatly reduce the size of the prey population. Sometimes, more than one kind of predator eats the same prey. Biologists can study the predator-prey interaction in the field or they can build a model of this interaction in the laboratory.

In this investigation you are to study predation as a limiting factor. You are to simulate the effects of predation upon a real population of *Daphnia*. You are to act as predator and compare the results of predation in this population of *Daphnia* with another population of *Daphnia* in which no predation occurs.

Materials *(per team of 2 students)*

Daphnia—60
beaker (100 mL)
petri dish
droppers—2
yeast—60 grains
jars (1 L)—2
baster
cow manure solution—1.6 L

FIGURE 1

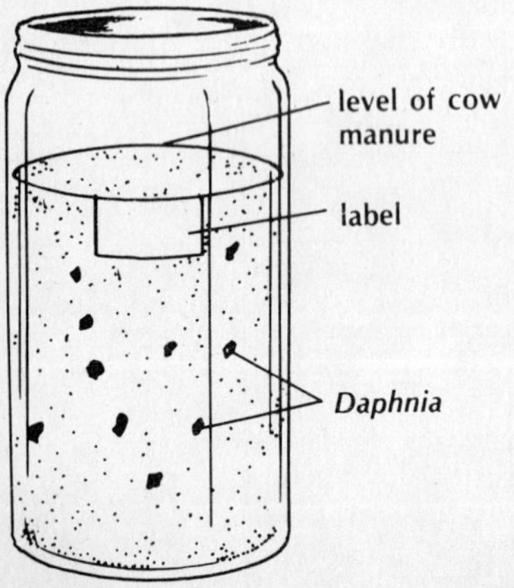

Procedure

Place 800 mL of cow manure solution in each of two jars. Label one jar "Population A" and the second jar "Population B." Place the label on each jar so the top of the label is aligned with the level of cow manure solution in the jar. See Figure 1.

Using a baster, remove some *Daphnia* culture from a source supplied by your teacher. Place the culture in a beaker. Transfer some of the *Daphnia* culture to a petri dish half. Remove the rubber bulb from the large end of a dropper and place the bulb over the small end of the dropper. See Figure 2. Using the dropper, transfer 30 *Daphnia* from the petri dish to jar A and 30 *Daphnia* to jar B. Put 5 grains of dry yeast in each jar. In a chart similar to Table 1, record the number of *Daphnia* placed in each jar. Place the jars on a shelf in the laboratory.

FIGURE 2

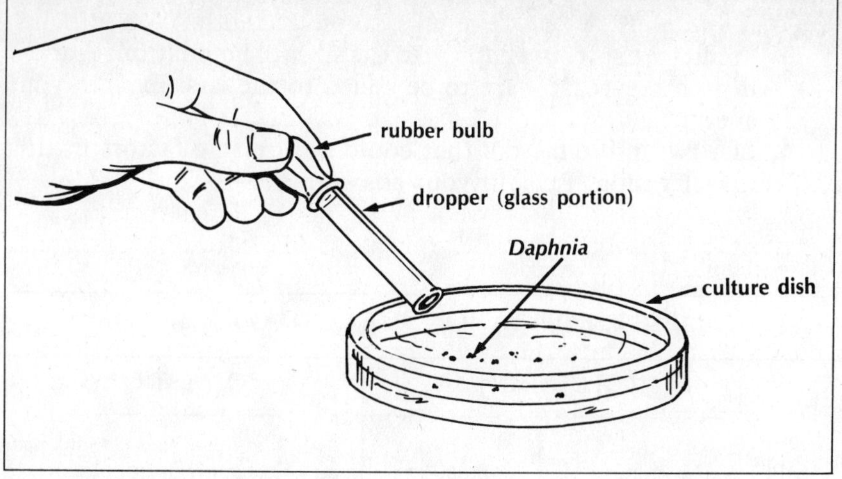

Population A. (No Predators)

On the next day of class (Day 1), use a baster to stir the *Daphnia* culture in the jar and remove exactly 80 mL of the solution. Place the solution in a beaker. Count the *Daphnia* in the beaker to estimate the population size of Population A by using the following steps.

1. Fill a petri dish top or bottom half full of the solution taken from jar A.
2. Count the number of *Daphnia* in the petri dish. To avoid recounting the same *Daphnia,* use the dropper to remove the *Daphnia* as you count.
3. As you remove the *Daphnia,* put them back in the jar and record the number as a slash mark in a chart similar to Table 2.
4. When all of the *Daphnia* have been counted in the petri dish, put the solution back in the jar.
5. Continue steps 1, 2, 3, and 4 until all of the water in the beaker has been used.
6. Multiply the number of *Daphnia* (slash marks in the chart) counted in the sample by 10 to determine the population size of Population A. HINT: Since your sample was 80 mL and there is 800 mL of liquid in the jar, the sample size was 0.1 of the population.

TABLE 1. POPULATION SIZE OF *DAPHNIA* ON DAY 0

	POPULATION A	POPULATION B
Number of *Daphnia*		

Population B. (Predators Present)

You are to simulate the role of a predator on this *Daphnia* population. Use the same procedure as you did for Population A except for one change. Instead of placing the *Daphnia* back in the jar when an 80 mL sample is counted, you are to place the *Daphnia* in a special container provided by your teacher. In this way, the *Daphnia* removed will be assumed to have been eaten by a predator. Repeat the procedure steps for Populations A and B on Day 3 and Day 5. Construct a graph similar to Figure 3 to show your data.

Formulating Generalizations

1. What were the population sizes of the *Daphnia* in Populations A and B on Day 0?
2. Why were the *Daphnia* returned to Population A after each count was made?
3. Why were the *Daphnia* not returned to Population B after each count was made?

FIGURE 3

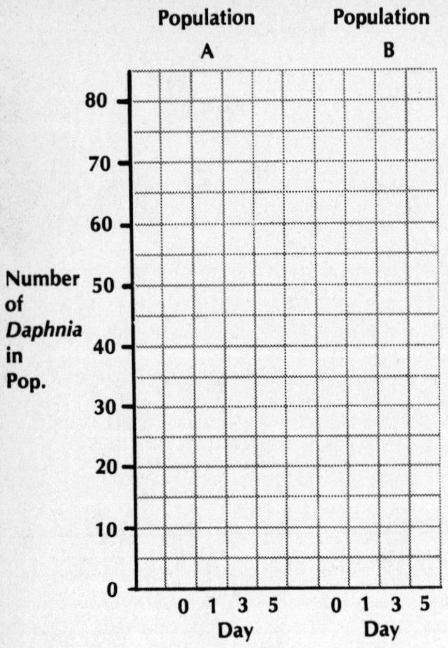

Combined Data of Populations

4. Predict what would happen to the sizes of Populations A and B if you were to continue this investigation for a month.
5. Predict what would happen to the sizes of Populations A and B if no more yeast were to be added to the jars. Explain your answer.
6. List two more factors that could be limiting factors in this investigation. Explain your answer.

TABLE 2. POPULATION SIZE ON DAYS 1, 3, 5

DAY OF SAMPLE	POPULATION A		POPULATION B	
	[A] Number of *Daphnia* in 80 mL sample	[B] Total Population (multiply [A] by 10)	[C] Number of *Daphnia* in 80 mL sample	[D] Total Population (multiply [C] by 10)
1				
2				
3				

Growth Of The Human Population In The United States

77

Many changes have resulted from technological advances. These changes have helped humans to "master" the environment. Development of vaccines, antibiotics, and other medicines enable humans to enjoy better health and live longer.

Humans can sometimes change the *physical* factors of their environment. If their home is too warm or too cold, they can set a thermostat which will turn on either a furnace or an air conditioner. Other living things adapt to their environment or die.

Humans also are affected by biological factors similar to those that affect other organisms. For example, humans are sometimes overcrowded. Some areas of the earth have no people while other areas have thousands of people per square mile. Crowding can lead to competition for food, natural resources, and even living space.

In this investigation you are to compute the human population densities in the United States for every decade from 1790 to 1990. You are to compute the change in human population in the United States per decade.

Materials *(per student)*

graph paper
ruler

Procedure

Population size can be measured as density. Density is calculated by dividing the population by the area. Population trends can be measured by comparing the growth rate of one year or decade with that of another. The rate of change in a population can be computed by using the formula.

$$\text{rate of change} = \frac{\Delta D}{\Delta T}$$

Δ means "amount of change," D is density, and T is time. Assume that in 1970, there were 30 rabbits per square km in a certain area and that in 1980, there were 45 rabbits per square km (Figure 1).

$$\frac{\text{current density} - \text{previous density}}{\text{change in time}} = \frac{45 - 30}{1990 - 1980}$$

$$\frac{15 \text{ rabbits/square km}}{10 \text{ years}} = 1.5 \text{ rabbits/square km/year}$$

FIGURE 1

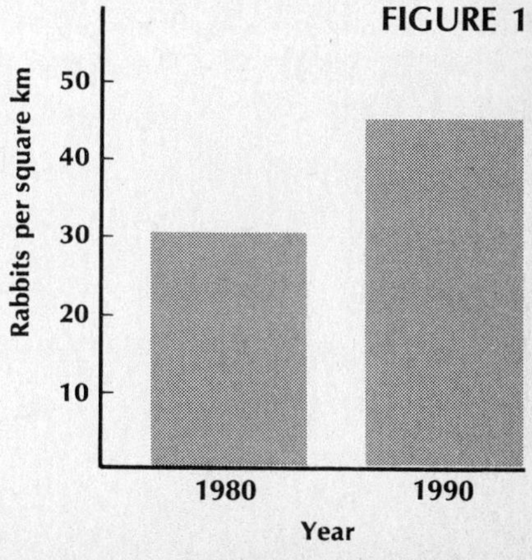

Because there are more rabbits in 1990 than in 1980, the rate of change is an increase. The rabbits are increasing at the new rate of 1.5 new rabbits per square km per year.

Using the data for the human population and land area of the United States since 1790 in Table 1, compute the population

TABLE 1. LAND AREA AND POPULATION OF THE UNITED STATES*				
YEAR	LAND AREA OF THE UNITED STATES (SQUARE KM)	POPULATION OF THE UNITED STATES	DENSITY PER SQUARE KM	RATE OF CHANGE PER YEAR
1790	2 239 692	3 929 214		
1800	2 239 692	5 308 483		
1810	4 355 935	7 239 881		
1820	4 531 107	9 638 453		
1830	4 531 107	12 866 020		
1840	4 531 107	17 069 453		
1850	7 614 709	23 191 876		
1860	7 691 367	31 443 321		
1870	7 691 367	39 818 449		
1880	7 691 367	50 189 209		
1890	7 691 367	62 979 766		
1900	7 691 870	76 212 168		
1910	7 691 173	92 228 496		
1920	7 691 111	106 021 537		
1930	7 710 762	123 202 624		
1940	7 710 762	132 164 569		
1950	9 200 214	151 325 798		
1960	9 170 959	179 323 175		
1970	9 168 660	202 302 031		
1980	9 168 660	226 542 203		
1990	9 168 660	248 709 873		

*Adapted from *The World Almanac and Book of Facts,* 1992 Edition, Newspaper Enterprise Association, Inc., New York, 1992.

density per square km for each decade. Also compute the rate of change in the human population in the United States every decade. Then construct two graphs. On Figure 2, show the population of the United States from 1790 to 1990. On Figure 3, show the population density from 1790 to 1990 and the rate of change at ten-year intervals.

Formulating Generalizations

1. Which of the three lines could you extend with reasonable accuracy to the year 2050? Explain.
2. How would the line showing the population of the United States compare with a graph of a hypothetical bacteria population?
3. From the population trend, which is higher, birth rate or death rate?
4. What other factors could cause the human population of an area to increase?
5. How are the three lines different? How are they similar? Why are there differences in the lines?
6. Can you account for a decrease in U.S. land area between 1950 and 1970?

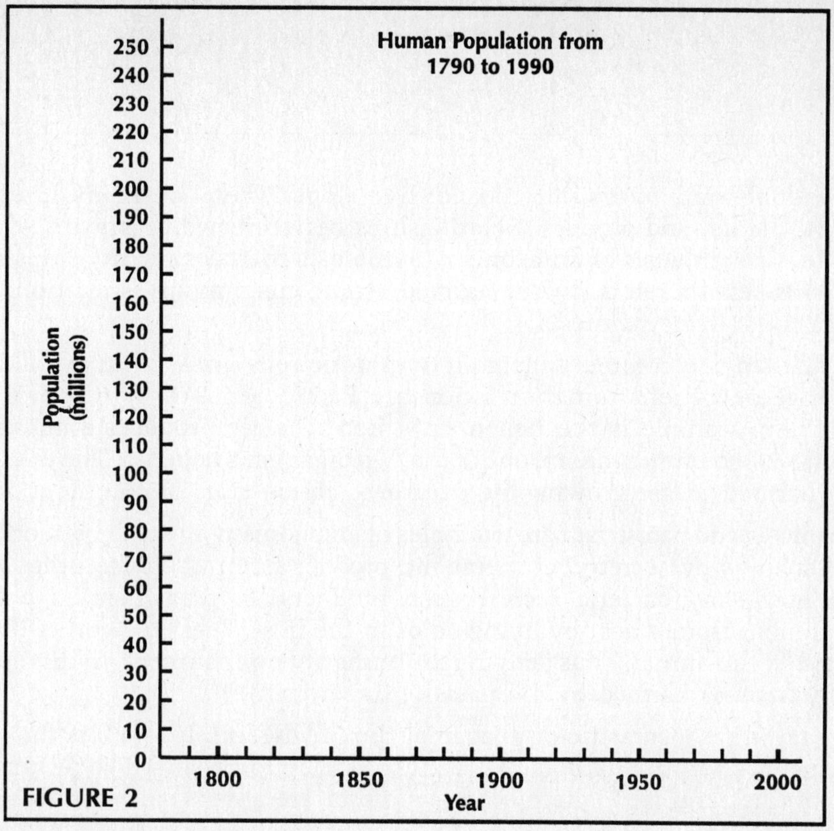

FIGURE 2

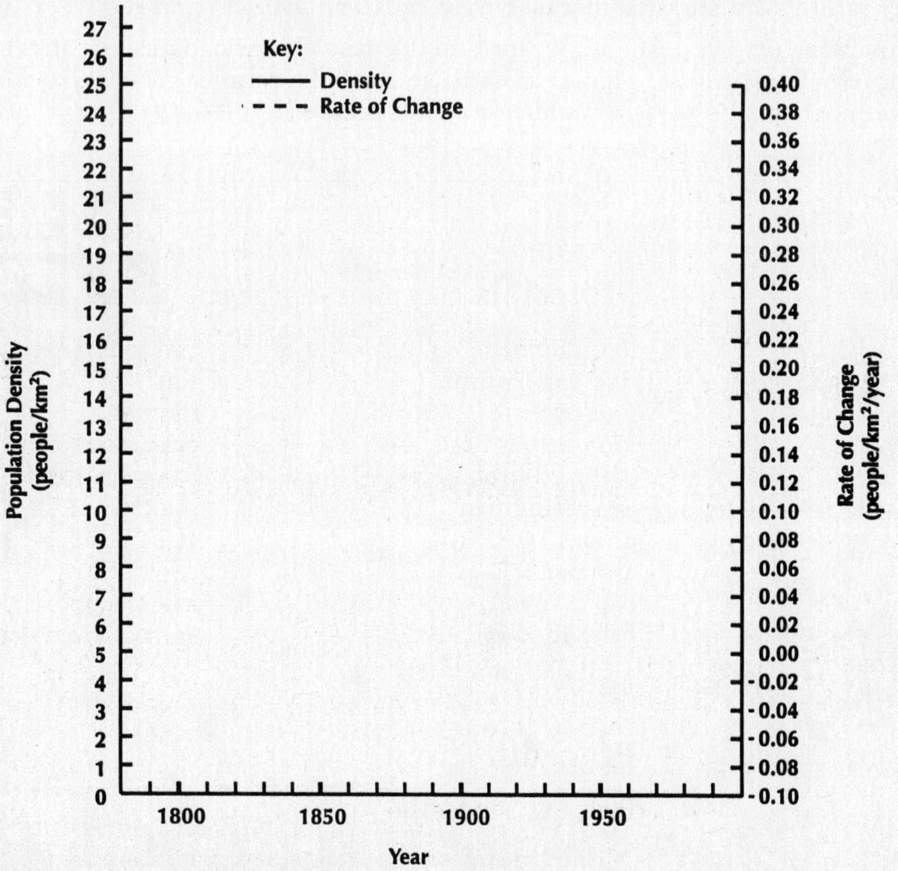

FIGURE 3

78 Interspecific Relationships Between Populations

Individuals in a community do not live alone. There are many interrelationships among animals, plants, and protists. Relationships between two organisms of different species are classified as symbiosis or antagonism. Symbiosis includes relationships in which one or both organisms benefit and neither is harmed. Antagonism includes relationships in which one or both organisms are harmed.

Mutualism and commensalism are symbiotic relationships. In mutualism, both organisms living together benefit from the relationship. Each depends on the other for something necessary for life. An example is the lichen. In a lichen, algae produces food and a fungus provides protection. In commensalism, one of the two organisms benefits. The other does not benefit but is not harmed. Algae growing on a turtle is an example of commensalism.

Antibiosis and parasitism are examples of antagonism. In antibiosis, one organism harms the other, such as by secreting a metabolic product harmful to the other. Some fungi, such as *Penicillium*, and bacteria secrete such products. In parasitism, one organism derives its nourishment from a host by living on or in the host. Beef tapeworms in humans absorb food digested by the human, thus denying the human of nourishment. In this type of relationship the host (human) is harmed by the parasite (tapeworm).

Monocystis is a parasitic protozoan of the earthworm. It inhabits the seminal vesicles. The intestine of a termite harbors many mutualistic protozoans. The protozoans digest cellulose eaten by the termite. If the protozoans die or are absent, the termite will die.

The larva of a frog (tadpole) houses many worm and protozoan parasites. They inhabit various organs of the body. Some biologists have classified various intestinal protozoans as commensals rather than parasites because they cause no visible damage.

In this investigation, you are to locate and identify specific parasites and mutualists inhabiting internal organs of a tadpole, an earthworm, and a termite. You are to compare the shape and numbers of the parasites and mutualists located.

FIGURE 1

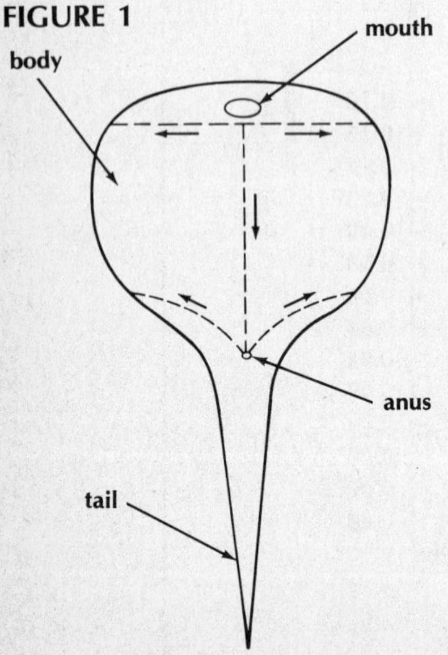

Ventral Surface of Tadpole

Materials *(per student or team)*

- live tadpole
- live earthworm
- live termite
- 95% ethyl alcohol—5 mL
- 0.5% chlorobutanol—10 mL
- dissecting pan
- probe
- dropper
- paper towel
- baby food jar
- dissecting pins
- scissors
- forceps
- petri dish halves—2
- Ringer's solution—8 mL
- scalpel
- glass slide
- coverslip
- microscope
- spring water—10 mL

Procedure

Part A. Tadpole

Place the tadpole in a baby food jar containing 10 mL of spring water and 10 mL of 0.5% chlorobutanol. Within a few minutes, the tadpole will become immobilized. This procedure is called narcotizing.

Place the narcotized tadpole on its dorsal surface in a dissecting pan. With scissors, make an incision through the mouth. **CAUTION:** *Always be careful when using scissors.* Proceed cutting down the midline of the chest and abdominal area to the anus (Figure 1). Cut two side flaps and open and fasten down the flaps with dissecting pins. This procedure will expose the entire digestive cavity. Use Figure 2 as a guide.

With scissors, cut the alimentary canal at the beginning of the esophagus and at the anus. Remove the alimentary canal gently with forceps and a probe. Place it in a petri dish containing 5 mL of Ringer's solution.

Separate the small intestine and the large intestine from the rest of the alimentary canal. Place the small intestine and the large intestine in separate petri dish halves. Add 4 to 5 drops of Ringer's solution to each organ. Macerate (chop) the tissue with a scalpel. **CAUTION:** *Always be careful when using a scalpel.*

Using a clean, dry slide, make a wet mount of the contents of the small intestine. Add a coverslip and observe the slide with a microscope. Locate and identify the parasites of the small intestine (Figure 3). Make sketches of each parasite. Make a slide of the contents of the large intestine and observe and identify the parasites.

Compare the parasites in the large intestine with those in the small intestine. In your notebook, expand Table 1 to include all the parasites, and record the parasites found in each organ. Place your data on the chalkboard. Record the class results in your table. Compare your data with the data of other members of the class.

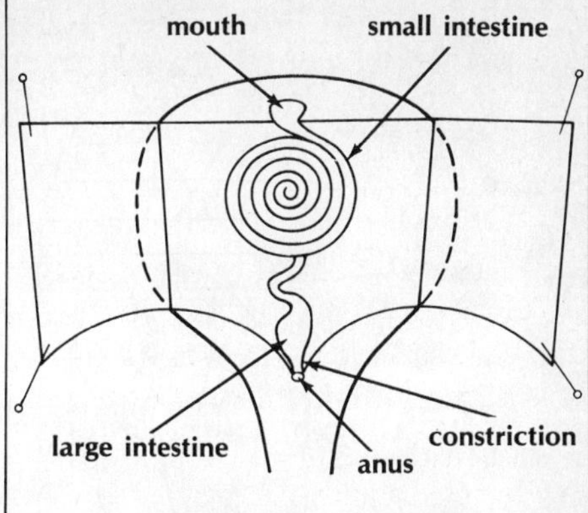

Digestive Cavity of Tadpole

FIGURE 2

Part B. Earthworm

Place a live earthworm on a wet paper towel in a dissecting pan. Anesthetize the worm with 95% ethyl alcohol by placing several drops of alcohol directly on the earthworm. **CAUTION:** *Alcohol is*

TABLE 1. TADPOLE PARASITES OBSERVED

STUDENT	*OPALINA*	
	LARGE INTESTINE	SMALL INTESTINE
Your data		
1		
2		
3		
Number of students observing the parasite		
Percentage of class observing the parasite		

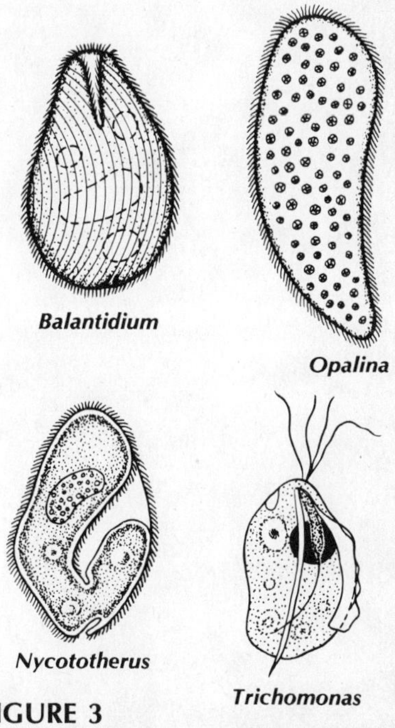

FIGURE 3

FIGURE 4

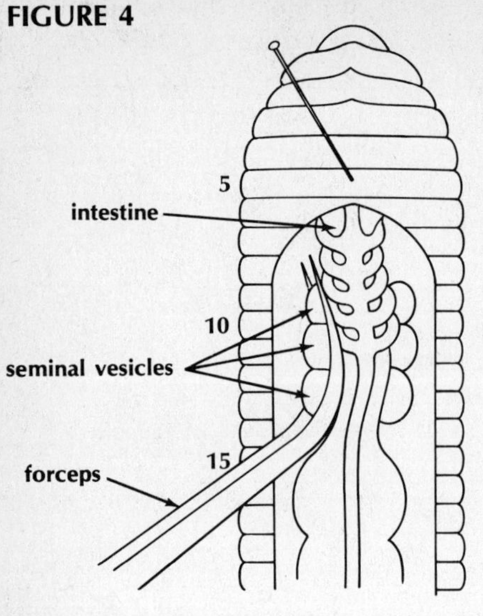

flammable. Be sure all flames in the laboratory are extinguished before proceeding. Avoid breathing fumes. Wrap the paper towel around the earthworm for a few minutes. When the worm is anesthetized, its body movements will be very slow. Place the earthworm on its ventral surface. Be sure the paper towel is moist to keep the worm from drying out.

Place a dissecting pin through the fifth segment from the anterior end. Stretch the worm and place a dissecting pin through segment 30.

With scissors, make a shallow longitudinal incision from segment 25 to segment 5. Keep the bottom blade of the scissors parallel to the dissecting pan and near the dorsal surface of the worm. Spread the body wall open and place dissecting pins into the body wall at intervals of 6 to 8 segments to hold it in place.

Place a pair of forceps beneath the lobes of the seminal vesicles (Figure 4). You may have to use a probe to lift them. Gently pull the forceps toward the dorsal surface of the worm to remove the seminal vesicles. Place the seminal vesicles in a small petri dish half. Add two drops of Ringer's solution to the petri dish. With a scalpel, macerate the tissue until it is cream-colored. This macerated, cream-colored tissue contains cells of the seminal vesicle as well as sperm cells in various stages of development. It also probably contains several stages of the life cycle of *Monocystis.*

Make a wet mount of the macerated seminal vesicle by adding a drop of macerated tissue to a clean, dry slide. Add a coverslip and observe the slide with low power, then high power of your microscope.

Locate and identify the various stages of *Monocystis* (Figure 5). Record the stages observed in your notebook in a table similar to Table 2. Record which stage is more numerous, less numerous, or entirely absent. Make sketches of the stages observed. Place your data on the chalkboard. Compare your data with the data of other members of the class.

Part C. Termite

Place a live termite in the center of a petri dish. Using forceps and a probe, separate the head from the rest of the body by a gentle pulling

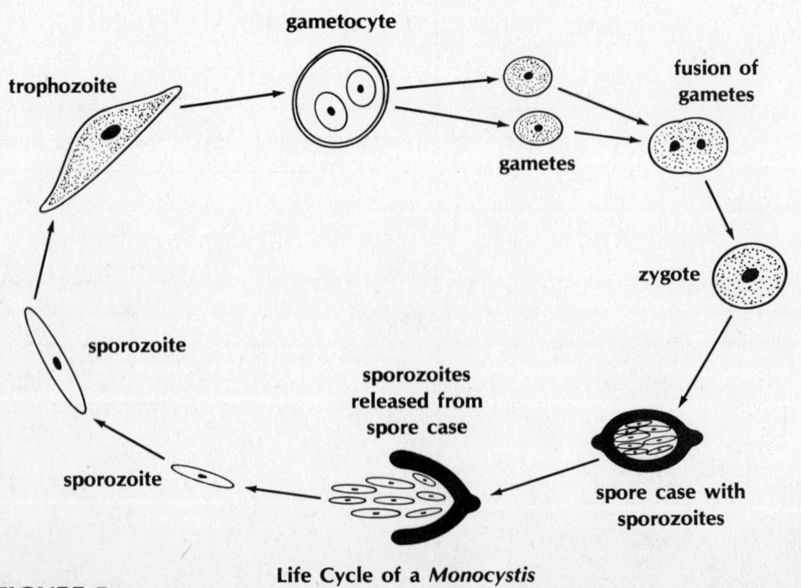

Life Cycle of a *Monocystis*

FIGURE 5

action. The intestines should come out intact (Figure 6). Tease out the intestines with a probe and add 2 drops of Ringer's solution. Macerate the tissue. Add another drop of Ringer's solution to the macerated tissue. Stir the macerated tissue with a probe. **CAUTION:** *Always be careful with sharp instruments such as a probe.*

Make a wet mount of the macerated tissue. Add a coverslip and observe the slide with low power, then high power of your microscope. Locate and identify various protozoans that inhabit the intestine of the termite (Figure 7). Make sketches of the protozoans you observe.

FIGURE 6

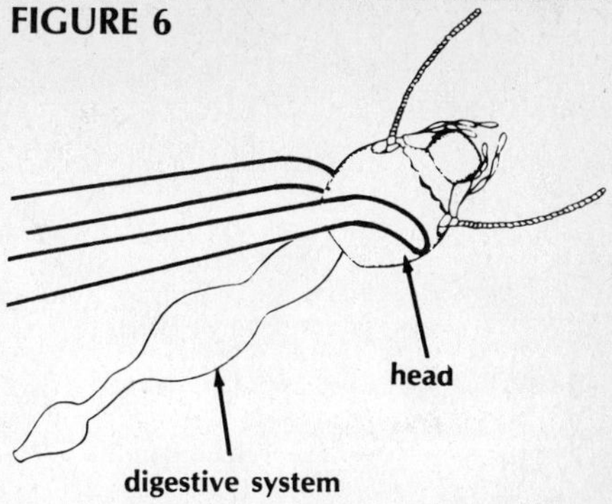

TABLE 2. NUMBERS OF EACH STAGE OF *MONOCYSTIS* OBSERVED IN THE EARTHWORM						
STUDENT	SPORE CASE WITH SPOROZOITE	SPOROZOITE	TROPHOZOITE	GAMETOCYTE	GAMETE	ZYGOTE
Your Data						
1						
2						
3						
number of students observing the stage of *Monocystis*						
percentage of class observing the stage of *Monocystis*						

TABLE 3. NUMBERS OF EACH TERMITE PROTOZOAN OBSERVED				
STUDENT	PROTOZOANS			
	Trichonympha	*Holomastigotes*	*Streblomastix*	*Stephanonympha*
Your data				
1				
2				
Number of students observing the parasite				
Percentage of class observing the protozoan				

FIGURE 7

Record in your notebook in a table similar to Table 3 the number of each species observed. Place your data on the chalkboard and record class data in the table. Compare your data with the data of other members of the class.

Formulating Generalizations

1. Arrange the stages of *Monocystis* in order from greatest to least according to the number observed. How do your data compare with class data?
2. *Monocystis* is a parasite that is thought to derive its nourishment from fatlike compounds. On what tissues or cells do you think it is parasitic?
3. How do you think *Monocystis* gets into the seminal vesicle of young or "uninfected" worms?
4. Arrange the various protozoans observed in the termite in order from greatest to least according to the number observed. How do your data compare with class data? If they are different, explain why.
5. Young termites need the protozoans. How do you think they get the protozoans in their digestive tracts?
6. Why do you think the protozoans found in the termite's intestine have such long cilia?
7. Intestinal protozoa in frogs release enzymes that digest cells lining the intestine. Why would a large population of protozoans be harmful to the frog?
8. Arrange the various parasites observed in the tadpole in order from greatest to least according to the number observed. How do your data compare to class data? If they are different, explain why.
9. Distinguish between a mutualist and a parasite.
10. How would you classify the protozoa inhabiting the termite's digestive tract, parasite or mutualist? Explain.

Physical Factors Of Soil

79

Soil is a major factor influencing the survival of many living things. Many organisms live in the soil. Other organisms are anchored in soil and obtain water and minerals from the soil. Still other organisms depend on these soil-dependent organisms for food. The physical properties of a particular kind of soil determine the kinds of plants that grow in the soil and the kinds of animals that live in or on it.

In this investigation, you are to analyze the physical characteristics of soil and relate them to the organisms living in the soil.

Materials *(per team of four students)*

soil samples—3 or 4
ring stand and ring
clothespin, wooden snap-type
burner
balance
20-cm cloth squares—3
specimen jar
beaker
water
ruler
can

Procedure

Perform the following tests to study the physical properties of soil. Record the data in your notebook in a table similar to Table 1.

Part A. Particle Size

Fill a specimen jar half full of soil; add water until the jar is full. Cover the jar with a lid and shake until the large soil particles break apart. Set the jar aside and let the particles settle overnight. Using a ruler, measure the depth of each particle type. Record the relative amounts of gravel, coarse sand, fine sand, silt, and clay in the settled sample (Figure 1).

FIGURE 1

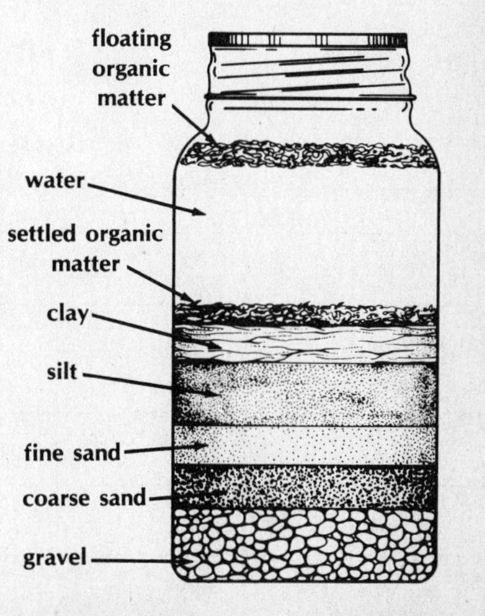

Part B. Water Content

Water content is the amount of water in soil at any given time. Soak a 20-cm cloth square in water. Allow excess water to drip from the cloth and determine the mass of the cloth. Wrap a soil sample in the wet cloth and determine its mass. Place the sample where it will dry completely. After the sample has dried, redetermine its mass. Calculate the water content as a percent of the wet mass of the soil: percent of water content =

$$\frac{\text{loss in mass of soil}}{\text{dry mass of soil} - \text{dry mass of cloth}} \times 100$$

Part C. Water-Holding Capacity

Water-holding capacity is a measure of the amount of water that soil can hold when saturated. Soil is saturated when it has soaked up all the water it can hold. Determine the mass of a wet 20-cm cloth

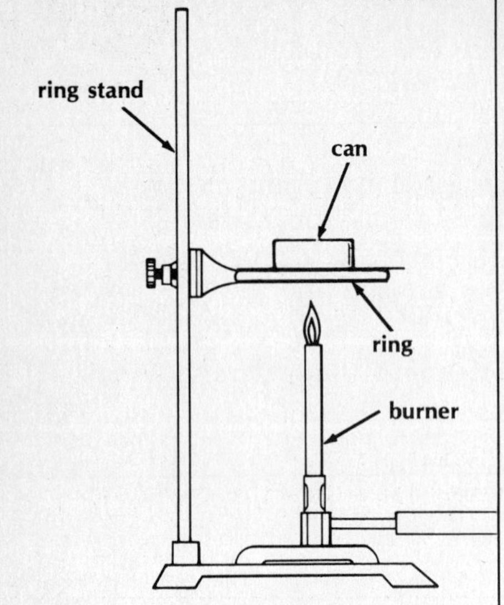

FIGURE 2

square as you did in Part B. Place half of the massed, dried soil sample from Part B in a 20-cm cloth square. Place the soil sample and cloth in a beaker of water for five to ten minutes or until the soil is saturated. Remove the soil sample from the beaker and allow excess water to drain from it through the cloth. Find the mass of the saturated sample and subtract the mass of the wet cloth. Calculate the water-holding capacity as a percent of the dry mass:

$$\text{water holding capacity} = \frac{\text{gain in mass}}{\text{dry mass}} \times 100$$

Part D. Organic Matter Content

Place the other half of the massed, dried soil sample in a can. Heat the sample over a burner until the organic materials ignite and burn completely (Figure 2). **CAUTION:** *Always be careful around open flames. Secure all loose hair and clothing before proceeding.* The contents of the crucible are the nonorganic materials of the soil. Allow the contents of the crucible to cool, then remass the sample. **CAUTION:** *Do not touch the hot can with your fingers. Pick up the can with a wooden, snap-type clothespin.* Calculate the amount of organic matter as a percent of the dry mass:

$$\text{percent of organic matter} = \frac{\text{loss of mass (burning)}}{\text{mass of dry sample}} \times 100$$

Formulating Generalizations

1. How is soil important to plants? To animals?
2. How do the water content and water-holding capacity of the soil determine which organisms can live in a community?
3. Which type of soil particle made up the greatest amount of your soil sample? The least amount?
4. Which type of soil particle was most closely packed?
5. Which were the least closely packed?
6. How does the degree of packing of particles affect microscopic organisms in the soil?
7. How does the type of soil particles in a sample affect water drainage?
8. How does organic material get into soil?
9. What is decayed organic matter called?
10. How does the amount of organic matter in soil change its water holding capacity? Explain.

TABLE 1. SOIL SAMPLE DATA

	AMOUNT OF EACH PARTICLE TYPE							
PLOT LOCATION	GRAVEL	COARSE SAND	FINE SAND	SILT	CLAY	WATER CONTENT	WATER-HOLDING CAPACITY	ORGANIC MATTER CONTENT

Effect Of Temperature On Seed Germination

80

A biome is a group of communities with the same major life forms. Temperature range is one factor that determines the type of biome an area will be. Living things have a temperature range in which they can survive. The lowest temperature tolerated is the minimum temperature. The highest temperature tolerated is the maximum temperature. Between the minimum and maximum temperatures tolerated is a narrow range of temperatures at which the organism functions most efficiently. This range is called the optimum temperature range. A biome must have the proper temperature range, and preferably the optimum temperature range, in order for an organism to exist there.

In this investigation, you are to observe and record the effects of temperature variations on seed germination. You are to determine which of three environments has the optimum temperature.

Materials *(per student or team)*

seeds (same type)—75
beaker—100-mL
1% household bleach solution—25 mL
forceps
paper towels—4
25-cm cloth squares—3
rubber bands—6
water
clock or watch with second hand
refrigerator
incubator

Procedure

Place 75 seeds of the same type in a 100-mL beaker containing 25 mL of 1% household bleach solution. **CAUTION:** *Bleach can damage skin and clothes. If spillage occurs, rinse with water and call your teacher. Avoid breathing fumes.* Allow the seeds to stand in this solution for two minutes to kill any fungi on the seed coats. Drain the bleach from the beaker and place the seeds on a clean paper towel. Blot the seeds dry.

Using forceps, place 25 seeds into each of three "rag doll" germinators. **CAUTION:** *Always be careful when using sharp instruments such as forceps.* A "rag doll" germinator is a piece of cloth saturated with water (Figure 1). The cloth holds moisture necessary for seed germination. When the seeds are placed in the "rag doll," fold *in order* flap A, flap B, then flap C. Roll the "rag doll" in the indicated direction. Secure the folded "rag dolls" with rubber bands and label them with your name and the environment in which the seeds will be placed.

Store the "rag doll" germinators in containers provided by your teacher. Place one germinator in a refrigerator at 4°C, another at room temperature (about 20°C), and the third in an incubator at 37°C.

Make counts of the total number of seeds that have germinated each day for eight days. Seeds have germinated if you can see a small embryo plant growing through the seed coat. Unroll the germinators and count germinated seeds. Record the data in a table in your lab notebook similar to Table 1. Multiply the number of seeds germinated by four to give you the percentage of seeds that have germinated. (Twenty-five is one fourth of a hundred and you used 25 seeds.) Roll the germinators again. Collect data from other students with the same type of seed. Construct a bar graph of your data and the class data (Figure 2). Each graph is to show the percentage of total seeds germinated each day.

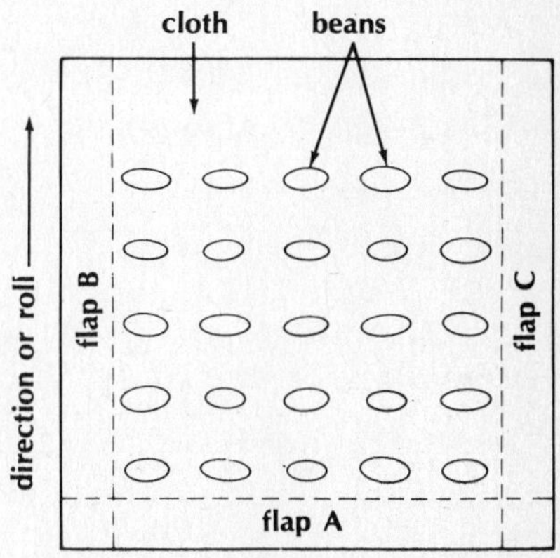

Rag Doll Germinator

FIGURE 1

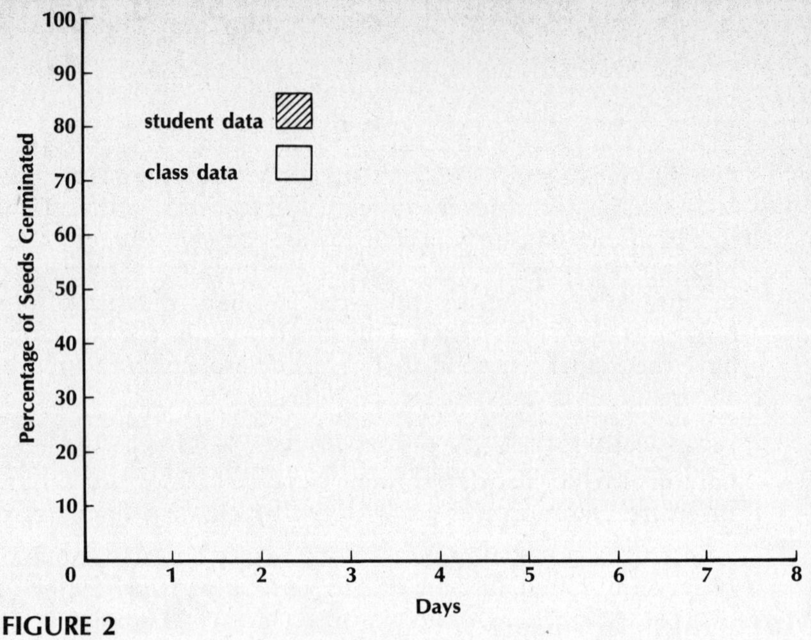

FIGURE 2

Formulating Generalizations

1. At which temperature did the greatest number of your seeds germinate? Why?
2. At which temperature did the least number of your seeds germinate? Why?
3. From class data, do all kinds of seeds germinate best at the same temperature?
4. List some factors other than temperature which might cause variation in seed germination time.
5. How does the germination rate of your seeds compare with data of other students testing the same type of seed?
6. Why is the expected percent of germination usually listed on a seed package?
7. Why will 100% of the seeds not always germinate?
8. Which seeds would probably germinate faster in an incubator, seeds from tundra plants or seeds from a tropical rain forest plant? Explain.
9. Suppose you were given several thousand seeds from an unknown environment. How could you find out the minimum, optimum, and maximum temperatures at which these seeds grow?

TABLE 1. NUMBER AND PERCENTAGE OF GERMINATED SEEDS AT (   )°C TEMPERATURE

DAY	NUMBER OF SEEDS GERMINATED	× 4	PERCENTAGE OF GERMINATION
1	10	40	40
2	12	48	48
8			

Field Studies Of A Freshwater Ecosystem

81

A freshwater stream is the habitat for many living things. Many organisms exchange gases with the water environment.

Living things are found in a freshwater stream throughout the entire year. However, the population density of each species does not remain the same all year. Changes in the chemical and physical characteristics of the stream influence what organisms will inhabit a certain area. For example, rocks, a physical factor of a stream, are habitats for many bottom-dwelling organisms. If the number of sizes of rocks change, available habitat for many bottom-dwelling organisms changes. Changes in chemical factors, such as the concentrations of oxygen and carbon dioxide, also determine what type of organism can inhabit the stream. Behavior patterns of entire communities are affected by changes in the physical and chemical environment.

In this investigation, you are to set up seven stations on a freshwater stream. You are to observe, distinguish, and record various physical factors of the stream. You are to observe, describe, and identify the organisms of the stream. From the collected data on physical factors and the organisms, you are to compare and analyze the relationship of the physical factors to the organisms.

Materials *(per team of ten students)*

Field Materials

hammer
stakes or large nails—14
cord—100 m
meter sticks—3
white lid from jar
graph paper—8 sheets
capped plastic bottle
baby food jars—3 to 4 dozen
small jars—4
medium jars—4
large jars—4
Celsius thermometers—2
100-mL sample bottles—1 to 2 dozen
phenolphthalein—25 mL
pipette with 0.1 mL graduations
0.4% sodium hydroxide—50 mL
pH kit
large plastic bags—1 dozen
household sieve, large
hand lens
70% ethyl alcohol—4 to 6 liters
net, 1.5 × 3 meters
white enamel trays, large—2
forceps
glass marker
watch with second hand

Classroom Analysis

microscopes—3
stereomicroscopes—3
coverslips—3
glass slides—3
hand lens
dropper

Procedure

Working in teams of ten, you are to study a 30-meter section of a stream. The beginning and end of your 30-meter section will be the beginning or end of another team's section (Figure 1).

FIGURE 1

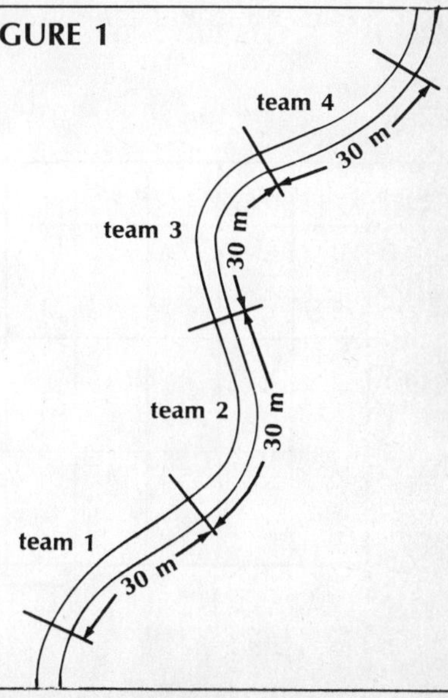

Choose seven areas or stations for study along your team's stream section. Among these stations should be rapids, deep pools, and slow moving areas. Determine your seven stations before proceeding any further. Mark the seven areas by driving two stakes opposite one

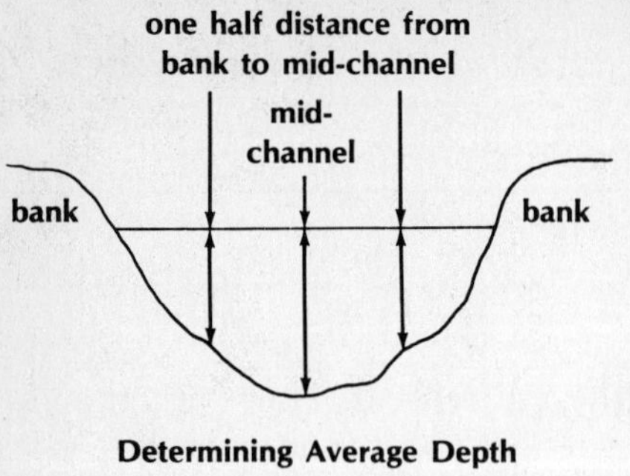

FIGURE 2

another along both banks of the stream at each station. Stretch a piece of cord from one stake to the other at each station. Do not turn over rocks on the bottom of the stream as you are setting up your stations. Disturbing rocks will interfere with certain physical and chemical samples that you are to obtain.

Part A. Physical Factors

Type of Bottom

Observe the bottom of the stream at each station. Record the type of bottom (substratum). Classify the bottom materials of the stream at each station as one of the following:

1. loose rock or gravel (easily moved)
2. attached rock (embedded in mud)
3. bedrock
4. sand
5. mud or silt
6. other

Depth and Width

Determine the average depth and width of the stream at each station. To determine the average depth, measure the depth at three points. Measure the depth at mid-channel and at one half the distance from mid-channel to each bank (Figure 2). Record the three depths for each station in your notebook. Add the three depths and divide by four. Dividing by four compensates for the narrow depth near the banks.

To determine the average width, measure the distance across the channel at three places near the station. Select areas within 3 meters of the station. If possible, select an area that is wide, one that is narrow, and one that is half-way between wide and narrow. Add the three distances and divide by three.

Record the average widths and depths in your notebook. Compare your averages for each station with other members of the class. Construct graphs showing the average width and depth at each station.

Volume of Flow

Determine the volume of flow of the stream at each station. Place a capped plastic bottle in mid-channel at a station. Record in your notebook the time (in seconds) it takes the plastic bottle to travel a measured distance. Using the following formula, calculate the volume of flow at each station in cubic meters per second:

$$R = \frac{WDaL}{T}$$

R = volume of flow (cubic meters per second); W = average width of stream (in meters); D = average depth of stream (in meters); a = constant for bottom type [0.9 for smooth (bedrock, sand, or silt bottom) or 0.8 for rough (gravel or rocky bottom)]; L = length of measured distance traveled by the bottle (in meters); and T = time for the bottle to travel measured distance (in seconds).

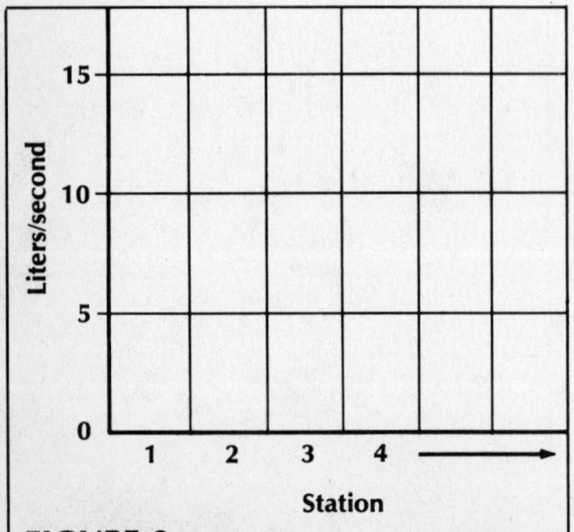

FIGURE 3

Calculate the volume of flow at each station in liters per second using the following formula:

$$R = \frac{WDaL}{T} \times 1000$$

Record the values in your lab notebook. Compare your data with other members of the class. Construct a bar graph showing the volume of flow in liters per second at each station (Figure 3).

Color and Turbidity of Water

Obtain a water sample from each station. Place the water in a small baby food jar. Record in your notebook the color of the water as clear, light, or dark and the station from which the sample was taken.

Determine the turbidity of the water at each station by placing a Secchi disc in the deeper pools. Make a Secchi disc by attaching a white jar lid to a meter stick (Figure 4). If the disc is slightly visible at a depth of 1.3 or more meters the water is clear. If the disc is slightly visible from 0.3 to 1.3 meters, the water is slightly turbid. If the disc is visible only from zero to 0.3 meters, the water is turbid. Record the turbidity at each station in your notebook. Compare your data with other members of the class.

Temperature

Using a Celsius thermometer, determine the air temperature 0.3 meters above the water level at mid-channel of each station. Keep the thermometer shaded from direct sunlight. Determine the water temperature at each station by securing a water sample in a small jar from the surface at mid-channel. Determine the temperature. Record the temperature for each station in your notebook. Determine the temperatures (air and water) at half-hourly intervals during the study. Plot the temperatures for each station on graphs (Figure 5). Use one graph for air temperatures and another graph for water temperatures. Compare your data with the data of other members of the class.

Bank

Determine the height in meters of both banks at each station. Use the widths and depths determined earlier and the bank heights to sketch a cross section of each channel (Figure 6). Describe plant cover and soil or rock composition of banks at each station.

FIGURE 4

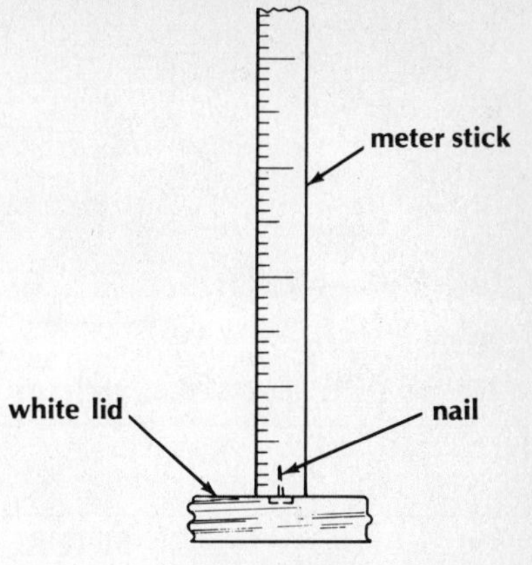

Secchi Disc

FIGURE 5

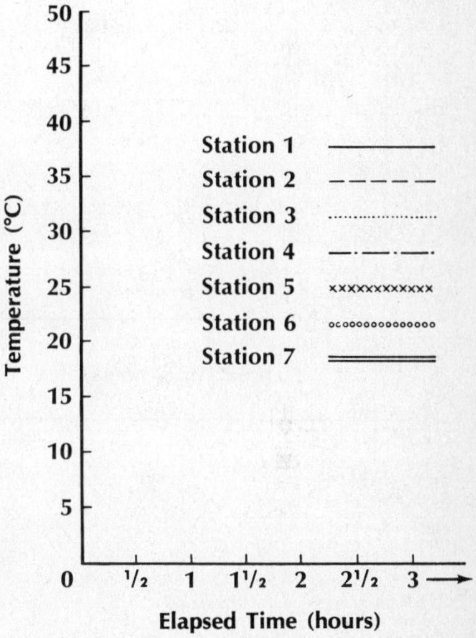

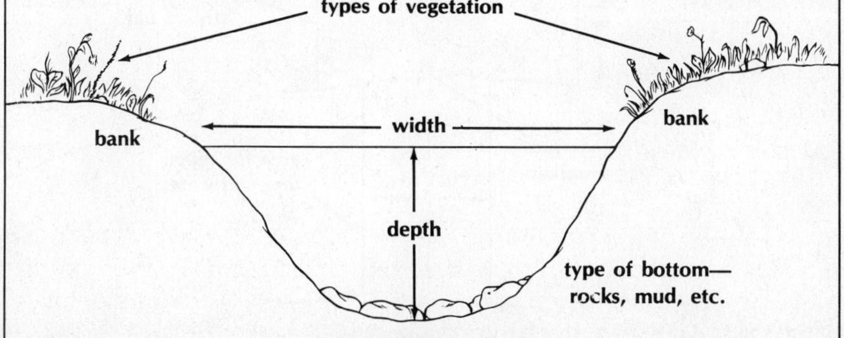

Cross Section of Stream

FIGURE 6

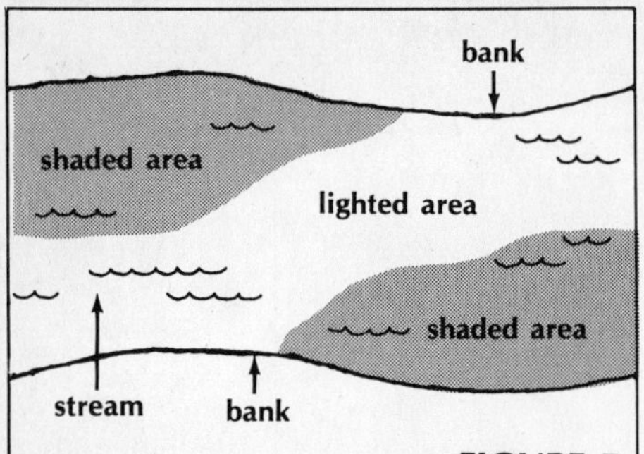

FIGURE 7

Shade and Cover

Determine the percentage of shade from overhanging trees that is present over your section of the stream. Record this data when the sun is shining. Make a drawing in your notebook similar to Figure 7. Label the parts of the stream that are shaded and lighted.

FIGURE 8

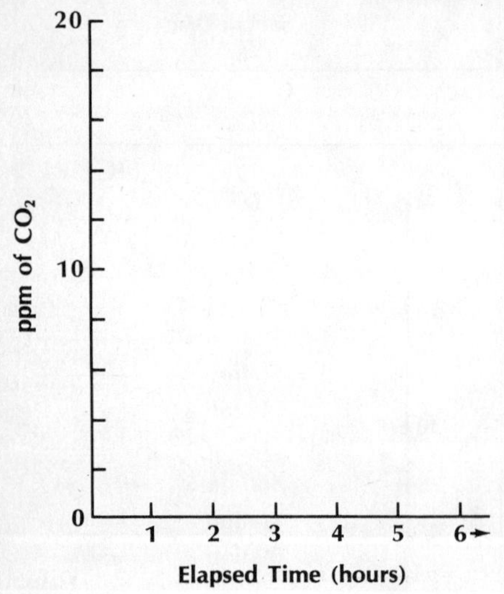

Part B. Chemical Analysis

Carbon Dioxide Content

To determine the amount of carbon dioxide, collect a 100-mL water sample from each station. Do not allow any air to "bubble" into the collecting jar. Add 3 drops of phenolphthalein indicator to each water sample. If the sample turns pink, pour out the contents of the collecting jar. Add water to the jar and rinse several times. Obtain another sample from the same station. Add 3 drops of phenolphthalein to the sample. With a pipette, add 0.4% sodium hydroxide solution one drop at a time until a pink color develops. **CAUTION:** *Sodium hydroxide may cause burns. If spillage occurs, rinse with water and call your teacher.* Add sodium hydroxide until the pink color remains for one minute.

Mix the water sample after each drop of sodium hydroxide is added by swirling or rotating the container with a circular motion of the wrist. However, any agitation of the surface of the sample can add gases to the sample; therefore, avoid excessive shaking of the sample. Record the milliliters of sodium hydroxide solution used in the sample for each station. Collect a water sample every hour at each station and determine the carbon dioxide content.

Compute the parts per million (ppm) of carbon dioxide (Investigation 58) in the water samples from each station by multiplying the milliliters of sodium hydroxide by 100. Construct a graph showing the ppm of CO_2 at each station each hour (Figure 8).

pH of the Water

Determine the pH of the water at each station at least once during the study. Place 5 mL of a water sample into a test tube. Add 3 drops of wide range pH indicator to the test tube. Cover the test tube with a rubber stopper and shake gently. Using charts with the pH kit, determine the pH of the water.

FIGURE 9

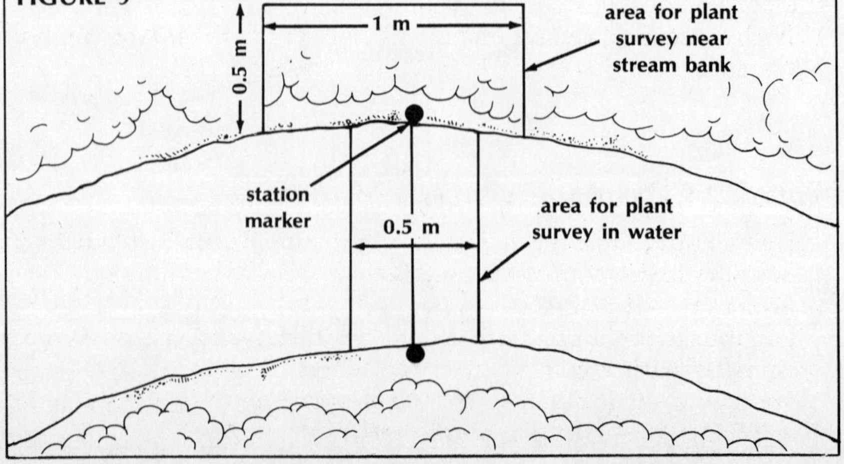

Part C. Organisms

Plants and Plantlike Organisms

Record kinds and numbers of seed plants, ferns, mosses, and/or algae growing near the edge of four stations. List the water plants as completely submerged, floating, or emergent (rooted in the bottom with stem and/or leaves above or on the surface of the water). Collect samples of each seed plant, fern, and moss. Collect one specimen of each plant type. Place the specimens in plastic bags for identification (see Figure 9).

Record the percentage of rocks at each station that are covered with algae. Collect samples of algae in small baby food jars for identification later.

Protozoa

Scrape debris from some rocks or decaying vegetation at each station. Place the material from each station along with 25 mL of stream water into a small baby food jar for identification later.

Bottom-Dwelling Animals

Holding a household sieve downstream from a submerged, loose rock, turn the rock over. The current will drive any organisms into the sieve. Transfer the organisms to jars containing 70% ethyl alcohol. Examine the bottom of the rock with a hand lens for small sluggish or attached organisms. Add them to the jar of alcohol.

Record the number of each type of organism found on the bottom of a rock. Repeat this procedure with three or four rocks at each station. Put all specimens from the same station in the same container. The specimens are to be taken to the classroom for identification.

Collect larger animals such as fish and snakes with a large net. While two students hold the net across the stream, the others should move quickly from upstream toward the net dislodging the rocks. Animals should be driven into the net. Place the collected organisms in large enamel trays for field identification. Determine the number of each kind of organism. After observation, select a few to take to the classroom for careful observation. Return the rest to the stream. Place the samples for lab identification in large jars or aquaria containing stream water. Refrigerate the containers upon returning to school.

Locate an area near each station in which the bottom contains mud or silt. Fill a medium jar one-third full of stream water. Fill the jar to the top with mud or silt from the sample area. Shake the material in the jar. Pour the material from the jar into a household sieve. Swirl the sieve in water to remove small soil particles. Place the contents on a white enamel tray. Examine the dead and decaying vegetation for the presence of animals and algae.

With forceps, place the organisms in containers for later analysis. Mark each container with the station number.

Part D. Classroom Analysis of Biota

Using taxonomic keys supplied by your teacher, identify the specimens found at each station. List and record the number of each organism found at each station.

For microscopic specimens, make wet mounts and observe the specimens with a compound microscope.

For macroscopic organisms, use a stereomicroscope or hand lens to observe the specimens if necessary.

Formulating Generalizations

1. In which area were insects more abundant, rapids or deeper pools? Why?
2. Why should you expect fewer aquatic insects in the stream in late summer than in early spring?
3. In which area were algae more abundant, rapids or deeper pools? Why?
4. Why should you expect more algae in the stream in late summer or early spring than at other times?
5. What physical factors are necessary for excessive algae growth?
6. Why are larger animals such as fish and turtles found in deeper pools?
7. Did the type of bottom at various stations have any bearing on the types of organisms found? Why?
8. What special adaptations do plants and animals that live in either pools or rapids have?
9. Is there any difference in the rate of flow at each station? Should there be any difference? Why?
10. How does the color and turbidity of the water affect the presence or absence of certain organisms?
11. If the stream remains turbid for a month, do you think all first order consumers would die or migrate? Explain.
12. Were there any differences in air and water temperatures throughout the study?
13. What physical factors could cause changes in the temperatures?
14. How do bank height, plant cover, and composition of the bank at each station affect erosion?
15. How does the amount of shade and light affect the organisms in the stream?
16. Would any other physical factors change if there were prolonged shading and cloudiness over each station?
17. Did the ppm of carbon dioxide change throughout the study? Explain.
18. Should you expect a change in carbon dioxide content or the pH throughout the study?
19. What factors could cause changes in the pH and carbon dioxide content?
20. Could the organisms present affect the pH and carbon dioxide content?
21. How can the pH and carbon dioxide content affect the life forms?
22. Which phylum of animals is widely represented in the rapids? In the deeper pools? Explain.
23. Which plant type is most widely represented, floating, emergent, or submerged? Why?
24. Did you capture all the animals beneath rocks by using the sieve?
25. If you were instructed to compute the density of animals per cubic meter of stream or square meter of stream bottom, how would you determine this accurately?

Field Study Of A Terrestrial Ecosystem

82

There is a constant interaction among plants, animals, protists, and the environment. Plants provide food, shelter, and oxygen to other organisms in the community. Animals are the chief consumers in a community. Some animals eat only certain types of plants. Therefore, these animals are found in association with certain plant types. Many protists, such as bacteria and fungi, are parasites on plants and animals. Other bacteria and fungi decompose dead parts of plants and animals.

Abiotic factors also influence the plant, animal, and protist populations of a community. Factors such as soil, water, and temperature help determine the organisms that live in a certain area. Some organisms can withstand slight changes in the environment; others cannot. Thus, changes determine the distribution of organisms.

In a field study, measurements of the physical factors and organisms present are made in ways that may look unimportant. However, the study in total gives a clear picture of an ecological community.

In this investigation, you are to sample and identify various organisms found on a 30 by 30 meter plot. You are to analyze and describe the effects of the physical factors on the plant and animal population.

Materials *(per team of ten students)*

Field Work

- steel measuring tape—30 m
- cord—300 m
- wooden stakes—12
- hammer
- graph paper—6 sheets
- pencil
- compass
- protractor
- meter stick
- transparent tape
- string—1 ball
- spike
- moss, tree, shrub, fern, mammal, reptile, amphibian, and insect keys
- insect net
- ethyl acetate
- 70% ethyl alcohol—500 mL
- baby food jars—60
- large plastic bags—12
- small shovel
- water
- pH soil kit
  - soft drink cans—9
- containers with 100 mL of water—9
- Celsius thermometers—2
- absorbent cotton
- clock or watch with second hand

Classroom Analysis

- Berlese funnels—6
- short stem funnels—6
- rubber tubing, 10 cm—6
- pinch clamps—6
- cheesecloth squares, 10 cm × 10 cm—6
- rubber bands—6
- water
- iron stands—6
- cooked rice—36 grains
- pasteurized spring water —1 liter
- microscopes—4
- stereomicroscopes—4
- glass slides—4
- coverslips—4
- masking tape
- filter paper strips 2 cm × 6 cm—9
- watch glasses—9
- 200-mL beakers—9
- crucibles or tin cans—9
  - burners—4
- balance
- cloth squares, 20 cm × 20 cm

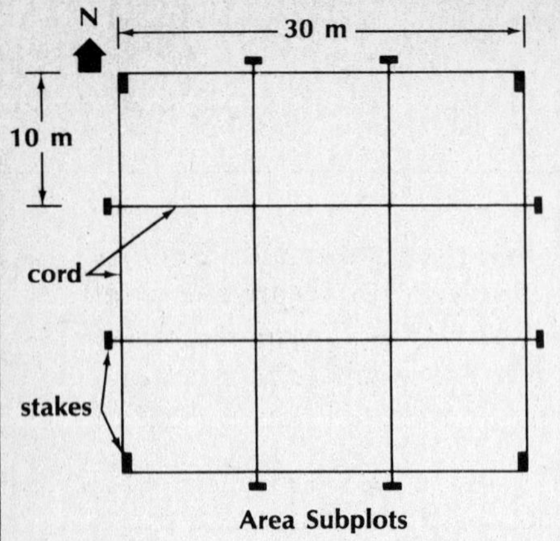

FIGURE 1

Procedure

Part A. Selection and Layout of a Plot

Working in teams of ten, select a plot as your study area. With a steel measuring tape, measure an area 30 m by 30 m. Your area can border another team's plot giving a common boundary. Drive four stakes into the ground at the four corners of your plot. Attach cord to one stake and loop it around the other stakes to enclose your plot. Disturb the enclosed area as little as possible. Divide the plot into nine equal subplots by driving stakes at 10-m distances around the plot and joining opposite stakes with cord (Figure 1). Number each subplot for identification.

On a sheet of graph paper, make a sketch of your plot noting prominent land features such as streams, trails, and open areas. With a compass, determine the north direction and indicate it with an arrow on your sketch.

Measure the angle of the slope of each subplot by using an Abney level. Construct an Abney level as shown in Figure 2 with a protractor, meter stick, tape, string, and spike. Hold the meter stick parallel to the slope of the subplot while another team member observes from a distance to make sure the slope and meter stick are parallel. Read the angle on the protractor made by the string. From the position of the protractor, 90° is at the bottom; therefore, when the slope is zero, the reading will be 90°. Thus, to determine the actual angle of the slope, subtract the angle reading from 90°. If the protractor reads 60°, angle of the slope = 90° − 60° = 30°.

Part B. Plant Communities

Observe the types of plants in your plot and each subplot. For sampling purposes, there are four types of plants:

(a) Trees—woody plants with one main stem, about 0.5 to 30 m in height
(b) Shrubs—low, woody plants with two or more main stems protruding from the ground about 0.5 to 3.0 m in height
(c) Herbaceous plants—nonwoody, green plants such as ferns and grasses that die in winter, about 0.1 to 1 m in height
(d) Floor covering—litter from fallen leaves and stems; mosses, lichens, and fungi

In sampling the plants *within each subplot,* use the following divisions:

Trees—10 m × 10 m
Shrubs—4 m × 4 m
Herbs—1 m × 1 m
Floor covering—20 cm × 20 cm

Sample one of each type of plant area in each subplot.

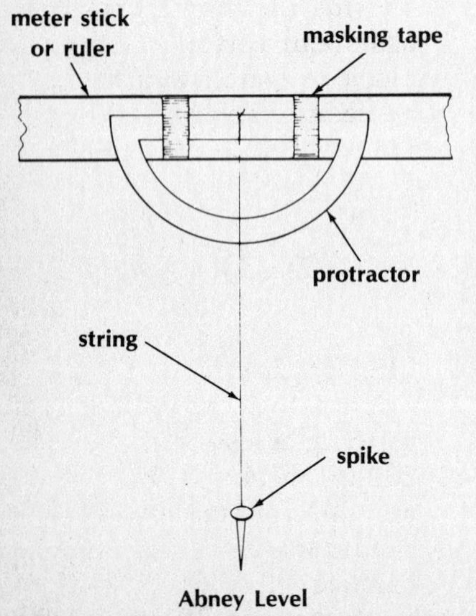

FIGURE 2

Frequency of Plant Types

Check the appropriate size of sample area in each subplot for the presence of each plant type. Record in your notebook in a table similar to Table 1 whether or not each type is found in each subplot. Determine the frequency (percentage) of each plant type in

Effects Of A Pollutant On Protozoan Populations

84

Humans introduce substances into the environment which decrease its purity or cleanliness. This decrease in cleanliness is called pollution. Pollution injures the health of both humans and other organisms. The ability of many plants, animals, and protists to survive in a polluted environment is greatly reduced.

The harmful substances introduced into the environment are called pollutants. Pollutants may be solids, liquids, or gases. Humans, both accidently and purposefully, pour wastes from industries, farms, and homes into streams, rivers, and lakes. These pollutants may cause imbalances in food chains. Some members of the chain are harmed or killed, and others increase their numbers dramatically.

In this investigation, you are to observe the changes in four cultures over a short period of time. You are to decide whether a pollutant is harmful or helpful to the organisms in the cultures by counting and recording changes in numbers of organisms.

Materials *(per student or team)*

baby food jars—4
droppers—4
glass slides—2
Euglena culture—1
Blepharisma culture—1
boiled rice grains—8
test tubes—4
graph paper—3 sheets
stoppers—4
microscope
boiled tap water—50 mL
solutions:
  1% copper sulfate—50 mL
  fertilizer—50 mL
  milk—50 mL
coverslip

Procedure

Prepare four baby food jars as follows. Label the jars with your name and the numbers one to four. Into jar one pour 50 mL copper sulfate solution and two grains of rice. Into jar two pour 50 mL fertilizer and two grains of rice. Into jar three pour 50 mL milk and two grains of rice. Into jar four pour 50 mL boiled tap water and two grains of rice. Jar four will function as the unpolluted control. Using a dropper, add ten drops of *Euglena* culture and ten drops of *Blepharisma* culture to each jar. To prevent evaporation, set the lids over the jars. Do not screw the lids onto the jars. Place the jars in a lighted area.

Make a wet mount of the pure *Euglena* culture and observe *Euglena* under low power of your microscope. Make a sketch of the *Euglena* in your notebook. Repeat this procedure with the *Blepharisma* culture.

Observe *Euglena* and *Blepharisma* in your "polluted" cultures (jars one, two, and three) on days one, three, five, and seven. Record the color and odor of the material in each jar in a table similar to Table 1. Stir the contents of each jar by charging and discharging the culture fluid with a clean dropper several times. Use low power of your compound microscope to observe *Euglena* and *Blepharisma*. Count and record the number of each organism in one field of view. Because *Blepharisma* move more rapidly than *Euglena*, count any *Blepharisma* that move through the field as well as those in the field.

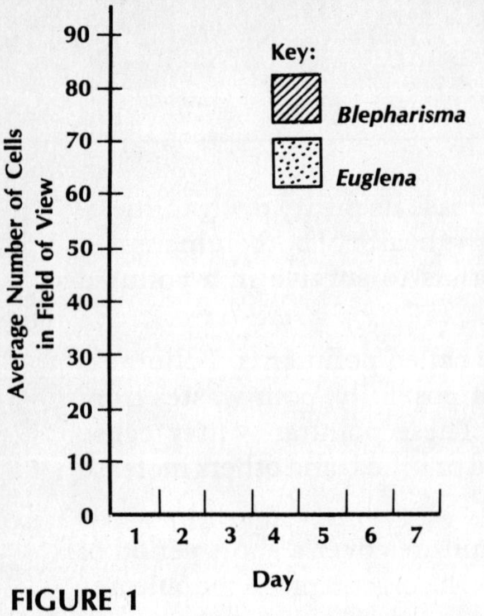

FIGURE 1

TABLE 1. OBSERVATIONS OF ORGANISMS

ORGANISM	DAY	NUMBER OF ORGANISMS IN EACH FIELD					AVERAGE	COLOR AND ODOR OF CULTURE
		1	2	3	4	5		
Euglena	1							
Blepharisma								
Euglena	3							
Blepharisma								
Euglena	5							
Blepharisma								
Euglena	7							
Blepharisma								

If too many protozoa are present to count accurately, make a dilution by adding one drop of culture and nine drops of boiled tap water to a test tube. Stopper and shake the tube gently. Make a count of the *Euglena* and *Blepharisma* in five fields of view. Counts made of diluted cultures must be multiplied by 10. Record your data in a table similar to Table 1.

Repeat this procedure with each culture. At the end of the seven days, construct bar graphs (Figure 1) showing the average number of *Euglena* and *Blepharisma* in five fields of view for each culture. Make four separate graphs, one for each culture.

Formulating Generalizations

1. Distinguish between a pollutant and pollution.
2. Which jars contained substances that could be considered pollutants? Name the pollutants.
3. Which of the substances acted as pollutants in the cultures of *Euglena* and *Blepharisma*? Explain.
4. What characteristics of the cultures would cause humans to call these materials pollutants?
5. Of the pollutants tested, were any non-harmful if ingested by humans? If so, why is this substance considered a pollutant in this investigation?
6. How could each of the pollutants studied enter a fresh water lake or stream?
7. Which jars showed any color change during the experiment? How did the colors change?
8. Why did the color changes occur?
9. In which jar were the *Euglena* and *Blepharisma* most numerous? Why?
10. In which jar were the organisms least numerous? Explain.
11. Which of the jars had the most disagreeable odor? Explain.
12. Will the odor eventually disappear? Explain.